INTRODUCTION TO 3D GRAPHICS & ANIMATION USING MAYA

ADAM WATKINS

CHARLES RIVER MEDIA

Boston, Massachusetts

Cover Design: Tyler Creative

CHARLES RIVER MEDIA
25 Thomson Place
Boston, Massachusetts 02210
617-757-7900
617-757-7969 (FAX)
crminfo@thomson.com
www.charlesriver.com

This book is printed on acid-free paper.

Adam Watkins. *Introduction to 3D Graphics & Animation Using Maya*
ISBN: 1-58450-485-4
Library of Congress Cataloging-in-Publication Data
Watkins, Adam.
 Introduction to 3D graphics & animation using Maya / Adam Watkins.
    p. cm.
 Includes bibliographical references and index.
 ISBN 1-58450-485-4 (pbk. with cd-rom : alk. paper)
 1. Computer animation. 2. Maya (Computer file) 3. Computer graphics.
 I. Title.
 TR897.7.W377 2006
 006.6'96--dc22
                    2006006348

Printed in Canada
06 7 6 5 4 3 2 First Edition

CHARLES RIVER MEDIA titles are available for site license or bulk purchase by institutions, user groups, corporations, etc. For additional information, please contact the Special Sales Department at 800-347-7707.

Requests for replacement of a defective CD-ROM must be accompanied by the original disc, your mailing address, telephone number, date of purchase, and purchase price. Please state the nature of the problem, and send the information to CHARLES RIVER MEDIA, 25 Thomson Place, Boston, Massachusetts 02210. CRM's sole obligation to the purchaser is to replace the disc, based on defective materials or faulty workmanship, but not on the operation or functionality of the product.

CONTENTS

PREFACE

This book intends to provide a holistic approach to 3D animation using Maya. Most major areas of animation are covered: modeling, UV mapping, texturing, rendering, rigging, and animation. By design, the book can be used by an individual user working at home or by a student in the classroom. Each chapter is broken down into a bit of theory and a bit of tutorial: the tutorials can be attempted on your own or in a classroom lab situation. If you are using the book as classroom support, be sure to check out the suggested pacing in the appendices at the end of the book.

ABOUT THE TUTORIALS

It is important to know which buttons to push and which pull-down menus to use; however, that is only one part of the overall success of good modelers, texture artists, or animators. Therefore each chapter starts with a bit of theory, and each tutorial contains frequent interludes that help explain the "why" of what you have just done.

These "why" sections—indicated by a light bulb icon—include important tips on how to use a tool, and the reasons we are using that particular tool. Be sure to take note of these sections, as they will help you move beyond the simple following of a 3D recipe, and enable you to begin creating your own full-blown creations.

NOTE ON THE CD-ROM

The companion CD-ROM includes files that show the results of the tutorials and all the steps in between. If you find a part of the tutorial unclear or would like to see a bit more of the steps in action, be sure to take a look at the files on the CD-ROM.

THE 3D WORKFLOW

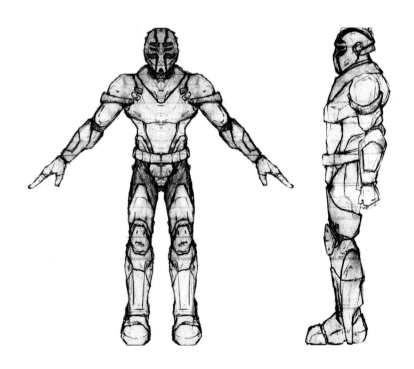

Some General Terms

Before we go any further, let's take a moment to make sure that we're speaking the same language. 3D, like any other field, is full of jargon that folks throw around like yesterday's dirty socks.

Most of us have built some sort of real-time model—plastic airplanes or cars, or models of ecosystems for a junior-high science class. Either way, the point of building models is not to really re-create the target object, but rather to create a representation of it. A computer model is the same—it is a collection of digital instructions interpreted by the computer to form the geometrical appearance of an object. The geometry of models exists only in the computer's digital space. They are files like Word files or Photoshop files. Models can be transferred over the Internet, stored on a disk, backed up on a CD, or corrupted. In all reality, it's just another collection of 1s and 0s. However, this collection of 1s and 0s is the basis for most all effective 3D. It's the building block of the rest of the 3D concepts to follow. But remember, a model is a representation of an object; don't try to make it into the actual object. Be frugal with your modeling; although it's important, good (as in highly detailed) models don't necessarily make for good 3D projects. Plan your time carefully to include all the areas of 3D. Employers looking for generalists can be much more impressed by a good model that is textured, lit, rendered, and animated well, than by just a good model (see Chapter 3).

After models are created, textures are applied. Textures are like a colored shrink-wrap or veneer applied over the surface of the model. Some textures allow the model to be clear like some sort of invisibility cape, and others make a model appear bumpy, shiny, coarse, or anything else. Some textures (displacement maps) even change the geometry of the model. Textures can be projected like a slide through a slide projector, laid over like a blanket, shrink-wrapped, or tacked down to parts around model geometry. Textures take the same ball of geometry and change the object from a golf ball, to a tennis ball, to a baseball, to a basketball, to an earth ball, to the actual Earth. See Chapters 8 and 9 for more on the tremendous power of texturing.

No matter how exquisite your model is or the textures are, without light it's like radio, heard but not seen. 3D light, like everything else in digital space, is virtual. It is comprised of a set of algorithms that attempt to imitate light as it occurs in the real world. And even though tremendous strides have been made in the way 3D applications handle lighting instruments (the objects that actually produce the light) and the way those light particles (or waves) behave within digital space, a tremendous amount of artistry and interpretation is still needed to produce effectively lit scenes. Lighting is one of the most powerful, yet most often overlooked areas of 3D. See Chapter 10, for more about the theory behind lighting design and the practical applications of these theories.

Some 3D is illustrative in nature. Some 3D's purpose is to create beautiful still figures. Other 3D is narrative in purpose like animation. Although the same 3D application is used to create both stills and animations, ultimately, the goal and media of the two is different. Animation is bringing the geometry of models to life; giving them life, a motion personality. Animation is a complex process, and even the simplest ideas of a bouncing ball require careful study of the world around us and the physics of weight. To top it all off, the most believable is the animation that transcends the heavy technical requirements of animation to a level of organic movement. You will usually find that you will spend about one-fourth of your time doing everything else in animation, and three-fourths of your time animating. It is a challenging, but tremendously rewarding aspect of 3D, and Chapters 10–14 are dedicated to animation.

After a scene is modeled, textured, lit, and sometimes animated, the computer must paint the geometry, color, and light we have given it. This rendering that the computer produces is usually our final still or animation. There is a lot of different ways to render, everything from the most photorealistic to cartoon shading.

Keep in mind as you work that complex scenes take large amounts of time to render. Remember that after your work is finished, the computer still has a lot of work to interpret all your instructions, and sometimes even the fastest computers will take a *long* time to do so. Finishing up your lighting and clicking the "render" button as your client walks in the door is a very bad idea. (It is my experience that clients are usually unimpressed by a black screen.) There's a lot more to discuss about rendering, so a whole chapter is dedicated to it (Chapter 12); check it out.

BUILDING A 3D PROJECT

Now with all those definitions laid out in such linear fashion, it is important to note that 3D *is not a linear process*. Figure 1.1 shows a chart of the quasi-linear nature of the 3D process.

The first step to a 3D project is to plan, plan, plan. You might want to get in and do it, which is an important thing to do when just starting in on 3D, but sooner or later, you will want to actually do a completed project. Every hour spent developing effective plans for a project saves 10 hours in actual production time. The planning process consists of lots of drawings.

Michelangelo had volumes and volumes of sketches. Today, these sketches are masterpieces of art. To him, they were means toward an end. Some were studies of the form and shape of anatomy, objects, or people. Others were layout plans, or drafts for composition, balance, and design. Although some artists of today can create fantastic pieces of artwork based on reactions to what they've just laid on canvas, many of the great artists take time to plan how their final project is to be laid out.

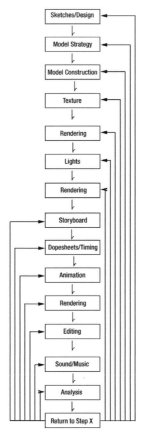

FIGURE 1.1   3D process.

3D should be no different. If the final project is a still image of a set of gears and cogs, sketches on how the cogs look, how they will be laid together to form a cohesive image, and notes on color and lighting are important. If the final project is a character, sketches of the character, its personality, and form provide a valuable visual resource during those tedious modeling hours (Figure 1.2). If the final project is an animation, many minutes of final footage can be saved if an effective storyboard is laid out with careful attention paid to camera angles, timing, and shot composition (Figure 1.3).

"Bah, a few extra minutes of footage, or a few extra renderings? That's not the end of the world!" you might say. It might not seem so now, but when a few extra renderings take 10–12 hours, and a few extra minutes turns into days to render four complex scenes, those 45 minutes it would have taken to make a sketch would have been well worth the time.

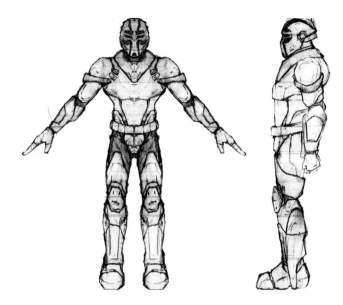

FIGURE 1.2   Game model character style sheet.

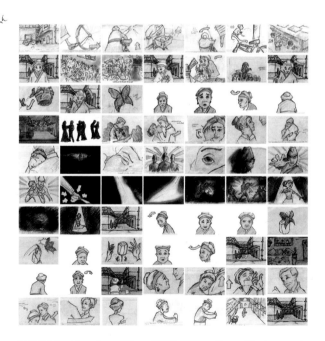

FIGURE 1.3   Storyboard from UIW's Willem Keetell's class project.

After the form of the model and composition of the shot has been worked and reworked on paper, it is time for strategizing the modeling process. Later, we will look at a lot of different ways to model, and it is easy to get caught up in the intricacies of the folds of skin under the eyes or the pock marks on the surface of the gear. But do not be seduced by the dark side! Modeling is fun, but it is only a part of the final project. Many people spend so much time creating perfect models that they never get around to texturing or animating the model and end up with a portfolio full of models but no finished projects, which works fine if you only plan to apply for modeling jobs, but disastrous if you goal is broader. Will the backside of the model ever be seen? Will the model or camera be moving when it is in the shot? How well lit is it? What kind of modeling can be done with textures? Ask yourself all of these questions before you start modeling. There is really no use in creating model parts if they are not seen. And there is no use spending hours on details if they flash through the shot with high motion blur in less than a second.

When all the planning a strategizing is done, it is time to actually touch the computer. The first step in the computer phase of 3D is to model. If planned effectively, modeling can be a fun process of sculpting, lathing, and creating that really can't be done the same way in any other media. Sometimes, you will find that your software or your modeling skills are not quite up to the task of realizing the original design. Thus, the "return to Step X" cycle begins. Redesign a bit, and then remodel.

After the models geometry is created, the texturing process begins. Sometimes texturing involves using stock textures (keep "canned" textures to a minimum), while at other times, it is creating your own through photographs or other figures. At still other times, creating textures is done through drawing your own textures in some other image creation program (for example, Photoshop, Illustrator, and so on). After the textures are created, the focus shifts to mapping those textures to the geometry of the model. Sometimes during this process, you will find that the texture needs altering or that the texture does not cover up flaws in the modeling that you thought it would, so some back tracking is needed.

When applying textures, do many interim renderings to see how the texture is falling across the surface of the model. Then model, texture, render, re-texture, re-render, sometime re-model, re-render, re-texture, re-render. . . you get the idea. When you render at this stage, be sure to use faster rendering algorithms; this is only a preview.

After applying the textures to the model, dive into the lighting of the project. Spend good time on lighting as good lighting can bring the most boring of models and textures to life, or it can kill the most vibrant of designs. Again, render often here. Oftentimes, during the lighting phase, you may find that the mood lighting you use is dulling the colors of the textures, so be sure to make adjustments to the textures.

Now, if the project calls for a still, a final render is in order. If the project is an animation, make sure that the storyboard is well worked and understood. If the animation calls for *sound-sync* (matching motion to sound) then building a *dope sheet* is an important step (Figure 1.4). Create your dope sheets to match your needs. Dope sheets are basically a way to map out the motion planned to the sound planned over the frames needed.

SPOON DESIGN & PRODUCTION						
Time	Frames	Action Description	Dialogue	Animation	Background	Camera Instruction

FIGURE 1.4   A sample dope sheet.

After you have mapped out how the timing works, it's time to start putting time into your project. Animation is sometimes called 4D, with time as the forth dimension. How you time your animations and how you design the movement is what gives animations personalities, what makes them interesting, and what makes them art. Since the last half of this book is devoted to animation, we leave this discussion until then. The key is to remember that animation, too, is a means to a finished project end and will obviously undergo revision after it is rendered.

When all of the rough footage from animations is finally done (probably created as *playblasts* instead of renderings), you will probably have many QuickTime movies, depending on how many shots are planned in your storyboard. (Playblasts are nonrendered outputs that enable you to put together a series of frames quickly without the need to spend the processing time of rendering.) The time has come to figure out which parts of the animation are truly needed to drive the story and which need to be left on the virtual cutting floor. We all fall in love with our projects; especially when we are pleased with a new technique we learned or when it is going well overall. However, audiences don't always share our love of newfound techniques and are usually bored if the elements we include do not facilitate in pushing the story forward. Plan on some significant time for editing. Good editing does not come quickly or easily, and usually several different editing sessions are needed to trim away unnecessary clips that made it past the storyboard cutting stages. It is during the editing process that you can begin to see whether all the elements listed previously have come together. If not, backup, rework, and try again.

Often, during the editing process, sound is added as an afterthought. However, sound is so important that it really deserves its own mention and category step. Animations work best when there is a clear concept of sound from the beginning of the project. Sound can help dictate motions, timing, and feeling. Take some time to create a sound *design*. Be careful not to just use stock sounds over the top of a creation. Putting stock sound over the top of a meticulously created 3D animation that took you weeks or months to painstakingly and lovingly create is like buying the whitest flour from Nebraska, the finest cocoa beans from South America, the purest sugar from Hawaii, and then getting water from the gutter to make a cake.

The biggest issue for many computer artists is the lack of outside feedback and influence. It's easy to get buried in the project at hand and finish the project without ever getting advice. After you have finished a good edit and a good sound design, realize that the work is still in process and get feedback—lots of it. You will be surprised how much your friends, family, and colleagues can help. Do not assume that when they say, "I don't understand what's happening there," they are telling you they do not understand the medium of 3D; it means you are not as clear as you should be in communicating your story. Besides getting friends or acquaintances to look at projects, get advice from those who know about 3D. There are a variety of newsgroups, forums, and other listservs that will allow you to post work for criticism. Usually the criticism that comes from these sources is constructive and comes from very knowledgeable sources. Sometimes a few well-placed constructive criticisms can take you in far more interesting and successful directions on a project. When the critique comes, and it always *does* come, disregard that which is of no use and adhere to the valid. After criticism, you might find that you need to rework clear back to the storyboard stage, or you might find that it's just a small matter of a tighter edit. Either way, the 3D cycle continues.

Now that we have looked at all the times to return to another step, it needs to be said that there is also a time to stop. The last step of the process is to know when to stop and let the project stand. There is always something that could be done a little bit better, but there are other stories to tell, more motion to study, and ideas to explore.

TUTORIAL INTRODUCTION AND EXPLANATION

One fallacy that exists all over the 3D world is: "You must know software *x*. If you don't, you'll never be able to create good work, and you'll never be able to get a job!" This sort of thinking comes from people who really do not understand the industry. Although there are some boutique-level animation houses that are looking for a Maya Master, or a Lightwave Lunatic, most of the largest employers of animators and the houses where animators would most like to work use some sort of proprietary software.

That is, you cannot get it anywhere and can only learn it when you get hired. Additionally, most studios that do use software available to the public often make sure of several packages within the same gig. Some software does certain things better than others—but none do *everything* better than everyone else. Studios are looking for good modelers, texturers, animators, and so on. They can always train you to use a new piece of software, but if you do not have the basic conceptual skills—well, you are of no use.

Further, the Web is littered with people creating absolutely horrible projects with the most incredible pieces of software and other folks creating amazing projects with free or very inexpensive packages. The rule is "content over tool."

However, ultimately, the big dichotomy is that you must know *some* piece of software to show you know the concepts that transcend the software. In this book, we will be using Maya as our medium; as the particular brand of paintbrush to create our masterpieces. As you are learning, stay focused on the concepts—do not go software chasing. You can show your mastery of 3D with most any application to get hired. After you get hired, these concepts could be translated to other packages; and if you really understand the tenets of good 3D modeling, texturing, and animation technique, you can quickly migrate to whatever package is in vogue or in use at the studio where you get hired.

The goal of the tutorials in this book is that you understand concepts, techniques, and strategies of 3D—not just one software. Then, with a firm understanding of the core issues of 3D, with a couple hours of fiddling, you can use any software to create your masterpieces.

THE MAYA PHILOSOPHY

So now that we have talked a bit about general workflow, let's look for a moment at how Maya approaches the 3D process and how this process is presented to the user through the Maya interface.

Nodes

Maya uses a very interesting, very powerful, very flexible, and potentially very troublesome method of executing commands called the *node system*. Maya thinks of each command you give it (creating a shape, tweaking a shape, applying a texture, binding skin, and so on) as a node. It keeps track of each command (node) you give it in something called *history*.

Think of history as a long list of nodes. Think of nodes as equations. Maya keeps track of these nodes in a linear fashion; it calculates what things should look like with the first node, and then with the result of that node, moves on to the next and calculates what the scene should look like after that, and so on. The power of this system is that you can jump back to most any spot along the history and change any particular node. This does not mean you are undoing back to that point; you are simply changing that particular part of the long series of equations.

When you make a change to the node, Maya automatically recalculates all of the nodes that took place after that node to produce the new result. It is as if you were working in Photoshop and 16 steps back, you made a color adjustment to one part of the image, and now you needed that changed. A node system would allow you to access that node—that point in time—adjust the color, and then all of the other changes, painting, filters, and so on that you had applied afterward would be applied again automatically.

The problem is that it makes Maya (and your hardware) work pretty hard to keep track of and continue to calculate a huge collection of instructions every time you do something to your scene. And, since it is generally a linear process of interpreting those nodes, the order that the nodes are resolved ends up being very important.

Later, we will look at deleting, reordering, and indeed clearing all the nodes so that you can essentially freeze time and tell Maya, "OK, don't worry about anything we've done before—just worry about this particular mesh as it now stands."

Effectively understanding the node system of Maya ultimately is critical to success with the application. Unfortunately, it does not make a whole lot of sense until you see it in action; so for now, keep it in mind that nodes are at work, and keep a watch for where you think they are involved. We will take a close look at nodes throughout the tutorials.

The Maya Interface

We are not going to cover the entire interface in this book; information on the interface is easily found in the Help documents that come with Maya, and there is no need to include it all again here. What we are going to cover in this book are a few of the core parts of the interface that we will be using in some upcoming tutorials.

The interface is big; it can be powerful; but it can also get in the way. Be aware that there are loads and loads of buttons nested all over the place and that too casual clicking can activate or deactivate something that you need or is important.

Figure 1.5 shows an overview of the interface and how it breaks down. Many of these tools we will use pull-down menus for instead. Most of them we will access via keyboard shortcuts as they are much, much faster.

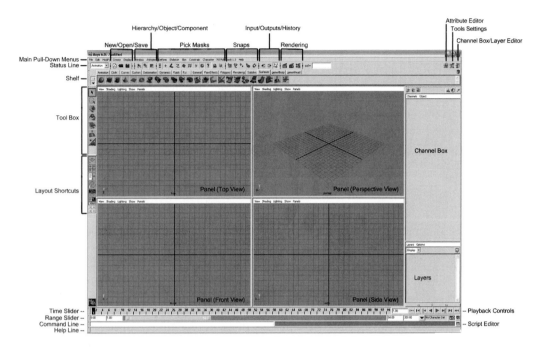

Attribute Editor
Tools Settings
Channel Box/Layer Editor

FIGURE 1.5   Maya interface overview.

As we progress with the discussion of tools throughout this book, remember that Maya provides a bit of help within the interface. If you let your mouse rest over buttons within the interface, a small yellow box will pop up with information on what that button is. Similarly, on the bottom of the interface is an area called the Help Line. The Help Line will often provide information on how to use a particular tool or alert you when there are problems. It also will show the name of any tool upon which your mouse is resting. In Maya 7, there is a box at the bottom of the Attributes Editor (bottom right corner) called Notes: that can provide some added insight into how a tool works.

Menu Sets

The Maya interface is so vast, in fact, that it can not hold all of the pull-down menus visible at any one time. Maya has various *menu sets*. These menu sets actually change the pull-down menus available at the top of the interface based upon what functions you are involved in.

Figure 1.6 shows some menu sets. Notice that they are fairly intuitively broken down into the general workflow sections of a 3D project. When you change the menu settings, the pull-down menus to the right of the Window will also change (Figure 1.7).

FIGURE 1.6 Change the menu set in the top left corner of the interface.

FIGURE 1.7 The entire collection of pull-down menus right of Window will change depending on the menu set within which you are working.

Pull-Down Menus

Commands that are available to use in Maya are nested within its many pull-down menus. These pull-down menus work as pull-down menus do in any program except for a few refinements.

The first is that when you select a pull-down menu, you will notice at the top of that are three small bars (Figure 1.8). If you select that bar, you can tear away that menu into a floating palette. This can be incredibly useful if you are going to be revisiting a collection of tools for a short amount of time. With the floating palette, you can have those tools at your beck and call, and you can close the palette just as quickly.

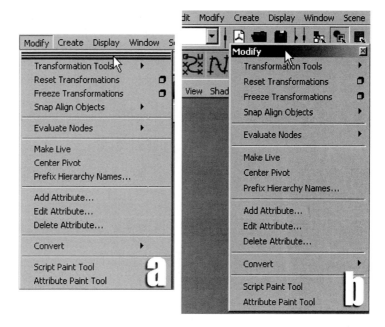

FIGURE 1.8   Tearing off floating palettes.

Additionally, within the pull-down menus many tools have more than just the name of the tool. Many tools will have next to their names small shadowed boxes. This box is referred to as the option box. When you are moving your mouse down a pull-down menu, remember that you cannot only select a tool or command, but move out to the option box to show some additional options for how that tool is to operate (Figure 1.9).

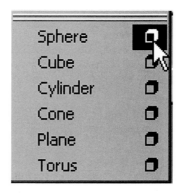

FIGURE 1.9   The option box within a pull-down menu.

The fact that an option box is present usually indicates that the tool can and should be adjusted. Keep in mind that changes you make within the option box remain changed until you reset them to default or change them to new values. So if you have not used a tool before, or it has been a while since you used the tool, go ahead and open its option box, and select Edit > Reset Settings (from within the option box window), to get the options back to their defaults. (Figure 1.10).

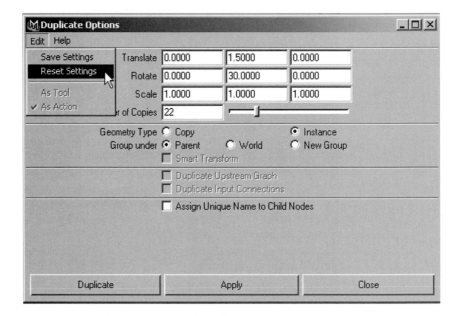

FIGURE 1.10   Resetting settings within an Option window.

ORGANIZING PROJECTS

It is important to understand how to organize objects within Maya. Although there are lots of ways to organize projects, and much of organization is personal preference, a couple of tools are used in most all organization schemes: Layers and manipulating the Outliner.

Layers

Figure 1.11 shows the three buttons at the top right corner of the Maya interface. From left to right these buttons define what is to be displayed in the space that the Channel Box (at the far right of the interface), by default, occupies: Show or Hide Attribute Editor, Show or Hide the tool Settings, Show or Hide the Channel Box/Layer Editor.

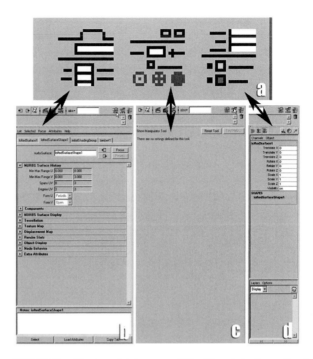

FIGURE 1.11   The top right corner of the Maya interface, allowing you to define whether to display the Channel Box/Layer Editor, Attribute Editor, or Tool Settings.

Note that the far right button shows two things: the Channel Box and Layer Editor. The Channel Box will be discussed at length later—basically, it contains information on the editable channels for a selected object; it also shows the nodes of the object in the INPUTS area.

Beneath the Channel Box is the Layer Editor. You can hide the Layer Editor (or the Channel Box for that matter) with the three buttons at the top of the Channel Box (Figure 1.12). The three buttons there allow for both Channel Box and Layer Editor to be displayed, or to only show one at a time.

The Layer Editor allows you to create, modify, hide, or display layers of your project. Layers contain objects. Layers can be used in the rendering process—you can choose to render or not render objects by layers or choose to render layers to different files for compositing later. Additionally, layers can be used to hide, show, or *template* objects while you are still editing your 3D world.

To create a layer, select the Layers pull-down menu and select Create Layer (Figure 1.13). Clicking the small button at the top right corner of the Layer Editor will also create a new layer.

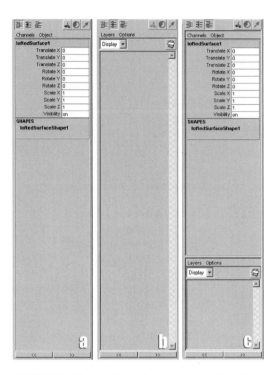

FIGURE 1.12   Channel Box with buttons to allow for showing or hiding of just the Channel Box, just the Layer Editor, or both.

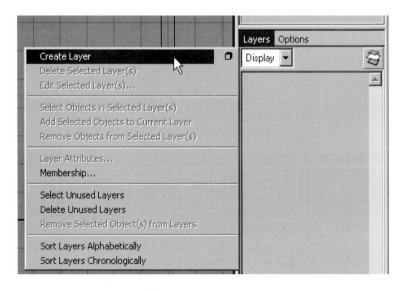

FIGURE 1.13   Creating a new layer.

This will create a layer called layer1 that you will see appear in the editor. Double-click this name to open a dialog box shown in Figure 1.14. Within this dialog box, you can change the name of a layer (make sure to use underscores instead of spaces); you can change whether a layer is visible or not (although there are better places to do this); and you can decide what color the wireframe of the objects in that layer will appear as.

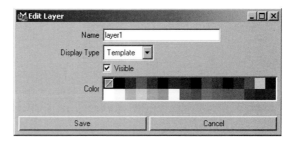

FIGURE 1.14 Changing the name of a layer.

Next to the name of the layer are two columns. The first with a V in it defines the visibility of the layer. Clicking on the V turns the visibility of that layer (and consequently all the objects contained in that layer) off.

The second column is blank by default but will turn to a T or R as you click the space (Figure 1.15).

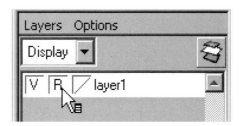

FIGURE 1.15 The Template/Reference column of the Layer Editor.

T stands for Template. A templated layer (or object) appears as a salmon-colored wireframe. This object cannot be selected or altered and does not render; however, it can be a great resource as a sort of construction object that assists in the building of other forms.

R stands for Reference. Making a layer referenced makes the objects appear as normal; however, these objects cannot be selected or altered. This works great when you have an object or group of objects placed and you know they should not be moved. Similarly, if you are animating a character with joints, you will not want to accidentally select the mesh—placing the mesh on a referenced layer keeps it out of reach.

Finally, to make objects part of a layer, select the object, right-click on the layer, and select Add Selected Object from the drop-down menu (Figure 1.16).

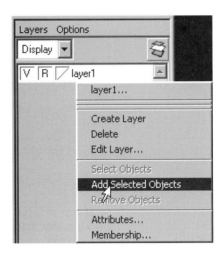

FIGURE 1.16   Adding an object to a layer.

Hierarchies and the Outliner

The Outliner is available at any time by selecting Window > Outliner. The Outliner often is underutilized by beginning 3D artists working in Maya. At its most basic, the Outliner simply gives a list of the objects within your scene. Within the Outliner, you can select objects or group, rename them, and more importantly, you can group or reorder hierarchies. In the course of the tutorials, you will have lots of chances to see the Outliner in action.

Consider Figure 1.17. In this screenshot of the Outliner, the object East_Wall is selected. Notice however, that East_Wall is also part of a group called Walls. In Maya, the grouping function is actually quite powerful as it actually creates a null object (an empty object with no geometry of its own), and makes the objects grouped together children of it. We will talk much more of this hierarchy function in the tutorials contained in Chapters 2 and 3.

The important thing to notice is that Walls (the group) is not selected; even though it appears highlighted. When something in the Outliner appears highlighted green, it indicates that an object that is a child of it is selected. The actual object that is selected will be highlighted gray (closer to blue on a Mac).

FIGURE 1.17   Screenshot of the Outliner. East-Wall
is selected (highlighted gray) within the group Walls
(highlighted green on-screen).

CONCLUSION

Now that you have had a chance to look at the general 3D process and
learned a bit about how Maya thinks, organizes, and presents 3D space to
you, it is time to get your virtual hands dirty and get working on using
Maya to create great work.

CHAPTER

2

UNDERSTANDING THE DIGITAL 3D WORLD

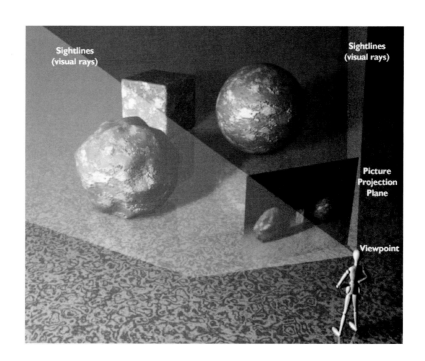

A rt has been and continues to be an evolutionary process. Although it has probably been around for as long as humankind has, the goals and methods have changed dramatically from the French cave paintings of Lascaux to the Egyptian *Geese of Medum* to Hokusai's *The Great Wave* to Botticelli's *The Birth of Venus* to Ingres' *Grande Odalisque* to Rothko's *Four Darks in Red* to the work of John Lasseter and his crew in *Toy Story*, *Toy Story 2*, and *The Incredibles*. All of these methods of depicting real or mystical three-dimensional occurrences on a 2D plane have been new steps in new directions.

The 3D World around Us

With two eyes, our brain is able to take the two different figures each eye sends to process visual cues of depth. Perspective in art is the attempt to fool the eye into understanding depth, distance, and relative position on a 2D space. The understanding of how to depict depth on the 2D plane of a painting or drawing has been one of the most important developments in art history and the foundation upon which 3D applications of today are built.

The basis of perspective is that the surface of a painting or drawing acts as an invisible plane that sits perpendicular to the viewer, called the *projection plane*. The viewer stands at a point referred to as the *viewpoint*.

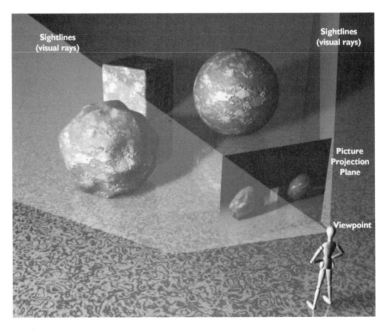

FIGURE 2.1   Projection plane, viewpoint, and perspective.

As the viewer looks through the projection plane, he sees a horizon usually depicted by a straight line, which includes a vanishing point. The vanishing point is the point at which all parallel lines also parallel to the viewer converge. As perspective advanced, artists realized that lines not parallel to the viewer had their own vanishing points, some of which were out of the projection plane (Figure 2.1). These are a lot of terms to throw out at the beginning of this discussion, but they all come in handy.

WHAT IS DIGITAL SPACE?

An important idea behind perspective is that every shape and object depicted on the projection plane sends a ray to the viewpoint, or our eye. Computer 3D applications, including Maya, rely heavily on this concept through a rendering process called *raytracing*. Imagine that all objects in a scene emit these theoretical rays. On their way to the viewpoint, they will pass through the projection plane, which in the case of computers is the screen. In theory, the screen records what shade, hue, and intensity that pixel on your monitor will appear. Raytracing works backward by working down these rays to the objects while considering whether the visible light is from a source or reflected. There are many different ways besides raytracing that computers actually use to figure out what should be displayed on your screen (see the following section), but it makes for a good way to picture how the computer is painting or projecting the 3D objects present in its digital space.

Digital Space through Project Windows and Virtual Cameras

The forms of perspective that we most readily accept are the linear forms that most closely resemble the world around us. Because of this, most of the figures we see done in 3D art have been displayed in perspective projection. However, although perspective is what is best for finally understanding a composition, it is not always the best way to view digital space when creating that composition.

In Maya, you can look at the same digital space and the objects contained in that space from a variety of different viewpoints. By default, you can view the scene from top, front, and side views. Although you can look at the digital space in perspective from all of these points, perspective provides some obstacles between you and the 3D application.

When the computer projects the space in perspective, it is showing you all three dimensions on your 2D screen. The problem is, your mouse can move in only two dimensions across the projection plane of your screen. So, when your mouse clicks on an object, it becomes very difficult for the application to decide whether you are just moving an object horizontally (x) and vertically (y), or whether you are attempting to move it in depth (z) as well. What Maya does is create a view plane, a plane that is perpendicular to your view, and moves the objects along this changing view plane. To rectify this, 3D applications use something called an *orthographic view* or projection.

Orthographic projections are views in which the parallel lines in the model do not converge on a vanishing point like they do in perspective; instead, they remain parallel or at right angles with the projection plane (*ortho* means "at right angles to"). Essentially, it means that you are only being shown two of the three dimensions.

In Maya, the default view of the 3D space is a big perspective view. However, by hitting the Spacebar quickly, you will see the perspective view (top right corner) as well as three orthographic views (Figure 2.2).

Note that new to Maya 7 is a new tool in the top right corner of the perspective view (as seen in Figure 2.2). Each of the cone shapes contained in that tool indicates a different orthographic view. By clicking on them, Maya will convert the view panel to show that orthographic view. Clicking on the cube in the center shifts back to the perspective view. It makes for some cool eye candy; but is also quite functional.

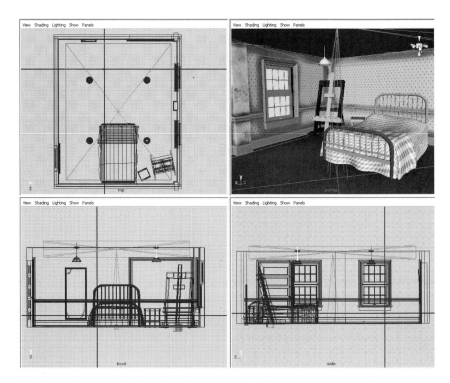

FIGURE 2.2   With a quick Spacebar click, you can see both perspective and orthographic views of your 3D space. Pressing the Spacebar again will bring a view panel back to full screen.

The advantages of orthographic viewpoints include the ease in which you can align objects. You can quickly and confidently position all the objects so that they are sitting on the ground plane from a side view. Or, from a top view, you can move furniture around without worrying about whether it is dropping through the floor. However, one orthographic view by itself is fairly useless as you cannot tell depth. So the best use of orthographic views is one in which you have multiple orthographic views open so that you can adjust the vertical aspects from one angle, the horizontal from another and the depth from the third—a view for each dimension. Maya creates orthographic cameras for each of these views as can be seen in the Outliner (Window > Outliner—a panel that lists the objects in the scene—more on the Outliner later). Perspective cameras are the views from which 3D projects are usually finally rendered and presented through.

To show any one view panel full screen, move your mouse over it and press the Spacebar again. Pressing the Spacebar again takes you back to the four-panel view.

Computers Drawing Methods

As you give the computer directions on what to do in its digital space, the computer tries to let you know what is going on by drawing or rendering the information on your screen. We have already looked at the ways the computer attempts to show the shapes of the objects, but there are also a variety of ways that it tries to show the form.

Rendering refers to the way the computer draws or paints on the projection plane (your computer screen) the information it has. 3D is the process of creating the world and then telling the computer to paint it for you and how to paint it. Sometimes the way you will want the computer to paint or render for you is in beautifully finished ways. However, at other times, more informative forms of illustration will be necessary.

The most intuitive form of rendering is shaded rendering with its various algorithms. Shaded rendering forms are those in which you see an object that is shaded to show roundness of form or source of light. Figure 2.3 shows a variety of shaded rendering formats. We will talk much more on some of the higher end rendering methods (Raytracing, Raydiosity, and so on) in Chapter 9, but for now, the more photorealistic the rendering, the longer it takes the computer to figure out how to paint and actually paint all the details of an image; so long, in fact, that those forms are not really feasible for easy maneuvering and modeling within digital space.

There are some forms of shaded rendering that are fairly feasible for the hardware technology of today to handle. The most popular form of late is the technology developed by SGI (Silicon Graphics Inc.) called OpenGL. OpenGL is a fast rendering algorithm that can be very effectively sped up by the right hardware. Most all video cards now come OpenGL

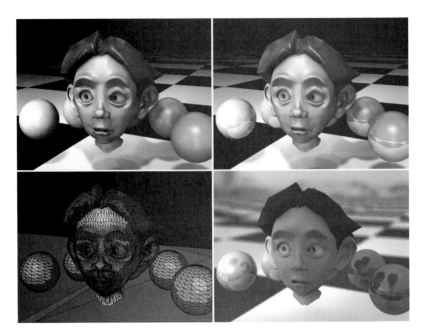

FIGURE 2.3   Rendering comparisons between varieties of shaded renderings.

accelerated. OpenGL is powerful in its ability to quickly draw lit models that show at least a reasonable facsimile of textures applied to the model's surface. It is still a rough form in many instances but gives a good idea of overall color and position. The point of all of these low-end shaded renderers is to provide the modeler a quick look at roughly how the light and texture falls across the surface of the objects present through the hardware; the video card essentially can draw this rendering in real time.

Sometimes, understanding the form is more important than seeing color and light on the surface. For instance, a typical exercise in most every beginning drawing course is to *draw through* the object. That is, the student draws the backsides of the objects through the space presenting the front side. The motive behind this exercise is to better understand the form. Maya's key method of allowing this is to display things as Wireframe.

By pressing 4, 5, 6, and 7 on your keyboard, you can toggle between the different display modes. Pressing 4 will display the model as wireframe (Figure 2.4).

Imagine this wireframe view as essentially the wire you would use under a paper-mache form. On a technical note, it actually defines the edges of each polygon or *isoparm* of the form. The wireframe mode allows for a quick look at your geometry and how the polygons are assembled. It allows for direct selection through an object and allows you to see objects that may be behind or inside other objects.

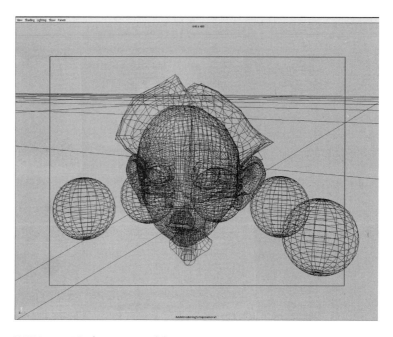

FIGURE 2.4   Wireframe view of the 3D scene.

Perhaps the biggest benefit to wireframe is the speed in which they redraw. As models become more complex and Maya has to deal with more and more information, it takes longer and longer for it to draw the information you have given it. Sometimes, the models become so complex that using the OpenGL shaded displays just takes too long.

Pressing 4 displays the scene as wireframe; pressing 5 displays it as Smooth Shade, which essentially is an opaque surface rendering with minimal texture information (usually simple colors). Pressing 6 uses Smooth Shade but adds Hardware texturing, which can give you a preview of bitmapped-based images used to define color or bump in the scene. Pressing 7 shows the scene with Smooth Shading and lighting. Note that this lighting is really an approximation and does not do a good job with some of the more sophisticated aspects of light like shadows or decay. Figure 2.5 gives a brief look at how the different display modes appear. Be sure to check out this figure and Figure 2.4 in their color versions on the CD-ROM.

ON THE CD

Also new to Maya 7 is the ability to show an object as a Bounding Box or Point. Bounding boxes are simply a box that would surround (bound) all the geometry of an object. Point shows the vertices or control vertices of a form. Neither are particularly useful unless you have an amazingly complex model; which you probably will not have over the course of working through this book. However, if you need them, they can be called up under the View pull-down menu of any view panel.

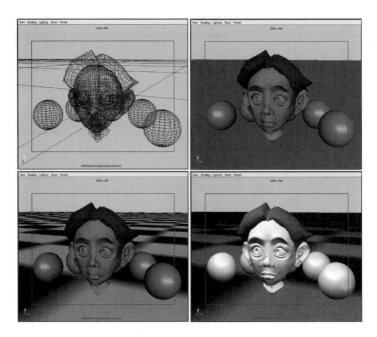

FIGURE 2.5 From top left clockwise: 4: Wireframe, 5: Smooth Shaded, 6: Smooth Shaded with Hardware Texturing, and 7: Smooth Shaded with lights.

Moving in the Digital 3D Universe

Computers work in mathematical equations and algorithms. Because of this and to be able to communicate with you, they think of digital space in terms of a measurable 3D axis with x, y, and z planes. This *Euclidean geometry model* depicts x as horizontal, y as vertical, and z represents depth. These values can be positive or negative, depending on their relative position to the center of the digital universe where all values of x, y, and z are 0. This is why the default screen of most all 3D applications (including Maya's) includes at least one grid and small key at somewhere to let you know how it is displaying the digital space (Figure 2.6). In Maya, the grid is right in the middle of the screen, and the key is at the bottom left of each view panel.

Maya thinks of all the objects, parts of objects, vertices of objects, or points on that object as a series of three numbers *(x, y, z)*. Although the user does not usually need to concern himself with the exact numbers involved, it is still important to know which values represent which direction as most every 3D application allows for the manual entering of numeric values. Further, understanding how computers think and keep track of digital space helps to understand how the computer shows it to the user. This is especially important in Maya, since (as you will soon see), Maya will sometimes simply provide three input fields with no clue as to what they are. With few exceptions, these are *xyz* coordinates.

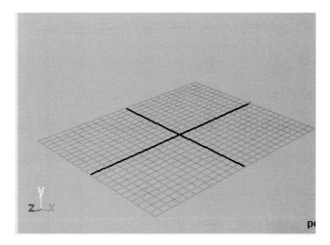

FIGURE 2.6   Default plane and axis key.

Figure 2.7 shows a cube with an object center at (0,0,0). Each side of the cube is two units long, so each of the vertices of this cube is at (1,1,1), (−1,1,1), (1,−1,1), (1,1,−1), (−1,−1,1), (1,−1,−1), (−1,1,−1), or (−1,−1,−1).

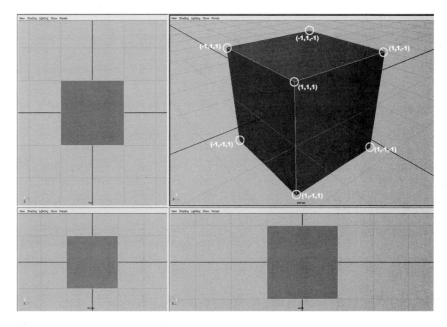

FIGURE 2.7   Two-unit-wide cube sitting at (0,0,0). Note that each of the vertices (corners of the cube) have an xyz coordinate value.

It is important to keep in mind that as much as we are using those right-brained functions of creativity, the computer is essentially a left-brained thinker. This is important to remember as we try to tell the computer where to position objects.

When Maya shows shapes in 3D space rendered in perspective (as it is in Figure 2.7), it is interpreting space on a 2D plane. Since our mouse can only move in two dimensions across the plane of the screen, if we simply reach in with our mouse and grab hold of the object with a Translate tool and attempt to move it, Maya makes its best attempt at interpreting which of the three dimensions we want to move the object through.

Using the typical four-view method shown in Figure 2.7, we are given orthographic views of the object. That is, other than in the persp (perspective) View Panel, we are only presented with two dimensions in each window. This simplified view of the objects present in digital space assists in clarifying to Maya how the object is to move. If we want to move the object along the horizon sideways (x-axis) or in depth (z-axis), we simply look at the view that shows the top of the objects, and no matter how we move it from this view point, it will not move the object up and down. This is an effective tool if you are arranging furniture in a room and do not want the furniture to end up floating above the plane of the floor. Similarly, if you grab an object from the front view, you can move it up and down (y-axis) and sideways (x-axis) but not affect its depth, and from the side view, you can affect the up and down (y-axis) and depth (z-axis) position of the object without moving it in its relative side-to-side position. This will make much more sense after you get into creating forms in upcoming tutorials.

Moving about in the Space

Among the most important things to be able to understand is where you are and what you are looking at within Maya's 3D space. Remember that Maya thinks about each of the View Panels as the viewfinder of a camera. These cameras are sitting in space and showing you the 3D world that you are about to manipulate. Being able to move these cameras (through the viewfinder) is key to survival in the digital realm.

When using Maya, it is critical to have a three-button mouse. Yes, yes, Apple has been adamant that you only need one button for years, but not when it comes to Maya. If you are on a Mac, buy a three-button mouse. If you are on a PC, be sure you really have three buttons— not two buttons and a scroll wheel. Although you can use the scroll wheel as a button, it speeds the entire process up if you have a true three-button mouse.

The Alt key (Command key on a Mac) will be your best friend. Most heavy Maya user's keyboard's Alt key is nearly completely worn away because of constant use, with their thumbs just permanently resting there. Holding the Alt key down essentially says to Maya, "Hey! I'm going to move the camera that I'm looking through now."

Alt-Left-Mouse-Button (Alt-LMB) will allow you to *tumble* your camera around either the active object, or the world's center. *Tumbling* is synonymous with rotating the camera as it stays fixed on a given point. Tumbling the camera allows you to rotate around a point in space. This allows you to move around, over, or under an object. Note that this tool only works in perspective view.

Alt-Middle-Mouse-Button (Alt-MMB) allows you to *track* the camera. *Tracking* is what most people would think of as moving the camera without rotating it. Think of the camera at any time as resting on tracks, when you Alt-MMB-drag, the camera will move along those tracks. This allows you to move along your scene to look at another point in space. Tracking works in perspective and orthographic views.

Alt-Right-Mouse-Button (Alt-RMB) or Alt-LMB+MMB allows you to *dolly* your camera. This means you are moving your camera closer or farther away from the object or point of interest. It is not changing the focal length; it is not using the zoom lens on the camera; it is actually moving the camera closer. Dolly works in perspective and orthographic views.

 There are other tools to control the camera including the ability to roll it (as in a dutch-tilt, or actually change the aperture of the virtual lens); but for now, and in most situations, the ability to tumble (Alt-LMB), track (Alt-MMB), and dolly (Alt-RMB) are very efficient at getting you around your scene.

Mastering Model Movement and Manipulation

When a sculptor undertakes an ambitious public commission project, he usually uses a very wide variety of techniques and tools. When a painter undertakes a challenging piece of trompe l'oeil, even though it is a definite style of painting, he still uses a wide variety of brush sizes, medium, paints, and techniques. So it is with digital art. The techniques described in the previous chapter are all different methods and tools on the digital palette. No one single tool or method will produce a good finished project; only combinations of the right tools at the right time will produce the right model.

Because of the immense power that emerges from using a variety of modeling techniques, it becomes necessary to assemble the different segments of your model into one coherent shape. To do this, an understanding of how to move, manipulate, and organize shapes within digital space must be had.

TOOLBOX

Before we begin jumping into digital space again, it would be prudent to discuss the idea of tools. As you work in 3D, you have a mouse that roams about the screen, scurrying hither and yon carrying out your orders. The orders carried out by this mouse are largely dependent on what sort of tools you are using. Maya (like most 3D applications) has a Toolbox (really the name) that contains some commonly used tools (Figure 2.8). The Toolbox is located in the top left corner of the interface.

FIGURE 2.8   Maya's Toolbox.

Some tools are for moving objects, some for resizing, others for rotating, and still others for altering polygon structure and a host of other functions. Each tool has a separate function and cannot do the functions of any other tools. This may seem obvious, but when you reach a point of utter frustration, the first thing to do is check that you are using the right tool for the right job.

Positioning Objects in Axis-Defined Space

The first tool to discuss is the Move Tool. In Maya, you use the Move Tool to *translate* an object in space. It is actually a bit more than that, as it will also allow you to select an object to be translated.

Within any view panel, a selected object will let you know it is selected by highlighting its polygons, or its isoparms (more on these terms later) in green, and by displaying a Pivot or manipulator in the center of the object. This manipulator is where you click to translate the object. However, the manipulator actually is several tools in one (Figure 2.9).

Notice that the manipulator is essentially three handles to indicate the *x, y,* and *z* (X Handle = red, Y Handle = green, and Z Handle = blue).

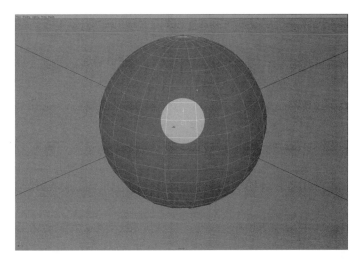

FIGURE 2.9   Maya object Pivot (sometimes referred to as manipulator).

There is a fourth handle indicated by the yellow box in the center called the Center Handle. This yellow box actually indicates the plane from which you are viewing the object.

With the Move tool activated, if you click and drag on the Center Handle (yellow box), the object will move along this image plane. In perspective view, this means it may be moving in x, y, and z directions. In orthographic views (top, side, or front), grabbing the manipulator in the center will move it in the two dimensions available in that view panel.

Each of the red, green, and blue handles (Translate X Handle, Translate Y Handle, and Translate Z Handle) can be used to translate (move) the object as well. If you click and drag the Translate Y Handle (green), for instance, you can constrain the translation so that it only moves in the Y direction. Note that when you have a handle selected, it will highlight yellow. The same is true for the other two handles.

Additionally, the Move Tool allows for a few other tricks. If you Control-click on any one of the directional handles, you can temporarily turn off the ability to translate the object in that direction. You will know because the Center Handle will change to reflect the directions that the object can still be translated along. Figure 2.10 shows the Center Handle after Control-clicking the Y handle.

Now, using the Move Tool, if you click-drag the Center handle, the object will only move in the x and z directions. Try it.

Control-click back on the Center Handle to enable all directions again.

 Hotkey Alert   *The Move Tool's keyboard short cut is w (lowercase).*

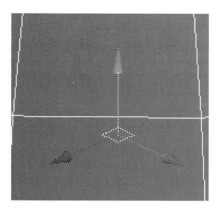

FIGURE 2.10   The Move Tool allows you to turn off a direction of translation. This figure shows the y direction turned off.

Rotation Functions

Besides being able to move objects around digital space, we can also rotate the objects around the object's axes. In Maya, this is done with the Rotate Tool. Each object has its own axis around which it rotates.

Like object movement, Maya allows for the unconstrained free rotation of objects, or a constrained rotation for those situations in which you want the car to be facing North instead of East, but you do not want it sitting on only two tires.

You can select an object while the Rotate Tool is active by clicking on it. When an object is selected and you are in the Rotate Tool, it will highlight in green, and you will have a new manipulator in the middle of the object (Figure 2.11).

By click-dragging in the middle of the Rotation manipulator, you can freely rotate the object in all three directions. However, ultimately this can be fairly tough to control, so constraining your rotation is usually preferable.

Like the Move Tool, the Rotate Tool's manipulator has four handles. They are represented by circles: a red Rotate X Handle, a green Rotate Y Handle, a blue Rotate Z Handle, and a yellow Rotate View Axis Handle.

When you click on any of these circles, they will highlight yellow to indicate you have got a hold on it. When you click-drag a handle, you will rotate the object around the respective axis. Note that each handle's color indicates which axis the object will rotate around.

 Hotkey Alert *The Rotate Tool's keyboard shortcut is e (lowercase).*

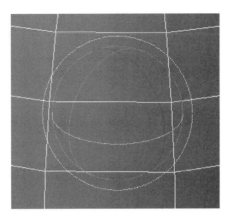

FIGURE 2.11   The Rotate Tool's manipulator.

Scale Functions and Relative Sizes

After objects are created, we can define and alter their size. Consistent with the Move and Rotate Tools, the Scale Tool in Maya allows you to manipulate the size of an object. It allows you to select an object directly and has four handles: Scale X Handle, Scale Y Handle, Scale Z Handle, and a Center Scale Handle (Figure 2.12).

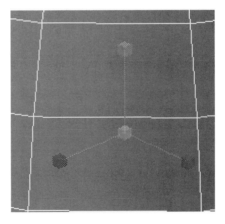

FIGURE 2.12   The Scale Tool's manipulator.

As you would expect, each of these handles allow you to scale the object in one direction. The notable exception is the Center Scale Handle. By click-dragging that handle, you can scale the object proportionally in all directions.

The Scale Tool's keyboard shortcut is r (lowercase).

Universal Manipulator

New to Maya 7 is a tool that by itself nearly makes Maya 7 worth the up-grade. Right below the Scale Tool in the Toolbox is the new Universal Manipulator tool, which is a fusion of the Move, Scale, and Rotate tools combined … plus some.

Here is the way it works. Select an object and activate the Universal Manipulator. The object will be surrounded with a bounding box that has manipulators on each of its edges and at the vertices. Additionally, the traditional move manipulator will be at the center (Figure 2.13).

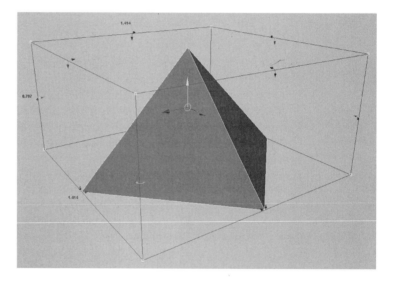

FIGURE 2.13   The Universal Manipulator with a selected object.

Now, with this one tool, you can move the object by clicking on the manipulator in the center, rotate the object by grabbing any of the curved arrows along the edges, and scale the object by grabbing any of the blue dots at the vertices of the bounding box. Give it a try.

A few added perks of this tool occur when you press the Ctrl or Shift key. While using the rotation manipulator handles, hold the Shift key down to constrain the rotation to 5-degree increments (note the blue number value letting you know how far you have rotated). Similarly, while using the rotation manipulator handles, hold the Ctrl key down to rotate not around the object center (as it does by default) but rather around the bounding box's opposite edge.

When using the scale manipulators (small blue boxes at each corner of the bounding box), by default, the object scales around the vertex opposite of the one you are dragging. Hold the Shift key down to scale around the object center, and hold the Ctrl key down to scale along just one axis.

If you are a long-time user of Maya, it might take a bit to get used to the power of this tool, but it is worth it. Manipulating objects position, scale and rotation becomes much more fluid with this new tool.

 Hotkey Alert *Ctrl-t activates the Universal Manipulator.*

Manipulating the Manipulator

By default, the manipulator is in the center of the object's 3D space. However, you might not always want it there. For instance, when creating a door, ultimately, you want the door to rotate around its hinges along its edge, and not around its center. Similarly, if you are creating a pillar, it is much easier to scale it up from its bottom so that it grows up from the floor.

Maya allows for some simple manipulator location alterations. Simply press Insert (on a PC) or Home (on a Mac). When you do this, the manipulator (regardless of whether you are in the Translate, Rotate, or Scale Tool), will change to look like Figure 2.14.

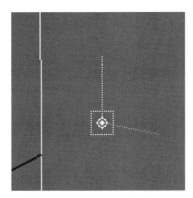

FIGURE 2.14   Moving the manipulator.

Now treat the manipulator as though you were using the Move Tool. You can do a constrained movement by grabbing any of the colored posts or move it freely with the center handle. After you have the manipulator placed where you want it, press Insert (Home on Mac) again, and that will lock the manipulator into that new location.

You will look at this technique much more in tutorials to come.

Hotkey Alert *To move the manipulator, press Insert (or Home on a Mac). Be sure to press Insert again to move out of this mode. Also note that holding the d key down allows you to adjust the manipulator; releasing the d key returns you to the last tool you were using.*

ENOUGH THEORY ALREADY

We have covered an awful lot of ethereal theory of how the computer thinks and communicates in digital space. This knowledge is important in order to be able to quickly communicate what you want the computer to do, but enough is enough. Now that we know how the computer takes instructions, let's look at how to plan for these instructions and how to give the instructions to Maya. Through the course of this book, we will be looking at several minitutorials to illustrate particular techniques. In addition, we will be working on one long tutorial that runs through the entire length of the book that will make use of all the techniques covered.

In each of the tutorials, the actual steps of the tutorial will be numbered. To make sure that more than just the "do this, and then do thats" are covered, there will be "Why?" boxes. These boxes will cover a bit of the theory behind the tool, or the rationale behind the workflow. Although these are not critical to getting through the tutorial, they are important to understand what is really going on. Remember the goal is not to just finish the tutorial, but to master the tools and concepts covered in the tutorial so you can create your own masterpieces of 3D.

If you are having problems with any of the steps, be sure to take a look at the CD-ROM. There you will find Maya files saved at various points in the tutorial. In addition, you can find all the figures of the book in full-color to get a more detailed read on the imagery.

So, without further ado, read on to get started putting the theory into practice and start creating.

MAYA'S MENU SET

Throughout the coming chapters, we will talk much more about the various parts of Maya's interface. However, there are a few things we should talk about right off the bat to make sure that they do not get in the way of the learning process.

Maya is so complex that there are actually several collections of pull-down menus. If you take a look at the top of the Maya interface, you will see File, Edit, Modify, Create, Display, and Window. These pull-down menus are a constant; they will always (unless you hide them) be visible. Within these menus are most of the tools you might need to access at various times during your construction process.

Beyond those, and depending on whether you are using Maya Complete or Maya Unlimited, you will have between four and six different menu sets. If you look at the very top left corner of your interface (Figure 2.15), you will see a pop-down menu that allows you to pick which menu set to display. The default is often Animation; although the first thing you usually do on a project is model.

FIGURE 2.15   Menu Set pop-down menu.

Depending on which menu set you have selected, the number of menus and the content of those menus after Window will change. Intuitively, the pull-down menus for each set will correspond to the tools you will need for Modeling, Animating, or Rendering your project.

In the course of the coming tutorials, sometimes it will be very important to know in which menu set you should be working. If it is a menu set specific pull-down menu, it will be indicated with a ? mark. So, Modeling ? Edit Polygons > Extrude Face (Options) means to find the Edit Polygons within the Modeling menu set and choose Extrude Face with options (or the little shadowed box).

TUTORIAL 2.1   PRIMITIVE MAN

Objectives:

1. Learn to create primitive polygonal shapes.
2. Use the Translate, Rotate, and Scale Tools.
3. Adjust manipulator location.
4. Explore the power of groups.

So this is not the sexiest of tutorials and the results look a bit primitive. However, at the end of this, you should have a good idea of how to move around Maya's 3D space and how to move your objects around that space.

Define Your Project.

Maya keeps track of files within Projects. A Project is actually just a collection of folders that contains various elements to be used. It can contain multiple scene files (what you would think of as Maya files), bitmapped files used for textures, movie files used as projections, sound files for lip-sync, and completed rendered sequential stills.

As Maya does not actually nest files—rather it links to them—having a proper file structure is a very important point. Making sure that you have control over where your Projects are and making sure Maya knows which project you are working within is absolutely critical, especially when you start to work with other artists. If you are working in a lab situation, make sure to define your Project before you do anything else every time you sit down at a computer. Do not take it for granted that no one else has used the machine or changed the defined project.

Step 1: Create space on your hard drive to save your Maya files. You might create a folder on your desktop called "Maya Tutorials" or something like that. This way, you can keep all your projects nested here.
Step 2: Within Maya, Select File > Project > New.
Step 3: Enter Primitive_Man into the Name input field.

To ensure true cross platform compatibility, Maya prefers to use underscores instead of spaces. In some places, Maya is pickier than others, but it is a good habit to get into to just always use underscores.

Step 4: Next to the Location input field click the Browse ... button. Find the Maya Tutorials folder on your desktop and press OK.
Step 5: Click the Use Defaults button.

The Use Defaults button essentially creates a bunch of folders that Maya knows. Although you could choose to store all your textures in a folder called "Fred," the defaults are intuitive and understood by other artists.

Step 6: Click Accept.

When you click Accept, it might take a second before Maya moves on. What it is doing is creating all those folders in the directory you told it to. Take a look in your Maya Tutorials folder, and you will find a new folder called Primitive_Man that contains a whole slew of folders in it. This is your new, ready-to-go project file.

Step 7: Create a new file to make sure that you have no other unknown objects in your scene. Select File > New.
Step 8: Save the file. Select File > Save As ... Save the file as Tutorial_2_1.

There are a couple of reasons to save right away. The first is that it helps you to check whether you have your project defined correctly. The directory that it should take you to is one called "scenes," which should be in your Primitive_Man folder. If it takes you to another directory, you will want to go back and redefine your project (you can do this with File > Project > Set. . .). The other reason is that Maya does crash. Getting in the habit of saving early and saving often is a good one. After you have done this initial Save As, you can then just hit Ctrl-S or Command-S (on a Mac) to save.

New Shapes

Step 9: Select Create > Polygon Primitives > Sphere (Options). The default settings should match Figure 2.16; if they do not, select Edit > Reset Settings within the Polygon Sphere Options window. Click Create.

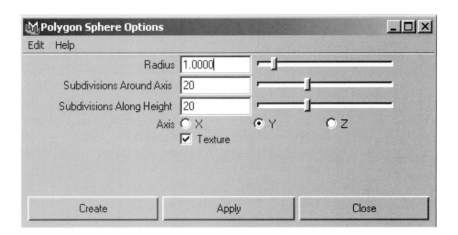

FIGURE 2.16   The Polygon Sphere Options window.

As indicated earlier, Maya works hard to maintain a consistent user experience; it wants to make sure that the settings are the same as when you sat down last. Unfortunately, this can be a problem if you are in a lab situation, or sometimes if it's been a while since you have accessed a certain tool. In general, if it has been a while since you have used a tool (or the first time), it is not a bad idea to take a second and reset the settings.

Notice that we are creating a sphere that has a radius of one unit with 20 subdivisions in both axis and height. In this case, subdivisions are polygons. It is creating a sphere that has 20 rows of polygons around its axis and 20 rows of polygons from pole to pole. We will talk much more of polygons later.

Step 10: Press the Spacebar to split your view panel into the standard four view (one perspective camera and three orthographic views).

 Understanding your form and where it is in regards to the other objects in the scene is a big deal in 3D. Making sure that you have four views of the scene will help.

Step 11: Press f on your keyboard to frame the object. Note that it frames the object in the view panel in which your mouse is currently. So, you can move your mouse over each window pressing f in each to frame the sphere in that view panel.

Step 12: With your mouse resting in the persp window, press 5 to see a shaded view of your model.

 Traditionally, many artists work with the persp window shaded (an opaque display of the geometry), but leave the top, front, and side as wireframe. Partly, this is to allow you to quickly see whether objects are inside or behind other objects in the orthographic views that do not allow you to rotate around the objects, and partly it's to make sure to leave as much video card processing power in the intuitive persp view panel.

Step 13: Select the Move Tool (w on your keyboard) and translate the sphere up 15 units in the Y direction. Make sure that you do this by grabbing the Translate Y Handle (the green handle with a cone on the tip) so that you know the object is moving only in the Y direction. You will know you have translated 15 units by looking in the Channel Box (Figure 2.17).

 The Channel Box (accessible by clicking the button where the mouse rests in Figure 2.17) allows you to see the channels that control the object that is selected. Notice that you can select any of those input fields and numerically enter a value. Be sure you press Enter on your keyboard (not your number pad) to have the value stick.

Also note that the Channel Box also keeps track of the nodes (remember the discussion in Chapter 1) associated with a particular object. They are listed as Inputs. The only node so far associated with this sphere is polysphere1.

Step 14: Rename the sphere (currently named pSphere1) to "Head." Do this is the Channel Box by double-clicking on pSphere1 (Figure 2.18).

 Naming seems to be a grungy little thing to do when you are busy trying to create ART. However, naming as you go along is a nice habit to get into. Partly, this is because in the workplace, an artist rarely works alone and rarely is the only one to work on a file. It is in very poor taste to pass a file along to a co-worker with 100 objects with names like pCube15, pSphere4, and so on … Name as you go.

Step 15: Create a new cube (Dreave > Polygon Primitives > Cube [Options]). Reset the tool (Edit > Reset Settings), and press Create.

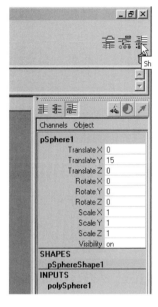

FIGURE 2.17   The Channel Box with the sphere translated up 15 units in the Y direction.

FIGURE 2.18   Renaming pSphere1 to Head.

Step 16: Rename the pCube1 to "Chest." Do this in the Channel Box.

Step 17: Translate the cube up in the y direction (with the Move Tool and by dragging on the Translate Y Handle) so that it sits underneath the head. The exact amount is not important; for this exercise you can just eyeball it.

Step 18: Press r (lowercase) on your keyboard to change to the Scale Tool. Scale the Chest object so that it roughly matches Figure 2.19. You will probably need to use all of the Scale X, Scale Y, and Scale Z Handles to get it to look about right.

Step 19: Duplicate Chest. With Chest selected, choose Edit > Duplicate (Options). Be sure to reset the settings (Edit > Reset Settings)—they should match Figure 2.20—and click Duplicate.

Why?

The Duplication tool can be one of the most amazing time saving tools in your arsenal, but it can also be a nightmare if the settings are not just right. The default settings should be set to make an exact copy of the object and leave the newly duplicated form in the same place. However, you can change these settings to make as many copies as you would like. If you forget that you have changed the settings (or the person on the machine before you changed them), you could find that you were accidentally duplicated 12 copies of the Chest without your knowledge. Resetting the settings avoids this danger.

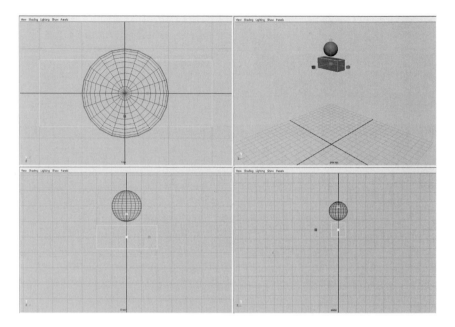

FIGURE 2.19 Chest translated and scaled into place.

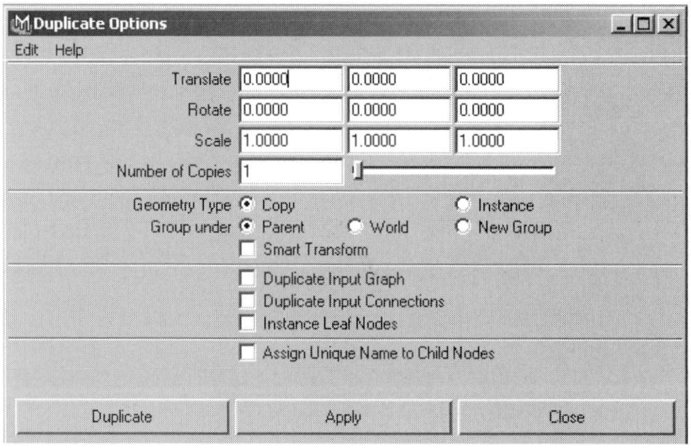

FIGURE 2.20 Default Duplicate settings to duplicate Chest.

Step 20: Translate and scale Chest1 (the newly duplicated Chest) into place to match Figure 2.21. Notice that the newly duplicated Chest1 is sitting at exactly the same spot as the original Chest and that you can not see that there are two shapes until you use the Move Tool to move it down.

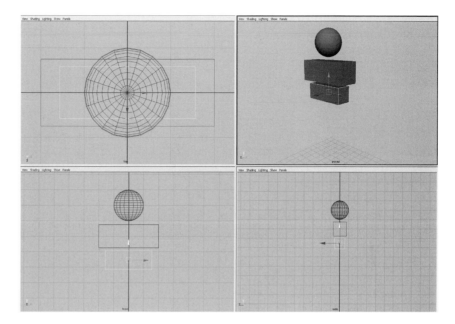

FIGURE 2.21   Duplicated, translated, and scaled Chest1.

Step 21: Duplicate (Ctrl-d or Edit > Duplicate) Chest1, rename to Abs, and translate and scale into position to match Figure 2.22.

Step 22: Duplicate (Ctrl-d) Abs and rename to Trunk. Translate and scale into position to match Figure 2.22.

Step 23: Create three spheres (Create > Polygon Primitives > Sphere) to be the hip, knee, and ankle; two cylinders (Create > Polygon Primitives > Cylinder (Options)—be sure to reset this tool as it is the first time you have used it—to be the thigh and shin; and two cubes (Create > Polygon Primitives > Cube) to be the foot and toe. Translate and scale them to their respective parts. Together all of these primitives will create the leg. Be sure to name each shape as you go so that you have R_Hip, R_Thigh, R_Knee, R_Shin, R_Ankle, R_Foot, and R_Toe. It should look roughly like Figure 2.23.

The Power of Groups

Step 24: Select the objects that are the leg. Select the R_Hip and then hold the Shift key down and select R_Thigh, R_Knee, R_Shin, R_Ankle, R_Foot, and R_Toe (all the objects that are the right leg). This will high-light each of the objects white with the last object selected being high-lighted green.

Take a look at the Outliner (Window > Outliner…). You will see that all of the se-
Why? *lected objects are highlighted gray.*

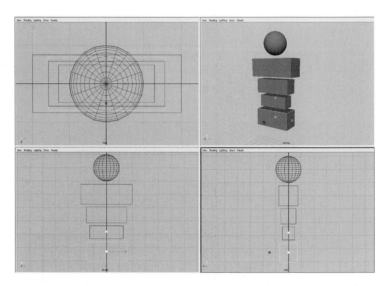

FIGURE 2.22   Completed torso comprised of Head, Chest, Chest1, Abs, and Trunk.

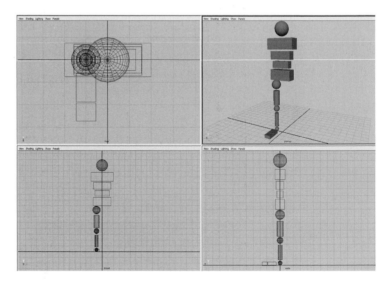

FIGURE 2.23   Completed right leg.

Step 25: Group the leg together. Press Ctrl-g (or select Edit > Group). A few things will happen. The entire group (one entity) will highlight green, and the Channel Box will show that the selected element is called group1.

Take a look at the Outliner now. A new null object called group1 has been created that when expanded includes (as children) all of the leg parts.
Why?

Step 26: Rename group1 to R_Leg.

Grouping can be an incredibly time-saving technique. It allows you to quickly select, modify, duplicate, or animate multiple objects at once. We will talk more about groups in later chapters, but for now it's important to note how to select a group.
Why?
    Click away from any object in the scene to deselect everything. Now click on any one object within the leg (it will highlight green). Now, press the up arrow key on your keyboard. Immediately, the entire leg will highlight green (also take a look at what is happening in the Outliner when you do this). Pressing the up arrow key selects up the hierarchy to move from selecting part of the leg to selecting the group R_Leg. See the idea?

Step 27: Adjust the pivot. Press w to activate the Move Tool and select any part of the leg. Press the up arrow key to select the group R_Leg. Note that the manipulator for the group is sitting at (0,0,0). This is because within the Group options, the new group is set to have its Group Pivot at "Origin" or (0,0,0). To fix this so that the manipulator (and, ultimately, the pivot point of the leg) is more intuitive, press Insert (Home on a Mac) on your keyboard. Move the pivot up to the center of the R_Shin object and press Insert again (Figure 2.24).

Ultimately, you will want to make sure that the leg rotates around the hip joint. Although there would need to be some other hierarchy work done to this leg to make sure that the shin rotates with the knee, and so on. . . .placing the pivot manipulator of the entire leg on the hip is an important first step. Be sure as you are moving the manipulator for the group to the hip that you take a look in all of your orthographic views to make sure it really gets to the right place in 3D space.
Why?

Step 28: Duplicate the group. Making sure that R_Leg (the group) is selected (take a glance at the Channel Box to see what is selected); press Ctrl-d (or Edit > Duplicate). This will create a new group called R_Leg1 that also contains all of the objects within that group. Rename this new group L_Leg.

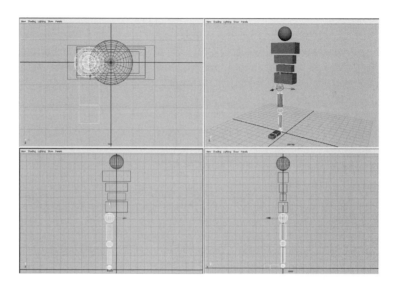

FIGURE 2.24   New leg with newly positioned pivot.

Step 29: With the Move Tool, move the group L_Leg over with the Translate X Handle (Figure 2.25). Select each part of the L_Leg group and rename it (in the Channel Box) to be L_Hip, L_Thigh, L_Knee, and so on.

Step 30: Make the leg and arm. (This is really a lazy, but quick way, to finish of the character.) Select either leg group (make sure that you have the group by pressing the up arrow key) and duplicate it. Rename it L_Arm.

Step 31: Move the L_Arm group up into position (Figure 2.26).

Step 32: Rename each object in the arm to L_Shoulder, L_UpperArm, L_Elbow, L_Forearm, L_Wrist, L_Hand, and L_Fingers.

Step 33: Scale the arm down to size. With L_Arm still selected, switch to the Scale Tool (keyboard shortcut r) and drag the Center Handle so that the arm scales down proportionally in all directions. Scale it so that the L_Wrist object is about at the hip.

Why? *Note that you are scaling the single group of multiple objects. When you use the Scale Tool to scale a group, all the objects proportionally scale down or up while maintaining their relative positions to other objects in the group. As an experiment, select all of the objects within the group (Shift-select to add to the selection). Because all the objects are selected, but not the group, if you now use the Scale Tool to scale, you will find all the objects scale right in their space in the world, thus increasing the space between objects. This ability to maintain spacing within the group is another benefit of using the Group functions.*

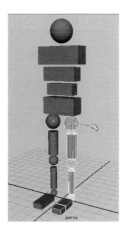

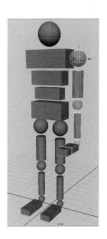

FIGURE 2.25   Duplicated, named, and placed L_Leg group.

FIGURE 2.26   The arm (that was a leg) translated into position.

Step 34: Rotate the arm to an outstretched position. Make sure that you have the group L_Arm selected and press e on your keyboard to activate the Rotate Tool. Note in Figure 2.27 that the manipulator for the arm will show as the Rotate X, Rotate Y, and Rotate Z handles. To rotate the arm up, you would want to grab the blue handle (the Rotate Z) handle. Instead of doing that, rotate the group in the Channel Box numerically: Change the Rotate Z input field to 90.

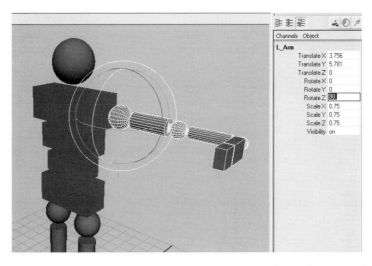

FIGURE 2.27   Rotated Arm. Note that the rotation would take place around the group's z-axis (using the blue Rotate Z handle) if you had not rotated it via the Channel Box.

Step 35: Rotate and translate the L_Hand and L_Finger objects into place. Scale to taste (Figure 2.28). You can do this numerically in the Channel Box or eyeball it with the Rotate Tool.

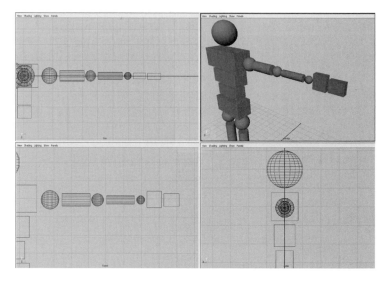

FIGURE 2.28   Rotated, scaled, and translated hand and finger.

Which view you do this sort of function in is largely personal taste. The easiest way to see whether everything is aligned in this case is to do the rotating, scaling, and translating in the top view panel as you know that the hand and finger are already aligned in the y direction.

Step 36: Duplicate L_Arm, rename it R_Arm, and position it on the other side of the body. Also be sure to rename all the individual objects to reflect the right side of the body (R_Shoulder, R_UpperArm, and so on). See Figure 2.29.

In this tutorial, you've done some pretty basic stuff. And in fact, this primitive man in his present state is fairly useless for anything beyond this basic exercise. He is not organized for animation and is really too simple to even justify a render. But, hopefully, through the process of this tutorial, you have picked up the basics of moving around in 3D space and moving (translating), rotating, and scaling objects within that space.

For now, save your file.

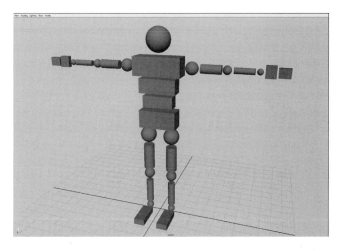

FIGURE 2.29   Completed primitive man.

CHALLENGES, EXERCISES, OR ASSIGNMENTS

1. Create a girlfriend for primitive man. What primitive forms might help indicate a symbolic difference in gender-specific clothing?
2. How would you organize (as in grouping) primitive man so that he is ready for animation? *Hint:* Think groups of groups.
3. Using primitive forms and the techniques described in this chapter, model the simple architectural form shown in Figure 2.30.

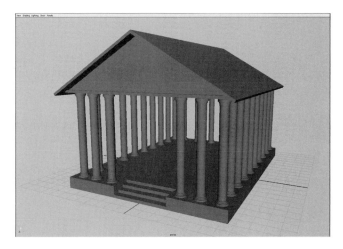

FIGURE 2.30   Primitive temple for Challenge 3.

CHAPTER

3

CARVING OUT MODELING BASICS—BASIC POLYGONAL MODELING

EFFICIENT MODELING

Figure 3.1 shows a simple but elegant digital character design by Mike Clayton. It is excellent in a lot of ways: it's just a good design; he has carefully used the same shape for all parts of the body; this same shape is composed of some very simple geometric 3D elements. Because he carefully *designed* the character, he already has a great idea of how to *construct* the character. Now not every character or other model is going to be as neat as the one the artists cleverly constructed, but sketches like the one presented in Figure 3.1 solve a great deal of the problems encountered as people try to put polygons together to form an interesting shape—that of "what are the shapes?"

FIGURE 3.1   Mike Clayton character design.

After the shapes are understood enough in your mind to be understood on paper, you can begin to make them understood digitally. For instance, in the sketch, the shape used over and over is a sphere combined with a sort of distorted cylinder. A strategy can quickly be developed as to what methods of which sorts of modeling to use after the component shapes of a model are decided upon. Following is a brief description of some of the kinds of digital geometry that presently exist. Following the descriptions are very specific looks at how to get started with some of the more basic techniques.

MODELING TYPES

Maya, as one of the high-end 3D packages, has a fairly robust collection of modeling tools. There are always new packages, and new versions of old software packages will continue to challenge Maya. This is great for consumers, as the tools that find their way to the market place and find acceptance, often end up migrating to different packages. Competition is great.

At its core, Maya, like most 3D packages, makes use of several types of modeling methodologies. Following is a brief overview of them.

Polygonal Modeling

Ultimately, every shape in Maya ends up a polygon. Rendering engines simply need to see these elements as polygons to draw them. All of the modeling methods allow different ways to control a form, but when Maya finally gets ready to render these forms, it uses a process called *tessellation* to break the forms down into triangular polygons.

Because of this, perhaps the most basic form of modeling is polygonal modeling. Polygonal modeling is the idea that you directly manipulate polygons and their components to make the desired form. With polygonal modeling, you (through Maya) take 2D shapes called polygons (usually four sided or three sided) and organize them in digital space to form the shells of 3D shapes. Figure 3.2 shows a cube made up of a combination of six squares. Likewise, Figure 3.3 shows the same principle in action using six triangles to make a pyramid.

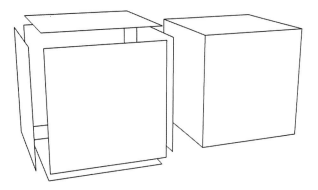

FIGURE 3.2   Polygon cube made of 2D square polygons.

For simple shapes like the pyramid and square shown in Figures 3.2 and 3.3, polygon modeling makes perfect sense. However, one rule of computer polygons is that they cannot be bent. They can be organized in any angle in relation to the next polygon, but the 2D shape itself cannot be bent. So, for an object like a sphere, many polygons (both square and triangular) are needed to create the round shape. If there are few polygons (Figure 3.4), then the sphere is not very round. As the number of

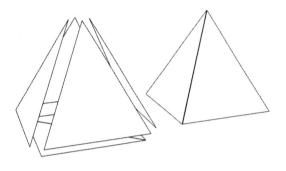

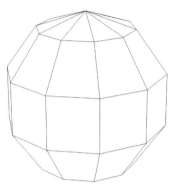

FIGURE 3.3   Polygon pyramid made of 2D triangular polygons.

FIGURE 3.4   Blocky polygon sphere made from few polygons.

polygons increases, the sphere becomes more like the EPCOT Center at Disney World (Figure 3.5). In fact, to make a well-rounded sphere, it takes a very large amount of polygons (Figure 3.6).

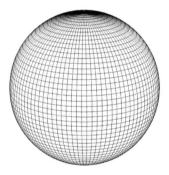

FIGURE 3.5   More rounded polygon sphere made from medium number of polygons.

FIGURE 3.6   Very round sphere from large amount of polygons.

The problem is, the more polygons that are present in the model, the heavier it is. That is, the harder the computer must work to keep track of the extra information. For one sphere, a large amount of polygons is no problem; however, as models become more complex, the poly-count (number of polygons) can begin to really add up. When the poly-count gets high, the computer slows down; the animator gets frustrated; the animator's coffee consumption rises; the animator's hair begins to disappear; the animator's spouse, kids, and pets begin to be neglected; and. . . the point is that high poly-counts are bad news. Lower polygon counts keep computers running quickly and the project rendering goes more quickly. This is the reason why most games (which use OpenGL or DirectX, real-time rendering engines) have fairly low poly-counts for each character. As the hardware technology advances, the sophistication of game models increases as well. Game modelers are experts at low-poly modeling. But no matter what sort of project you are working toward, when using polygon modelers, good sketches and story boards become invaluable in planning where the extra polygons are needed, and where to leave them out.

NURBS Modeling

NURBS (sometimes called free-form polygons) is actually an acronym for Non-Uniform Rational B-Splines. Each application (including Maya) handles NURBS slightly different than the next. However, the core idea for all applications is that NURBS are 3D objects created from one or more *splines*.

The technical explanations of splines are that they are a sequence of three-dimensionally placed vertices that are connected by lines. The links between the vertices are sometimes referred to as *interpolation*. The most basic types of splines are made with straight lines (linear interpolation); however, other types of splines have interpolations that are curves (cubic interpolation). The beauty of these spline-based curves is that they do not contain any sharp corners unless you tell them to. Spline creation works much the same way as vector-based drawing programs work (that is, Illustrator or Freehand). See the tutorial at the end of this chapter for some examples of spline creation and editing.

Splines themselves are actually one-dimensional, although they can be built in 3D space. They are no-dimensional because they have no geometry of their own and will not render in rendering engines. However, when splines are created and arranged in conjunction with a NURBS function, they can become the wire inside of Chinese lanterns, spun around as though they were on a lathe or extruded like those Playdough toys of old to create 3D shapes (Figure 3.7).

The real power of NURBS objects is that since they can be built from very curvilinear splines, they can be tremendously helpful in creating organic forms quickly. For instance, to create the vase shown at the right side of Figure 3.7, you would have to manipulate an awful lot of polygons—especially to get the nice smooth line. But creating with NURBS allows for quick definition and the creation of organic shapes.

Having said all that, it is important to point out that NURBS themselves have no actual polygons of their own as you work with them—just splines and surfaces. However, all rendering engines actually use polygons to define a surface. So the NURBS surfaces/objects you create must be converted to polygons when your 3D application gets ready to render through the aforementioned process of tessellation.

FIGURE 3.7   Variety of splines and the shapes they can create.

Most rendering engines only render triangle (three-sided) polygons. Therefore, if you have created a four-sided polygon, or an *n*-sided polygon (as some 3D applications allow), your software must tessellate the polygons down into three-sided polygons. Similarly, when your software is showing your NURBS surface or gets ready to render it, the software must decide how the three-sided polygons would be created across the surface of your shape.

Luckily for us, Maya does all of this behind the scenes—without us worrying or having to bother with how it happens. Maya allows you to see the tessellation and adjust it if you need to; but generally, most shapes work out just fine, and Maya takes care of all the under-the-hood stuff.

Subdivision Surfaces

Technically, for most applications, this is actually a kind of polygonal modeling. However, for some, like Maya, *subdivision surfaces* are a strange sort of hybrid between polygons and NURBS; although Maya does use something called a Smooth Proxy, which works very much like subdivision surfaces work in most other applications.

In all applications, the basic idea is this: You can use polygonal tools to create a basic shape using a relatively few number of polygons. This low-poly version is often referred to as a *cage*. A subdivision surface will take this cage, subdivide the extant polygons, and bend them to create smoother surfaces. This allows you to essentially control large amounts of polygons with a relatively few.

Figure 3.8 shows an example of a subdivision surface at work. The first figure shows the low-poly cage created by UIW student Jennifer Barton; the second shows what this low-poly surface becomes once a subdivision-surface function is applied to it; and the third shows the rendered result. Notice the low-poly cage that sits outside of a much smoother surface beneath.

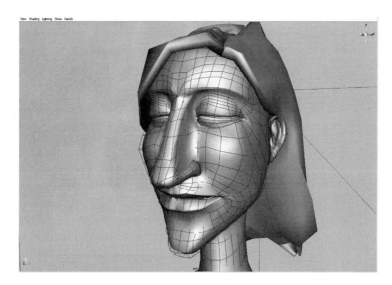

FIGURE 3.8   Subdivision surfaces create smooth, complex, high-poly models from low-poly cages.

The real power of this method is that you can continue to control and modify the smoothed subdivided surface by altering the low-poly cage! Details can continue to be added, new joints created, and various designs explored quickly with the power of this tool.

PRIMITIVES

Every 3D application has a collection of shapes that it makes very well. These stock shapes, whether polygon or NURBS-based, are called *primitives*. Maya has a fairly standard collection of primitives—Sphere, Cube, Cylinder, Cone, Plane, and Torus and new to Maya 7 are Platonic Solids, Soccer Ball, Helix, Pipe, Pyramid, and Prism (Figure 3.9).

Now, although these shapes are the most basic of the 3D shapes available, do not underestimate the power of them. Primitives render quickly and are usually optimized as far as poly-count goes. In general, primitives are most useful as starting collections of polygons; they are most useful when you tweak, bend, and extrude them into new dynamic forms.

For the first tutorial, we will look at using primitives as the building blocks to create the general outline of the room and some very basic versions of the furniture.

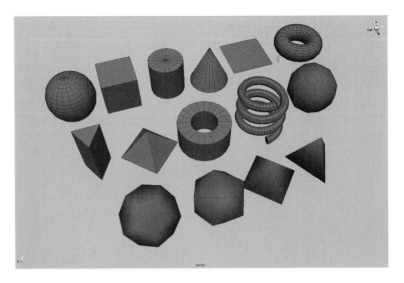

FIGURE 3.9   Maya's primitive collection.

TUTORIAL 3.1   ROOM PRIMITIVES

Objectives:

1. Use primitives to create the general shape of the room.
2. Use the align and snap tools to get crisp joints where objects meet.
3. Work effectively with the Channel Box to work accurately in scale and position.
4. Work with basic node-altering capabilities within the Channel Box inputs area.

Now to the nitty-gritty. A rendering of the models that we'll use for the project that arcs across all the chapters is shown in Figure 3.10. Through the rest of this chapter and the next, we'll be using a variety of modeling techniques to create those shapes.

Define Your Project

Why?

You will be creating the room and characters over a number of tutorials. In fact, you will be making parts of the room in different files to make the construction a little cleaner. So, you are going to have many Maya files that eventually will all come together in a master file to create the finished product. While you work, though, all the various Maya files will need access to the same collection of texture files. This is where having a project file set up with multiple scene files comes in handy. We will create a new project here in this step and save all of the Maya files involved in the project into its scenes folder.

FIGURE 3.10   The room final render from Amazing Wooden Man project.

Step 1: Select File > Project > New. In the New Project dialogue box, enter "Amazing_Wooden_Man" into the Name input field.

Step 2: Next to the Location input field, click the Browse…button. Find the Maya Tutorials folder on your desktop and click OK.

Step 3: Click the Use Defaults button to tell Maya to create and use the default folders for storage of all the assets.

Step 4: Click Accept.

Step 5: Create a new file (File > New) and then save it (File > Save As…) as Tutorial_3_1.

The directory it should be trying to save to should be the scenes folder within your Amazing_Wooden_Man directory (project file).

Step 6: Create the floor. Create a plane 12 feet wide by 20 feet deep. Create > Polygon Primitives > Plane (Options). Change the Width = 12, the Height = 20, the Subdivision Along Width = 1, the Subdivision Along Height = 1 (Figure 3.11). Click Create.

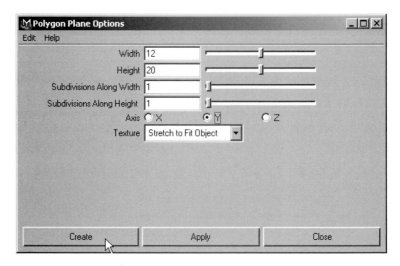

FIGURE 3.11   The Polygon Plane Options window for the plane that will be the floor.

Maya deals in nebulous units. You can define these units as whatever you would like. For this tutorial, we will assume that these units are feet. This makes for easy manipulation as each unit is represented by a square on the grid.

Also note that (as discussed earlier), the subdivisions indicate how many polygons to have the object contain. Since there will not be a lot of deformation on the floor, there is no need to have any more than one polygon to represent the entire floor.

Step 7: Rename the pPlane1 to "Floor" in the Channel Box.
Step 8: Duplicate the Floor object and rename it to Ceiling.
Step 9: Move Ceiling up 8 units. In the Channel Box, with Ceiling selected, enter 8 in the Translate Y input field.

Still with the assumption that each unit is one foot, we are simply telling the ceiling to be eight feet high.

Step 10: Create the North_Wall. Create > Polygon Primitives > Cube (Options). In the Polygon Cube Options window enter Width = 12, Height = 8, and Depth = .5. Note that the Subdivisions input fields should all have 1 as their value. Rename this new pCube1 to North_Wall.

We know the width of the room is 12 feet and its height is 8 feet (thus, the Width = 12 and Height = 8). The .5 value is defining the wall as 6 inches deep.

Step 11: Move the wall into place. Use the Move tool (or the Channel Box) to move the North_Wall to the "north" (Z = −10) end of the room. Be sure to translate it up 4 units so the bottom of the wall actually sits on the floor (Figure 3.12).

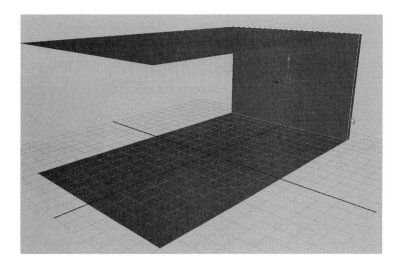

FIGURE 3.12   North_Wall renamed and positioned.

All new objects are placed at the world origin (0,0,0). Since you numerically entered the size of the room, you know that 10 feet in the Z direction will put the wall right at the edge of the room. Note that we are assuming that the room is oriented on a standard North-South-East-West organization as we look at it from the top view panel.

Why?

Step 12: Duplicate North_Wall. Rename to South_Wall and move into position on the south end of the room (Z = 10) with either the Move tool or by numerically entering 10 in the Translate Z input field in the Channel Box.

Step 13: Create a new cube to be used as the East Wall. Choose Create > Polygon Primitives > Cube (Options). Change the settings to Width = .5, Height = 8, and Depth = 20. Click Create. Rename cube to East_Wall.

Note that you are creating a new cube rather than simply duplicating an extant wall and rotating it. This is because we want to keep this sort of architectural thing as clean and exact as we can.

Why?

The Channel Box shows input field for Scale—not Size. So when you define the size of an object in the options box, the actual Scale inputs will show up as 1 (as in "this object is 1 times the size it was when it was created"). Changing the Scale input to 2 does not make the object 2 units big, but makes it twice the size it was when it was created.

So, in this case, since you know exactly the size of the room, it makes sense to create the objects at exactly the right size, so you know the exact measurements.

Step 14: Position the East_Wall. The Channel Box should read Translate X = 6 and Translate Y = 4 (Figure 3.13).

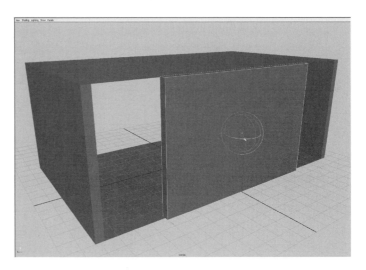

FIGURE 3.13   Positioned East_Wall.

Note that there is a problem. If you look at the corners where the East_Wall matches the North_Wall or South_Wall, you can see a gap (Figure 3.14). This is because you are working with walls that have thickness (6 inches worth). To fix this, you will need to make the East_Wall longer.

Step 15: Resize the East_Wall to a Width = 20.5. Do this by changing the node that created the shape East_Wall. In the Channel Box, look for the INPUTS area. There will be the list of nodes used to create the object East_Wall. There should be only one there now—polyCube2. Click that node, and new input fields will appear (Figure 3.15). These are the same input fields you altered when you created the cube. Here you can make adjustments. Change the Depth input field to 20.5.

Each of the south and north walls are .5 units thick and are sitting with their centers on the edge of the floor. So, there is .25 feet sticking off the end of the floor. .25 × 2 yields .5 units (or feet in this case). Because the East_Wall's pivot is at the center of the wall, adding .5 units to its Depth setting will increase its size .25 units in both the north and south directions.

FIGURE 3.14   Problem area of the wall's gap.

FIGURE 3.15   The INPUTS area of the East_Wall Channel Box with the polyCube2 node accessible to editing.

Step 16: Duplicate East_Wall, rename it West_Wall, and translate it into place. The Channel Box for West_Wall should read Translate X = –6, Translate Y = 4 and Translate Z = 0 (Figure 3.16).

Why? *This looks suspiciously like a box; a box that took 16 steps to produce. It is a box, but it is a box with depth in its walls—and this is important. When we get to cutting windows and doorways out of the walls, we will need the depth to the walls. Further,*

later we will be adjusting the floor so that it also includes a hallway and some other things; if we just had a flattened cube, it would be more difficult to get the geometry we needed.

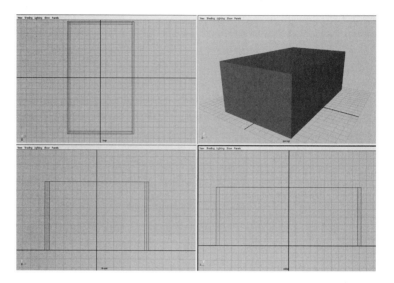

FIGURE 3.16   Completed basic walls.

Organizing

 As you move along, it is easier to organize as you go than it is to try and organize everything at the end. Additionally, it is a bit of insurance in case you need to turn your file over to someone else. Always having clean files with clean hierarchy is a good idea.

Step 17: Create a new layer. In the Layer Editor, click the new layer button or select Layers > Create Layer. Name this new layer Ceiling_Layer.

 Why the name Ceiling_Layer; why not just Ceiling? The name Ceiling is already tied up with an object named Ceiling. Essentially, what this means is that there is a node within this file with that name, and Maya will not allow any other nodes (including layer nodes) to share the same name.

Step 18: Assign the object Ceiling to the layer Ceiling_Layer. Select the object Ceiling (either in the View Panel or in the Outliner). Right-click on Ceiling_Layer in the Layer Editor and select Add Selected Objects from the pop-down menu.
Step 19: Create a Walls_Layer and add all the walls to that layer.
Step 20: Create a Floor_Layer and add the floor to it.

Now, you can quickly click the V on the Ceiling_Layer, and the ceiling will vanish. It is still there, of course, but it just is not being shown. This allows you to work in-side the room without the ceiling impeding your view. For that matter, since you have layers for walls and floor, you can choose to hide or show any of those objects quickly in the Layers Editor.

Step 21: Hide (turn off visibility) for the Ceiling_Layer.
Step 22: Save.

The Power of Snapping

 There are some other details you will want to add to the model at this point. To make sure these new details are accurately placed, the next few steps will use some of Maya's snapping tools.

Step 23: Create a new polygon cube (Create > Polygon Primitives > Cube (Options)) that is Width = 2, Height = 8, Depth = 2. Rename the cube to NW_Pillar.

 Essentially this will be a square pillar that will sit in the corners of the room. The pillar is 2' × 2' and 8' tall.

Step 24: Snap the pillars manipulator (pivot) to the outside corner. In the top view panel, press Insert. With the Move Tool active, hold v (lower-case) down and move the manipulator to the top left corner of the pillar (Figure 3.17). Press Insert again to lock in the new manipulator position.

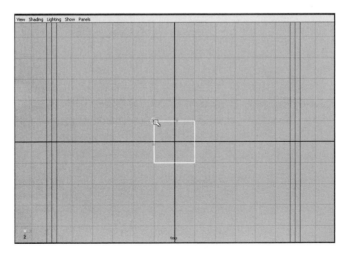

FIGURE 3.17   Snapped manipulator.

Holding the v key down is the keyboard shortcut for Snap to Point (in this case point is a vertex). Notice that at the top of the interface (Figure 3.18), you can see the Snap tools. From left to right, these are Snap to Grid, Snap to Curve, Snap to Point, Snap to View Plane, and Make the Selected Object Live. We will look at more of these snap tools later. For now, you want to make sure that the manipulator is on a corner of the pillar; this will allow you to snap the pillar into the corner of the room.

FIGURE 3.18   Snap tools (Snap to Grid, Snap to Curve, Snap to Point, Snap to View Plane, and Make the Selected Object Live).

Step 25: Snap the pillar into the northwest corner of the room. Activate the Move Tool (w on your keyboard) and hold the v down to snap to point. Use the Center Handle to move the pillar over so that it snaps to the outside edge of the walls (Figure 3.19).

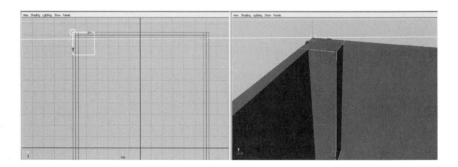

FIGURE 3.19   Snapped pillar using Snap to Point (v) and the Move Tool (w).

Step 26: Make sure that the NW_Pillar also is snapped to the top of the walls. You can see this in the persp View Panel or the front View Panel. If it is not, move it there.

Step 27: Duplicate NW_Pillar and name the new pillar NE_Pillar.

Step 28: Move the manipulator to the top right corner of the pillar (as seen from the top View Panel). Be sure to use Snap to Point (v).

Step 29: Snap NE_Pillar to the northeast corner of the room. Again, make sure that you snap to the outside corner of the walls.

Step 30: Select both pillars and add them to the Walls_Layer.

Step 31: Save.

Step 32: Create and snap into place three additional cubes into the scene to match Figure 3.20. The exact dimensions are unimportant; just visually match the approximate sizes.

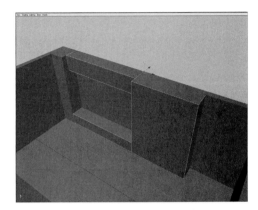

FIGURE 3.20   Added architectural geometry.

Step 33: Add a bathroom. Do this by creating three more walls, a floor, and a ceiling. Name them BR_Floor, BR_Ceiling, BR_North_Wall, BR_South_Wall, and BR_West_Wall (Figure 3.21).

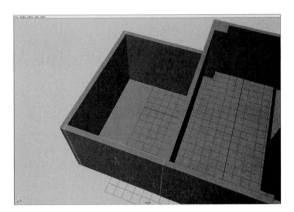

FIGURE 3.21   Added bathroom.

Step 34: Create new layers to intuitively place the new bathroom objects in. Add them to the layers.

Step 35: Create two more walls for the hall. Do not create a new floor (Figure 3.22).

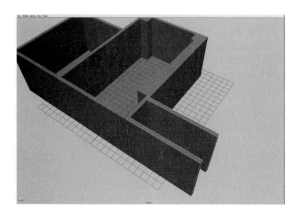

FIGURE 3.22   Added hall.

Step 36: Create a new layer for the hall and add the objects to it.
Step 37: Save.

Tutorial Conclusion

True, it looks pretty sparse right now. Not to worry, though. In the next chapter you will start to cut shapes out of the walls to make doorways and windows. In addition, we will look at editing things on a component level to allow for much more interesting shapes.

CHALLENGES, EXERCISES, OR ASSIGNMENTS

Use a book on interior design or find an architectural magazine. Find a room that has multiple photos (so that you can really see what is happening in the room). Make a sketch of the ground plan and start to lay it out using the methods we have looked at so far. This will probably only include walls, but it will start to give you a good idea of proportions for the room.

4

POLYGONAL MODELING AND COMPONENT EDITING

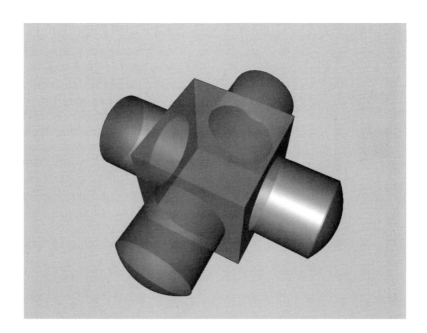

In the last chapter, you used basic forms to create the outline of the room. However, that room is particularly problematic as there is no way to get in or out. In this chapter, we will start out by looking at Boolean functions to get the right doorways.

Additionally, in this chapter we will move beyond the macro and into the micro so that you can start manipulating individual polygons and not be limited to simply moving, rotating, or scaling collections of polygons.

BOOLEAN

Remember those Library Technology courses during your first years of college? If not, have you tried finding that online "needle +straight – record" in the haystack? Boolean searching is the idea of searching for one or more terms that are qualified by making sure that the term is coupled with or excludes other terms. Boolean modeling is the same idea. Boolean lets you take one object (A) and add or subtract another object (B) to produce a third object that is the sum, difference, or intersection of the two source shapes. Maya's Boolean functions for polygons are in the Modeling | Polygons > Boolean pull-down menu.

The best way to understand how Boolean modeling works is to see examples of it in action. Figure 4.1 shows an example of Boolean addition (A plus B). By using Boolean, the two shapes become one mesh of polygons. This might not seem like a big thing since it looks like the two intersecting objects. However, what is actually happening is that most computers think of models as just shells. Even though a ball might look like a solid marble ball, it's really a hollow egg painted like marble. So, when several objects are intersecting, the 3D application keeps track of the shells of all the shapes that intersect. Figure 4.2 shows a shape with intersecting shapes with a semitransparent texture applied.

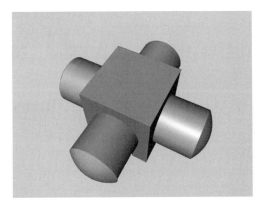

FIGURE 4.1 Simple Boolean union.

Compare this with Figure 4.3, which is the same shape made with a Boolean function. When Maya uses Boolean union (Modeling | Polygons > Booleans > Union), it forgets all the polygons that might be contained by shapes inside of other shapes and just remembers the shell that goes around the entire group of shapes. Think of intersecting shapes like taking solid chunks of clay in the form of the original shapes and squishing them together into the desired form. All the original polygons are still there, just inside one another. Now paper-mache over the entire shape and remove the clay from inside the dried mache shell. This shell of the outside shape is like Boolean union. You can see the difference in Figures 4.2 and 4.3 and how the computer renders each.

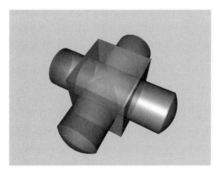

FIGURE 4.2   Intersecting shapes with transparent texture.

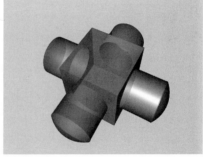

FIGURE 4.3   Boolean union with transparent texture.

Boolean difference takes one shape and subtracts its geometry from another. Think of magic shapes that can be inserted into any shape. These magic shapes would then surround parts of the shape into which they were inserted. When these magic shapes are told to, they disappear taking with them any polygons that may be within them. Figure 4.4 shows a

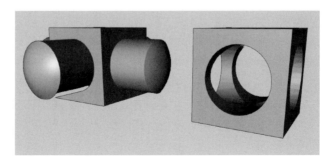

FIGURE 4.4   Boolean difference.

Boolean difference and its resultant shape. It is easy to see how Boolean difference allows for the creation of shapes that would be very difficult to create any other way.

Another powerful form of Boolean modeling is Boolean intersection (A*B). This takes two (or more) intersecting shapes and gets rid of all the polygons that are not in direct contact with the polygons of another shape. Figure 4.5 shows a Boolean intersection.

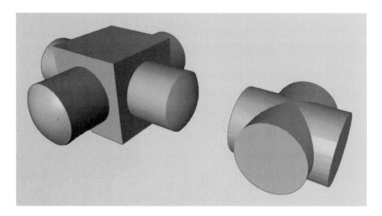

FIGURE 4.5   Boolean intersection.

Some Boolean Caveats

There are some tricks to working with Boolean modeling. Before we get to that, it is important that Maya will only do polygon-based Boolean functions with polygons (although you can do NURBS Boolean functions with Modeling | Edit NURBS > Booleans). Next, notice that if you tell the computer, "Perform a Boolean subtraction on that sphere and cube," when the sphere and cube look like Figure 4.6, the computer does the math to subtract the polygon shape of the rough sphere on the cube and the result ends up looking like Figure 4.7.

So, in order to get a good round hole (if that's the intended goal), it is probably a good idea to use high poly-count shapes or to *subdivide* the low-poly models that you have (more on subdividing or smoothing later).

TUTORIAL 4.1   **BOOLEAN FUNCTIONS IN THE ROOM**

Objectives:

1. Explore how Boolean functions work.
2. Use Boolean functions to create doorways and window holes.

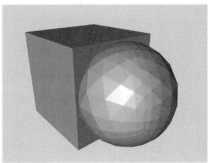

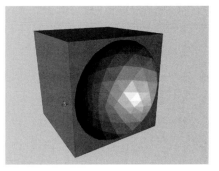

FIGURE 4.6   Low-poly sphere and square.

FIGURE 4.7   Result of low-poly Boolean subtraction.

In this tutorial, you will put Boolean functions to the test to get a look at how they work, what their power is, and what the drawbacks could be.

Define Your Project

Step 1: Set your project. No need to create a project new, but do make sure that the project Maya thinks you are working in is indeed the Amazing_Wooden_Man project. Do this by choosing File > Project > Set…. Then make sure that your Amazing_Wooden_Man folder (inside your desktop folder Maya Projects) is selected and press OK.

Step 2: Open Tutorial_3_1. Just select File > Open, and Maya should take you right to your scenes folder inside your Amazing_Wooden_Man project folder. Click Open.

Step 3: Save the file as Tutorial_4_1. File > Save As….

You could simply continue to work along and continue to save over that last version of your file as this tutorial is just another continuation of the last chapter's tutorial. However, this process can begin to help you get in the habit of sequential saving. This is the idea that instead of continually working on one Maya file, as you save, you save each time under a different name (or the same name with a new number on the end). This can be very handy if you end up with a corrupted Maya file (heaven forbid), or you simply want to go back to an earlier version of a model to work from there. Sequential saving is good.

Step 4: Create the door hole. Create a new cube that is Width = 3, Height = 6.75, and Depth = 2.

This object is going to be the shape we subtract from walls to make the holes where the doors will go. This shape will not actually be the door, and it will not be seen after it has

been used in the Boolean operation. The size is based on the idea that the whole in a wall where a door would sit would be 6'8" (6.75 units) tall and 3' wide and needs to be thicker than the wall, which is around 6", so 2' as a depth should be plenty.

Step 5: Name this Front_Door_Hole.

Step 6: Snap the manipulator to the bottom center of the Front_Door_Hole object. Press Insert and then hold the v down to Snap to Point. Grab the manipulator by the green peg (the y direction) and move downward (Figure 4.8).

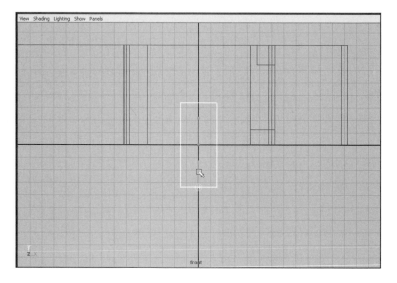

FIGURE 4.8   Moved manipulator for Front_Door_Hole.

Well, the why is that you want to be able to snap this hole right to the floor and having the manipulator on the bottom will make it easy to move the object right up so it is sitting on the floor (with the Snap to Grid (x) being activated).

The "how" of this step is that by moving the manipulator just in the y direction, the manipulator is snapping down to where the point is—but only in the y direction; so it does not snap to any of the corners and remains in the middle of the door when looking at it in the top View Panel.

Step 7: Snap the Front_Door_Hole on the grid and move it to penetrate the front wall of the hallway. Activate the Move Tool (w), and hold x down to activate Snap to Grid. Translate the object up so that it goes through the front wall (Figure 4.9).

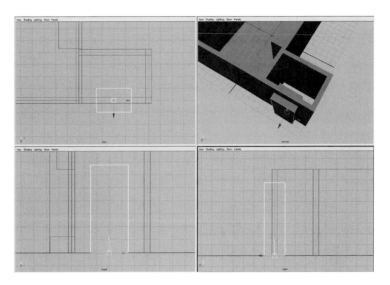

FIGURE 4.9   Placed Front_Door_Hole.

 Note that for this to work well, the object that is to make the hole, Front_Door_Hole, has to go completely through the object it is going to make the hole in (in this case Hall_South_Wall). If not, the hole will only go partway through the wall.
Why?

Step 8: Select the Hall_South_Wall and then shift-select the Front_Door_Hole.

 Maya understands that the first shape you select is the shape to be subtracted from—the second is the shape to do the subtracting.
Why?

Step 9: Select Modeling | Polygons > Booleans > Difference (Figure 4.10).

 Some things to notice: First, you indeed have a hole in the door. Second, the manipulator is unintuitively back at the origin (0,0,0).
Why?

Step 10: Reset the manipulator. Choose Modify > Center Pivot.

 This moves the manipulator (pivot) back so that it is at the geometric center of the wall with a hole in it.
Why?

Step 11: For fun, move the hole. In the Outliner (Window > Outliner), select the (now) group Front_Door_Hole. In the persp View Panel, use the Move Tool to move the manipulator along the x direction. The hole will move!

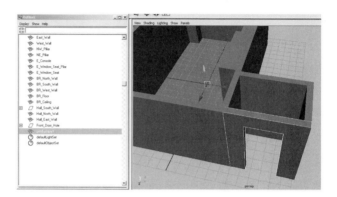

FIGURE 4.10   Result of the Boolean function for the front door.

This is one of the manifestations of the power of history. Take a look in the Outliner (Window > Outliner) and see that Hall_South_Wall and Front_Door_ Hole are actually now null objects containing a transform node. See that a new object has appeared in the Outliner called polySurface1. If you select polySurface1 (in the Outliner) and look in the Channel Box, you will see that under INPUTS, there is now a node called polyBoolOp1.

Why?

As long as this polySurface maintains its history, you can make changes to either of the objects involved in the Boolean operation (resize the hole, move the hole, resize or move the wall, and so on.) and the history will recompute the result.

Step 12: Undo the hole move. Press z on your keyboard to undo.
Step 13: Delete the history from polySurface1. With polySurface1 selected choose Edit > Delete by Type > History.

History can be a lot of help; however, this history also leaves a lot of junk hanging around—especially in your Outliner. In this case, you have the largely useless Hall_South_Wall and Front_Door_Hole groups. There are ways to delete all the history in a scene (Edit > Delete All by Type > History) and ways to make sure that no history is ever being recorded; but often you will want to have history for some objects (especially when you start working with characters), so its better to do a little house cleaning of unnecessary history as you go along.

Why?

Step 14: Rename polySurface1 to "S_Entryway."

Step 15: Repeat for the West_Wall. Create a hole object, position it, use Boolean difference, delete history, rename to "W_Bathroom_Wall," and Modify > Center Pivot. (Figure 4.11)

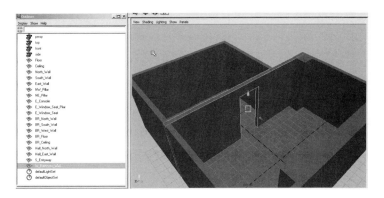

FIGURE 4.11 New W_Bathroom_Wall.

Step 16: Repeat again on the East_Wall to make a hole for the window (Figure 4.12). Do not worry about renaming the new shape; you will need it for the next step. However, do make sure that you delete the history.

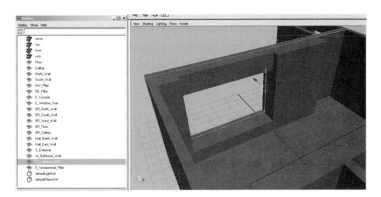

FIGURE 4.12 Wall with hole for window created from Boolean difference.

Step 17: Create a new hole object for the entry way from the hall into the room (Figure 4.13).

Step 18: In the Outliner, select the object that is the wall with the window hole (polySurface1) and then Ctrl-click (Command-click on a Mac) the hole object (probably pCube1). Choose Modeling | Polygons > Booleans > Difference.

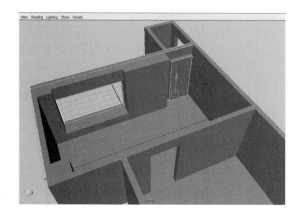

FIGURE 4.13   New hole object for entryway doorway.

In the View Panels, if you have an object selected, you can add to that selection by Shift-clicking an additional object. However, in the Outliner, Shift-click adds not only the object you are clicking on, but all the objects between it and the first object you selected (as happens in standard Windows or Mac interfaces). Ctrl-clicking will add a second object to a selection without grabbing all the objects in between.

Step 19: Delete the history and rename it "E_Wall" (Figure 4.14). Center the pivot.

Step 20: Save.

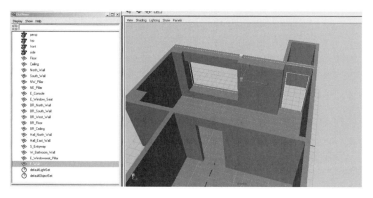

FIGURE 4.14   Completed, renamed E_Wall with a clean history and centered pivot.

A Bit of Reorganizing

Before we get going too much further, let's take a moment to reorganize. You have already created some layers, which are a good start; however, the Outliner is starting to get quite a list of objects; and over the next few tutorials it is going to accumulate quite a few more. A bit of extra organizing will help keep the Outliner tidy as well.

Why?

Step 21: Add E_Wall, W_Bathroom_Wall to the layer BR_Walls_Layer (select the walls in the View Panel or the Outliner and then right-click on BR_Walls_Layer in the Layer Editor and select Add Selected Objects).
Step 22: Add S_Entryway to the Hall_Layers layer (if you have it organized that way).

When you Boolean objects, Maya creates a new object that did not previously exist. These newly created objects are not assigned to any layer by default—thus, the need to reassign the walls to their appropriate layers.

Why?

Step 23: With your Outliner open, select all of your walls (including those involved in the hall and entryway area). Do this with combinations of Shift-clicking and Ctrl-clicking (Command-clicking on a Mac). This will actually be most everything except the floors and ceilings.
Step 24: Press Ctrl-g (or Edit > Group) to group them all together.
Step 25: Rename the group "Walls."

Why create this added group? Well, it is largely a personal preference, but I like to work out of the Outliner when selecting objects; it is just more accurate than always hoping you are clicking on the desired object in the View Panel. By grouping objects, the Outliner will display fewer things when these groups are collapsed (showing the + sign). You can still see each of the individual walls by clicking on the + sign, but they can just as easily be hidden by clicking the – sign on an expanded group.

Why?

Note that these groupings in the Outliner do not change to which layer they are assigned. So you can still choose to hide or show groups of walls in the Layer Editor at any time.

Step 26: Group all the floors and ceilings. Name this group "Floors_ &_Ceilings."
Step 27: Save.

Tutorial Conclusion

So, in this brief tutorial you have cut out holes for windows and doors. You also did some organizing as you went. Booleans can indeed be a handy way to work with getting the shapes you need. However, ultimately, you want to be able to move beyond just working with objects; you will want to be able to edit an object by adjusting the parts that make the object. But first, you need to understand a bit about what the anatomy of a polygon is.

THE POLYGON AND ITS COMPONENTS

Meet your friend the polygon (Figure 4.15). Let's spend a little time getting to know it and its parts.

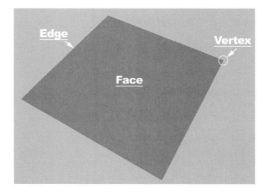

FIGURE 4.15   The polygon and its components.

Polygons are the building blocks that rendering engines see when they attempt to draw the scene you have created. As discussed earlier, they are best thought of as metal plates that do not bend but are able to be connected to other polygons at an angle. The more polygons there are, the more places to bend there are. Thus, potentially higher polygon forms are smoother forms but also are much heavier.

The polygons can be broken down into various components—in fact this is what Maya calls the various parts of a polygon—components. The component that we see when we look at a polygon is the *face*. The face is the big flat part of the polygon. It has no depth; it is infinitely thin. However, it does occupy space in other directions. Although this is a broad simplification of face topology, think of a face as having a front and backside. The front of a face is called the *normal* (this is actually an over simplification, but works well when getting started with 3D). You can choose to show or hide the normals of a mesh (a collection of polygons and, thus, a collection of faces) by choosing Display > Polygon Components > Normals. The normal will appear as a thin line shooting out from the middle of the face. We will look much more at normals and their implications later in this chapter, and in Chapter 6 when we get working with textures.

Faces are surrounded by the intuitively named *edges*. Edges simply define the boundary of a face. Edges can be selected scaled, moved, or rotated. Edges are the connections where polygons can be welded together. When two polygons are connected, they share an edge.

Edges are flanked on each end by a *vertex*. A vertex (vertices for plural) is a point in space with no mass or size of its own. Vertices simply define the ends of edges. Much of modeling is the process of adjusting vertices because when you move a vertex, it changes the edge and, thus, changes the shape of the face. Vertices are shared between two or more polygons if they are a solid mesh. Although technically a vertex could be shared by an infinite number of polygons, you will want to aim at trying to make sure that each vertex is shared by four polygons (much more about this later).

Component Mode and Selecting Components

At the top of your interface, to the right of the Menu Set selector and the New/Open/Save, is a whole slew of tools to allow you to select and filter your selection of components. Figure 4.16 shows the Select by Component Type button selected.

FIGURE 4.16   The Component selection and filter tools built into Maya's interface.

When you are in this tool, you cannot select entire objects (or entire meshes of polygons—or NURBS), but you can select the individual components that make up a polygon mesh, a NURBS surface, or a CV curve, and so on.

 In practice, unless you need to filter what you are selecting (as in, "I want to marquee around this mesh, but only select the vertices and edges"), you probably should not use these tools. There are other ways to select components that are quicker and allow for quick return to moving entire objects. But, as you work, some tools leave you within Component node, and you suddenly cannot select objects; if this happens, take a look at these tools and make sure that you are in Select by Object mode (the tool to the left of Select by Component).

In general, being in Select by Object mode is preferable. While in this tool, you can still select components with a right mouse click on the object (Figure 4.17).

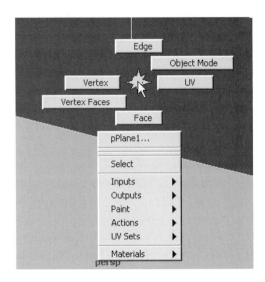

FIGURE 4.17   Right-clicking on an object allows for the selection of components.

When you right-click on an object (any object including curves, NURBS, or polygon meshes), a marking menu appears. Marking menus are there to give you a new collection of tools right where your mouse is. In this case, this marking menu allows you to define what you want to select or modify. Just move the mouse over the component type with which you want to work.

After you have selected a component type (say Vertex), the vertices of the mesh will become visible (probably purple colored); you then can marquee or directly select any of these vertices and proceed to translate, rotate, or scale them.

When selecting components, the same selection rules of selecting objects apply. Namely, you can Shift-select to add vertices to your present selection of vertices. Or, if you Shift-select vertices that are already selected, Maya will then deselect them. Ctrl-selecting deselects components, and Shift-Ctrl-Select will add to a selection without deselecting anything.

So why is this important? Consider the following quick example:

Figure 4.18 shows the front doorway of your room model this far. While in Select by Object mode, if you click on the doorway and try to translate it, you will move the entire wall; which is useful, but what happens if you want to change the height of the doorway, or the shape?

By right-clicking on the wall (Figure 4.19), you can tell Maya that you want to work with the vertices of this shape. In this case, there will be vertices around the doorway as there are polygons on the inside of the doorway connecting to the polygons that make up the walls.

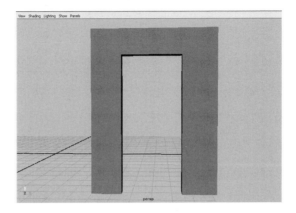

FIGURE 4.18   Doorway with deleted history.

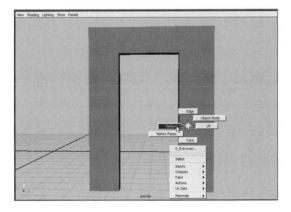

FIGURE 4.19   Defining that vertices are the components to be selected and modified.

Now, the vertices all show up in purple. By marqueeing around the desired vertices (say the four at the top of the doorway), you can make the doorway taller by simply translating the selected vertices up in the y direction with the Move Tool. Or, as you can see in Figure 4.20, you can even deform the entire shape of the doorway.

Even though these screenshots showed the components of the form being modified, Maya is still in Select by Object mode. And if you click on another object, you will be selecting the entire object.

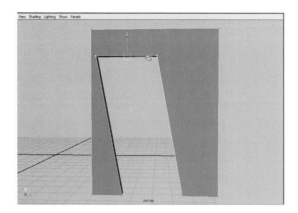

FIGURE 4.20   Deformed doorway created by moving the vertices that make the top of the shape.

After you are done modifying vertices of an object in this type, you can right-click on the active object again and select Object Mode from the Marking Menu to select the entire mesh again.

 Sometimes, when right-clicking on an object with the intent to select in Object Mode again, Maya can be a bit picky. If you just right-click in the middle of a polygon, Maya sometimes will give you an unexpected marking menu. If this happens, release the mouse and instead right-click on an edge, and you will get the expected marking menu that allows you to choose Object Mode.

Extruding Faces and Edges

So being able to work with components and adjust polygons is an important part of the 3D process. However, more powerful is the ability to quickly create new polygons (and their components) quickly. This frees you from the world of primitives to create new and interesting forms.

Here is the idea; Figure 4.21 shows a plain old primitive cube (polygonal) with a face selected (right-click on the object and select Face from the marking menu; then click on a face).

Modeling | Edit Polygons > Extrude Face extrudes the face off of the edges upon which it previously sat. When the Extrude Face tool is activated, a new collection of tools appears as shown in Figure 4.22. This one set of handles allows you to move, scale, or rotate the extruded face (translate by dragging the cones, scale by dragging the cubes, and rotate by dragging the blue circle that surrounds them all). By dragging out along the z-axis with the Translate Z Handle (within the Extrude Tool—no need to activate the Move Tool), you can see that the edges of the extruded face now have another polygon between them and the old edges (Figure 4.22).

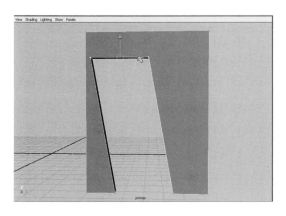

FIGURE 4.21   Primitive cube with selected face.

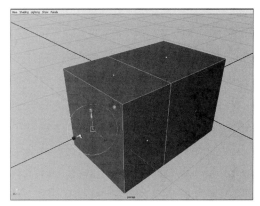

FIGURE 4.22   Extruded face.

This new face can be scaled, translated, or moved further with the Extrude Face Tool or with the regular Move, Rotate, or Scale Tools. Note that is important that after you invoke the Extrude Face Tool, you *must* do something with the newly extruded face. If you do not, you are left with extra polygons between the old and new faces; this causes all sorts of problems later when you get to smoothing surfaces or other subdivision techniques.

Take a look at Figures 4.23–4.26. These show a progression of continued extrusions that create the ever cliché spaceship. Make a new file, create a cube, and try making your own to get a feel for how the Extrude Face Tool works.

FIGURE 4.23   Getting started with the spaceship.

There is tremendous power in being able to extrude new faces (later we will look at extruding new edges). Really play with this a little bit building a whole squadron of these insipid spaceships. (Do not include them on your reel, of course, but it does help to master the Extrude Face technique.) Let's look at some useful ways to use the Extrude Face Tool.

FIGURE 4.24 Continued extrusions, including extruding into the form to create holes.

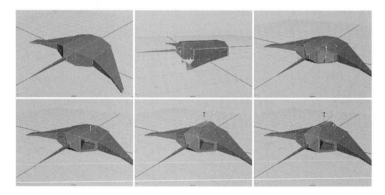

FIGURE 4.25 Continued extrusions to add details.

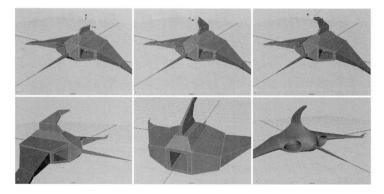

FIGURE 4.26 Finishing touches. Note the last figure has a smoothed version of the mesh as a teaser. More on this later.

TUTORIAL 4.2

CREATING A TABLE WITH COMPONENT EDITING AND EXTRUDE FACES

Objectives:

1. Become familiar with the nature of components and how to select and manipulate them.
2. Use the Extrude Face tool to create added visual interest.
3. Use the Cut Faces tool to add needed geometry.
4. Explore Merge Vertices and other geometry-cleaning techniques.
5. Create the table for the Amazing_Wooden_Man room.

Step 1: Define your project. You know the drill, just make sure that Maya knows you are working on a scene that belongs with the Amazing_Wooden_Man project by choosing File > Project > Set.

Step 2: Create a new file. File > New.

Step 3: Save the file as "Table." File > Save should prompt you with a dialog box asking you for the name of the file. Make sure that you are saving to the scenes folder of the Amazing_Wooden_Man project file.

In this tutorial, you will make the base of the table and the table top two separate objects. Although this table could easily be constructed as one solid object, it will be easier to texture as two. Further note that we are not going to be too concerned about creating this table too big. In fact, the table—as we create it—will probably be larger than the entire room after it is imported. Not to worry, though, we can easily scale it down to fit. For now, it is more important that we have a good-sized grid with which to work. Because of this, this tutorial will generally not list specific sizes and numerical values for objects and distances. The important thing is the general shape and the use of the tools. Eyeball the table; make changes as you see fit.

Step 4: Create a primitive cube (polygonal). Create > Polygon Primitives > Cube (Options). Reset the settings (Edit > Reset Settings) and press Create. Rename to "Table_Base."

Why?

Be sure to reset the settings in the options window (Edit > Reset Settings) as Maya probably remembers the last time you created the cube, and that was to create a tall thin shape that was to be the hole in a wall.

Step 5: Use the Scale tool to scale the cube so that it approximates Figure 4.27 (approximately six times in the Scale Y (Figure 4.27).

Step 6: Right-click on the object and select Vertex from the marking menu.

Step 7: Marquee around the bottom four vertices. You can do this in most any tool (Move, Scale, Rotate, or Select).

Step 8: Use the Scale Tool to scale these vertices together to get a tapered shape (Figure 4.28).

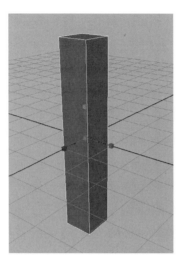

FIGURE 4.27   Base shape started.

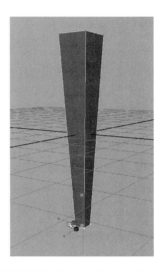

FIGURE 4.28   Tapered base achieved through scaling the bottom vertices.

Step 9: Switch to the Move Tool (w) and adjust these points by moving them up in the y direction to make the base a bit stumpier.

Step 10: Right-click on Table_Base again and select Face from the marking menu.

Step 11: Select the face that is on the very bottom of the shape (Figure 4.29).

Step 12: Extrude the face. Select Modeling | Edit Polygons > Extrude Face.

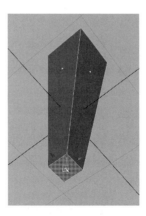

FIGURE 4.29   Selecting the face tat will become the very bottom feet of the Table_Base.

This will display the fancy handle that indicates you are in the Extrude Face tool.
Why? *Remember that this one tool will allow you to move, scale, and rotate the face.*

Step 13: Using the Extrude Face handles, translate with the Translate Y handle (green cone) the new face downward to approximate Figure 4.30.
Step 14: Use the Scale handles to scale this same face outward as shown in Figure 4.31. You can also uniformly scale the face by clicking once on any of the scale manipulator handles (cubes) and then click-drag the new gray cube in the middle of the tool.

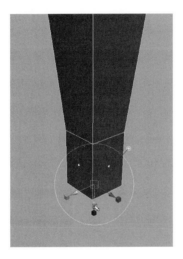

FIGURE 4.30   Extruded face pulled away with the Translate Y handle.

FIGURE 4.31   Scaled face to create a broad base.

Step 15: Select Modeling | Edit Polygons > Extrude Face again; or press the g key.

 Hotkey Alert *Pressing g activates the last used tool. In this case, the last used tool was the Extrude Face tool.*

Step 16: Using the Translate Y handle, move this newly extruded face down to give the base a bit of thickness (Figure 4.32).
Step 17: View the model in the top View Panel.
Step 18: Right-click on Table_Base and select Object Mode from the marking menu.

 You are about to use the Cut Faces tool, and you want to have it not only cut through one polygon, but to cut through the entire object. Maya can also be fairly
Why? *picky about which mode it must be in to use certain tools. Cut Faces tool happens to be one of those that works well in Object Mode.*

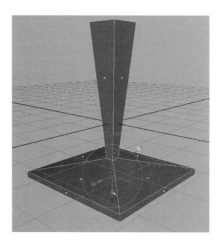

FIGURE 4.32   Added thickness through an additional extruded face.

Step 19: Activate the Cut Faces tool. Modeling | Edit Polygons > Cut Faces Tool (Options). Reset the settings (Edit > Reset Settings) and click Enter Cut Tool and Close.

The Cut Faces tool allows you to, well, cut faces. What this means is that you can split extant polygons into new collections of polygons. Imagine this tool as an Xacto that will allow you to cut through the objects, leaving a new set of edges in its wake.

In this case, you'll be creating four new feet off the base. To get this, you need to cut the base form four times to yield four new polygons at each of the corners. You can then extrude each of those to create the feet.

Step 20: In the top view, hold the Shift key down (to constrain the cut to be a flat 90 degrees). Click-drag horizontally to define the direction you want the cut to go (Figure 4.33).

Step 21: Repeat the process to create three more cuts (Figure 4.34).

In the persp View Panel, rotate down and take a look at the bottom of the form. You will see that this Cut Faces operation has cut all the way through to the bottom. Ultimately, this is the area of interest as the four new polygons on the corners of the base are the ones you will be extruding to create new feet. However, if you had split just the bottom face (instead of cutting all the way through the object), you would end up with some undesirable geometry around the base (essentially five-sided faces).

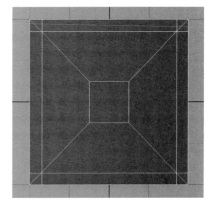

FIGURE 4.33   Using the Cut Faces Tool to cut through the object.

FIGURE 4.34   Finished sliced-up base.

Cleaning Up

Step 22: In the persp View Panel, zoom in on one of the corners. Notice that these cuts made for some messy geometry. There is a triangle and three points where there ought to really be one.

Step 23: Right-click on Table_Base and select Vertex from the marking menu. Select the three vertices that should be one (Figure 4.35)

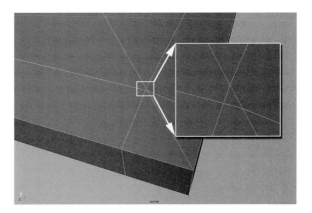

FIGURE 4.35   The dirty geometry to be cleaned.

Remember that when selecting vertices, you can select through an object to select vertices on the back side of the poly-mesh. Make sure that when you select these three vertices that you have not selected through the object to snag stuff on the back. View the object in wireframe if you wish. If you have selected some unwanted components, Ctrl-marquee around the vertices that should not be included.

Step 24: Merge the vertices. Modeling | Editing Polygons > Merge Vertices (Options). Change the Distance setting to 1. Hit MergeVertex (Figure 4.36).

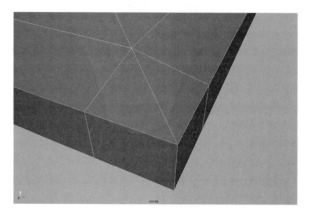

FIGURE 4.36   The results of a successful Merge Vertex function.

The Merge Vertex (or Vertices) tool allows you to take several vertices and move/merge them together into one. This automatically gets rid of unneeded faces and edges. The way it works is by taking each selected vertex and checking to see whether there are any other selected vertices within the volume defined by the Distance setting. In this case, 1 is a completely arbitrary value; it could be 100 in this case, as you know that only three vertices are selected and all three of those need to be merged. However, if this value is too small, it will interpret that some points are not meant to be merged, and they will not be included.

Step 25: Delete the unneeded edge. Right-click on the object and choose Edge from the marking menu. Select the edge that splits the two triangles and delete it (Figure 4.37).

In reality, this is largely cosmetic. The nature of the remaining polygon on the corner actually has some problems (namely five different polys share the same vertex at the top, which may not be a huge problem in this case, but can be a real issue in more complex models, so it is a good idea to avoid them if you can). So when Maya interpolates at rendering, it will essentially subdivide that polygon right down the same edge you just deleted. But, it does keep the mesh clean as you move forward with the modeling process.

Step 26: Repeat for each of the other corners (Figure 4.38).

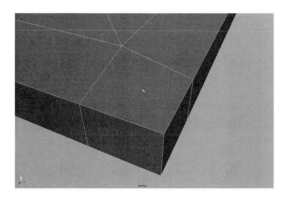

FIGURE 4.37   Deleted edge.

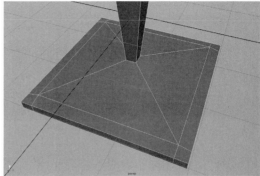

FIGURE 4.38   Cleaned-up base.

Creating Feet

Now that you have clean (four-sided polygons) geometry, the feet will be easy to create.

Step 27: Select the faces that will become the feet. Right-click Table_Base and choose Face from the marking menu. Click and then Shift-click on each of the four faces shown in Figure 4.39.

Step 28: Extrude and adjust to create the foot. Extrude Face (Modeling | Edit Polygons > Extrude Face). Dolly closer into the shape so that you can see the face well and then use Extrude Face manipulator handles to create a shape similar to Figure 4.40.

FIGURE 4.39   Selected faces for creation of the foot.

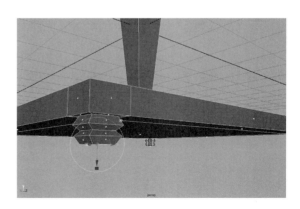

FIGURE 4.40   Completed foot.

Why only work on one? Since four corners are selected, when you begin working on **Why?** *one corner and extrude it, the others will extrude as well. As long as you are within*

the Extrude Faces handle to manipulate the face, the other faces will change as well relative to their own location. In this way, you can do four legs at once.

Table Base Finishing Touches

Step 29: Finish the table base by creating a new extrusion off the top of the base for the tabletop to sit upon (Figure 4.41). Just select the face at the top of the table and select Modeling | Edit Polygons > Extrude Face. Use the Extrude Face manipulator to pull the face up to the desire height.

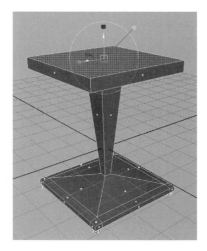

FIGURE 4.41   Completed table base.

Creating the Tabletop

Step 30: Create a new polygon primitive cube. Scale it and translate it into position (Figure 4.42). Rename to "Tabletop."
Step 31: Select the face on the top of the table.
Step 32: Extrude Face and use the scale handles to scale the extruded face to match Figure 4.43.

Notice that in the final render of this scene there is a small trough in the table top that indicates where the material changes from the bumpy stone-like material to the wooden frame. This is the process of creating that.

Why?

Step 33: Extrude face again; use the translate handles to move straight down (Figure 4.44).
Step 34: Extrude face again, scale in (very slightly).
Step 35: Extrude face again, use the translate handles to move the face back up to the level of the table, thus creating the small trough (Figure 4.45).

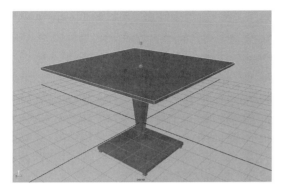

FIGURE 4.42   New tabletop.

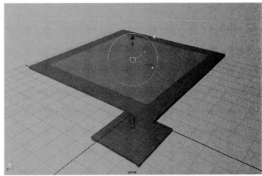

FIGURE 4.43   Extruded table top.

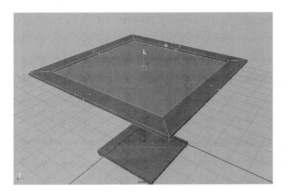

FIGURE 4.44   Creating the recede.

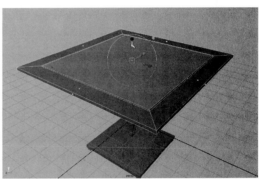

FIGURE 4.45   Trough completed.

Organize

Step 36: Choose Edit > Delete All by Type > History.

To keep things clean, and because there really is no usable history to use in the future, deleting all the history in the scene will strip both the Tabletop and
Why? *Table_Base of unnecessary nodes.*

Step 37: Save.
Step 38: Open Tutorial_4_1.mb (File > Open).
Step 39: File > Import (Options). Reset the settings (Edit > Reset Settings).
Step 40: Turn on Group. Click Import.

By turning on group, you get Maya to automatically create a group making all the objects that you are about to import children of that group.

Step 41: Choose Table.mb from the Import dialog box.

This will import the work done on the model Table.mb into the room. Note that it is too big and is sticking through the floor. A bit of adjusting left to do.

Step 42: In the Outliner, select group and rename to Table. (It should include two objects named Table:Tabletop and Table:Table_Base.)
Step 43: Scale and translate the group Table into place in the room (Figure 4.47).

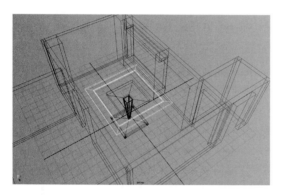

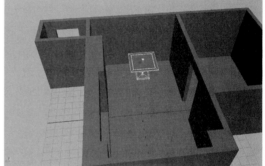

FIGURE 4.46   Imported table.

FIGURE 4.47   Finished placed table.

Step 44: Create a new layer called "Furniture." Add the Table group to it.
Step 45: File > Save as. Save as Tutorial_4_2.

Tutorial Conclusion

Seems like a lot of steps for a table. Indeed, it does take a while to explain and get the hang of how the extrude functions work. However, after you understand and are comfortable with extruded faces, there are very few shapes you cannot hash out quickly.

CHALLENGES, EXERCISES, OR ASSIGNMENTS

1. Figure 4.48 is a close-up shot of the bottom of the table you created in Tutorial 4.2. The details were done with simple extrusions. Add these details—or ones like them—to the table.

2. Using the tools we have covered so far, most of the lamps, lamp shades, and sconces are possible to create. Figure 4.49 shows these

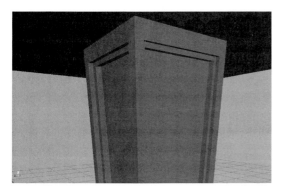

FIGURE 4.48   Details on table from further extrudes.

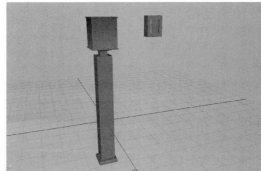

FIGURE 4.49   Lamps and shades.

lamps, and Figure 4.50 shows them in place. Model these; remember that they may be created with a combination of extrudes and Boolean functions.

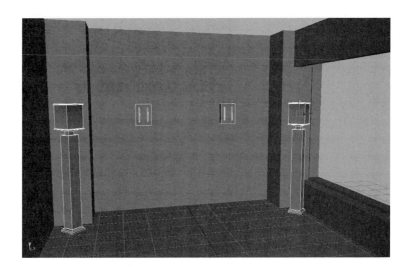

FIGURE 4.50   Lamps and shades placed.

3. Using extrusions and Booleans, create the acoustic panels in the room and the headboard for the bead (Figures 4.51 and 4.52).

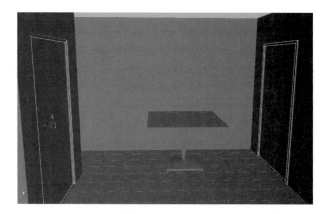

FIGURE 4.51   Acoustic panels.

FIGURE 4.52   Headboard.

ON THE CD

4. Rename and organize everything in the scene. Make sure that you have appropriate levels and groups. To see an example solution, take a look at Tutorial_4_2-Extra.mb on the CD-ROM.

BEGINNING NURBS
MODELING

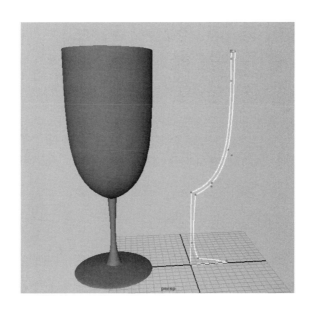

In the next chapter we shall return to the ever-interesting world of polygonal modeling—more importantly, we will look at ways to get much more organic forms using the initially blocky methodology that polygonal modeling offers. But, for now, we will take a cursory look at how Maya handles NURBS surfaces.

NURBS surfaces are objects created from splines or—as Maya calls them—curves. These objects are altered in ways different than polygonal modeling. Instead of faces, vertices, and edges, NURBS surfaces are controllable through Control Vertices, Isoparms, and Hulls. With History in action, you can also adjust the surfaces by altering the curves that created them. To get a better idea of how surfaces work, take a look at these synopses:

CURVES

Curves are the basic building blocks of NURBS surfaces. Maya only creates one type of curve; however, there are two ways (and ways within those ways) to create these curves: the CV Curve tool and the EP Curve tool. But before we get into how to create curves, let's take a look at the anatomy of a curve.

Figure 5.1 shows a curve (it does not really matter how it was created). This object can be translated, rotated, or scaled like any other object.

If you right-click on this curve, you can select the components that make up this curve (much like you did with polygonal objects). The relevant components of a curve are all found in this marking menu (Figure 5.2).

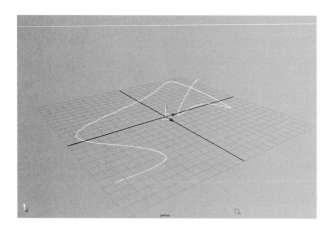

FIGURE 5.1 A curve (pretty exciting).

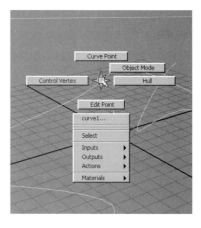

FIGURE 5.2 Marking menu displayed when a curve is right-clicked. This lists the important components of a curve.

Control Vertex

Figure 5.3 shows the curve with the Control Vertices revealed. A control vertex (CV) can be thought of as a magnet. The position and number of magnets determines how the curve (think of this as a filament of metal) winds along its course. If you move these CVs, you do not move anything directly on the curve, but it does influence how the curve's shape appears. Figure 5.3 (a–b) shows the before and after of moving one of the CVs and the resulting curve.

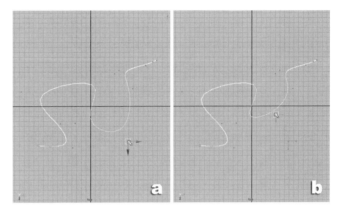

FIGURE 5.3   Control vertices. Although not directly on the line, they still control the shape of the curve.

Curve Point

Theoretically, along a given curve in Maya, there are a large number of curve points. When you snap to a curve (hold the c key down), or use Point on Curve deformers, these Curve Points provide a location for Maya to keep track of. However, they are of little use in editing a curve or surface, so we will move along.

Hull...

Hulls are very useful when they are on a surface (a NURBS surface, that is). They are essentially a collection (usually) of a ring of control vertices. Hulls can be rotated, scaled, and translated *as a unit*. So, when there are several hulls that are part of a surface, this provides a quick way to work with a bunch of CVs at once. But, when working with curves, it is less useful, as you might as well translate, scale, or rotate the entire curve since there is only one hull. Figure 5.4 shows the hull for the illustration curve.

Edit Point

Maya defines Edit Points as "a point that lies on a curve or surface (spline) where polynomials are joined." Translation: Edit Points are the points along a curve that the curve defines as important points that it passes through. Although you can create a curve by creating edit points, Maya is essentially finding a curve that matches those points. Editing with Edit Points (ironically) is not a good way of making adjustments to curve shapes—editing Control Vertices is still the preferred method. Edit Points appear as x's on the curve (Figure 5.5).

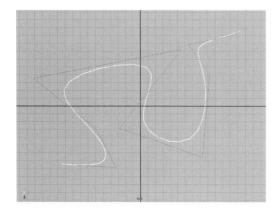

FIGURE 5.4   Hull of a curve.

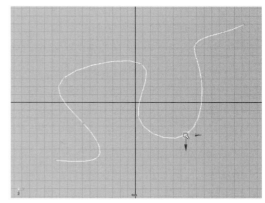

FIGURE 5.5   Edit Points.

CREATING CURVES

The two tools for creating curves are found under the Create pull-down menu: CV Curve Tool and EP Curve Tool. As you would guess, CV Curve Tool allows for the creation of curves by defining the control vertices; and the EP Curve Tool does so by defining the Edit Points. Since the best way to edit curves really is through editing the CVs of the curve, this will be the preferred method that you will use to create the curves needed to create NURBS surfaces.

When you select Create > CV Curve Tool, the Channel Box area will change to show the tool settings (Figure 5.6).

Note that there is a Reset Tool button that works just like Reset Settings for other tools. Also note that the default setting for Curve Degree is set to 3 Cubic. Ironically, 3 Cubic is actually the setting you use to create curvilinear curves. Curve Degree defines how many CVs are set between spans of a curve (actually it is the number of CVs minus 1, but the technicalities of this are not important here).

Basically, the curve is broken down into spans. A span consists of two points; the control vertices are the controls that allow you to pull the line away from a direct line between points. A 3 Cubic curve has four CVs; essentially two that define the start and end of the curve, and two to define the curviness of the curve.

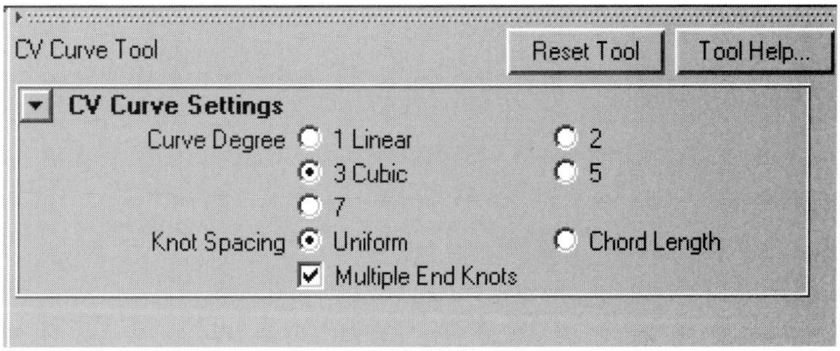

FIGURE 5.6   CV Curve Tool settings.

So, to create a 3 Cubic curve, you must create at least four CVs. Creating CVs within the CV Curve Tool is just a matter of clicking in any of the View Panels. When you do, the first CV will display as a box (Figure 5.7a), the second as a U (Figure 5.7b), and the third and fourth as dots (Figure 5.7c and 5.7d). Notice that you will just get lines until you have created the fourth CV. When you are done creating a curve (by defining at least four CVs), press Enter to exit the tool.

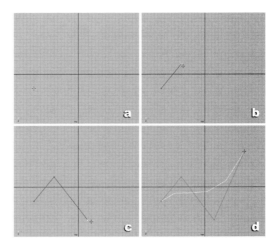

FIGURE 5.7   (a) First CV creates a box. (b) Second CV creates a U. (c) Third creates a dot. (d) Fourth creates the last CV and, thus, defines the curve.

You do not have to stop at four CVs, though. When creating a curve with the CV Curve tool, you can continue to click and continue to create CVs that will create added spans that are all connected together to create one large curve. When you are done creating a curve with as many CVs as you need, press Enter to exit the tool and complete the curve.

Linear Curves

It sounds like an oxymoron, but you can use the CV Curve tool to create straight lines. Do this by activating the CV Curve tool (Create > CV Curve tool) and choosing 1 Linear in the Curve Degree section of the tool options. 1 Linear means that there are two CVs to define the curve—one at the beginning and one at the end of the span. Since there are no CVs between them, the curve is just a straight line. Like a 3 Cubic CV curve, you can make multiple spans by continuing to place CVs, only think of this as simply defining where the next corner of the rectilinear line will occur (Figure 5.8).

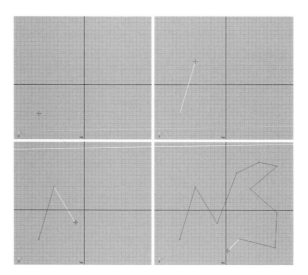

FIGURE 5.8   Creating a linear curve with 1 Linear curves.

A Few Curve Tips

A few notes about using the CV Curve Tool:

- When creating the CVs that define the curve, you can snap the new CVs to the grid (x) to curves (c) or to points (v).
- If you click and drag, you can create a point and then shift it before it is placed and before you have to move on to the next CV.

- If you do not like the placement of a CV, you can immediately click z to undo its placement and then place another instead. Remember that the placement of these CVs is not permanent, and that after you have finished with a curve (press Enter to exit the Curve Tool), you can come back and adjust them by right-clicking the curve and selecting Control Vertex from the marking menu. This makes the CVs selectable so that you can select and translate the previously positioned CVs.
- Curves can be open or closed. However, do not try to close it yourself while within the CV Curve tool. Although visually it might appear that the curve is closed; you will actually have created two CVs right on top of each other, and you will not have a closed curve. To close a curve, create the general curve (except for the last connecting CV). Then press Enter to exit the tool. Select Modeling | Edit Curves > Open/Close Curves, and Maya will sew the curve up to create a closed shape.
- Remember that Maya remembers your last settings for any tool. So if you change the Curve Degree settings to create a rectilinear line, be sure you change it back to 3 Cubic to create a curvilinear curve.
- Generally, most all curves (rectilinear or curvilinear) that you will need to create can be most easily created and edited with 1 Linear or 3 Cubic as the Curve Degree settings. So although there are other options available, usually you can leave those alone.
- When creating curves with 3 Cubic activated, you can still create sharp, rectilinear corners for your curve. Simply place multiple CVs right on top of each other. With the metaphor that the CVs are magnets, more magnets mean more attractive power, and so the line attracts in very tightly to create a sharp corner for the curve. The best way to do this is to make sure to use the snap tools—especially the Snap to Grid (x). This will allow you to ensure that you are snapping the multiple CVs truly in the same spot. Generally three CVs on the same spot makes for a perfect hard corner.

NURBS SURFACES

Now that we have taken a look at how curves work, let's take a look at how curves are used to create NURBS surfaces. Not all of the surfaces Maya's NURBS create are of tremendous use; and some are of no use to us in the room tutorial on which we are working. However, for future reference, a brief synopsis of each will be included here.

Revolve Surface

Revolve surfaces work much like a wooden lathe. You define the profile of a shape. Usually, creating the profile with the inner edge right on the *y*-axis makes for easier revolving. When the curve is complete, Modeling |

Surfaces > Revolve will take the curve and spin it around the world's axis with the resulting shape being a symmetrical 3D realization of the curve created (Figure 5.9).

Note that because of history, if you select CVs on the curve and move them, the revolved surface that was created with that curve will dynamically update (Figure 5.10).

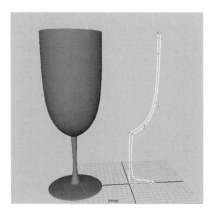

FIGURE 5.9   Curve used to create a revolve NURBS form.

FIGURE 5.10   The power of history. Since the curve at right was used to create the revolved surface at left, when the curve is altered, the geometry of the surface is changed as well.

Loft Surface

Lofted surfaces are created from two or more curves. To create such a surface, simply select the curves in the order that they are to define the surface and select Modeling | Surfaces > Loft. The resulting shape (Figure 5.11) is also editable by changing the curves that were used to create the surface.

Planar Surface

The hole-filler of surfaces is Modeling | Surfaces > Planar. Planar surfaces will take any planar, closed curve, and fill it with a flat surface. It essentially fills the curve in (Figure 5.12).

Extrude Surface

Extrude surfaces also make use of two curves (Modeling | Surfaces > Extrude). The first curve defines the cross section of the surface, and the second curve dictates the path that cross section is to follow (Figure 5.13).

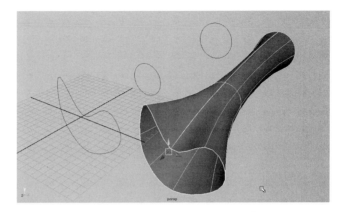

FIGURE 5.11   Quick illustration of a loft surface.

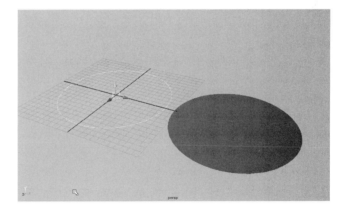

FIGURE 5.12   Planar example.

FIGURE 5.13   Extruded surface.

Birail Surface

A spectacularly powerful surface creating tool that allows for the quick creation of really complex forms. The basic idea is that one curve is run along two rails to create a surface. The interesting thing about creating Birail surfaces is that the method of creation is an interactive tool. After you have your curves created, selecting one of the Birail Tools (Modeling | Surfaces > Birail >) will activate the tool. When one of the Birail Tools is activated, take a look at the Help Line (at the bottom of the interface) for details on what rails to select when (Figure 5.14).

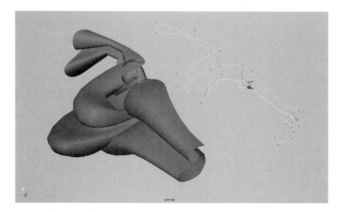

FIGURE 5.14   Abstract form created from Birail Tool. Note that there are much more pragmatic uses of this tool as well.

Boundary Surface

Figure 5.15 shows four curves on the far left. These curves can occupy any sort of 3D space. Boundary surfaces create a NURBS surface between

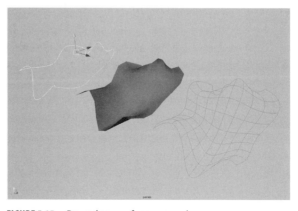

FIGURE 5.15   Boundary surface example.

those curves. Some important caveats about boundaries: First make sure that the ends of the curves are snapped together (do this by snapping to curve (c) when creating a curve). Second, in general, you want to make sure that curves across from each other on the surface are made of the same number of CVs.

Square Surface

At first glance, it seems like Square surfaces are the same as Boundary surfaces. Like Boundary surfaces, you select four curves with intersecting ends. The difference is that Square surfaces work hard to maintain continuity with other surfaces. Specifically, this applies when one of the curves was created as a curve on surface—select an object, click the magnet icon at the top of the interface (near the snap tools) and then draw a CV curve right on the surface of that object and click the magnet to turn the active object off. When one of the curves is a curve on surface, then the surface that the Square Surface makes has a much smoother transition as it connects to the original surface.

Figure 5.16 is an illustration of this. In the background you can see the curves used—including one that is a curve on surface. The top is a Square surface created with those curves, and the bottom is a Boundary surface created with those curves. You can see the transition onto the sphere is much different.

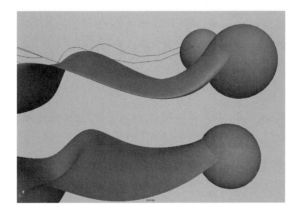

FIGURE 5.16   Square surface illustration. The top example is a Square surface with the curves shown in the background; the bottom is a Boundary surface.

Bevel and Bevel Plus

These are really amazingly robust tools. They are essentially variations of each other—and so will be presented together here. At its core, the Bevel surfaces are meant to take a single curve, extrude it, and bevel the extrusion. However, with Bevel Plus (options), you can also make sure that the surface puts caps on the front and end of the extrusion and that the bevel connects the caps and extrusion. Further, you can vary greatly what sort of bevel is created (Figure 5.17).

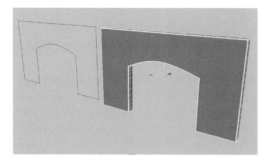

FIGURE 5.17   A look at Bevel Plus. The right-hand image shows variations on the different types of profiles possible with the Bevel Plus Tool.

A BIT ABOUT THE NURBS STRATEGY

Most every 3D package handles polygons and polygonal modeling in very similar ways. However, although most 3D packages have NURBS, the actual editing and construction capabilities of them vary widely. Maya's NURBS implementation strategy is among the most powerful in the industry; but it is quite unique. Further, when Maya's NURBS first came out, people were very excited about NURBS modeling techniques as they seemed a quick way to create smooth organic meshes. However, as of late, NURBS modeling has fallen a bit out of vogue, and poly modeling is the weapon of choice for most.

Because of this, we will not be spending a huge amount of time with NURBS. For organic shapes, this author prefers polygonal modeling because of its quasi-direct capability of controlling the polygon topology (the way the polygons are organized). It just provides more power to get the mesh right for things like textures and animating.

But, having said all that, there are some shapes and functions that just work best, quickest and easiest with NURBS functions. Maya lets you use NURBS methodology (creating shapes from curves) to actually create polygon meshes so you can still work with most of your scene in polygon world.

In the tutorials in the rest of this chapter we will be looking at a variety of ways to use NURBS construction methods to create some needed shapes in the room. Again, as with most things we have looked at, we are not analyzing the *only* way to create the forms we are making; and you may choose to use alternate methods later to create these shapes. But consider the possibilities of these tools for the time being.

TUTORIAL 5.1   CREATING VASES

Objectives:

1. Create CV curves.
2. Use NURBS to create organic curvilinear shapes.
3. Edit NURBS objects at a component level.

Step 1: Define your project (File > Project > Set…, and so on…). This file will still sit the scenes folder of your Amazing_Wooden_Man project.
Step 2: Create a new file (File > New). Save it as Vases.

Creating Curves

Step 3: Make the side View Panel full screen (press Spacebar to swap to a four view, and then with your mouse over the side View Panel, press Spacebar again).

When creating curves, you almost always want to avoid doing so in the persp View Panel. This is not an absolute rule and with certain situations, especially Boundary surfaces, working with curves in the persp View Panel is preferable. However, in most cases you want to be working with only two dimensions as you create curves to be used to create surfaces. Orthographic views provide ease of snapping and allow you to quickly and easily see the sorts of profiles that these curves will need to be to get clean meshes.

Step 4: Create > CV Curve Tool(Options).
Step 5: In the Tool Settings (where the Channel Box usually resides), click the Reset Tool button. Make sure that Curve Degree is set to 3 Cubic.
Step 6: Your mouse should have turned into a little + sign. This indicates Maya is ready to place CVs. Click and release five or six times to create the general outline of a vase.
Step 7: As you approach where the profile will reach the floor, press and hold the x (to Snap to Grid). Click three times (still holding the x key down) to place three CVs on the same grid intersection (Figure 5.18).

Sometimes, when placing multiple CVs at the same spot, you actually have to slow your clicking. If you click too quickly, Maya does not always place three distinctive

CVs. So slow down a bit, click, then click again (watch for the white part of the curve to shorten), and then click again (the white part of the curve will shrink again). Also be sure that in situations like this (where you are going to revolve the curve) that you keep all the vertices on one side of the y-axis.

Take a look at each of the progressing screen shots in Figure 5.18. Notice that with each added CV, the white part of the curve becomes shorter and shorter. What is happening there is Maya is indicating that it is being pulled tighter and tighter into that position in space.

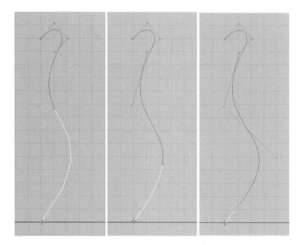

FIGURE 5.18   Creating the vase profile. Note that creating the three points snapped to the same position in space will be the start of a crisp edge.

Step 8: Create two more hard corners by holding the x key down and clicking three times at the world origin, and again three more clicks a unit or so up in the y direction. See Figure 5.19 for reference.

The y-axis will become the axis around which this curve will be revolved. Making sure that the points along this plane are clean and that the curve does not spill over will make for much tidier geometry.

Step 9: Still within the same tool and still working on the same curve, continue to place CVs up the inside of the vase to give the vase thickness. When you have moved up so you are close to the first point—but not at it, press Enter on your keyboard to exit the CV Curve tool (Figure 5.19).

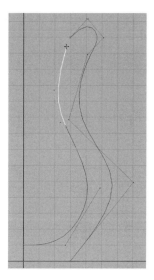

FIGURE 5.19   Finishing off the curve. Note that you do not click on the first CV. Just get to a reasonable distance from it.

Remember that you want to let Maya do the curve closing. If (while creating the curve) you click on the position of the very first CV, Maya does not close the curve, it simply puts another CV at that point. Visually, it will appear that the curve is closed, but it is not, and your geometry will suffer with splits and unintended creases.

Why?

Step 10: Select Modeling | Edit Curves > Open/Close Curves (Options). Reset the tool and press Open/Close.

This will close the curve off. If you take a look in the View Panel, you will see that you now have a closed shape.

Why?

Step 11: Select Modeling | Surfaces > Revolve (Options). Reset the settings. Make sure that the Axis Preset is set to Y (the axis you carefully drew around) and click Revolve (Figure 5.20).

Adjusting

Step 12: With the Translate tool, click away from the vase, and then click the vase surface.

This makes sure that you are just selecting the surface, and not the new surface and the curve.

Why?

Step 13: Rename the new surface (called revolvedSurface1) to Vase. Do this in either the Channel Box or the Outliner.

Step 14: Translate (with the Move Tool) the vase in the z direction enough to let you see the curve that created the surface.

Step 15: Right-click on the curve and select Control Vertex from the marking menu.

Step 16: Marquee and translate CVs into position to make the vase look like the form you want (Figure 5.21).

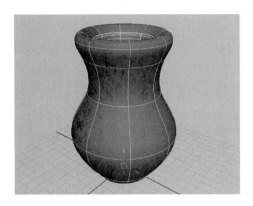

FIGURE 5.20   Revolved vase.

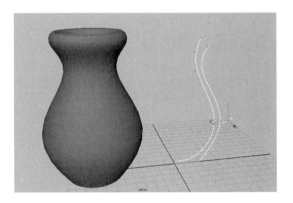

FIGURE 5.21   Adjusted vase tweaked by adjusting the curve that made the surface.

The key here is that the history is active. The curve and Vase are tied together—the curve is actually an input for the Vase surface. Thus changes made to the curve change the form of the form it created.

Why?

Step 17: Delete the curve. Right-click the curve and select Object Mode. Press delete.

You no longer need the curve. And, actually, there are other ways to change the shape of the vase that you will use in the coming steps. Deleting unneeded curves prevents unwanted selection and editing down the road.

Why?

Other Adjusting Methods

Step 18: Duplicate Vase.

Step 19: Translate Vase1 a bit so you can see both forms.

Step 20: Right-click on Vase1 and choose Control Vertex from the marking menu.

Step 21: Marquee around the control vertices (purple dots) that define the fattest part of the vase. They will highlight yellow. Use the Translate tool to move those vertices up in the y direction (Figure 5.22).

Step 22: Select the vertices around the neck of the vase. Use the Scale tool to scale them proportionally (use the Center handle) smaller (Figure 5.23).

FIGURE 5.22 Adjusting the shape of a vase by moving control vertices.

FIGURE 5.23 Scaling control vertices to further alter shape.

Step 23: Have fun. Continue to duplicate Vase and work with the Control Vertices for the surfaces to create new variations. All of the shapes shown in Figure 5.24 were created from the same base Vase with variations to the surfaces CVs.

FIGURE 5.24 Variations of vases created through editing CVs.

Step 24: Save.

Step 25: Open your latest version of the room (Figure 5.25 shows Tutorial_4_2-Extra.mb).
Step 26: Import Vases.mb (File > Import).
Step 27: Place your vase around the room to taste (Figure 5.25).

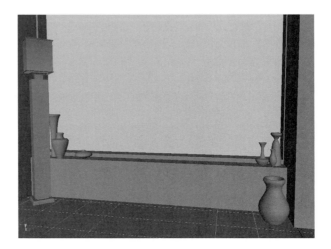

FIGURE 5.25   Placed vases

Step 28: Save.

Tutorial Conclusion

Pretty fun, huh? NURBS work incredibly well for this sort of shape. Smooth curves seem to flow effortlessly from your mouse. These shapes are symmetrical, but you can pull and push control vertices however you want in pursuit of a desired shape. But ultimately, these shapes are fairly limited in use (after you get past vases, goblets, and wine glasses) in practice. It just gets to be too cumbersome to push and pull these magnet-like CVs in an attempt to control the curved surface below.

However, let's take a look at some other uses for NURBS that may not seem like the kind of surfaces you would expect to create.

TUTORIAL 5.2   TRIM

Objectives:

1. Use CV Curve tool to create curvilinear and rectilinear lines together.
2. Use Loft NURBS to create doorway trim.

3. Create doorway trim, crown molding, and floor trim.

Step 1: Define your project (still working in Amazing_Wooden_Man).
Step 2: Create a new Maya file (File > New).
Step 3: Save it as Door_Trim.

Yep, you guessed it, this tutorial will be creating door trim; or the jam of the door-way. It may not seem like NURBS would make this shape, but it actually works very well.

Why?

Step 4: Create a new polygon primitive cube (Create > Polygon Primitives > Cube (Options)) that is Width = 200, Height =10, Depth = 50.

This is largely an arbitrary size. This cube is going to serve as a guide to help you understand how the trim is to be shaped so that it works on the front and back of the wall. True, we know that the walls in the room are at .5 units thick; but if you made a cube that size, the grid (which is set so each block is one unit), is too big for the kind of snapping we need. So creating this wall with a thickness 100x the real size gives us proportions, but gives us a tight grid to work on. From the top View Panel, think of what you are seeing as a chunk of wall 6 inches thick and 100 inches long. Remember that at this point the absolute size does not matter—we can always rescale after the shape is right; but the proportion is everything.

Why?

Step 5: Translate the cube over so that its edge is on the yz-axis (the center).
Step 6: Make the top View Panel full-screen.

You are about to draw the profile or cross section of the trim. That is, if you took the door trim and cut it with a band saw, and then looked straight at the surface you cut (perpendicular to how the blade ran), you would see this shape. This is similar to the profiles you would see for trim at a home improvement store. Doing this from an orthographic view is important, and the top View Panel ends up being the most intuitive.

Why?

Step 7: Choose Create > CV Curve Tool. Make sure that the tool settings are set for 3 Cubic.
Step 8: Draw a curve to represent the profile (approximation is okay). Figure 5.26 shows the curve drawn with notes on how many CVs were snapped and placed at each point (the numbers do not represent the order in which the CVs were placed). Remember that pressing the x key down snaps to the grid and will keep multiple CVs right on top of each other.

Note that there are some places where the corner needs to be very sharp, and so have 3 CVs. Other places where a corner needs to be tight—but not a hard angle

Why?

have less—like 2. Also note that the points both before and after a sharp corner have multiple CVs.

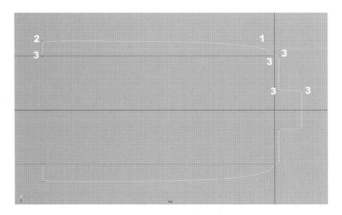

FIGURE 5.26   Profile for door jamb. Note the number of CVs placed on top of each other to create sharp corners.

Step 9: In Object Mode, rotate the curve 45 degrees in *z*. Or enter 45 in the Rotate Z input field of the Channel Box.

 The plan is to create one of these curves at each corner of the door frame. By lofting them together, you will get a great looking frame. However, if you try and leave these curves flat, the door frame will be two dimensional—as thin as paper—along the top. But, if you just rotate the curves at the top corners of the door, the actual width of the frame will change from the flat versions at the bottom. By rotating this curve to start with (and the last curve that will also be on the floor), you maintain a constant size all the way around the door.

Step 10: Duplicate the curve as an instance. Select Edit > Duplicate (Options). Here, change the Geometry Type to Instance.

 Instances are a powerful tool within 3D applications. An instance is not a copy of an object, rather Maya is simply displaying the same object twice. What this means is that if you have 499 instances of one cupcake, if you adjust the polygons on the first cupcake, all 499 will be updated as well.

In this case, creating instances creates flexibility in the door frame. If, for example, you decide that the actual jam part should be deeper, you only need to adjust it on this first curve, and all the other curves (and the resultant lofted surface) will automatically update to reflect the change.

Step 11: Translate curve2 (the new instance) up 675 units in y.

 Again, this is a largely arbitrary value as there will be lots of adjustment to come, but this gets the curves into rough approximations of where they need to be to create the door trim.
Why?

Step 12: Rotate it in the Channel Box so that Rotate Z = –45 (Figure 5.27).
Step 13: Select curve1, duplicate (as an instance) and change the Channel Box setting for this new curve3 to Translate X = 300, Translate Y = 675, and Rotate Z = –135.
Step 14: Select curve1, duplicate (as an instance) and change the Channel Box settings for this new curve4 to Translate X = 300, Rotate Z = –225 (Figure 5.28).

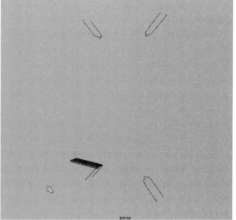

FIGURE 5.27   Rotated curve2.   **FIGURE 5.28**   Placed curves.

 *The Translate values are approximately 100x the 6'8" height and 3' width of the doorways you made in the last chapter's tutorials. The trim will look a bit bulky right here at first; but no worries—because of the instances, it will be easy to adjust.*
Why?

Step 15: Select curve1, shift-select curve2, shift-select curve3, and shift-select curve4.

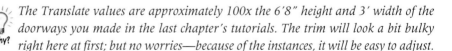 *The order in which you select curves determines which order Maya uses them as lofting guides. Since these are numbered, Maya can usually figure it out; however, it is good practice to select curves in the order you want them lofted together.*
Why?

Step 16: Select Modeling | Surfaces > Loft (Options).

Step 17: Change the Surface Degree setting to Linear. Press Loft (Figure 5.29).

FIGURE 5.29   Initial door trim.

Similar to curve degrees when creating CV curves, the Surface Degree setting determines how the surface is to interpolate between curves. The default—Cubic—creates a nice smooth curved interpolation, which works great if you are dealing with natural forms. However, in this case, you are making a man-made door trim—you want hard corners and straight lines. Thus Linear is the best choice here.

Step 18: Organize. Rename the newly created loftedSurface1 to "Door-Trim." Create a new layer called Trim, and make DoorTrim a member of it. Reference the layer Trim (by clicking the second column in the Layers Editor) until it shows an R.

Step 19: Select curve1 and rotate it back to Rotate Z = 0 in the Channel Box.

In the next step, you are going to adjust the trim so that it's a bit more refined. Adjusting the curve is a bit tricky when it is rotated 45 degrees, so flattening it back out becomes only a temporary (but necessary) step.

Step 20: Right-click on curve1 and select Control Vertex. Marquee around the outside left CVs and use the Translate Tool to move them inward (Figure 5.30). Notice that as you do this, all of the instanced curves will change, as will DoorTrim. Adjust to taste.

Step 21: Rotate (in Object Mode), curve1 back to Rotate Z = 45.

Step 22: Delete all history. Edit > Delete All by Type > History.

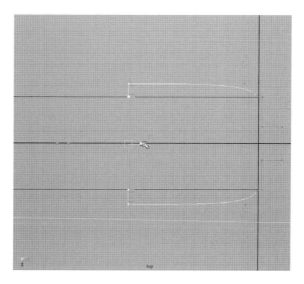

FIGURE 5.30   Adjusting door frame through curve CV manipulation.

This may be a controversial choice, but it is preferred to delete the curves. After they have served their purpose, and you have made adjustments to the surface to get the form you want, there is little reason for the curves. Most other adjustments at this point can be made through the components of the surface, and the curves just tend to get in the way.

Why?

Step 23: Delete curve1, curve2, curve3, and curve4.

Step 24: Make the Trim layer a nonreferenced layer (turn off the R).

Step 25: Save.

Step 26: Open your latest version of the room (the image here is listed as Tutorial_5_1.mb on the included CD-ROM) Import Door_Trim.mb.

ON THE CD

Step 27: Place the DoorTrim object in a doorway. The imported version will be huge! So make sure and scale it down.

Step 28: Edit > Duplicate (Options). Reset settings (the duplicates of the door way should not be instances). Press Duplicate.

Step 29: Translate the duplicated door into position. Repeat for any other doorways (Figure 5.31).

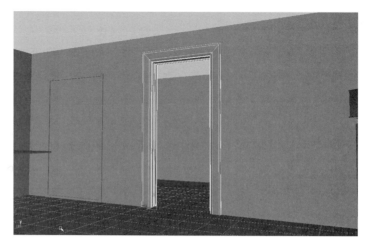

FIGURE 5.31 Placed doorway trims.

Tutorial Conclusion

The detail possible with this sort of method really starts to make scenes look sophisticated. All sorts of trims and moldings become possible when you have control over curve construction and linear loft creation.

CHALLENGES, EXERCISES, OR ASSIGNMENTS

1. Figure 5.32 is a curve made for crown molding in the room. Figure 5.33 shows the layout of the curves. Create crown molding or any

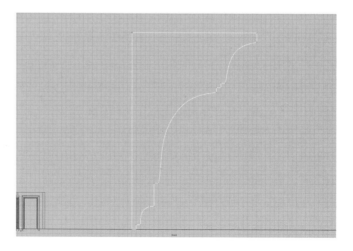

FIGURE 5.32 Curve for crown molding.

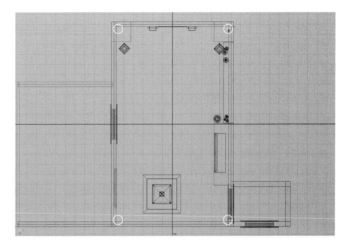

FIGURE 5.33   Layout of crown molding curves.

other upper molding for your room. Note that in Modeling _ Surface > Loft (Options), there is a Parameterization for Close to have the lofted surface loft back to the first curve when it is done with the last. Also note that this trim is created as part of Tutorial_5_1, although it is far too large. After the curve is created, it is resized to match the room.

2. Create a floorboard in the same way.
3. Consider Figure 5.34. How would you construct a window like this using the techniques covered in this chapter?

FIGURE 5.34   Window using NURBS surfaces.

4. Use these NURBS techniques to construct the details and trim in the room you began in Chapter 2.

5. Consider the frame in Figure 5.35. Using the techniques covered in this chapter, how could you make such a thing?

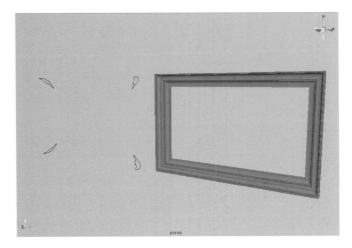

FIGURE 5.35   Frame.

6. Using the techniques covered thus far; make the bedspread for a bed (Figure 5.36). (*Hint:* see Bed Construction.mb for how the author did it.)

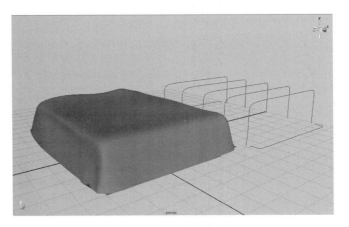

FIGURE 5.36   Bed.

6

ADVANCED POLYGONAL MODELING

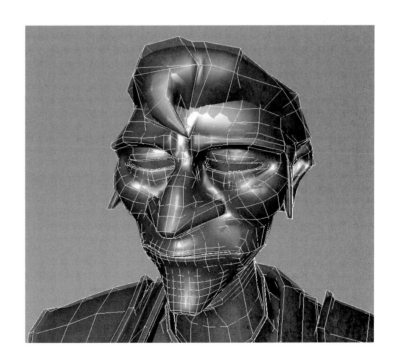

So far, you have looked at creating simple forms using NURBS objects and some very basic forms using potentially extraordinarily powerful tools like the Extrude Face tool. Indeed, we have only just begun to see the power of polygonal modeling.

In this chapter, we will be looking in more detail at how to control your model through Maya's polygonal modeling tools. Specifically, you will use tools that allow for the true control of polygonal topology. More importantly, you will have a chance to use tools like the Smooth Proxy that allow your models to break through the boxy look to create much more dynamic and curvilinear forms.

Control over Editable Components

The key to modeling polygonally is to have components where you need them. That is, if you need to make an area more round, or more sharp, or have a different curvature, you must have components (vertices, edges, faces) there to edit. This may seem like it could go without being said, but it comes into play again and again when dealing with complex forms.

So how do you ensure that you have the necessary components needed to create a given shape? On one hand, if you have a simple cube, you only have eight vertices to manipulate—this certainly limits the complexity of the form you can create. Conversely, you could simply create a highly dense polygonal sphere with hundreds of thousands of polygons—surely that would provide enough points to edit. Yes, it does provide a ton of vertices, each just waiting to be pulled and pushed; however, it means that to get the form you want—each and every vertex *must* be edited leaving you with countless hours of endless tweaking. Clearly, there has to be an effective method in between that will provide enough vertices to create complex forms, but not so many as to make the process impossible.

Actually, there are several methods. Maya provides several ways to add editable components to an object and to collapse unneeded editable components as well.

Options Windows

When you create a polygon primitive (a cube, for example) you can select the Options window and define not just the size (width, height, and depth), but also how many subdivisions are on that object (Subdivisions Along Width, Subdivisions Along Height, and Subdivisions Along Depth). Figure 6.1 shows the Polygon Cube Option window and the cube resulting from setting the subdivisions to 4, 1, and 2, respectively.

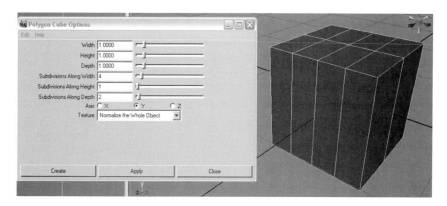

FIGURE 6.1   Using the Options window to create necessary geometry.

In some cases, if you can plan appropriately, having the right number of subdivisions can save time as you work. However, oftentimes you need Maya to be more flexible as you need to add subdivisions as you're modeling.

Via Nodes (Inputs)

Early in the modeling process, you can also make use of Maya's node system to adjust the node that created your shape to add subdivisions (and the resulting new edges and vertices). With polygon primitives selected (and with history active), the Channel Box (far right of the interface) will show the INPUTS of that shape. In the case of Figure 6.2, one of the INPUTS is polyCube1. By clicking on that cube, some of the options chosen in the Options windows are available for further refinement. In Figure 6.2, the Subdivision Height setting was set to 6, and you can see the resultant cube.

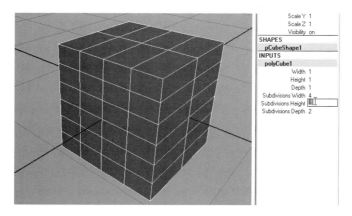

FIGURE 6.2   Using the INPUTS of a shape to increase subdivisions and add edges and vertices.

This adds flexibility, and often is a great way to get a whole lot of subdivisions when needed. However, Maya places them at equal distance from each other; and often you will need more specific placement. Luckily there are other methods available.

Cut Faces Tool

In the last chapter, we looked at using the Cut Faces Tool to place a cut that cuts completely through the object (Figure 6.3). This allows for precision cuts that can help maintain nice quadrangle-based topology; it also allows for exact placement of the new subdivision. Use the tool by selecting Modeling | Edit Polygons > Cut Faces Tool. This will change your mouse symbol. Click and drag to define the line that will cut through the object; holding Shift down will constrain the cut angle.

This tool works best when you are in object mode. If you are in polygon mode, this tool will let you cut just one polygon, or just a collection—but this can result in undesirable topology. Make sure that your object highlights in green (as it does when the entire object is selected) before using this tool.

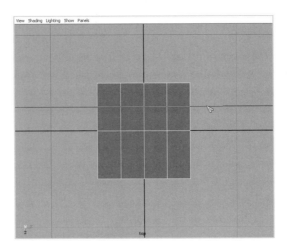

FIGURE 6.3   The Cut Faces Tool in action.

Split Polygon Tool

Although the Cut Faces Tool allows for clean, quick subdivisions where they are needed; it only does so in one long straight line. Sometimes, the added geometry is needed in less-than-linear placement. The Split Polygon Tool (Modeling | Edit Polygons > Split Polygon Tool) will allow you to click on an edge and then click on another edge to split that polygon with a new edge. Continue working around edges to continue the split. Press Enter on your keyboard to tell Maya you are done with the tool (Figure 6.4).

Remember that getting your topology right is important. Do not stop at the point that Figure 6.4 shows. In order to avoid five-sided polygons (or triangles for that matter), keep splitting around the form until you get back to the first click on the first edge that you started on.

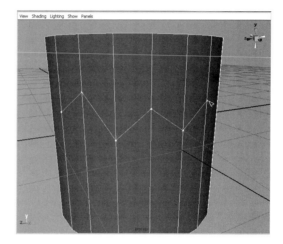

FIGURE 6.4   Split Polygon Tool in action.

Split Edge Ring Tool

Maya 7 has added some very important (and needed) tools to allow for quick addition of subdivision and accompanying vertices and edges. The first is the Split Edge Ring Tool (Modeling | Edit Polygons > Split Edge Ring Tool).

Notice that in most shapes, the edges of polygons can be thought of as a loop that goes around the form. Maya actually differentiates between something called a loop and something called a ring. A ring of edges is really the collection of edges that do not actually touch each other (that in a most basic situation run parallel to each other). In Figure 6.5, the edge ring is highlighted for illustration purposes. For now, the core idea here is that Maya will allow you to split an edge ring (a ring of edges). This creates a new ring of subdivisions, edges, and points.

Figure 6.5 shows this tool in action. The tool has been selected, and then, by clicking on an edge, you can see the new ring that Maya will create when the mouse is released. Notice that it follows the nonstraight line of edges right above it. As the mouse moves closer to the flat line of edges at the bottom of this shape, the new ring would become flatter.

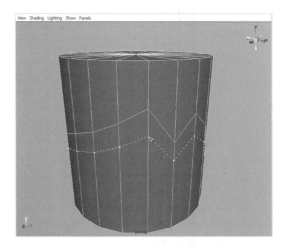

FIGURE 6.5 The Split Edge Ring Tool in action. Notice with the new ring you can create without having to laboriously use the Split Polygon Tool.

Duplicate Edge Loop Tool

A sister to the Split Edge Ring Tool, the Duplicate Edge Loop Tool (Modeling | Edit Polygons > Duplicate Edge Loop Tool) allows you to duplicate an edge loop. The idea here is that rather than splitting a ring of edges, you are duplicating a loop of edges. A loop of edges can be thought of as the single file row of edges that loop around a surface.

With this tool, you click and drag on an edge loop, and a new loop will be duplicated above and below the loop (Figure 6.6).

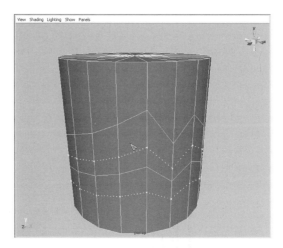

FIGURE 6.6 Duplicate Edge Loop Tool in action.

The Duplicate Edge Loop Tool and the Split Edge Ring Tool are welcome additions that become incredibly useful when it comes time to model organic forms. Much, much more on this later.

Subdivision and Smoothing

Maya provides several ways to take a low-poly model and systematically increase the density of polygons based upon the extant topology. The first is the Subdivide (Modeling | Edit Polygons > Subdivide).

A quick illustration of this can be seen in Figure 6.7. Figure 6.7a shows a low-poly mesh. Figure 6.7b shows the model with the Subdivide command implemented. Notice that each polygon has been split to create several others.

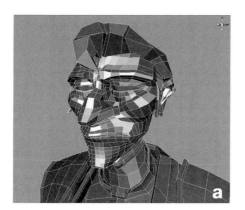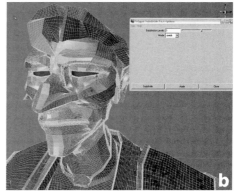

FIGURE 6.7   (a) Low-poly version of model (b) Subdivided model. Model by Will Keetell.

There are lots and lots of polygons; plenty there to push and pull. But in general, the need is not just to have more polygons; often it is to have more polygons to make a surface look smoother and more organic.

Because of this, Maya has available the Smooth tool (Modeling | Polygons > Smooth). If you check the options, you can decide what the Subdivision Level should be. Each subdivision indicates that you want Maya to take each polygon and subdivide it once (actually cuts it into fours—for quadrangle faces) and then take these new polygons and tweak them to small angles. The result is a smoothed version of the mesh (Figure 6.8).

This is tremendously powerful. It means that the modeler can work with a low number of polygons and then use the Smooth function to get a high-poly, but smoother mesh. Tweaking the higher number of polygons in an attempt to get a smooth mesh would be tremendously time consuming; and this allows for complex forms with minimal polygonal alteration.

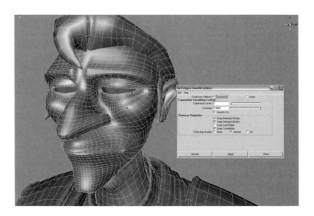

FIGURE 6.8 Using the Smooth function to create a smooth mesh from a low-poly mesh. Model by Will Keetell.

SMOOTH PROXY

But it gets even better. Built into Maya is the ability to create interactive low-poly versions of higher-poly models. These Smooth Proxies (as shown in Figure 6.9) can be thought of as (and are often called) cages. The idea is that this low-poly cage surrounds a higher-poly mesh and as you pull the low-poly cage around, it deforms the higher-poly mesh beneath. Maya makes the low-poly version 75 percent transparent, to allow you to see through the cage to the high-poly version (although this is an editable attribute).

In Figure 6.9, the low-poly cage is selected (appears in green on-screen), although you can see beneath a smoother version.

Figure 6.10 shows the power of this. For illustrative purposes, the low-poly cage has been moved to the side and an opaque texture placed on it to make it easier to see the difference between the two versions. Notice that the low-poly version on the right has some points selected and moved; the high-poly version on the left immediately updates the mesh to reflect the change.

This tool is pretty fun; let's take a look at it in action with a few added pieces to the room.

 Hotkey Alert *The keyboard shortcut for Smooth Proxy is Ctrl-` (that is the tilde button at the top left corner of your keyboard). After a Smooth Proxy has been activated, you can toggle between the low-poly and high-poly versions of the model with the tilde key (Shift-` shows both). Further, when the high-poly version is visible and selected, pressing the Page Up button will increase the number of subdivisions, and pressing the Page Down button will decrease them. However, use with prudence; if you turn the subdivisions up too far, your computer will slow to a crawl and might even crash.*

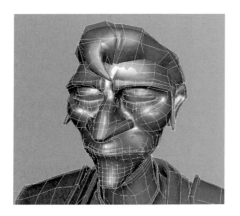

FIGURE 6.9   A Smooth Proxy created.

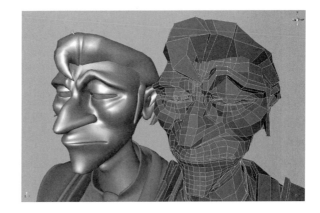

FIGURE 6.10   The Smooth Proxy relationship in action.

TUTORIAL 6.1   MODELING A SINK WITH SMOOTH PROXY

Objectives:

1. Take control of poly organization through

    - Adjusting subdivisions of polygonal primitives
    - Changing nodes settings
    - Cut Face Tool
    - Split Polygon Tool

2. Use Smooth Proxy to create smoother and more complex forms from low-poly meshes.
3. Use Poly Crease Tool to add crispness to smoothed forms.

Step 1: Set your project. If you are just continuing on from the last chapter, you may not need to do this; but if you have worked on any other project, or anyone else has worked on your machine, set the project. File > Project > Set. . . find your Amazing_Wooden_Man folder and press set.
Step 2: Create a new file. File > New.
Step 3: Save as Sink. This should automatically try and save to the Scenes folder of your Amazing_Wooden_Man project; if not, reset your project.

Roughing Out the Shape

Step 4: Create the base form. Create a cube that is 9 units in the X, .5 units in the Y, and 2.5 units in the Z. This can be done two ways; either create a cube (Create > Polygon Primitives > Cube [Options]) and then change the width, height, and depth to 9, 0.5, 2.5, respectively. Or create a default polygon cube and change the Scale X, Scale Y, and Scale Z in the Channel Box to 9, 0.5, 2.5.

Either method can work. Some prefer the second as it provides the size of the object to be seen easily in the Channel Box (even though technically this is just the number of times larger or smaller than the original shape was when it was created). The choice is up to you.

Step 5: Rename to Sink.
Step 6: Create sink subdivisions. Select the new cube (if it is not already). In the Channel Box, in the INPUTS, click on the polyCube1 input node. This will expand the node. Change the Subdivision width to 3.

This will be a single sink in the middle of a counter. By creating three subdivisions, we can begin to work with a smaller collection of polygons right in the middle of the counter. This will allow for easier manipulation and cleaner geometry ultimately.

Step 7: Adjust the center subdivision to be wider. Right-click on the cube in the View Panel and select Vertex. Select the vertices in the new subdivisions. Use the scale tool to resize out along the x-axis to widen the collection of polygons in the middle (Figure 6.11).

Because you added the subdivisions via the INPUTS, you were unable to determine how big the subdivisions were from each other. It is not difficult to adjust them, however, although you do need to do it via component mode as you did in Step 7.

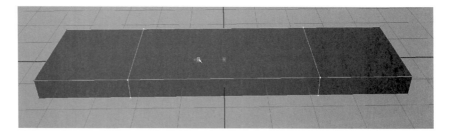

FIGURE 6.11   Widening the center polygons.

Step 8: Create a Smooth Proxy. Switch to Object mode (right-click on Sink, select Object Mode from Marking Menu). Select Modeling | Polygons > Smooth Proxy (Options). Reset settings (Edit > Reset Settings) and click Smooth (Figure 6.12).

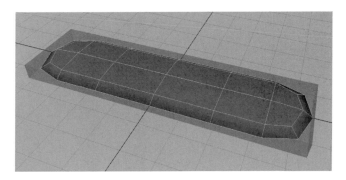

FIGURE 6.12   Smoothed sink.

Why now is a good question. Eventually, this sink will be smoothed to create the form we need. Smoothing early in the process will give you a chance to see how the changes you make to the low-poly version of this mesh effects the high-poly version. You could certainly wait until everything was done to smooth the form, but it is much more intuitive to see how added subdivisions add to your model.

Why are we smoothing at all? This is also a good question. Eventually the sink will be a very curvilinear form. Using the basic polygonal tools covered up to now will always result in a blocky form. Smoothing it will help add the smooth curved interesting forms desired.

True, at this point, it looks like we made a blocky surfboard out of a cube; that is not all that impressive. Not to fear, though, as we control the subdivisions further, the form will take place.

Step 9: Press the ~ (tilde) button on your keyboard. This toggles between your low-poly and high-poly version of the model. Press that key until you are left with the original low-poly version. Notice that it is semi-transparent, which will actually help in the modeling process.

Step 10: Extrude the basic sink shape. Select the face in the center top of the Sink shape (right-click, select Face from Marking Menu). Use the Extrude Face Tool (Modeling | Edit Polygons > Extrude Face) to extrude a new face.

Step 11: Resize newly extruded face. With the Extrude Face Tool still active, use the scale manipulator handles (the colored cubes) to resize the face without moving it (Figure 6.13).

Extruding the face only in scale like this helps to create clean geometry. Notice that now there are four polygons surrounding that face, but the other faces on the outside edges are unaffected.

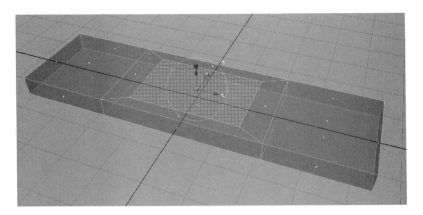

FIGURE 6.13 Extruded/resized face.

Step 12: Extrude face again and move down to create basin. Press g on your keyboard to activate the last used tool (in this case the Extrude Face tool) and then use the Move handles to drop the face downward to create the sink basin (Figure 6.14).

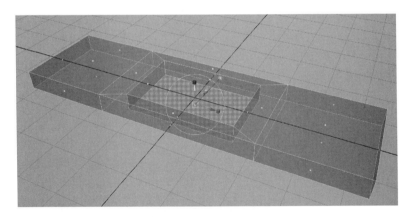

FIGURE 6.14 Creating the sink basin with additional extruded faces.

Step 13: Press the tilde key (~) to display a smoothed version of sink.

Looks pretty ugly, eh? It lacks shape and really makes you wonder whether this tutorial is any good. Not to worry, though. This shows what happens to the smoothed shape when the subdivisions and extrusions are far apart. All the globbiness will be gone as we add and control the subdivisions on the shape.

Step 14: Press ~ again to get back to the low-poly version.

Step 15: Use the Cut Faces Tool to add a subdivision through the middle of the basic segment of the sink. Make sure that you are in Object mode and select Modeling | Edit Polygons > Cut Faces Tool. In the top View Panel, click and drag from above to below the sink right in the middle (Figure 6.15).

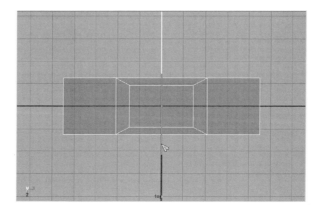

FIGURE 6.15   Adding a subdivision through center of sink.

Using the Cut Faces Tool will provide a clean cut that goes all the way through the object. This provides you with two new collections of vertices in the middle of the basin that will allow for some rounding off of that form.

Why?

Step 16: Reshape the sink. Switch to Vertex mode and reshape the basin to roughly look like Figure 6.16. Note that you can do this by moving vertices or scaling collections of vertices.

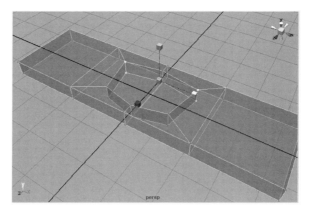

FIGURE 6.16   Reshaped basin done in Vertex mode.

For a quick look, switch to Object mode, and press ` to see the smoothed version. You can start to see the shape of the sink begin to emerge with these additional subdivisions and vertex tweaks. Be sure that you press ` again to get back to the low-poly version.

Step 17: Use the Duplicate Edge Loop Tool to provide additional subdivisions. Switch to Object mode and select Modeling | Edit Polygons > Duplicate Edge Loop Tool. The mouse pointer will change to indicate you are in a new tool now. Click and drag on the center subdivision. Two new dotted green lines will appear to indicate the proposed new location of the new edge loop. Release the mouse when your View Panel appears close to Figure 6.17.

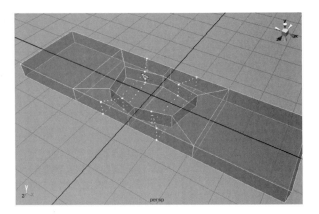

FIGURE 6.17   Using the Duplicate Edge Loop Tool to create new subdivisions as loops.

Note that these new subdivisions are not in straight lines as the Cut Faces Tool would have done. Rather, these are a balance of the center loop of edges and the next loop of edges on the edge of the sink. Further, note that you have created two subdivisions in one function.

This tool can be a bit unwieldy at times in its present incarnation. Often moving your mouse left to right will make the tool unresponsive; rather move your mouse up and down even though the new edge loops might be moving outward and inward along the surface.

Step 18: Tweak new subdivisions to add extra shape to the basin. Do this in Vertex mode using the Move and Scale Tools (Figure 6.18).

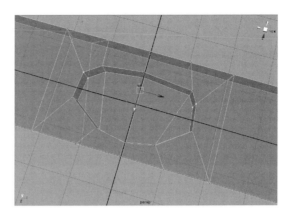

FIGURE 6.18   Further refining basin shape.

 An exact match of Figure 6.18 is not important. Move and scale your vertices to taste; the important issue to learn here is that these new subdivisions allow for needed additional geometry and vertices that allow for more sophisticated shapes.

Sharpening Shapes

Step 19: Press Shift-` to show both the low-poly and high-poly versions of the Sink. Figure 6.19 shows the results so far from the top View Panel.

Why?
Notice that in the middle area where new subdivisions have been added to create the sink, the form is much more refined, whereas areas like the far left and right of the countertop are rounded off into blunt rounded shapes.

This largely has to do with how far the subdivisions are from each other in the low-poly version. Consider the distance between subdivisions around the sink compared to the distance between the left edge of the sink and the far left edge of the counter.

This is important as it indicates how the edges of the counter can be tightened up. If new subdivisions can be created closer to the outside edges, the ends will become tighter as the distance between the end edges and the next edge become narrower.

Step 20: Cut new subdivisions close to the two outside edges. Use the Cut Faces Tool (Modeling | Edit Polygons > Cut Faces Tool) and cut through the entire form (of the low-poly version) near the outside edges (Figure 6.19).

Why?
Note that as you cut through the object to create a new subdivision, suddenly the edge of the counter tightens.

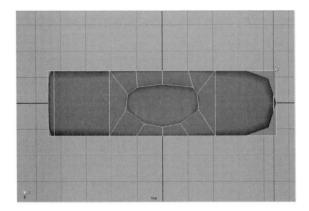

FIGURE 6.19 Adding new subdivisions to the low-poly and, thus, tightening up edges of the smooth version.

Step 21: Add definition to the Sink basin with added geometry. Press ` until the low-poly version of the Sink is visible. Select Modeling | Edit Polygons > Split Edge Ring Tool. Click on one of the edges that make up the inside of the basin (Figure 6.20). The dotted green line indicates the proposed cut in the edge ring. Release the mouse to create a ring close to the top of the basin.

The edge of the counters are nice and crisp (well, crisper anyway); but other areas (like around the sink basin) are still lacking definition. By adding this new ring of edges, the sink basin will begin to have some added definition. Press ` to take a look at the high-poly shape to see the results.

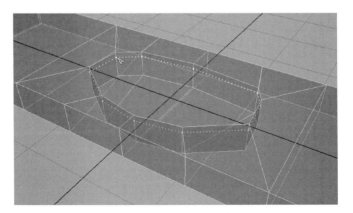

FIGURE 6.20 Using the Split Edge Ring Tool to create added sub-divisions that follow the shape of the sink.

Step 22: Repeat toward the bottom of the basin to further define the form (Figure 6.21).

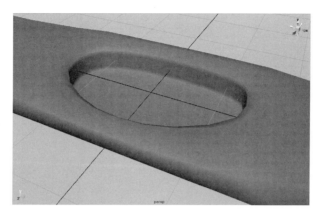

FIGURE 6.21   Added geometry at the bottom of basin.

Step 23: Select the front edges. Press Shift-` to show both low- and high-poly versions of the Sink. Select the low-poly version and change to Edge mode (right-click on the object and select Edge from the Marking Menu). Select the edges (top and bottom) that define the front edge of the sink (Figure 6.22).

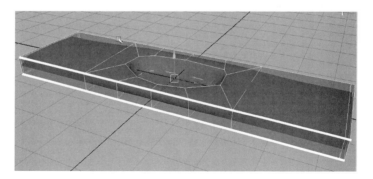

FIGURE 6.22   Selected edges that make up the front of counter top. (Highlighted in white for emphasis).

Technically, the soft edge of the counter front could be solved by extruding out another face as we did on the sides. However, in the interest of exploring a larger chunk of the Maya toolset, you will be making use of the Poly Crease Tool to do this. As is the case with most methods, this is not the only way to achieve this result.

Step 24: Use the Poly Crease tool to sharpen the edge of the low-poly mesh. Choose Modeling | Polygons > Poly Crease Tool. MMB-drag in your persp View Panel (Figure 6.23).

Notice that the edge will appear to get fatter (the peach line will get thicker), but more importantly, the subdivided polygons of the smooth version will then tighten up to the edge. With the metaphor that the low-poly shape is a magnetic cage surrounding a high-poly mesh of metal, you have just increased the magnetic power of those front edges of the cage.

FIGURE 6.23   Using the Poly Crease Tool to add definition to the smoothed version of the sink and counter.

Step 25: Use the tools covered thus far to tweak and add geometry to make your form approximate Figure 6.24.

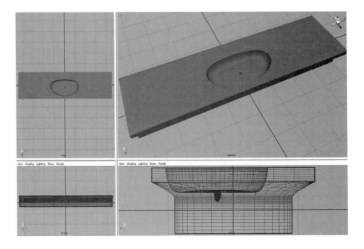

FIGURE 6.24   Finished counter top shape.

Press the ` button to show the high-poly version. Select it, and then press the Page Up button. This will increase the number of smoothed subdivisions. Quickly, the form can take a very definitive shape.

Step 26: Add other geometry to finish off the form (Figure 6.25).
Step 27: Save.
Step 28: Open Tutorial_5_2.
Step 29: Save as Tutorial_6_1.
Step 30: Import Sink.mb (File > Import).
Step 31: Resize and place the group into the bathroom (Figure 6.26).

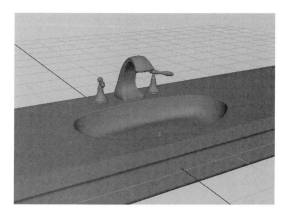

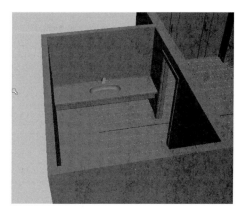

FIGURE 6.25   Added Faucet. . . .modeled using standard extrusions and some lofted NURBS surfaces.

FIGURE 6.26   Placed completed sink.

Tutorial Conclusion

Seems like a lot of text for a simple sink. However, quite a few tools have been covered here. In fact, the kind of complex form that the sink and its basin represent with its harsh edges and soft edges can be used to create all sorts of beautiful and complex forms. Take a close look at that faucet, and you can get an idea of the industrial design that becomes quick and easy to make and edit.

These techniques of the Cut Faces Tool and the new Duplicate Edge Loop Tool and Split Edge Ring Tool become immensely important when it comes time to model organic forms like faces and human characteristics. Having control of when new geometry comes into play, and where it goes, is the key to effective polygonal modeling.

Conclusion

And with that, we leave modeling for the time being. We will look at it much more when we deal with organic modeling later; but for now, it is time to move on and begin to add some visual depth to this collection of polygons. In the coming chapters, you will create color, visual tactile characteristics, and lighting. The fun has just begun.

CHALLENGES, EXERCISES, OR ASSIGNMENTS

1. Using the methods discovered in this chapter, model a chair similar to that shown in Figure 6.27. Place it in your room. Note, depending on your furniture choices, you may have to resize your room (make wider or thinner).
2. Find some good research, and using methods described so far, model a toilet for the bathroom (Figure 6.28). This actually ends up being a surprisingly complex shape, so make sure that you have good images to guide you.

FIGURE 6.27   Chair modeled with Smooth Proxy.

FIGURE 6.28   Toilet using polygonal modeling.

3. Add a shower stall. Put a shower head inside of it. Do not model tiles or anything like that on the floor—not even a drain. We will take care of that later with textures (Figure 6.29).

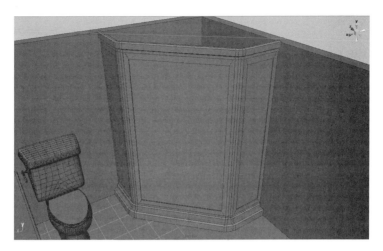

FIGURE 6.29   Added shower stall.

ON THE CD

4. Finally add any other details as you see fit to the room. Consider the bed—what techniques might you use to create the pillows and so on? For hints, take a look at Bed Construction.mb on the CD-ROM. Add details like light switches, props on shelves and countertops, and front doors.

SHADERS, MATERIALS, AND TEXTURES AND BASIC NURBS TEXTURING

In the first six chapters you have created at least one room through a variety of modeling techniques. NURBS modeling and Polygonal modeling are really some of the core techniques used in all 3D applications. They are certainly not the only techniques, but techniques that will serve you well regardless of your final application of choice or employer's choice.

For now we are going to make a short diversion to talk specifically about how to add color to your gray plastic room. This is actually a two-part process: part texture and part lighting. For this chapter, we will start by diving into the details of the texturing part.

What Is Texturing?

An example from the author: While in grad school, I used to visit a painter friend of mine whose studio was down the hall. On one visit I noticed a "Peanuts" cartoon strip tacked to the wall. On the next visit, he had a banana peel tacked in the same spot. The visit after that he had a postcard of another artist tacked to the same place. Upon examining the postcard further, I realized it and all the other objects were not actually tacked there, but had been painted on the wall in *trompe l'oiel*. Visiting a few weeks later, I noticed a smallish basketball sitting on the floor but when I reached down to play with it, I realized it was a bowling ball that he had painted to look like a basketball.

This is how texturing works. When you model within a 3D application, the gray object that the application shows you is simply a collection of colorless polygons. Texturing is a sort of veneer that goes over the top of the polygons to make the polygons look like a recognizable object with a tactile surface. Some textures actually make changes to the polygons they are laid over (that is, displacement maps), but more on that in Chapter 8.

Texturing will be how you make the bedspread look like cloth but the lamp look like brushed metal. Consider the following brief illustration. Figure 7.1 shows nine spheres. This is actually the same sphere duplicated eight times with nothing but a different material assigned to each.

Before we get into the details of applying textures, it will be important that we understand some terms and theories first.

Materials, Shaders, Textures. . . What's the Difference?

Well, not much actually. These terms are often used interchangeably to mean the same thing. Someone will say that they are "texturing their model" or that they are "creating shaders" or "making materials," and often they are all referring to the same process of adding color and tactile characteristics to the visual appearance of their polygons.

FIGURE 7.1   Nothing but different materials can make a great deal of difference in a surface's visual complexity.

Technically, there is a difference between each of these terms. Shading is the term used to describe how Maya defines a surface when it renders it. Materials are the nodes that are applied to the surface of polygons that define characteristics such as color, bump, transparency, and so on. Textures are (usually) bitmapped files that further define characteristics like color and bump beyond simple solid tones or procedural calculations.

For our purposes here and to make sure we are speaking the same language, we will be creating materials to apply to surfaces. To make these materials further detailed, we will import textures (images) to help define certain characteristics of these materials.

GENERAL CHARACTERISTICS OF A MATERIAL

Many, many characteristics can be defined and tweaked in Maya (and in any 3D application for that matter). But it is worthwhile to take a minute and define some of the general terms and characteristics that materials will use.

Color: This is more than just a solid shade. Color represents any color information of a surface. This can come from procedural (mathematically generated) textures, from photographs of surfaces, or from traditional photographs as well. It is probably the most obvious of texture characteristics.

Bump: Bump can often be thought of as the tactile characteristic of a surface. That is, when you run your fingers over the surface, what does it *feel* like? In general, most 3D applications will use either color or black-and-white images as bump maps. Grayscale images are the most intuitive as you can clearly see that pixels closest to white are rendered raised, and those closest to black render as recessed.

Transparency: Can you see through the object? Remember that objects can be semitransparent as well.

Translucence: Different than transparency. Transparency deals with being able to see through an object, while translucency deals with how much light passes through an object. Think of the difference between glass (very transparent) and rice paper or a lamp shade (highly translucent).

Specular: The shininess of a surface. In real life, specular highlights are actually the result of reflections on a surface; but 3D allows you to fake this through specular definitions. Most 3D applications allow you to define the size and brightness of a specular highlight as well as the color.

Reflectivity: Most glossy surfaces have some sort of reflection to them. You can define a material as having high reflectivity (like a mirror), to very low, to none at all for completely matte objects.

MAYA'S MATERIALS

Maya uses a system of having several different types of materials that should be used at different times and in different situations. Depending on the installation of Maya that you have on your machine, the basic materials that are used in Maya software (the most common type of Maya rendering) are anisotropic, blinn, lambert, phong, and phong e. Sometimes the differences between these types of material have to do with the amount of specularity (or shininess) it has (lambert has none for instance). At other times, the difference is how the specular highlight appears (anisotropic produces shaped highlights); and at still other times, the difference lies in how the reflection qualities function.

The minute details of which material to use when are really beyond the scope of this book. In general, it is hard to go wrong in your choice until you get into extensive shader networks, so do not fret about it now. Also remember that you can change material types at any point, even for materials that have already been created and heavily defined.

The Hypershade

When looking at creating materials within Maya, keep in mind the node system described in earlier chapters. Maya works through a series of nodes or instructions to provide a final image either in your View Panel or through a rendering. Creating the materials that will be applied to objects is about creating and modifying nodes associated with that material.

To view materials and the nodes used to create them, Maya uses a tool called the Hypershade. Access this window at Window > Rendering Editors > Hypershade. This will open a new window similar to Figure 7.2.

 Remember that if you put your mouse over any tool in Maya, the bottom left corner of the Maya interface will display the name of that tool.

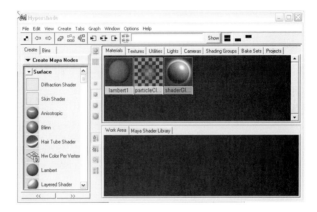

FIGURE 7.2   Hypershade.

Across the top of the Hypershade window is a collection of pull-down menus specific to materials and the Hypershade. They will be referred to with a Hypershade |.

Below that are a collection of tools represented by icons that allow you to largely control the Work Area.

Running along the left of the Hypershade is the Create Bar. This allows for the quick creation of new materials as well and new procedural nodes and other rendering nodes. Although this can be a quick way to snag a new material, it is full of really high-end stuff with which we will not be dealing. Do not get confused or seduced by the nodes that can be created there.

To the right of the Create Bar are some small buttons (new to Maya 7) that have to do with how the materials or shader networks are displayed.

To the right of these icons is a split screen. The top called (no kidding) Top Tabs, is essentially a shelf or a library of shelves that contain various nodes. It can contain materials ready to be applied to surfaces and textures ready to be plugged into materials, lights, cameras, and even projects. For most of what we are going to do, having the Materials tab the foremost will be just the setup you will need.

Below the Top Tab area, is the Bottom tab. Depending on your Maya installation, this will include only the Work Area tab or a few others including a Maya Shader Library tab. Because you want to generally avoid prebuilt materials in your own work, the Work Area tab is the only one of any import for our purposes.

So here is how all of these sections interact. Click Blinn in the Create Bar; this creates a new swatch in the Materials tab called blinn1. Usually, this will automatically also place the blinn1 swatch in the Work Area to allow you to work with it. If not, or if you want to work with a different material, middle-mouse-drag the material from the Material tab above to the Work Area below. The analogy is you store the materials up on the Materials shelf, but pull them down to the Work Area to actually do things with them. Finally, click on the Input and Output Connections button (eighth from the left—Figure 7.3) to show the nodes both coming in and out of the blinn1 material node.

FIGURE 7.3   The Input and Output Connections button. This will clean up the WorkArea and display the inputs and outputs of the selected material node.

Another important note about the Hypershade is that the Work Area allows for much of the same navigation as the View Panels do. Alt is your friend. Alt-MMB allows you to slide around in the space—or move your view of the nodes. Alt-LMB+MMB or Alt-RMB will allow you to zoom in and out, or make the node appear larger or smaller.

The Attributes Editor

The Hypershade is a powerful tool to creating and editing materials, and you will usually have it open when you are dealing with shading a scene. However, oftentimes, editing the nodes that exist within the Hypershade is easier done in the Attributes Editor. If you double-click a material (either in the Materials tab or the Work Area), the attributes of that material node will appear to the right of the View Panel or where the Channel Box usually lives (Figure 7.4).

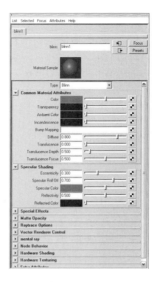

FIGURE 7.4   Attributes Editor showing the attributes of a material node.

The Attributes Editor shows you the various channels that are editable for a given material. Some are editable via a swatch, slider, and a button to allow for a texture to be imported (like the Color channel), but others—like the Bump Mapping channel—only allow for the importing of a texture to define how the bump attribute will be rendered. To look at how it all works, take a look at the following minitutorial.

TUTORIAL 7.1   CREATING A MATERIAL

Objectives:

1. See how Maya materials are created and edited in the Attributes Editor.
2. Explore the Hypershade to see how nodes are created and linked together.
3. Create a procedurally based texture for use in a material.

Step 1: Create a new file. File > New.

The project does not really matter for this tutorial as you will not be keeping this and is more of an exploration of the tools.

Why?

Step 2: Create a polygonal sphere. Create > Polygon Primitives > Sphere.

Step 3: Press 6 on your keyboard.

Remember that pressing 4 displays the window as wireframe, pressing 5 is flat shaded, pressing 6 is textured, and pressing 7 is lit. Although nothing will change visually when you press 6, it will allow you to see when you have actually placed a texture on the object.

Step 4: Create a new lambert shader. Right-click on the sphere and select Materials > Assign New Material > lambert from the pop-down menu (Figure 7.5).

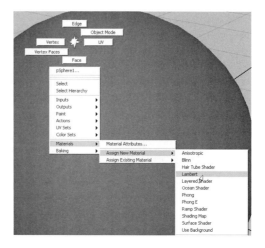

FIGURE 7.5   Creating a new material (automatically assigned to the sphere) by right-clicking on the object.

Right-clicking on an object and assigning a new material from the pop-down menu is one of several ways to create new materials. You can also create one by clicking on the type of material you want to create in the Create Bar in the Hypershade. We will explore other methods in tutorials to come.

When you create a new material in the way described in step 4, the Attributes Editor should automatically open up with the new material active. This makes the default gray shader (also a lambert) no longer attached to the object; it has been replaced with this one.

Step 5: Rename lambert2 to "Test_Material" in the lambert: input field.

When a new material is created, it simply keeps the name of the type of material it is. This becomes impossible to manage when you begin to have 10, 20, or 100 different materials. Renaming as you go becomes absolutely vital to effective work.

Step 6: Change the color of the material to red. In the Attributes Editor under Common Materials Attributes, you will see a Color channel. Right next to the word color is a grey rectangle swatch. Click this rectangle and in the Color Chooser that will appear, change the color to red and click Accept (Figure 7.6).

Notice that when you change the color, the swatch changes color, the Material Sample sphere changes color, and the sphere in the View Panel changes color. Since Test_Material is already assigned to the sphere, any changes you make to the material Test_Material will appear on the objects that have that material assigned to them.

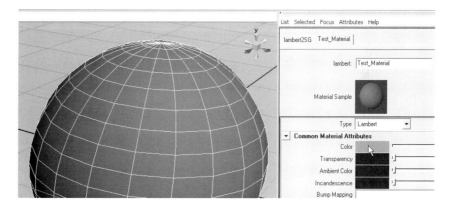

FIGURE 7.6   Changing the color of a material.

Step 7: Take a test render. Along the very top of the interface includes three buttons that allow for rendering (Figure 7.7). The furthest left

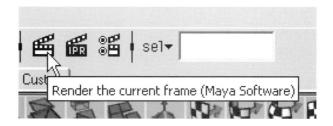

FIGURE 7.7   The Render the Current Frame button.

(Render the Current Frame) allows you to create a single framed render of whatever View Panel is active. Click that button to get a look at what the material on this sphere looks like.

If those buttons are invisible, remember that you can use Rendering | Render > Render Current Frame. . . to achieve the same effect.

Why?

Note that even though there have been no lights placed in this scene, we can still see the red sphere upon rendering. This is because Maya has a default lighting set that essentially adds a floodlight on top of the camera for rendering if there are no lights present in the scene.

Step 8: Add a Noise node to the Bump Mapping channel. In the Attributes Editor (in the Common Material Attributes) look for the Bump Mapping channel. At the far right of that channel is a small button that has checkers on it. Click this to indicate that you are going to use a texture to define how the Bump Mapping should appear. This will open a Create Render Node window (Figure 7.8).

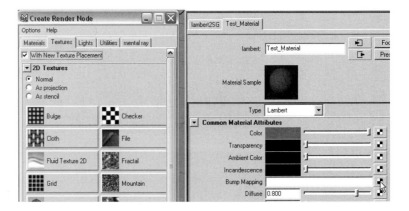

FIGURE 7.8 Creating a texture render node for a material.

The Create Render Node window is a fancy way of saying, "use this window to indicate what texture is to be used for this channel." It includes lots of procedural textures (textures created by Maya mathematically and not based upon a bitmapped image) as well as the ability to insert a bitmapped image (via the File button).

Why?

Step 9: Create a Noise Render node to define the Bump Mapping. Within the Create Render Node window, click the Noise button.

Note that a few things happen. First, the Attributes Editor will change to show the attributes of the last effected node, which in this case is a new Noise Bump node called "bump2d1." Second, notice that in the View Panel, it appears that nothing has changed; the sphere still looks red.

Why?

Step 10: Render the sphere to see what you have got (Figure 7.9).

By default, Maya uses the Color as the information it spends video card power on. Unless you change it (we will look at how to later), Maya will show the approximation of a material by simply displaying the color; which seems rather anticlimactic in this situation. However, after you render, you can quickly see the results of your labors.

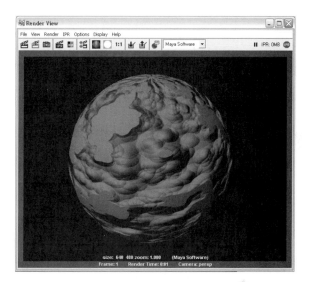

FIGURE 7.9   Rendered sphere with new bump applied.

Step 11: Open the Hypershade. Window > Rendering Editors > Hypershade....
Step 12: Click the Test_Material in the Materials tab.

Selecting a material in the Hypershade will display the attributes for that material in the Attributes Editor.

Step 13: Replace the red color with a texture. In the Attributes Editor, click the checkerboard button next to the Color channel to indicate that you want to use a texture to define the color. This will open the Create Render Node window again.
Step 14: Click the Mountain button.

Usually, these procedural built-in textures are not the best. Without a tremendous amount of altering, they end up with a very canned look; a look that everyone else has. But for this exploration of the process, a bit of generic texture choice will work just fine.

Step 15: Render (Figure 7.10).

 Note that the red is gone; when you use a texture to define a channel (in this case Color), this texture overwrites any color changes you have made. Note that the View Panel makes a very rough, quick approximation of what the color will look like, but the true nature and appearance of the material is not seen until you render.

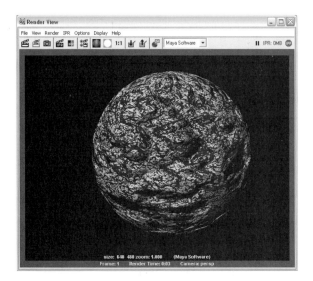

FIGURE 7.10   Rendered sphere with mountain as the color texture.

Step 16: Open Hypershade.

 On occasion, Maya's interface will display some errors and not show all the buttons it should in places like the Hypershade. If this happens to you, just restart Maya, and usually this problem is solved.

Step 17: Middle-mouse-drag the Test_Material from the Materials tab into the Work Area.
Step 18: Click the Input and Output Connection button at the top (Figure 7.11).

 Now in the Work Area you will be able to see all the nodes related to the Test_Material. Note that to the right of the material is something called lambert2SG; this is essentially the node that defines all the objects to which Test_Material is assigned.

To the left of the Test_Material node are the nodes that input or feed into Test_Material. At the top is the color texture mountain1 that was imported. Below it is the bump series of nodes. A bit more about this later.

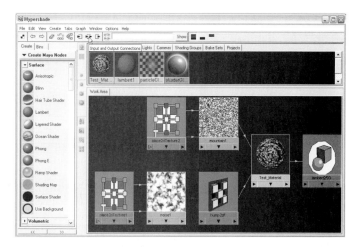

FIGURE 7.11   Hypershade displaying the shader network for Test_Material. Note that the mouse is over the Input and Output Connection button.

Tutorial Conclusion

Pretty exciting, eh? Hopefully, you can start to see how the workflow of constructing Maya materials works: Create a new material and then define relevant channels through color swatches or imported textures.

HYPERSHADE REVISITED

Now that there is a material constructed, let's take a closer look at what the Hypershade allows us to see and do. Try the following:

1. Click on the mountain1 node. In the Attributes Editor you will see the editable attributes of this procedural texture. For this particular procedural texture, you can change things like the Snow Color and Rock Color. If this were a bitmapped image, this node would allow you to change which image was used.
2. Click on the place2dTexture2 node (to the left of the mountain1 texture). In the Attributes Editor, you will see this node displayed. Notice that here you can define the coverage (how much of an object is covered by this node) and how much the node is translated or rotated (this would move the color across or rotate it across the surface of the object). We look at other ways to work with this node later.
3. Place your mouse over the green arrow that connects the mountain1 node to the Test_Material node (Figure 7.12). Note that over the mountain1 node a little white box will pop up to indicate what is going out of that node. In this case it will read "mountain1.outColor"

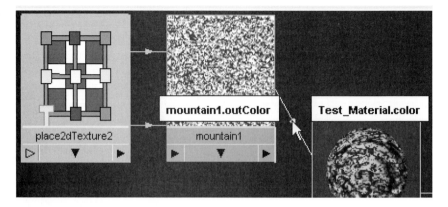

FIGURE 7.12 Screen hints that indicate the connection between Hypershade nodes.

indicating that the color of this node is going out to define the characteristic of the node it is attached to—in this case Test_Material. Over Test_Material a white box appears that reads Test_Material.color. If you ever want to understand how a material is working and how its nodes are feeding into on another, just let your mouse rest upon the connection arrows. Take a quick look and see how the other connections function by resting your mouse on the other arrows of this shader network.

If you ever want to break a connection, you can select the arrow and delete it or simply select a node and press delete, and the connection will be broken. You can establish links between nodes within the Hypershade manually as well, but clicking the checkerboard button in the Attributes Editor of a material is often an easier way to make the connections in just the right way.

4. Click on the bump2d1 node. In the Attributes Editor you will see a section called 2d Bump Attributes. This allows you to define how high your bump will appear. Change the Bump Depth value to something like .1 and do another render to see the change.

So look at how this can all be used in a more real-life situation. In the next tutorial we will take some of these concepts and start to bring the room from chapters past to life.

TUTORIAL 7.2   TEXTURING NURBS VASES

The way that NURBS and Polygon objects accept materials is just a little bit different. In this chapter, NURBS will be the target shape, and we will use a variety of techniques to texture surfaces (NURBS surfaces) within the room.

Objectives:

1. Create custom materials using procedural textures.
2. Create custom materials using bitmapped images.
3. Adjust bump heights/values for materials.
4. Adjust placement of materials across NURBS surfaces.

Before we get started on the tutorial, find the sourceimages folder on the included CD-ROM (Project Files > Amazing_Wooden_Man > sourceimages). Copy the contents of that folder into the sourceimages folder of your own project file on your hard drive.

The sourceimages folder is where Maya assumes texture files live. When you attempt to place any texture file within a material, Maya will automatically open to that location. Keeping all of your textures in this location makes it so that Maya always knows where to find them when it comes time to render, or when you need to work on another machine—just as long as you make sure to define your project. Always store your textures in your sourceimages folder. It will save you much pain and suffering in the long term.

Step 1: Define your project. Since the room we have been working on will be the object we continue to work with, set your project back to the Amazing_Wooden_Man project (File > Project > Set. . .).

Step 2: Open the most recent version of the room. In the case of this tutorial, you will be using the file named Tutorial_6_1-Extra, or you can use your own.

Step 3: Open the Hypershade. Window > Rendering Editors > Hypershade.

Step 4: Cleanup unwanted materials. Within the Hypershade, select Edit > Delete Unused Nodes.

As you have been building objects in separate Maya files, Maya has been building and importing multiple default materials. By default, all objects you create in a file will be assigned a lambert1 material. When you import objects from different Maya files, these multiple lambert1 materials come along for the ride. Although these extra materials technically do not do any harm; it keeps everything tidier if you clean up a bit before you begin the texturing process.

Do note that often you will end up texturing an object before you import it into a master file. Do make sure that when you do texture before importing that you are always careful to be creating new materials and naming them appropriately as you go along. This will help avoid conflicting names of nodes.

Step 5: Create a new Blinn material. In the Create bar, in the Create Maya Nodes section, click the Blinn tab. This will open a new material that can be seen in the Materials tab, in the Work Area and in the Attributes Editor.

 Why a blinn? Well, the material is going to be applied to a vase and so should have a bit of shininess to it. Some materials like lambert have no shine (specular highlight), and several other materials (anisotropic, phong, and phong e) do. Blinn materials tend to be a fairly rapid render, so for this first example that was picked as the shiny material to be used.

Step 6: Rename to Vase_Material. In the Attributes Editor, change blinn1 to Vase_Material.

 Why add "material" to the title? This is more than personal preference actually; Maya can sometimes actually end up with multiple nodes that share the same name. In many cases, this is never a problem, but occasionally, when you tell Maya to do something to an object (smooth it for instance) if there are multiple nodes called Vase, Maya can become confused and refuse to execute the command. By labeling materials as materials, you can help avoid future node name conflicts.

Step 7: Change the color to a cream color. In the Attributes Editor, click the swatch in the Color channel and use the Color Chooser to find a light cream color.

Step 8: Apply this material to a vase via the Hypershade. Pick a vase in your scene (select it by clicking on it in the View Panel or the Outliner) and press f to zoom in on it. In the Hypershade, right-click on the Vase_Material node (either in the Materials tab or the Work Area) and choose Assign Material to Selection from the Marking menu. Render to get a quick update of what you have so far.

Step 9: Make sure Vase_Material is shown in the Attributes Editor (if it is not, click the Vase_Material node in the Work Area of the Hypershade).

Step 10: Assign a Fractal node as the Bump Mapping. In the Bump Mapping channel, click the checkboard button to indicate you want to define a texture. In the Create Render Node window click the Fractal button.

Step 11: Clean up the Hypershade. Your Work Area may start to be a little jumbled as you add new nodes. Click the Input and Output Connection button to clean it up. You will be able to see the nodes and how they are connected to your Vase_Material. Render to see the progress (Figure 7.13).

 A bit intense, eh? The bump map is too high and too big. For that matter, why are we putting a bump map on a vase in the first place? Well, most every surface has some sort of tactile quality; whether we consciously recognize it or not.

Porcelain is one of those surfaces that seem smooth because of its high gloss, but do indeed have a bump to it. However, generally this bump is very gentle. But having it there will help avoid overly plastic looks. Note that the white parts of the fractal image render as raised.

FIGURE 7.13   Rendered vase with a pretty intense bump.

Step 12: Reduce the Bump Depth value. In the Hypershade's Work Area, click the bump2d1 node (the node that defines how high the bump is). In the Attributes Editor change the Bump Depth value from 1 to .005.
Step 13: Render (Figure 7.14).

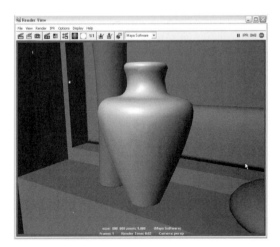

FIGURE 7.14   Rendered vase with a very low (but still present) bump map.

Step 14: Select another vase. Do this either in the Outliner or View Panel. Focus in on it.

Step 15: Right-click on the vase and select Materials > Assign New Material > Blinn from the Marking menu.

Step 16: Rename to Vase_Material_BlueTop. Do this in the Attributes Editor where the new blinn material should have opened to.

Well, this name simply is a bit more expressive of what the material will actually look like. If the new blinn is not visible in the Attributes Editor, find it in the Materials tab of the Hypershade. Click it there, and it will appear in the Attributes Editor.

Step 17: Create a file node for your color. In the Color channel, click the checkerboard button to tell Maya you want to use a texture map. In the Create Render Node window, click on the File button.

Step 18: Import the color texture map. The Attribute Editor should change to a file1 tab with an area called File Attributes. In the Image Name input field, click on the folder button (to show Maya where the file is you want to use).

If your project is set correctly, Maya should automatically open to your sourceimages folder. There, navigate and choose VaseColor.tif.

Step 19: Select Vase_Material_Bluetop in the Hypershade. This will re-open the material in the Hypershade.

Notice that the Color channel appears black, but the button that was checkerboard is now an input button. If you click that button, the Attributes Editor will change to show the node that defines the Color—in this case, it will be the node file1 that contains our VaseColor.tif file. For now, make sure that Attributes Editor shows the Vase_Material_Bluetop.

Step 20: Import a bump map. In the Bump Mapping channel, click the checkerboard button. In the Create Render Node window, click the File button. Back in the Attributes Editor, in the Image Name input field, click the folder button. Navigate to VaseBump.tif and click open. Take a render.

So now you have an image that defines the color in the Color channel and one that defines the bump in the Bump Mapping channel. However, when you render, the bump is still probably way too intense.

If in step 20, after you click the File Create Render Node, you are taken to bump2dx node in the attributes editor, be sure to click on the Bump Value tab to get to where you can define the bump texture.

Step 21: Display the shader network for Vase_Material_Bluetop. Select the material in the Materials tab, and click the Input and Output Connections button. This will display the shading network in the Work Area (Figure 7.15).

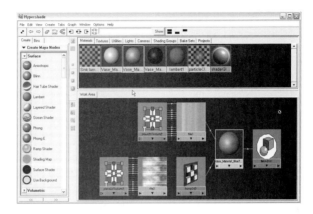

FIGURE 7.15   The shader network for our Vase_Material_Bluetop.

Step 22: Reduce the Bump Depth. Click on the bump2d2 node in the Work Area. In the Attributes Editor, the attributes for that node will be displayed. Change the Bump Depth value to .05. Render (Figure 7.16).

FIGURE 7.16   Finished Vase_Material_Bluetop.

Step 23: Create Materials assigned to other vases you have in the scene. Notice that in the sourceimages folder, there are color and bump texture maps for another few vases. Use those or create your own texture maps.

Although we will be talking more about creating texture maps later, for now, just note that an uncompressed TIFF (.tif) is often the best file format for any texture maps you create from scratch.

Step 24: Save.

 The results of this tutorial are saved as Tutorial_7_2.mb on the CD-ROM.

TUTORIAL 7.3   TEXTURING THE BEDSPREAD

There is much, much more to be known about Maya's texture system. In the last tutorial, we were content to create textures that sat upon surfaces as placed. But there is more power and flexibility to be had within this system. In this tutorial we will do a bit of extra texturing to some of the other NURBS surfaces in the scene and learn a bit more about how the system can be further manipulated.

Objectives:

1. Adjust the placetexture nodes to repeat and adjust textures.
2. Use bump and color texture maps independently to create various sizes textures in the same material.

Step 1: Set your project.
Step 2: Open your most recent version of the room. The version used for these figures is the result of Tutorial_7_2.mb.
Step 3: Create a new lambert material. In the Hypershade, click the lambert button in the Create Bar. This will place a new material in the Materials section in the Work Area, and open the material in the Attributes Editor.

 Lamberts are matte materials. There are no specular (shininess) qualities available with this sort of material. Neither is there any sort of reflectivity characteristic. It tends to work very well for things like cloth.

Remember that selecting material type is never permanent. In the Attributes Editor, when you have a material selected, you can change the Type to other kinds of materials.

Step 4: Rename the material to Bedspread_Material. Do this in the Attributes Editor.
Step 5: Define BedspreadColor.tif as the color texture map. In the Attributes Editor, click the color's checkerboard button, and then click the File button in the Create Render Node window. In the Attributes editor (in the file node) click the Image Name's folder button and choose BedspreadColor.tif from the sourceimages folder.

Step 6: Apply Bedspread_Material to the bedspread in the scene. You can do this using methods described earlier or by right-clicking on the bedspread in the View Panel and choosing Materials > Assign Existing Material > Bedspread_Material from the Marking menu.

Step 7: Render (Figure 7.17).

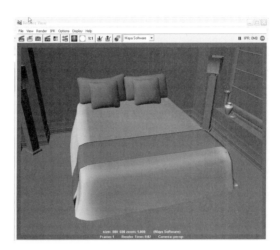

FIGURE 7.17   Bedspread as indicated with the color texture at the default size.

Pretty, err, moldy, eh? To get a better idea, open the file BedspreadColor.tif in Photoshop (or other image editing application). Notice that it is essentially a white file with a green stripe through it. Not only that, but it is a small file.

This is a good thing. Maya—like more 3D applications—will repeat a given texture and tile it out until it fills an object. The ability to repeat a texture across a surface makes for smaller texture files and takes a shorter time for Maya to load into memory and ultimately to render. So for repeating surfaces like the stripes this bed will have, a smaller texture like this is the ideal solution. We just need to tell Maya to tile the texture.

Step 8: Select the Bedspread_Material node in the Hypershade and click the Input and Output button.

Step 9: Click the place2dTexture node.

The place2dTexture node defines how the texture file is used within the material. In this case, we want to tell Maya to take the texture file just imported and repeat it several times across the material (which will make it appear tiled across the bedspread).

Why?

Step 10: Repeat the texture six times across the surface. In the Attributes Editor, look for the 2D Texture Placement Attributes section and the Repeat UV input fields. The first value is the U, and the second is the V. Enter 6 in the first input field.

UV is a way of wrapping around a surface. Think of U as the latitude lines and V as the longitude. UVs are a big part of texturing, and later we will be working with them quite a bit. However, in this case, we just need to tell the texture to repeat six times in the U direction of the texture.

A few things will happen when you do this. First, you will see the texture is replicated/tiled and can be seen in the file node in the Hypershade. Second, any object that has this material applied to it will update to show the repeating texture (Figure 7.18).

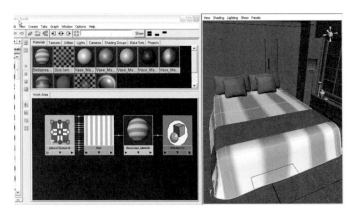

FIGURE 7.18   Results of increased Repeat UV values.

Step 11: Change the Rotate Frame input field to 90.

Rotate Frame takes the actual texture file and rotates it before applying it according to the UVs of the object. By changing the value of Rotate Frame to 90, you are essentially turning the BedspreadColor.tif file 90 degrees. Of course, this could be done in Photoshop as well, but the ability to dynamically change/rotate a texture within Maya can save you a lot of bouncing-between-applications time (Figure 7.19).

Step 12: Select the Bedspread_Material node in the Hypershade.
Step 13: Add a new node to the Bump Mapping channel. In the Attributes Editor, in the Bump Mapping channel, click the checkerboard button.
Step 14: Add a Cloth Texture Render node. In the Create Render Node window, click the Cloth button.
Step 15: In the Hypershade, select the Bedspread_Material node and click the Input and Output Connection button.

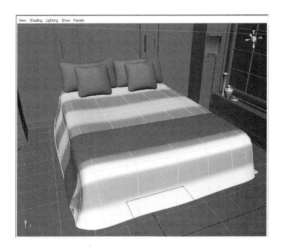

FIGURE 7.19 Results of the rotated frame.

 Cleaning up the Work Area often gives you a chance to really understand how your
Why? *material is being constructed.*

Step 16: Display the Bump Map in the View Panel. In the Attributes Editor expand the Hardware Texturing tab. Change the Textured Channel input field to Bump Map.

 Notice that the default there was Color Map. But when making adjustments to one
particular texture—in this case the bump—it does you little good to see the color in the
Why? *View Panel. By showing the Bump Map, you can get a better idea of changes you*
make to the texture and how they will affect the final render (Figure 7.20).

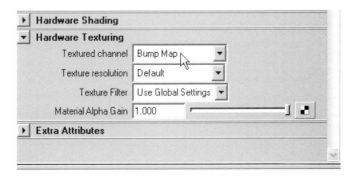

FIGURE 7.20 Altering the Hardware Texturing for a material to show
the Bump Map in the View Panels

This will make your View Panel look a little bit odd. Remember that you have not lost the color texture placed in earlier steps; Maya simply is not displaying it at this point. If you render, you will see your color map there (as well as this way too big bump map). But now, as changes are made to the bump's place2dTexture node, changes in the bump can be seen in the View Panel.

Step 17: Still in the Hardware Texturing section, change the Texture Resolution input field to "Highest (256 × 256)."

To keep the interface working smoothly, Maya keeps most of the textures displayed at a reasonably low value. However, when dealing with size and placement, sometimes selectively turning the resolution up will help give you a more detailed look at what a texture will look like at final render (Figure 7.21). If you have a beefy video card, you can keep these resolutions high; if not, be sure to turn the resolution back down after you have moved and scaled your textures into place.

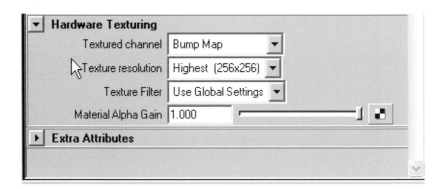

FIGURE 7.21 Changing the Texture Channel to show bump and increasing the resolution of the display.

Step 18: In the Hypershade, select the bumps place2dTexture node.

Remember that at this point there are two place2dTexture nodes; one that defines the color's placement and this new one that defines the bump's. Be sure you are clicking on the node connected to the cloth1 node, which is then connected to the bump2d node.

Step 19: Change the Repeat UV values to 200 and 200.

Notice that the default setting for this was already 4 and 4. However, that was still way too big. This bump should be very small and very subtle; just enough to make the spread look like it has a bit of tactile quality. Two hundred repetitions will make the bump quite small indeed.

Note that when you start changing these values to extreme values, the resolution cannot keep up with really small repetitions. So, in cases like this, as the Repeat UV values get higher and higher, which make the texture appear smaller and smaller, remember to take some test renderings as you go.

Step 20: Render (Figure 7.22).

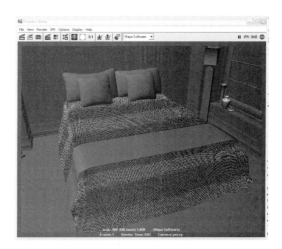

FIGURE 7.22   Render of the bedspread with the material constructed so far.

Step 21: Reduce the Bump Depth. In the Hypershade select the bump2d node. In the Attributes Editor change the Bump Depth to .01.
Step 22: Render.

ON THE CD

Step 23: Save. The results of this tutorial are saved on the CD-ROM as Tutorial_7_3.mb.

You may want to change the material's Texture channel back to Color (in the Hardware Texturing section of the Bedspread_Material node in the Attributes Editor). It is not necessary to do so but can make your scene look a little bit more like you would imagine it rendered.

Tutorial Conclusions

So there is a start. So far, you have created multiple materials and applied them to NURBS-based objects. In Tutorial 7.3 we looked at how to use separate place2dTexture nodes to control *independently* the size and rotation of a material's color and bump. But we are just getting started. In the next chapter, we will look at how to create custom textures for materials and how to gain absolute control over how that material wraps across polygonal-based objects.

CHALLENGES, EXERCISES, OR ASSIGNMENTS

1. At the base of the bed is another blanket folded across the length of the bed. In the sourceimages folder is an AfghanColor.tif file. Create a new Afghan_Material and use this color texture to approximate Figure 7.23. Use the cloth node for bump to give it some added tactile quality.

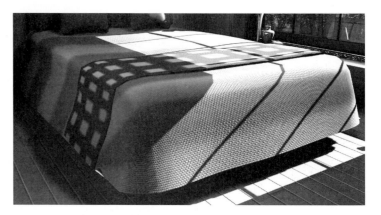

FIGURE 7.23   Finished afghan.

2. Create you own custom color textures for either the bedspread or the vases in this room. Create new materials to use the textures and apply them. Take frequent renders to see the ultimate output.

Maya 7.0 has a strange bug. Hopefully, by the time of this book's printing, this will be solved; but as of 7.0, Maya does not do well with any non-power-of-two textures; the textures will import and look skewed. To fix this, find the Maya.env file (located in My Documents/Maya/7.0/) and open it with Notepad (or some other text editor). Add the line:

```
MAYA_NON_POWER_TWO_OFF = 1
```

Resave. When you reopen Maya, textures will appear as they should.

8

TEXTURING POLYGONS AND UV MANIPULATION

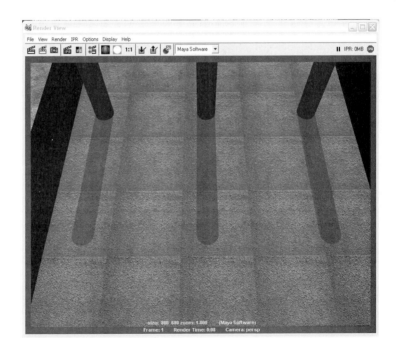

In Chapter 7, we tackled creating materials from scratch. You imported textures both as procedural textures and bitmapped-based files. These materials were placed on NURBS surfaces, and the size of the color and bump textures were edited independently.

In this chapter, we will continue on with this mode expanding it into the realm of polygons. Specifically, we will look at how to create materials that work well on polygonal surfaces and how to manipulate the information that defines how a material crawls across and sticks to a polygonal object.

But first, in your own work, you will want to avoid using prebuilt textures (either those available with your Maya installation or available via download); after all, who wants to hire someone whose demo reel is simply putting together other people's work? So, in this chapter, we will look at a few basic techniques to creating texture maps from scratch. That way, you will have all unique, dynamic, and ever-so-impressive materials.

TEXTURE TILING

Figure 8.1 shows a photo of some asphalt. Figure 8.2 shows the results of using this image as the texture for both the color and bump channels.

FIGURE 8.1   Photo of asphalt.

FIGURE 8.2   Results of using a photo as a tiled texture.

Notice that when tiled, the results are a little less than desirable. The tiles are visible, and the surface looks fairly unbelievable on the whole. It just does not work when you can see where one copy of the image ends and the next one begins.

One solution to this would be to simply have one image that covered the whole plain; this actually has some real benefits in that you can get some real-life grunge and imperfections across the surface. However, getting those images that include a big enough area to represent 20 yards of street, for example, are tough to get and start to become unreasonably large files.

A better solution is to indeed work with a smaller chunk of texture image, but find ways to make the texture seamless so that you cannot tell where one tile ends and the next one begins.

Figure 8.3 shows the same photo with the seams worked out, and Figure 8.4 shows the results of this texture.

FIGURE 8.3   Seamless texture.

FIGURE 8.4   Results of seamless texture.

TUTORIAL 8.1   CREATING SEAMLESS TEXTURES

Objectives:

1. Use a photo of a surface to create seamless texture ready for use in Maya.
2. Explore the Offset filter in Photoshop.
3. Briefly use the Clone Stamp Tool in Photoshop to work out seams.

This tutorial uses Photoshop. Although some of the specifics are unique to the application, many of the techniques here can be used in a variety of other image manipulation programs. So if you do not have access to Photoshop, still take a look at this tutorial for general techniques.

Step 1: Open Photoshop.

Step 2: Choose File > Open and choose the file Asphalt.tif from the CD-ROM. It is located in the Project Files > Chapter08 folder.

Why? *Or, you could also use your own photograph if you would like. Or, you can download some raw textures for learning's sake at places like 3D Café (look for the Free Stuff and the Textures).*

Note that this image is quite large (lots and lots of pixels); this is largely so you can get a good look at all the things happening in the tutorial. However, if your computer is having a hard time handling this large an image, go ahead and reduce the image size (Image > Image Size. . .).

Step 3: Crop the image to cut out really distinctive traits like the leaf at the bottom left corner (Figure 8.5).

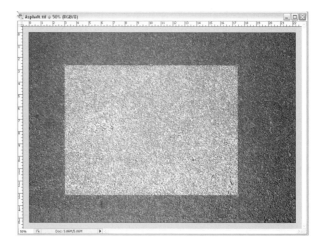

FIGURE 8.5 Cropping the source image a bit tighter to isolate a good tiling candidate.

Why? *Although things like dirt, leaves, and cracks help add some real authenticity to a surface, when the surface is created from a tiled texture, they can be a real distraction. Few things scream tiling like the same leaf repeated again and again laying in the same direction at the same distance from the other leaves. So the cropping drops out the leaves and the crack that runs across the bottom of the image.*

Also note that this cropping cuts out the corners of the image quite a bit. This is largely a limitation of this particular photo. The photo was taken in the middle of the day with a harsh sun overhead. The photo has a definite highlight in the middle with a very blue tint emerging as the highlight drops off. It is very difficult to work out that color gradient; so cropping down to an area where the color balance is more even gives us a much easier file with which to work.

Step 4: Choose Filter > Other > Offset. . . . In the Offset dialog box that comes up, the values there are largely arbitrary; just shift them so that the seams appear about in the middle of the image (Figure 8.6).

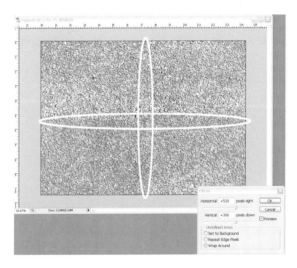

FIGURE 8.6   The Offset filter. The seams are highlighted here in this figure.

The problem with seamed textures is that the edge of one tile does not match up with the edge of the next. The Offset filter slides all the pixels across and down and then wraps the pixels that have slid off the palette back around the other side. What this does is make sure that now; the right side of the image matches the left side perfectly. The same goes for the top and bottom.

The seams are clearly still there, but they are in the middle of the image where you can get at them and work them out.

Step 5: Use the Clone Stamp Tool to clone out the seams. In case you have not used this tool, hold the Alt key down to establish a source region. Then—on another region of the image—click and drag, and the pixels of your source region will be cloned to the new location.

By cloning parts of the image over the seam, you can eliminate the hard edge in the middle. Be sure to experiment with different-sized brushes and redefine your source region often; you do not want to just duplicate all the pixels of the image an inch above where you are cloning.

Step 6: When you can no longer see the seams running through the middle of the texture, run the Offset filter again (Filter > Other > Offset ...). Check for any remaining seams.

Sometimes when working out old seams, you can inadvertently create new ones. Running the Offset filter one more time allows you to check to see whether you have any.

Step 7: Save the file as AsphaltColor.tif. The location does not matter.

Since you likely will not be using this project again, a simple place like your desktop will allow you to grab it in Maya, and you will not have to work with setting a new project or anything like that.

Step 8: For fun, in Maya, open a new File (File > New). Create a plane.
Step 9: Create a new material (lambert will work well), and import AsphaltColor.tif into its Color channel.
Step 10: In the Hypershade, select the place2dTexture node and increase the Repeat UV settings to something like 5 and 5.
Step 11: Render.

Tutorial Conclusion

See the idea there? No matter how many times you repeat the texture across the surface, you cannot see where one copy of the texture ends and the next one begins. True, when it gets repeated a lot of times, you can begin to see a repetition of the pattern—and there are ways to get rid of that as well through adding things like a Fractal node in the Diffuse Channel (diffuse acts much like a dirt layer). But no amount of diffuse will hide hard edges in a seamed texture.

In upcoming tutorials, or in your own work, you may need to take one of your photographs and work out the seams. It takes a little while, but the results are always worth while.

UVs

So what the heck is a UV? Well, it is not so much of a what as a where. UVs are coordinates; they define locations on an object where a texture can be pinned down. Usually, UVs are at the same location on an object as the vertices are. And when you create things like Polygon Primitives, that is exactly where they are.

However, as your model gets more complex, you may have created new points (via polygon or edge extrudes), and these new points often will not have UVs assigned where they should be. Additionally, even when UVs are assigned exactly where points are, it does not mean that is the way you want your texture distributed across your object.

Controlling your UVs, their placement, their rotation, and their proximity to one another is central to controlling your textures.

As we look at the UV Texture Editor, you may choose to follow along with the saved file on the CD-ROM. In the Project Files > Chapter08 folder is a file called CheckeredBall.mb. It is just a sphere with a slightly altered checkerboard procedural texture applied. But for some, it helps to not only see how a tool works but to actually mess with it themselves.

UV TEXTURE EDITOR

Maya's method of controlling UVs is through the UV Texture Editor (Window > UV Texture Editor. . .) shown in Figure 8.7. Figure 8.7 actually shows the UV Texture Editor open next to a selected Polygon Primitive Sphere with a simple material applied to it.

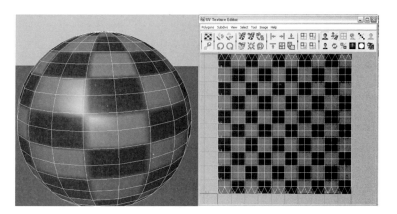

FIGURE 8.7   The UV Texture Editor open with a selected sphere. Notice that the polygons are unwrapped—laid out in the UV Texture Editor.

On the left you see the sphere and the polygons that make that sphere. On the right (in the UV Texture Editor), you see the grayish checkerboard texture in the background, and laid on top of it are white lines. These white lines indicate the polygons of the sphere. So you can see that each black check covers four polygons (this can be seen both in the UV Texture Editor and on the sphere itself).

The UV Texture Editor allows for navigation in much the same way as the View Panel or Hypershade does. Alt-MMB to move your view of the UVs around, and Alt-LMB+MMB or Alt-RMB allows you to zoom in and out.

Across the top of the UV Texture Layout is a collection of buttons that represent tools available in the pull-down menus above them. Since we are looking to understand the concepts—not the iconography—we will be referring to most of these tools by their names and where they can be found in the pull-down menus. However, as you work, you may find that tracking down which button represents which tool will help speed up your workflow.

Another similarity to the View Panel is that in the UV Texture Editor, right-clicking will bring up a Marking menu that allows you to choose which component you want to select.

Consider the following illustration of how UVs work. After right-clicking in the UV Texture Editor and selecting UVs from the Marking menu and then marqueeing around all the UVs of the sphere (still in the UV Texture Editor, although you could also select the UVs in the View Panel), the UVs are highlighted (Figure 8.8).

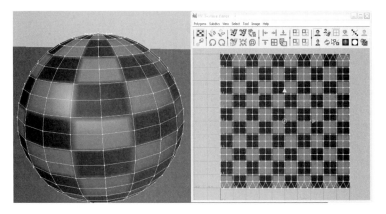

FIGURE 8.8   UVs can be selected in the UV Texture Editor.

By pressing r on the keyboard (shortcut for the Scale Tool), the UV Texture Editor will show a 2D Scale Tool manipulator. Then, a click-drag on the center handle will scale the UVs smaller (Figure 8.9) or larger (Figure 8.10). Notice that when the UVs go beyond the quadrant that the texture is in, the texture just repeats as tiles.

By pressing e on the keyboard (shortcut for the Rotation Tool), the UV Texture Editor provides you with manipulation handles that allow you to rotate the UVs across the texture (Figure 8.11).

Notice that the texture itself does not resize, move, or rotate. But the UVs can do all three across the surface of the texture. The texture space is

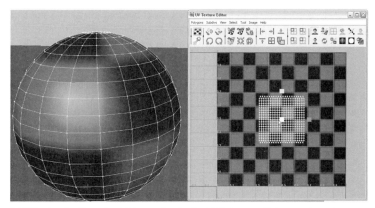

FIGURE 8.9   Scaling the UVs smaller in the UV Texture Editor makes the texture larger across the surface of the object.

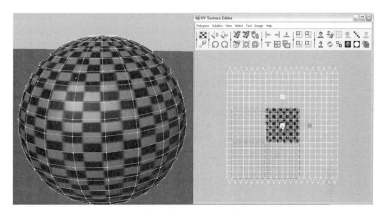

FIGURE 8.10   Scaling the UVs larger in the UV Texture Editor makes the texture smaller across the surface of the object.

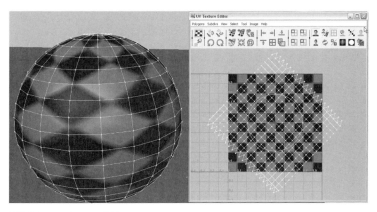

FIGURE 8.11   Rotated UVs.

finite and remains fixed; but the UVs can be adjusted however we need to within that texture space.

Assigning and Projecting Textures/UVs

So what happens when the way that the UVs are laid out do not suit the purpose of the project at hand? Or, what happens when you have created a custom shape (as we have in most of our room), and the polygon form is missing UVs or has none at all? The ability to assign, or reassign UVs is critical to defining a texture's placement.

In Maya 7, the core tools for assigning UVs live in Modeling | Polygon UVs pull-down menu. In Maya 6.5 and earlier, they live in Modeling | Edit Polygons > Texture. Coincidentally, many of the same commands available in the Polygon UVs menu are also available in the UV Texture Editor.

The basic idea is that you can *map* UVs of an object to a texture/shader. Or, as some like to think of it, you can map or project a shader to an object.

Figure 8.12 is the default mapping of the UVs for a primitive sphere.

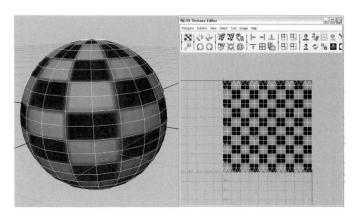

FIGURE 8.12   Default projection.

Planar Mapping

By selecting the sphere (in Object Mode) and choosing Modeling | Polygon UVs > Planar Mapping, we get the result shown in Figure 8.13. Notice that the way a planar project works is analogous to standing in front of a projector. The image being projected (in this case the checkered texture) looks fine on the parts of the surface that are closest to perpendicular to the projector. However, as you look at the polygons wrapping around the sphere, you start to see the texture smeared across the side.

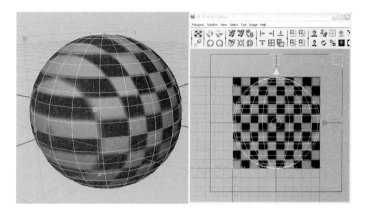

FIGURE 8.13   Planar Mapping.

Do notice that immediately after enacting a Planar Mapping, you will see some new manipulators around the object in the View Plan. By click-dragging these blue, green, or red squares, you can resize the mapping (and, subsequently, the size of the UVs in texture space).

Cylindrical Mapping

The enchilada of mapping techniques, Cylindrical Mapping (Modeling | Polygon UVs > Cylindrical Mapping) attempts to wrap the texture around the object like a tortilla. You can see the manipulators in the View Panel as a sort of half-pipe. Notice also in the UV Texture Editor that the mapping by default only wraps halfway around—namely the UVs are twice as wide as the texture (Figure 8.14).

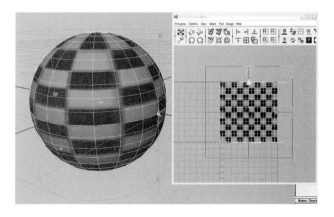

FIGURE 8.14   Cylindrical Mapping.

Just like the Planar Mapping, when you use Cylindrical Mapping, the manipulators for the mapping node are visible an editable in the View Panel. The red handles will allow you to wrap the mapping further around the object. As you do this (Figure 8.15), you will see the UVs narrow in the UV Texture Editor until the UVs are the same size as the texture when the mapping wraps all the way around the object.

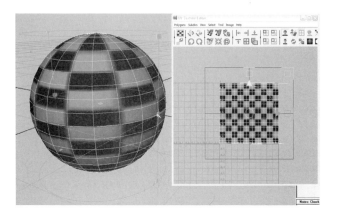

FIGURE 8.15   Using the Cylindrical Mapping manipulators to increase the coverage of the mapping and, thus, squeezing the UVs closer into the texture space.

Spherical Mapping

Pretty self-explanatory. This mapping attempts to wrap the texture around the object spherically. It usually causes a bit of pinching around the poles. Remember, you can use the node manipulators in the View Panel to wrap the mapping further around the object, thus avoiding tiling of the texture as the UVs fit further into the texture space (Figure 8.16).

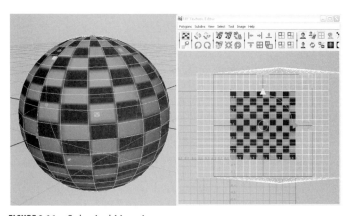

FIGURE 8.16   Spherical Mapping.

Automatic Mapping

When students first see this, they become very excited. "Automatic!" they say, "That'll make it easy!" Well, unfortunately Automatic Mapping is really rarely the solution. What it attempts to do is create multiple Planar Mappings on an object (between 3 and 12 depending on the settings you choose in the Automatic Mapping Options window). The result as seen in Figure 8.17 is a splitting of the UVs in to multiple chunks. The result (Figure 8.18) is really not what you want for most shapes.

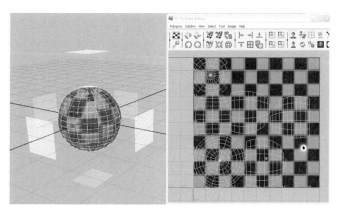

FIGURE 8.17   Results of Automatic Mapping.

FIGURE 8.18   Problems of splitting up UVs into multiple joints.

There are situations in which Automatic Mapping does indeed come in handy; but they are typically for very simple forms. Do not be seduced by the seeming simplicity of "automatic" anything.

Getting to It

This might still seem rather ethereal, abstract, and theoretical at this point. However, keep this illustration in mind as we tear into the tutorials to come. Although it might seem much ado about nothing for the room, it will be a very big issue when we deal with organic models.

TUTORIAL 8.2   TEXTURING THE SHOWER STALL

Objectives:

1. Create some simple non-texture-map materials with reflection.
2. See the difference between Maya software rendering and Maya raytracing.

3. Create a new tile texture and adjust its placement through effective UV manipulation.

Step 1: Set your project. We should still be working in Amazing_Wooden_Man.

Step 2: Open your latest version of the room.

 Or you can use Tutorial_7_3.mb if you want to follow the steps exactly as they appear here. However, you can certainly adjust the steps here to fit your version of the room—or even your version of an entirely different room.

Step 3: Save As . . . Tutorial_8_1.

Step 4: Find and focus in on the shower stall.

Step 5: Select all the non-tile parts and hide them. Figure 8.19 shows the non-tile parts selected (basically everything above the floor). Ctrl-h hides them.

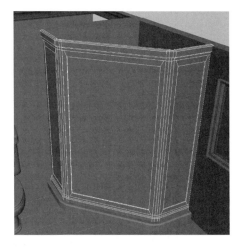

FIGURE 8.19   Hide these parts of the shower.

 Ctrl-h hides a selected object. Shift-Ctrl-h unhides the last hidden object.

Step 6: Open the Hypershade. Window > Rendering Editors > Hypershade ... .

Step 7: Create a new Blinn material. In the Hypershade, in the Create Bar, click the Blinn button in the Create Maya Nodes section.

 Blinn is one of several materials that have a specular highlight. We need this shine as this material will be the tile at the bottom of the shower floor.

Step 8: Rename the material to ShowerTile_Material. In the Attributes Editor, change the name.

If the Attributes Editor did not automatically pop up when you created the Blinn material, just click it in the Hypershade, and it will open up.

Step 9: Use the texture TileColor.tif to define the Color channel. In the Attributes Editor click the checkboard button and choose File from the Create Render Node window. Click the folder button in the file node (again in the Attributes Editor) and find TileColor.tif in the sourceimages folder.

Step 10: Use the texture TileBump.tif to define the Bump channel. Select the ShowerTile_Material Node in the Hypershade to open it in the Attributes Editor. Click the checkboard button in the Bump Mapping channel and press the File button in the Create Render Node window. Click the folder button in the file node (again in the Attributes Editor) and find TileBump.tif in the sourceimages folder.

Connecting Placement Nodes

Step 11: In the Hypershade, press the Input and Output Connections button. Your shader network should appear like Figure 8.20.

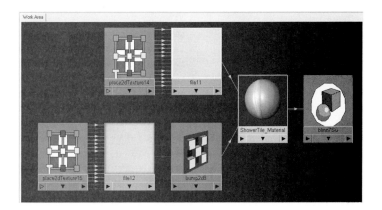

FIGURE 8.20   The shader network for ShowerTile_Material.

Step 12: Delete the place2dTexture node for the Color file node. In the Hypershade, in the shader network for ShowerTile_Material, look for the nodes that define the color (usually the top branch). Select the place2dTexture node and delete it.

Why? *Currently there are two nodes that define how many times a texture is repeated within a material; one for the color and one for the bump. This means that if we wanted to change the size of this tile (which we do), we would have to do it twice. In the following steps, we are going to connect both the color and bump to one place2dTexture node. Getting rid of one of the first steps of that process.*

Step 13: Connect the bump's place2dTexture node to the color branch of the network. Ctrl-MMB-drag from the output triangle of the place2dTexture node (bottom right corner of Figure 8.21a) to the input triangle of the color file node (bottom left corner of Figure 8.21b). The resulting shader network is shown in Figure 8.21c.

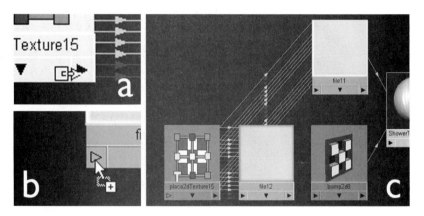

FIGURE 8.21 Connecting the place2dTexture node of the bump branch to the color's.

Why? *Pretty tricky and not very intuitive. And, actually, there are several ways to connect nodes within the Hypershade. But in this case, Ctrl-MMB-drag is the ticket. Remember in most all instances of connecting nodes in the Hypershade that you are connecting the output of one node (the triangle at the bottom right corner of the node) to the input of another node (the triangle at the bottom left corner of the node).*

The benefits of this are fairly substantial, though. Now, any changes made in the place2dTexture node will affect both the color and bump branches of the materials' network. In essence it links the sizes of those two textures together.

Step 14: In the Hypershade, select the place2DTexture node.
Step 15: In the Attributes Editor, change the Repeat UV input fields to 12 and 12.

Why? *The texture files were of one tile. When this material is applied to a surface, we want to have multiple tiles cover the surface.*

Step 16: Apply the ShowerTile_Material to the floor of the shower. In the View Panel, find the shower floor. Right-click it and select Materials > Assign Existing Material > ShowerTile_Material from the Marking menu. The results can be seen in Figure 8.22.

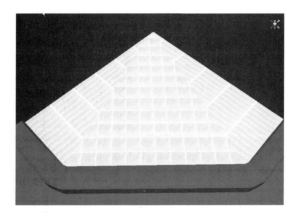

FIGURE 8.22   Applied material.

 If you do not see the material after it is applied to the surface, press 6 on your keyboard. Remember that you must have 6 to see imported texture files—by default it will display the color map.

Doesn't look quite right, does it? This has to do with how the shape was built. As this polygon was stretched, bent, and extruded, the once clean UVs were also deformed. To fix this, we need to remap the object.

Mapping

Step 17: Use Planar Projection to remap the texture. Select the shower floor and select Modeling | Polygon UVs > Planar Projection (Options). In the Mapping Direction section, click Y Axis. Click Project (Figure 8.23).

 The options window of the Planar Projection allows you to determine which axis the texture will be projected along. We want to make sure that the material is projected down onto the floor and not across the surface. The Mapping Direction allows us to define that.

Why?

Step 18: Select the face that is the floor of the bathroom (Figure 8.24). Remember, you need to right-click on the floor and select Face from the Marking menu before you can select a face.

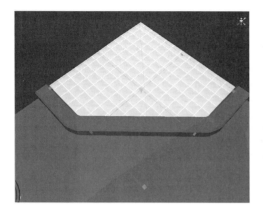

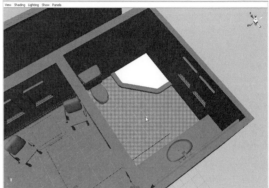

FIGURE 8.23   Results of a planar projection along the y-axis.

FIGURE 8.24   Selected floor of the bathroom.

 Maya allows you to assign shaders on a per-polygon basis. In this case, we will be attaching the same tile shader on the floor of the bathroom. We could remake the **Why?** *floor as another object, but we can assign this tile shader to just this section of the floor much easier.*

Step 19: In the Hypershade, right-click on the ShowerTile_Material and select Assign Material to Selection from the Marking menu.

 You could also have assigned it by right-clicking on the actual face (in the View Panel) and choosing Materials > Assign Existing Material > ShowerTile_Material **Why?** *as well.*

 If the floor appears completely white, just rotate your view a bit. Maya is trying to communicate that the texture has a specular highlight, and with large flat surfaces, this often is shown as a whiting out of the entire surface. As you rotate down and change your angle, you should be able to start to see the floor.

Step 20: Remap with Planar Mapping. With the bathroom floor face still selected, choose Modeling | Polygon UVs > Planar Mapping (Options). Again make sure to use Y Axis as the Mapping Direction.

Step 21: Resize the mapping to provide square tiles. Immediately, after you use Planar Mapping, the manipulators for that mapping will be visible (Figure 8.25). Click-drag the green and red handles to get the tiles square. You can use the blue handles in the corners of the manipulator to resize the mapping.

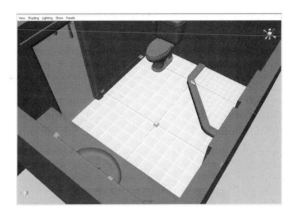

FIGURE 8.25   Using the mapping manipulators to resize the mapping.

Why?

These mapping manipulators are pretty handy. However, if you click on something else, the handles disappear. How do you get them back?

One way is to reproject. However, this Planar Mapping is actually an added node. If you select an object, the nodes of that object will appear in the INPUTS section of the Channels Box. For this floor, if you click it, you will see a node called polyPlanarProj2 (Figure 8.26). With the Show Manipulators Tool active (the eighth tool down in the Toolbox), when you select the polyPlanarProj2 node, the mapping manipulators will pop up again ready for your changing whims.

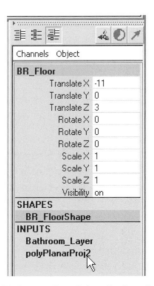

FIGURE 8.26   Regaining the handles through selecting the projection node in the Channels Box.

Step 22: Take a quick render (Figure 8.27).

Step 23: Reduce the bump. Select the bump2d node for ShowerTile_Material (do this in the Hypershade) and reduce the Bump Depth to 0.100. Rerender. Adjust to taste.

If you have been working in the Channels Box, you will need to double-click the bump2d node to get it to show up in the Attributes Editor.

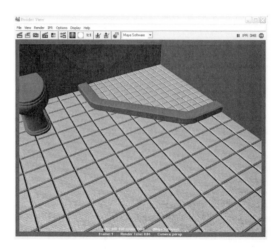

FIGURE 8.27   Rendered results.

Step 24: Unhide the rest of the shower. Press Shift-Ctrl-h to unhide the last hidden objects. You can also select the objects of the shower in the Outliner and then in the Channels Box change the Visibility input field from off to on.

Glass Materials

Step 25: Create a new Phong material.

Step 26: Rename it ShowerGlass_Material.

Step 27: Open it in the Attributes Editor.

Step 28: Adjust the color to a grayish blue. Click the color swatch in the color channel and pick a color in the Color Chooser. The HSV values used in this file were 198, .25, .7.

Step 29: Make the material semitransparent. In the Transparency channel, move the slider to about half-way (Figure 8.28).

Step 30: Import a Noise node as the bump. Click the checkboard button in the Bump Mapping channel and select Noise from the Create Render Node.

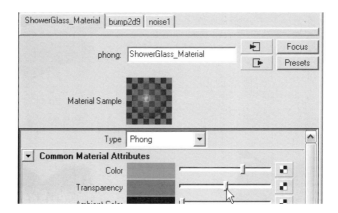

FIGURE 8.28 Making the ShowerGlass_Material semitransparent.

Step 31: In the Attributes Editor, in the Hardware Texturing section, change the Textured Channel to Bump Map.

With a transparent material, there is not much to see in the View Panel. Asking Maya to display the Bump Map gives you a little bit more information about what
Why? *the texture will finally look like.*

Step 32: Change the Texture resolution to Highest (256 × 256).

Since you are using a procedural texture (Noise), it can be kind of hard to reliably see the results in the View Panel with the lower Texture Resolution. Turning it up
Why? *makes things easier to see.*

Step 33: Adjust the Noise node to taste. In the Hypershade, choose ShowerGlass_Material and click the Input and Output Connections button. Select the noise node in the Work Area; this will open noise in the Attributes Editor. Change the settings to get a look that you like (Figure 8.29).
Step 34: Render (Figure 8.30).

Not too terribly impressive yet. Not to fear. Part of the reason the scene looks so flat is it has not been lit yet; it is being rendered using the default lighting setup, which
Why? *consists of a non-shadow-casting spotlight on top of the camera.*
    Another reason is that by default, Maya renders with a very low-quality setting of Maya Software (a rendering engine). Among the limitations of this rendering engine is the lack of reflections. We can fix that in the coming steps.

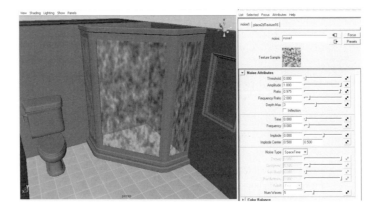

FIGURE 8.29   Glass texture with adjusted bump noise node.

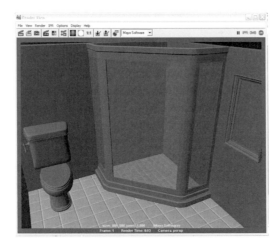

FIGURE 8.30   Rendered scene with glass.

Render Globals

Step 35: Open the Render Settings. In the top shelf, two buttons down from the Render the Current Frame button is the Open Render Settings button. You can also open the Render Settings with the pull-down menu Window > Rendering Editors > Render Settings … .

The Render Settings window allows you to change everything from the size of the render (Common tab, Image Size section) to what the renderer actually outputs in terms of channels (RGB, Alpha, Depth). Additionally, you can change settings of the active renderer here as well.

Why?

Step 36: Click the Maya Software tab.

Step 37: Open the Raytracing Quality section. Turn on the Raytracing checkbox (Figure 8.31).

By default, Maya uses Maya Software. Notice the Maya Software tab (next to the Common tab). Within the Maya Software tab, you can change the way that Maya Software works including whether or not it calculates reflections. Reflections are calculated by Raytracing. Because raytracing is slower (rendering a reflection of a room means rendering the room twice—once for the camera's view and once for the reflected object's view), Maya leaves it off by default. Turning it on will slow the rendering but give a more accurate interpretation.

Step 38: Render (Figure 8.32).

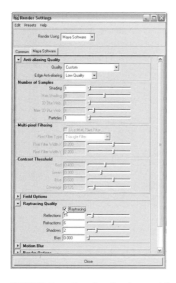

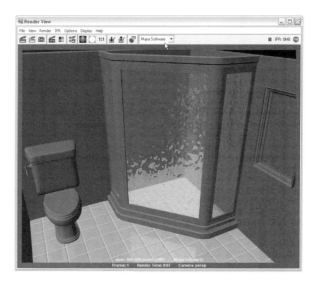

FIGURE 8.31   Render Settings with Raytracing turned on.

FIGURE 8.32   Rendering using raytracing. Notice the reflection in both the shower glass and the reflection from the floor.

Of course, it starts to point out flaws (for example, no shower head—need to add that), but it does start to make the space have much more dimension and a much better look.

Chrome

Step 39: Create a new Phong shader and name it Chrome_Material.

Step 40: Open Chrome in the Attributes Editor (via the Hypershade).

Step 41: Turn the Color channel off. Move the slider all the way to the left.

Truly reflective materials are the color of whatever they are reflecting. They have no color of their own.

Step 42: In the Attributes Editor, in the Specular Shading section, turn the Reflectivity channel to 1.

Step 43: Apply Chrome_Material to the chrome parts of the shower. Select the metal parts of the shower stall and in the Hypershade, right-click on Chrome_Material and select Assign Material to Selection from the Marking menu.

Step 44: Render.

FIGURE 8.33   Rendering of chrome added to shower.

There are some black splotches in this chrome, or there appears to be something weird in the reflection. This is because you have the default lighting still. You have a spotlight on top of the camera lighting that is in front of the camera; however, things behind the camera have no light on them at all. So when a surface like the metal part of the shower reflects the rest of the room, it is going to be reflecting some objects that appear totally black.

Porcelain

Step 45: Create a new Phong E material, and rename it Porcelain_Material.

Step 46: Change the Color to pure white (in the Attributes Editor, slide the Color slider all the way to the right).

Step 47: In the Specular Shading section, turn the Highlight Size to 0.
Step 48: In the Specular Shading section, turn the Reflectivity to .2

Porcelain is a fairly reflective surface. It is quite shiny, but that shine is really re-flections of light sources in the scene. To get the look right, turning off the specular attribute of this material (by turning the Highlight Size to 0), but turning the Re-flectivity on will give us believable surfaces.

Step 49: Render (Figure 8.34).

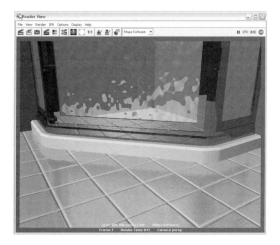

FIGURE 8.34   Rendered porcelain.

Tutorial Conclusion

Those are a lot of steps for just a few things textured. Luckily, since you now know the basic structure, we can move through the other areas much quicker. Now, you can create from scratch materials that use tex-ture maps (and you know how to create those texture maps as well). More importantly, you can control absolutely how the material falls across, wraps around, or stretches across a polygonal object.

TUTORIAL 8.3   TEXTURING THE MAIN ROOM

Objectives:

1. Add material to remaining objects in the room.
2. Work through details of different materials for different faces.

3. Create accurately spaced materials.

Step 1: Set the project.
Step 2: Open your most recent version of the room. This tutorial works on the results of Tutorial_8_1.mb.

Picture Frame

Step 3: Find a framed image in the room. Zoom in on that.

Some things to note about any of the wall hangings in Tutorial_8_1.mb: First notice that there are actually two objects there, the frame and a polygon plane. This is important as the polygon plane will actually be the object that gets textured to show the painting or photograph.

Step 4: Create a new Phong shader, and name it FrameLacquer_ Material.
Step 5: Change the color to very dark red.
Step 6: Change the Reflectivity to very low (.1). This is located in the Specular Shading section of the material in the Attributes Editor.

Why?

We want this lacquered surface to have a high gloss but not be so reflective that it looks like metal. Turning the reflectivity down will maintain a little bit of reflectivity but not overwhelm.

Step 7: Apply the material to the frame.
Step 8: Create a new material (Lambert), and name it KatiePhoto_Material.
Step 9: Import a texture into the Color channel. For the example, the file KatiePhoto.tif was used from the sourceimages folder.

You can use your own photo here if you would like. However, do make sure that you place a copy of it in your sourceimages folder and load it into your texture from there.

Step 10: Apply KatiePhoto_Material to the plane behind the frame (Figure 8.35).

Table

Step 11: Find and focus on the table.
Step 12: Create a new Phong E material, and name it TableLacquer_ Material.
Step 13: Change the color to a near black.
Step 14: Add a Noise node to the Bump Mapping channel.
Step 15: Reduce the Bump Depth to .010

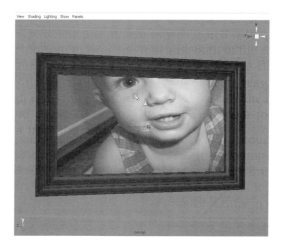

FIGURE 8.35   Using a photograph to texture a plane like, well, a photograph.

There are very few objects that are perfectly smooth. Especially big surfaces like this table should have just a little bit of bump. However, the table should not cut your hand as you run your finger over it; so setting a generic bump (like noise) with a very, very low value can add just enough variation to make the surface more believable.

Step 16: Reduce the Reflectivity to .2.

Lacquer should be reflective, but not too reflective. Reducing the value to .2 is largely arbitrary. After the scene is lit, you may find that several of these textures need to be tweaked and have their reflectivity settings turned up or down. The same for their other specular characteristics.

Step 17: Assign TableLacquer_Material to the table (both top and base).
Step 18: Duplicate the material TableLacquer_Material. Do this by selecting the material in the Hypershade. Then select Edit > Duplicate > Shader Network. This will create a new material called TableLacquer_Material1. This new material will be right next to the material it was duplicated from in the Materials tab.

Why duplicate? The inset is the same color but with a slightly different finish. By duplicating the shader network, you can be sure that you have the same color and the same bump map values. It saves time.

Step 19: Change the material type to Lambert. In the Attributes Editor for TableInset_Material, right at the top is the Type drop-down menu. Change this from Phong E to Lambert.

Step 20: Rename to TableInset_Material.

Step 21: Change the Bump Depth to .020.

Step 22: Select the inset face of the table (Figure 8.36).

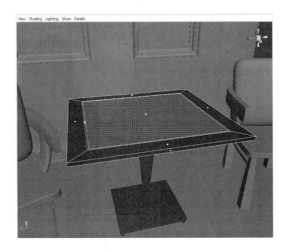

FIGURE 8.36 Selected inset face.

Step 23: In the Hypershade, right-click on TableInset_Material node and choose Assign Material to selection.

Floor

Step 24: Create a new Phong material. Name it WoodFloor_Material.

Step 25: Import WoodFloorColor.tif into the Color channel.

This file is located in sourceimages. Take a look at this texture in something like Photoshop. Notice that it is really a close-up of one small chunk of floor. In a case like the floor, oftentimes this works out just right. The bump texture will do most of the work, and the color map simply needs to provide some variation in color across the surface. So this one chunk of color will stretch across the entire floor.

Step 26: Use FloorBump.tif as the Bump Channel texture. Change the Bump Depth to .1.

Step 27: Have Maya display the Bump Map as the hardware textured channel. To do this, select the material. Then in the Attributes Editor, in the Hardware Texturing area, change the Textured Channel input field from Color Map to Bump Map.

Step 28: Select the floor.

Step 29: Choose the faces that make up the main bedroom area (Figure 8.37).

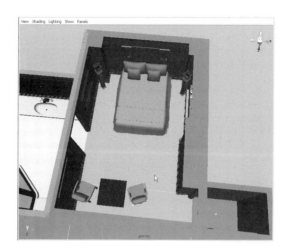

FIGURE 8.37   Select only the polygons that make up the main bedroom.

Step 30: Assign WoodFloor_Material to these faces (Figure 8.38).

Step 31: Make sure that the faces that are the wood floor are selected, and choose Modeling | Polygon UVs > Planar Mapping (Options).

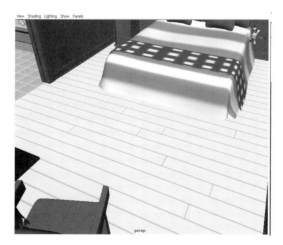

FIGURE 8.38   Assigned material to floor. Notice by having the bump map be the textured channel, we have a much better idea of scale.

The planks of this floor should be rotated and running the other direction. There are actually a couple of ways this could be accomplished. One is through the place2dTexture nodes for both the color and bump of this material, and the other is through simply controlling how the material is mapped across the surface.

Step 32: In the Polygon Planar Projection Options window, make sure that the Mapping Direction is set to Y Axis, and change the Image Rotation section to 90.

Pretty intuitive here. You are just telling Maya to project the material down along the y-axis and rotate it 90 degrees as you do. The results can be seen in Figure 8.39

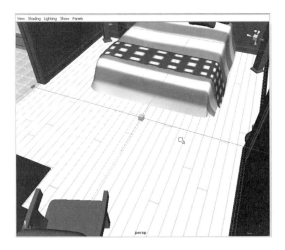

FIGURE 8.39   Results of the newly projected material.

Step 33: Adjust the Reflectivity to .1.
Step 34: Render (Figure 8.40).

Wall Paper

Step 35: Create a new Lambert material, and name it Wall_Material.
Step 36: Make the color a solid golden yellow (or whatever color you want really).
Step 37: Use a Grid node for the bump. The Grid is one of the nodes available in the Create Render Node window.
Step 38: In the Hypershade, double-click the grid1 node in the Work Area (you may need to open the Wall_Material in the Work Area and organize the graph by pressing the Input and Output Connections button).

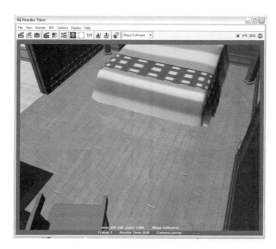

FIGURE 8.40   Rendered floor material.

We are going to adjust this grid node to create a stripe bump across our wallpaper. By double-clicking it in the Hypershade, this node will be opened in the Attributes Editor where we can manipulate it.

Why?

Step 39: Change the settings to U Width = .5, V Width = 1, and in the Effects area change the Filter Offset to .250. This will give you a soft stripe (Figure 8.41).

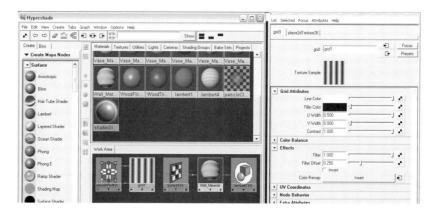

FIGURE 8.41   The shading network of Wall_Material and the edited attribute for the grid1 node used for the material's bump.

Step 40: Change the Textured Channel to Bump Map. Remember, do this in the Attributes Editor for the Wall_Material. The Textured Channel drop-down menu is in the Hardware Texturing section.

When this material is applied to the walls, it will need to be adjusted for each sur-
Why? *face so that the bump map is uniform across the objects. If you just throw the ma-*
terial on all the walls without adjusting, the same four stripes you see on the grid1
node will be stretched across long walls and shrunk across short ones. But without
being able to see the bump map (the grid that is now stripes), you cannot make the
necessary adjustments to the mapping.

Step 41: Pick a wall—any wall (except the walls that are shared with the
bathroom). Apply Wall_Material to it (Figure 8.42).

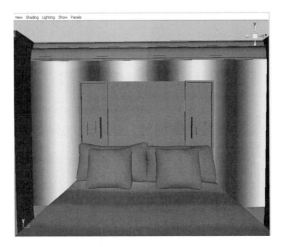

FIGURE 8.42   Wall_Material applied to a wall. Notice that
the four stripes are stretched all the way across it.

Step 42: Select the wall you just applied the material to and select Modeling
| Polygon UVs > Planar Mapping (Options). Change the Mapping Direction to
the appropriate axis (in the case of Figure 8.42, it's the z-axis, although it may
be different for yours depending on what wall you have chosen).

Step 43: Use the red manipulators of the projection node to resize the
material to approximately match Figure 8.43.

Step 44: Move to the next wall. Select it and assign Wall_Material to it.

Step 45: Reproject the mapping. Adjust the mapping using the planar
projection manipulator handles so that it matches the projection on the
first wall.

If the next wall has two surfaces visible (as the corner column in Figure 8.44 does),
make sure that you select one face, use Modeling | Polygon UVs > Planar Mapping
(Options) and adjust the projection axis. Adjust the projection to match and then re-
peat for the next face.

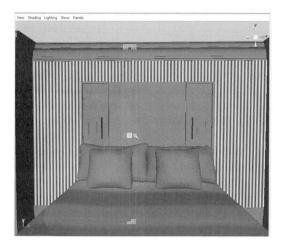

FIGURE 8.43   Adjusted planar projection to tighten the bump on the wall.

Step 46: Repeat the process moving around the room until you have all the walls complete. The only notable exception will be the West Walls (those that share the bathroom). Since you will be using a different material on the other side of that wall (that bathroom side); make sure that you

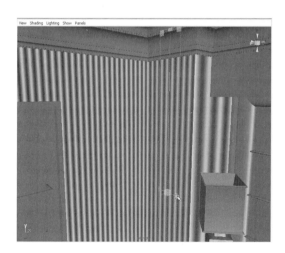

FIGURE 8.44   Adjusting projection for an individual plane to match.

assign this Wall_Material only to the faces in the room (select the faces and then assign the material). Figure 8.45 shows what it should look like.

Step 47: Change the Wall_Material's Textured Channel back to Color (or if this is unavailable, change it to Combined Textures).

FIGURE 8.45   Assigned and adjusted Wall_Material.

Why? *Ultimately, the color is going to have more to do with the overall look of the room than the bump. So getting back to seeing the color will help give you a better idea of what the final product will look like. You may choose to do this with the floor material, too.*

Tutorial Conclusion

Is it done? Not by a long shot. You will notice that there are still many materials to be created and applied. However, through these materials, you now know how to create new materials, how to apply them to an object, and how to project and control the mapping of those materials. Armed with this, you should be able to complete texturing all the floors, walls, and objects in the scene.

The renders will still appear a bit flat; this is largely because the scene has not been lit yet. However, in the next chapter, you will get a chance to start to make this scene have some real depth and feel like a real space.

Challenges, Exercises, or Assignments

1. In the sourceimages folder, you will find a file called FurnitureWood-Color.tif. Use this as the Color channel for a new Blinn material. Use it to texture the remaining trim and furniture in the room.

2. Figure 8.46 shows one of the acoustic panels in the room. Take a guess at how to create this and apply it to the panels and headboard in the room (if you get stuck, take a look at the Panel_Material node in the Tutorial_8_2.mb file on the CD-ROM).

ON THE CD

3. Create a new material (of your choosing) for the bathroom walls.

FIGURE 8.46   Panels with Panel_Material applied. Note this is a render to view the bump map.

Apply and adjust the mapping so all the walls have an evenly distributed material.

4. Check out Figure 8.47. It refines the shower stall. How would you create panes of tiles like that? (*Hint:* The Cut Faces Tool and assigning materials to specific faces comes in really handy here).

FIGURE 8.47   Refined shower stall.

5. What would a material for window glass look like? Create one, and assign it to the glass pane in the windows.
6. Figure 8.48 shows the numbers on the door. They have a brass/gold material created. Take a look at this image in color, and look at how the material is constructed. Create your own and apply it to your numbers.

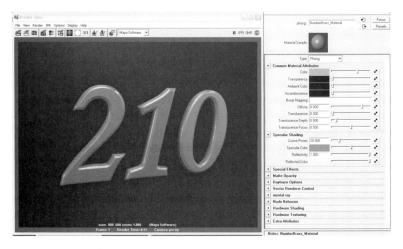

FIGURE 8.48 Gold/brass material.

7. Finish texturing the room to taste.

9

LIGHTING AND RENDERING

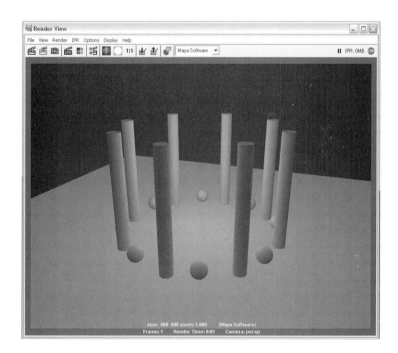

S o we have modeled the room using NURBS and polygons. We have created materials using built-in procedural textures and custom made bitmapped-based images. We have applied those materials to NURBS and polygonal objects in the room; and controlled how those materials are distributed across the surfaces. There is actually quite a bit more to be learned about modeling and texturing; but those techniques are best explored on very organic forms. So in the next few chapters we will look at organic modeling and texturing.

But for now, it is time to add a bit of realism to our scene. Yes, we have made valiant efforts by ensuring materials had bump maps attached; some may even have had diffuse channels activated. But the renderings still appear flat, and well, computery.

The pros never neglect lighting. Successful 3D movies, TV projects, commercials, and games all make careful use of lighting techniques and tools. However, when people are just learning 3D, lighting tends to be one of those areas to slap together at the last minute. Many a great project that a student has carefully designed, exquisitely planned, and expertly modeled and textured was ruined by slapping a few lights on without giving thought to the power of lighting.

In this chapter we will be looking carefully at many of the tools Maya provides for lighting. As is the case with most of this book, we have neither the space or time to cover everything that Maya does with lighting—but we will look at all the lighting types, and some important tools in defining shadows.

Tied with lighting is the rendering process, which will also be covered in this chapter. Remember that rendering is the process by which the computer actually draws this world that you have been creating and defining. Although sometimes a fairly accurate artist, the computer is pretty dumb and largely uninspired by default. You have to often help it along by telling it some of the specifics of how you wish it to draw your creation. In this chapter we will explore some of that communication.

A few notes about lighting instruments and light illumination in Maya. As soon as you place a light in Maya, the default lighting set is no longer used; that is, when you render, the default flood light that was attached to your camera is now off. In addition, you can finally make use of using 7 on your keyboard. This will suddenly give you a preview (in your View Panel) of what your lighting will look like.

Note, however, that this is just an estimate. While pressing 7 will show you some characteristics like general intensity and color, it will not give you details on shadows or decay (how the light falls off over a distance)—you have to wait for renders to get this information. But, as you begin to build your lights, do press 7 to get a peak at what your lighting setup might produce.

LIGHTING INSTRUMENTS

ON THE CD

To start with the exploration of lighting in Maya let us take a look at the instruments or types of lights that Maya allows us to place in a scene. To illustrate this we will be using the Maya file shown in Figure 9.1. This file (without lights) is available on the CD-ROM in the ProjectFiles > Chapter09 folder; it is called LightingSetup.mb. If you learn better by doing than reading, open the file and follow along.

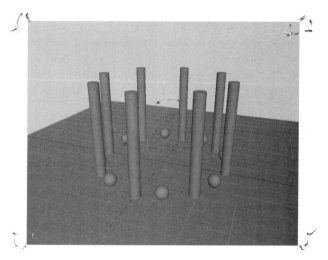

FIGURE 9.1   Scene before lighting.

Creating lights is done under the Create pull-down menu. Create > Lights > pulls up the different types of lights available in Maya. Below is an illustration of each light and some of the characteristics they allow you to change.

It is really impossible to talk of lighting and not talk of rendering engines. The following illustrations of the various lighting instruments are all rendered using Maya Software. Although there are other rendering engines widely used (mental ray, Renderman, etc.), Maya Software is still the primary rendering engine of most Maya users. So although we will look briefly at some mental ray options later, Maya Software is the tool of choice for now.

Ambient Light

Hardly ever a good idea, ambient light is light that comes from everywhere yet nowhere. Figure 9.2 shows the results of an Ambient light. The light was placed right in the middle of the circle of objects, and sure enough there is light; lots of it, even with the default light settings. The problem is what there is *not*.

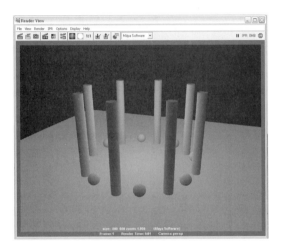

FIGURE 9.2   Results of Ambient light set within center of objects.

The first problem is there is no true dark side of the objects. Although the backsides of the objects are darker, they still have some light on them. Similarly, there are no shadows; and without using raytraced shadows (a very time-intensive method of generating shadows that we will talk more of later) this lighting instrument will not cast shadows.

In general, stay clear of this instrument. The first solution lots of students have to a scene that feels too dark is to throw an ambient light in the scene. This always tends to flatten the scene out and destroy a lot of the visual modeling they have tried so hard to achieve. Stay clear of it.

Directional Light

This light acts the most like sunlight of any of the lighting instruments. Think of it as a wall of light. It comes from an infinite distance away and casts light for an infinite distance. Additionally, the light rays all come toward the scene parallel to each other—there is no splay in the light.

A Directional Light (shown in Figure 9.3) actually has two parts to it: the light and a target null object. The idea here is that the light (represented by the green arrows) points toward the target null. Now, you can rotate the light like any other object using the Rotate Tool, but if you have a Directional Light (or any other lighting instrument in Maya) selected and have the Show Manipulators active (shown in Figure 9.3 as well), you will actually get two Move Tool manipulators—one for the light and one for the target null. As you move the target null, the light will turn to remain pointed at the target.

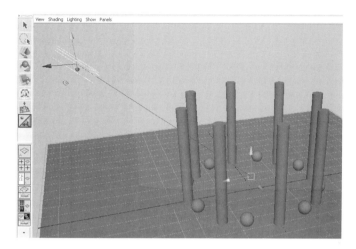

FIGURE 9.3   The Directional Light and the companion target null available with Show Manipulators active.

Figure 9.4 shows the results of a default Directional Light. Sure enough, there is indeed light coming from one direction, and unlike the Ambient light there is a true dark side of the objects. However, by default the results are still less than impressive—no depth and no shadows.

Like most objects in Maya, the attributes of a light are controlled in the Attributes Editor. Double-clicking the light in the Outliner, or selecting it in the View Panel will display the editable attributes in the Attributes Editor at the right of your interface. Figure 9.5 shows the Attributes Editor for the Directional Light used in Figure 9.4.

Notice that it is broken down into fairly intuitive sections. The first area, Directional Light Attributes allows you to change the type of light, the color and the intensity. Changing the color is self-explanatory and changing the intensity changes the brightness of the light.

Below that is the Shadows section. By default Maya's lights do not cast shadows (although this can be changed in the options window of any light when you create it). There are really two different kinds of shadows to be used. The first are called Depth Map Shadows. Usually Depth Map Shadows are the tool of choice because they render much more quickly than the second shadow type: Raytrace Shadows.

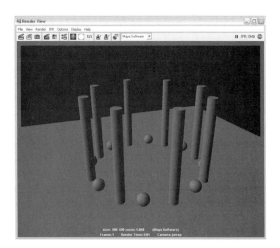

FIGURE 9.4   Rendering of scene with default settings for Directional Light.

FIGURE 9.5   Attributes Editor for Directional Light.

Depth Map Shadows

Depth Maps are actually images that indicate how far objects are from the camera—or in this case from each light. A Depth Map Shadow is the result of this image (stored temporarily by Maya as an .iff) that is rendered from the light's point of view. The depth map figures out which objects should be in shadow.

In the Depth Map Shadow Attributes section of the Attributes Editor, click on Use Depth Map Shadows to activate them. Note that one of the first options there is Resolution (you are creating an image after all). The lower this resolution, the smaller the depth map is and often the blockier your shadows will be.

Figure 9.6 shows the results of the Directional Light with an intensity of 3, Depth Map Shadows activated with the default 512 resolution. Notice the detail and how you can actually see the pixels of the depth map.

The issue of resolution in the depth map shadows is especially an issue with Directional Lights because you are dealing with a wall of light—the depth map has to be as large as the entire scene (rather than a much more limited size as other lights would have).

To fix the blotchy look of the depth map shadow, you can turn up the resolution. Figure 9.7 shows the results of turning the resolution up to 3500.

Of course, as you increase the Resolution setting, the rendering time increases as Maya has to create large images for the depth map. An alternative (shown in Figure 9.8) is to adjust the Filter Size setting. The Filter Size is a sort of blur applied to the depth map. The higher the filter size, the more the depth map is blurred. The result is a shadow with softer edges.

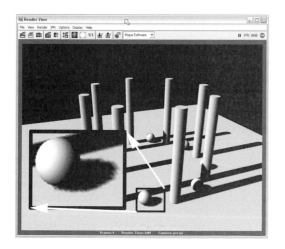

FIGURE 9.6   Default Resolution on Directional Light.

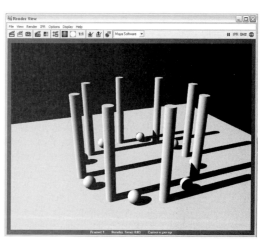

FIGURE 9.7   Depth Map Shadow with a resolution of 3500; notice the crisper shadows.

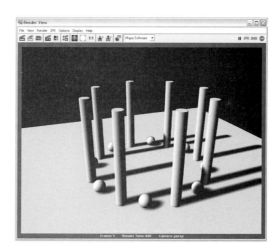

FIGURE 9.8   Rendering of Directional Light with a Resolution setting of 512 but a Filter Size of 4.

Both of these methods (increasing resolution and filter size) help eliminate the blocky shadows; although the results are much different. Usually, when using the Directional Light, you are trying to get the look of the sun; which typically casts very crisp shadows so often the increased Resolution setting is the best option for those situations.

Raytrace Shadows

Notice that in the Attributes Editor below the Depth Map Shadow Attributes is an area called Raytrace Shadow Attributes. Activating Use Ray Trace Shadows automatically deactivates Use Depth Map Shadows.

Although Ray Trace Shadows are more accurate than Depth Map Shadows and often produce a very fine result (Figure 9.9) that have shadows that are crisp next to the object and soften as the shadow stretches away (as shadows really do); notice that the screenshot shown in Figure 9.9 took 46 seconds to render as opposed to the 1 and 3 second renders provided with Depth Map Shadows.

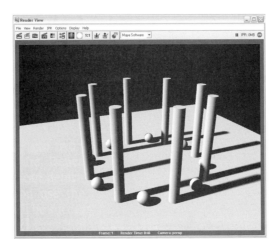

FIGURE 9.9   Results of Ray Trace Shadows.

Although the result is beautiful, it is rarely worth the penalty you take in increased rendering times. As your lighting schemes become more complex, the differences between depth map shadows and raytraced shadows become smaller and smaller. So in general, there is little need to descend into the time-sucking realms of raytraced shadows.

Caveat of Directional Lights

Figure 9.10a shows a Directional Light actually set within the circle of objects. Figure 9.10b shows the resulting render. Notice that even though the light is inside the objects, the outside left of the objects is still lit. This is because Directional Lights always come from an infinite distance; regardless of where you put the actual instrument. This is a little counterintuitive, but important to remember. It is also the reason why Directional Lights are sometimes a bit more difficult to control than some other types of lights.

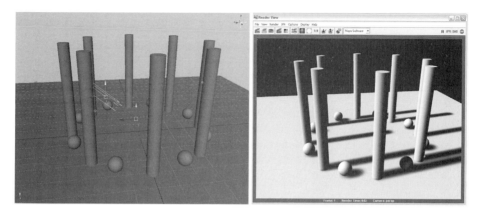

FIGURE 9.10   (a) Directional Light inside of objects, but (b) still illuminating the outside of them.

Point Light

Point lights act much like light bulbs. The light that comes from a Point light illuminates from a single point in space in all directions (Figure 9.11). Note that by default, a Point light casts no shadows. Also note that in the Attributes Editor you can see a new characteristic in the Point Light Attributes—Decay Rate.

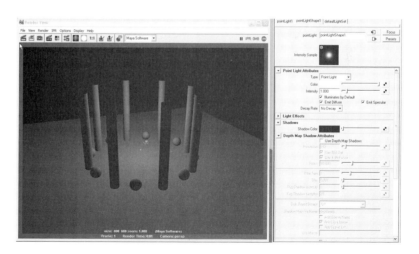

FIGURE 9.11   Default Point light settings and its results.

Decay Rate

Decay Rate is actually a fairly important idea in 3D. With the default setting of No Decay, a lighting instrument in 3D will theoretically throw light *forever*. That is, it never breaks down, never gets dim no matter how far it travels.

This is actually a big problem when dealing with lights like a Point light. With a Point light, you can imagine the illumination it gives off as a sphere. The closer to the Point light, the smaller the sphere (the smaller the volume and thus the less the light). As the light gets farther from the point light source, the sphere of light gets bigger, the volume gets larger, and thus the amount of light is more. This provides a situation in which the further you are from a light, the more light there is.

Of course this is not at all how lighting behaves in the real world. Turning on decay is almost always a good idea. Yes, it takes a little longer to set up the lighting as you cannot see accurately what the decay does in the View Panel and often it takes more lighting instruments to get final illumination; but the results are always more believable with corners that can remain dark (if you want them), and hot spots nearest the light (if you want them).

The types of decay available are Linear, Quadratic and Cubic. These are largely a reference to what a graph would look like if you mapped the decay over the distance. Essentially, quadratic decay is the most like light decays in the real world. However, it can be a bit tough to control. Cubic decay rate decays at a much faster rate than light decays in the real world and is very hard to work with. For most situations, linear decay is the author's tool of choice. It is a good combination of mimicking real-world decay while providing an easily altered and predicted rate.

In each of these situations, decaying the light means that the Intensity setting must be higher than it would without decay. So while a light with intensity of 1 and no decay will light any room, a light with Linear decay will need intensities of 2, 3, or 10 times higher (depending on the size of your scene).

Figure 9.12 shows the same LightingSetup scene with a Point light sitting in the middle (off the ground) of the objects. It has Linear decay

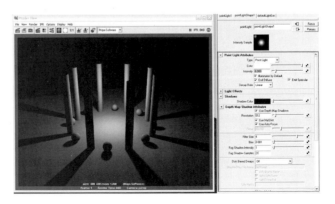

FIGURE 9.12   Point light with decay active.

and so a higher intensity (6) than Figure 9.11. Notice too that Use Depth Map Shadows are active.

Spot Light

The Spot Light uses many of the same techniques and tools that were seen in the Directional Light and the Point light. Again, the Spot Light's attributes (editable in the Attributes Editor) include color, intensity and decay as well as Depth Map Shadows. Notice, however, that the Spot Light also has Cone Angle, Penumbra Angle, and Dropoff in its Spot Light Attributes.

A Spot Light takes light from a point in space (think of it as a bulb) and shoots it outward in a cone-like shape. The Cone Angle is the size of that cone. Increase the Cone Angle and the light illuminates a broader area. The Penumbra Angle has to do with the focus (to use a theatre term) of the lighting instrument. 0 has a light with sharp focus and sharp edges; nonzero values soften the focus or edges of the light. Finally Dropoff deals with how the light diminishes from the center hotspot to the edge of the light.

To illustrate these characteristics consider Figure 9.13. It is a default Spot Light (with Depth Map Shadows turned on). Notice that there are two manipulators in the scene, one for the Spot Light (the green cone shape in the top left corner) and one for the target null (where the Spot Light is pointing at). Decay Rate is set to Linear and so the Intensity has been raised to 12.

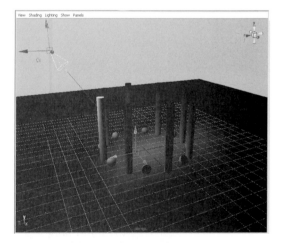

FIGURE 9.13   The Spot Light setup.

Figure 9.14a shows the rendering of the setup. Figure 9.14b shows the Cone Angle increased from the default 40 to 60. Notice the illuminated area is larger.

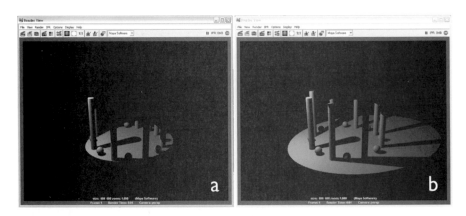

FIGURE 9.14   Difference in Cone Angle (a is set at 40 degrees with b set to 60).

Figure 9.15a shows the same setup only with a Penumbra Angle of 10. Figure 9.15b shows a Penumbra Angle of –10. Notice how soft the edges are in each of these renders.

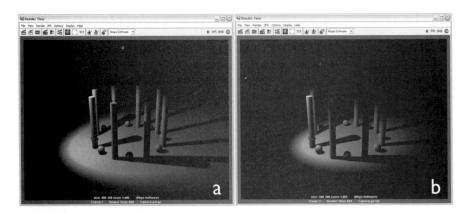

FIGURE 9.15   Varying Penumbra Angles (a is set to 10, b is at –10).

Aiming a Spot Light

Since Spot Lights have such a particular area of light, it is helpful to talk a bit about how to get them to light what you have in mind. The first method is to make sure you have Show Manipulators active for starters; but there is also a nifty trick available through the View Panels.

With a Spot Light (or any light or even object for that matter) selected select Panels > Look Through Selected (within the View Panel's pull-down menus). You will be given a view like Figure 9.16 which allows you to see, aim, and move around the scene from within the light. As you change your view in this mode, the light's aim will also change. It is a fairly intuitive way to make sure you are Spot Lighting the right spot in your scene.

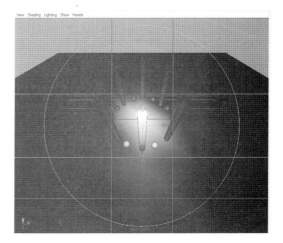

FIGURE 9.16   Selecting the Spot Light and using Look through Selected.

Area Lights

Area Lights really can develop some very sensitive lighting schemes. The closest analogy to real-life lighting is a light box—a box of lights that emits a soft wash of light. Figure 9.17 shows a simple setup and the rendering results.

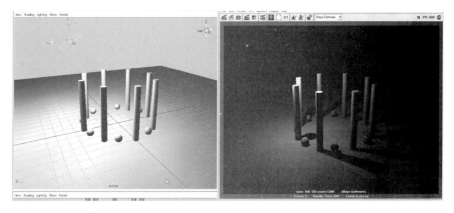

FIGURE 9.17   Area light in action.

With light the Directional and Spot Light, you can rotate the lighting instrument to aim the light. Remember you can do this by showing the manipulators. You can change the size of the area light with the standard Scale Tool. The bigger the Area light, the bigger the box of light.

A few caveats about the Area light. The light that comes off of an Area light splays outward. It does not just emerge as a long box of light. You will see why this is important once we start lighting the room; but in essence the core issue is that objects that are to the side (and a little ahead) of the area light will be illuminated as well.

In many other applications the Area light provides an even wash of light. In Maya this is not necessarily the case. The Area light has a hot spot—usually around the center of its illumination. This hotspot can be very problematic and often ends up looking like the light a Spot would emit. Because of this, to really take advantage of the Area light, it is usually used with a much more gentle touch than many of the other lights.

The advantages are indeed great. Raytracing or Maya Software do not calculate bounced light—that is, when Maya is rendering and it sees that light hits a surface, that light stops right there. It does not bounce of the surface to continue to light other objects in the scene as light does in real life. Although Mental Ray provides some radiosity rendering that does do this type of calculation for you—it is slow (really slow), and often is not the solution for animation or beginning 3D folks.

But, you can fake the characteristics of real light within Maya Software. The Area light is one of my favorite ways to simulate the bounced light that occurs in the real world. Need a wall to bounce sunlight coming in from a window on the opposite side of the room? Put an area light on the wall facing into the room. Need bounced light from a hardwood floor? Put an area light on the floor facing up. We will see this technique in action in the upcoming tutorial.

Volume Lights

The way that Volume Lights (Figure 9.18) works is that the light has a volumetric shape that surrounds it. By default this shape is a sphere, but it can also be a box, cylinder or cone. The important thing about this shape is that the light only exists within this volumetric shape. Objects outside the sphere (as in Figure 9.18) simply receive no light.

The great thing about this tool is that it provides a very visual way to see exactly how far the light is thrown; there is not much guesswork needed (as is sometimes the case with Maya's other lighting tools). Additionally, you can make a light that does not really act as a light would in real life. You can make it cast a very bright light in a very tight radius, but yet does not reach very far. In certain cases (as you will see in the upcoming tutorials), this is a truly valuable option.

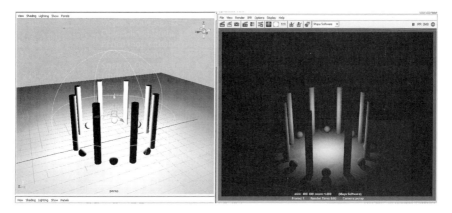

FIGURE 9.18   Volumetric Lights.

PUTTING THE TALK INTO PRACTICE

We have looked at the tools that Maya provides to illuminate your scene. Now we can start to take these tools and make some great-looking renderings.

The process of lighting can sometimes be a frustrating one for early students of 3D. What you see in the View Panel is seldom what you get in the final render. Because of this, it becomes quite important that you render often to see the results of you work. Additionally, the default settings for most lights (no shadows, and no fall off) is quite counterintuitive to getting a good-looking render. Sometimes, making sure that things are switched on (or off) for a light in the Attributes Editor can be the difference between a confusing mess and a delicately lit scene.

So hang in there, prepare to do a little bit of waiting when it comes time to refine your scene. But do not give up. Remember there is not much to see if your scene has not been lit well.

Ironically, lighting for night is actually easier than lighting for day. This largely is because you are using all artificial lighting which is easier to control in the 3D environment. So in Tutorial 9.1 we will light the scene for night, and then follow up with day-time lighting in Tutorial 9.2.

TUTORIAL 9.1	**LIGHTING THE SCENE FOR NIGHT**

Objectives:

1. Create Point, Volumetric, Spot, and Area lights.
2. Control falloff, intensity, and color of lighting objects.
3. Create a believably lit scene.

Step 1: Define your project.

Step 2: Open your last saved version of the room. In the case of this tutorial, we will be using Tutorial_8_2.mb as the basis scene. But use your own if you would like and adapt the ideas to come to your scene.

Step 3: Create a Point Light. Create > Lights > Point Light.

We are going to start by placing recessed lighting in the ceiling. This lighting situation would have a light bulb inside the recessed section that sticks out a little below the ceiling. As this is essentially a light that throws in all directions, a Point Light is the best candidate.

Step 4: Rename to "PotLight." In the Outliner, double-click the point-light object and change the name. Notice that this will also open the attributes of the light in the Attributes Editor.

Before we are all done, there will be many lights in this scene. Naming them as you go will make a huge difference when it comes time to make adjustments, or work with assigning certain surfaces to be lit (or not lit) by certain objects. It is always a good idea to name every object you create in any 3D application.

Step 5: Press 7 on your keyboard.

Remember that 7 will give you a rough estimate of how the scene looks lit with the lights you have placed. Pressing it right now will probably make your scene appear really dark because the one light you have created is sitting on the floor in the middle of the room.

Step 6: Position the light just under the ceiling. If it is not visible, make your Ceiling layer visible. Use the Move Tool to slide the PotLight up in the Y direction so that it sits very near the ceiling, but not through/in/above it (Figure 9.19).

Yes, we could go through and cut holes in the ceiling, create the metal cup shape that really exists in pot light situations; but because we will be working with the premise that the actual bulb dips below the surface of the ceiling, we can simply put the light just under the ceiling. This will save loads of time in modeling and make for a much quicker set up.

Step 7: Render.

Looking pretty nasty with the render huh? The Point Light by default shoots light all over the place with not falloff/decay and no shadows. The result is a very flat and unbelievable looking space.

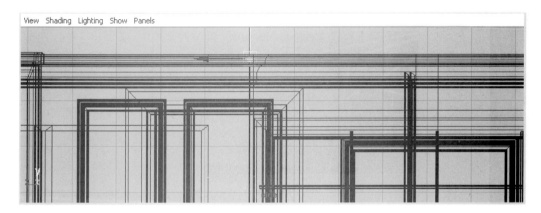

FIGURE 9.19 Positioning of the PotLight.

Step 8: Give PotLight an Intensity of 7, Decay Rate of Linear and shadows. If you cannot see the attributes of PotLight in the Attributes Editor, double-click Potlight in the Outliner. Once visible in the Attributes Editor, in the Point Light Attributes section change the Intensity to 7 (you can enter this in the input field or use the slider). Change the Decay Rate to Linear. Open the Shadows section and activate Use Depth Map Shadows. Enter 4 in the Filter Size input field (Figure 9.20).

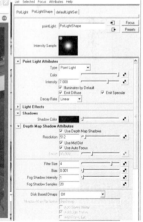

FIGURE 9.20 Altering the default settings for PotLight to give some believability to the setup.

 An intensity of 7 seems extreme right off the bat, but remember, as soon as you turn on any sort of decay, you do not have as much light in the room as the lighting in-

Why?

strument is not throwing as much. Activating decay will almost always need to be paired with an increase in intensity.

Activating the Use Depth Map Shadows is needed to get any sort of shadows at all. Turning the Filter Size up to 4 allows for some additional softness to the shadow, and allows you to keep the Resolution small without getting really jagged shadows.

Step 9: Render.

Gotta see what the scene looks like with the current lighting choices. But, it still looks a bit stark. Part of this starkness comes from totally black shadows that are the result of only one light in the scene. Hang on, and this will be fixed.

Light Geometry

Step 10: Create geometry to represent the light. Create form to taste; Figure 9.21 uses a sphere (slightly flattened) and a torus (both from Create > Polygon Primitives >). Name the sphere "Bulb."

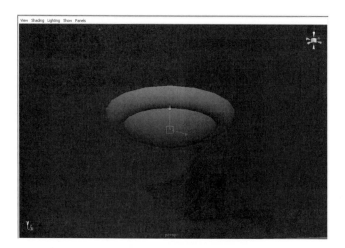

FIGURE 9.21   Geometry created to represent the light.

One of the things wrong with Figure 9.20 is that you can see what the light does, but you cannot see the light itself. Basically the room is being lit, but you cannot see the lighting instrument. Creating geometry to represent this light is important to the believability of the scene. This way, as the lighting does not only look right, it makes sense.

Do note that the actual PotLight is inside of the sphere.

Step 11: Render.

With the PotLight inside the sphere (Bulb), your scene should suddenly look very, very dark. This is because the sphere is blocking all the light that PotLight is giving off. The inside of that sphere is lit really well, but the room is not getting any light.

Step 12: Make the Bulb not cast shadows. Select the Bulb in the Outliner. In the Attributes Editor, you should see the attributes of Bulb; specifically, you will want to look for the tab that is the shape node (BulbShape). Within this node is a section called Render Stats. Expand this and click off Casts Shadows.

It is interesting that you can actually tell certain objects to cast shadows—or not. By telling this sphere to not cast shadows, you are telling the sphere to allow light to pass through it. This means that the PotLight within it will still be able to illuminate the room.

Step 13: Render.

Although the room is lit now, the actual geometry that represents the light is the darkest in the room. To fix this we must create some new materials.

Step 14: Create a new material to give light to the sphere. Create a new Lambert (either by right-clicking Bulb and selecting Materials > Create New Material > Lambert or through the create bar in the Hypershade). Name the material Light_Bulb_Material.
Step 15: Turn the Color and Ambient Colors up full blast. You may want to change the colors to slightly yellow.
Step 16: Open the Special Effects section of the material and turn the Glow Intensity to .1.

The Glow Intensity is a characteristic of materials that we have not looked at yet. It is pretty self-explanatory though—it adds a glow to the material that makes the object the material is applied to appear to have a glow.

A caveat about this though; remember that it is a post rendering effect. That means that Maya renders the scene, and then goes back and paints the glow on. The problem with this is that if you have any reflective surfaces that reflect an object with this material, the glow will not appear in the reflection. This is why you need to make sure Ambient Color is activated because that will be reflected. Having a material that has its own Ambient Color will help minimize the difference between the material itself and the reflected material.

Step 17: Render (Figure 9.22).

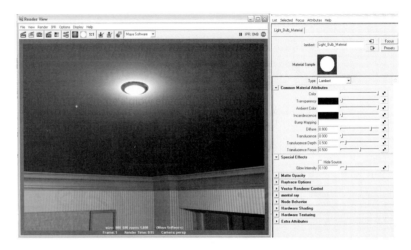

FIGURE 9.22   Rendered light object with bulb that does not cast shadows and a material that glows.

Step 18: Create/Apply any other materials to the geometry of the light.
Step 19: Group the PotLight, Bulb and any other geometry that is part of the overhead light.
Step 20: Center the pivot and rename the group to Overhead_ Light.

Duplicating and Adjusting

Step 21: Duplicate and move the new duplicates so that there are six lights in the room (Figure 9.23).

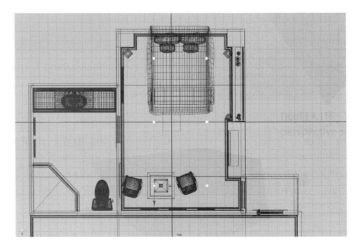

FIGURE 9.23   Placed Overhead_Lights.

Placing multiple light sources in the room like this does several good things for us. First it creates visual interest in the ceiling. Second, each of these placed lights will help soften and mellow the shadows cast by the other lights.

Why?

Step 22: Reduce the intensity of all the lights. In the Outliner, expand each of the Overhead_Lights groups. Ctrl-select each of the PotLights within each group. Show the Channel Box (where the Attributes Editor is probably currently visible) by clicking the Show Channel Box/Layer Editor button (very top corner of the interface). In the Channel Box, under the SHAPES area, in the PotLightShape Node, change the Intensity from 7 to 1.

 Now that you have 6 lights in the room, there is no need for each light to have such a high intensity. Reducing the intensity will help give a much more subtle look.

Why?

Note that the Intensity was changed via the Channel Box—not the Attributes Editor. Even if you have multiple lights selected, if you change any attributes in the Attribute Editor, Maya will change that attribute only for the last light selected. However, if you change a node characteristic in the Channels Box, it will change it for all objects (including lights) selected.

Step 23: Render (Figure 9.24).

 It will probably appear a little dark at this point. Not to worry, it is generally better to use more lights at less intensity to create your lighting scheme than few with high intensity. Since there are many lights yet to be placed, having early renderings that appear a little dark is not of great concern.

Why?

FIGURE 9.24   Rendered room with multiple Intensity = 1 light.

Step 24: Duplicate and place some more Overhead_Lights in the bathroom, above the window seat, in the entry way and wherever else you see fit.

This probably will not make a significant difference in how your scene generally appears (although areas like the entryway, hall and bathroom will go from black to having light); but since the same Overhead_Light is repeated several places in this scene, putting them in place now is a good time to do it.

Step 25: Organize your lights. Group lights by room, and create a new Layer. Assign all your lights to this layer.

As the number of lights you create increases, they can actually become a hassle if you need to add things or animate things in your scene. If all your lights are on a layer, you can easily make the layer not visible.

Volumetric Lights

Step 26: Create a new Point light.

We are going to do it wrong first to see why Volumetric Lights work better in this situation.

Step 27: Position it inside the shades at the headboard.
Step 28: Activate Shadows for the light (Depth Map Shadow); activate decay (Linear), and change the intensity to 5.
Step 29: Duplicate and position in the other shade.
Step 30: Render (Figure 9.25).

Pretty ugly. The problem is that if you reduce the intensity of the light so that the shadows on the ceiling are not so disproportionate, the light inside the shade ends up being too dark—so dark that there does not appear to be any light on in there at all.

Essentially, the solution here is to have a light with a very small area of illumination that does not throw all across the room, but still provides a very intense light inside the shade. Volumetric Lights to the rescue.

Step 31: Change each of these lights to Volumetric light. Select the light, and in the Attributes Editor, in the Volume Light Attributes Section change the Type from Point Light to Volume Light. All other settings (Intensity = 5, Use Depth Map Shadows) should remain the same.

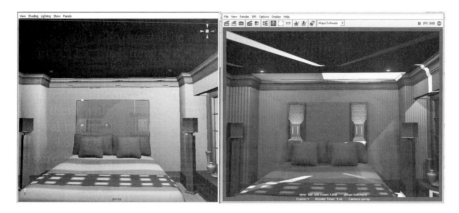

FIGURE 9.25   Results of using Point Lights inside of shades. Notice undesirable lights on ceiling.

Step 32: Scale each so that they approximate Figure 9.26. That is a light that brushes the ceiling. Rename the lights Headboard_Light and Headboard_Light2.

Step 33: Render.

Suddenly, you have a hot light inside the shade. But the shadows (and light) do not extend all over the room. The results are a bit of light on the ceiling, but no strange white bars of light.

Why?

FIGURE 9.26   Positioned and scaled Headboard_Light.

Step 34: Organize. Group the headboard lights together and add them to your Light Layer.

Translucency

Step 35: Create a Point light. Rename it Lamp_Light.
Step 36: Position it inside one of the lamps to either side of the bed.
Step 37: Change the setting to Intensity = 1.5, Decay Rate = Linear, Use Depth Map Shadows.
Step 38: Make the lamp shade not cast shadows. Remember that this is done by selecting the lamp shade, and then in the Attributes Editor, find the shape node for the shade. In the Render Stats section turn off Casts Shadows.
Step 39: Render (Figure 9.27).

FIGURE 9.27   Render of lamp shade not casting shadows. Something is still wrong, though.

Sure enough, as seen before, the lamp shade not casting shadows allows the light inside the shade to shine through. However, the look is still wrong. This is largely because the outside of the shade—the side we see—is opposite the light side. So the lamp shade—which should be glowing—looks dark.

The solution to this interestingly enough is not a lighting issue, but rather a materials issue. One solution would be to make the lamp shade have Incandescence or Ambient Color activated. This would make the surface appear to be lit; however, it would not be reacting to the lights around it. If you turned all the lights off, or choose to relight for daytime with light streaming in from the window, you would have to go back and reedit materials.

Instead, Maya provides something called Translucency. The idea of a translucent material is one that light may pass through. This is not transparent (we have seen the power of that with the shower); but translucent. Think of rice paper,

paper, or leaves. Light passes through all these surfaces, but you cannot see through them. Lamp shades are a perfect place to use translucent materials.

Step 40: Create a new Lambert material. Rename it Lamp_Shade_Material.
Step 41: Change the color to a yellowish-brown. Turn the Translucence to .5, Translucence Depth to 5, and Translucence Focus to 0 (Figure 9.28).
Step 42: Assign this material to the faces of the shade to be translucent.

Why? *The entire shade may not be transparent. If it is, just apply this material to the object. But in the case of our scene, the shade has metal parts at the top and bottom of the shade; selecting just the faces in the middle will make just that part of the shade have that translucent glow.*

Step 43: Render (Figure 9.28).

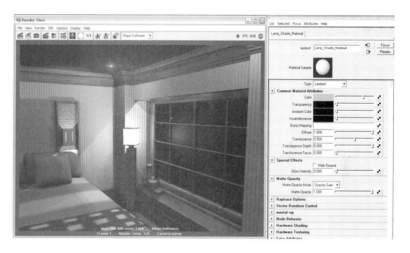

FIGURE 9.28   Rendered lamp shade making use of translucent materials.

Step 44: Duplicate and place Lamp_Light to the other side. You may choose to delete the second shade and duplicate the first to replace it with (Figure 9.29).

Why? *A bit of a caveat here. If you plan to use translucent materials, the organization of your polygons (topology) of your shades becomes important. For instance, the shades to begin with in this file had polygons both on the outside and inside. These double polygons can make for difficult-to-control translucent results—often artifacts (glowing lines) will appear across a surface.*

To fix the problem just delete the inside polygons so that you are left with only one set of polygons that will be translucent; the results are much easier to control.

FIGURE 9.29   Completed lamps.

Step 45: Group the new lights and shades together with the lamp bases. Add these to the Light Layer.

Lighting the Artwork with Spot Lights

Step 46: Create a new Spot Light. Create > Lights > Spot Light.
Step 47: Position the light over and in front of any of the hanging pictures in the room (Figure 9.30). Use the Move Tool to move the light into

FIGURE 9.30   Spot Light positioned to illuminate wall hanging.

position. Either rotate or use the Move Tool with Show Manipulators active to point the Spot Light at the picture.

 When you need to have clear control over how far a light is throwing or how wide the influence is, a Spot Light is often a good choice. In this case, a Spot Light will **Why?** *give us that pool of light that picture lights usually have.*

As you position this, using the Rotate versus the Move Tool is largely a personal preference issue. Using the Move Tool with Show Manipulators active is the easiest method. This method also becomes tremendously useful when you begin animating, so getting used to working with it now is a good thing.

Step 48: Adjust the attributes of the Spot Light. Change the Intensity = 5, the Decay Rate = Linear, the Cone Angle = 60, and Penumbra Angle = –10. Activate Use Depth Map Shadows.

 These values are found. That means, we entered a good guess, took a render, and then tweaked the settings, rendered, repeated, and so on. Lighting is often this way. **Why?** *Just because the values are provided here, does not mean that there is some secret to plucking values from the air. Adjust the settings to get the look you want.*

Step 49: Render (Figure 9.31).
Step 50: Create geometry to represent the light source. This includes creating the actual light bulb (in this case a simple flattened sphere with Casts Shadows turned off). A suggested form is seen in Figure 9.32.

FIGURE 9.31   Rendering with Spot Light.

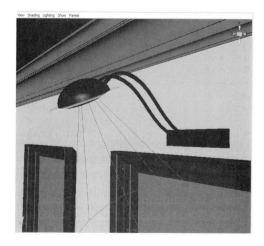

FIGURE 9.32   Geometry for the light.

Step 51: Group the geometry and the Spot Light. Call the group Picture_Light.

Step 52: Duplicate the Picture_Light and place it on other pictures in the scene.

Step 53: Save your file.

Step 54: Render to your heart's content.

Tutorial Conclusion

Further work could yet be done. Place lights in the scene in places where it is too dark. You may add new picture light, you may want to place additional lights in the ceiling. Remember lots of lights with lower intensity can often help give a scene a much more life-like appearance than few lights with high intensity. Tweak to your hearts content.

Figure 9.33 and Figure 9.34 are some renderings of the room with some additional lighting schemes for the night time. Be sure to check these images out in color on the CD-ROM. The results of this tutorial are found on the CD-ROM saved as the file Tutorial_9_1.mb.

ON THE CD

FIGURE 9.33   Night-time renderings.

FIGURE 9.34   Further night-time renderings.

TUTORIAL 9.2   DAYTIME LIGHTING

Interestingly enough, daytime lighting is a bit tougher than night time. Largely this is because there are less light sources, but yet the room is still brighter than the night time scene. If rendering engines all calculated bounced light with any sort of speed, this would not be such a hassle; but to avoid rendering delays we will need to fake the bouncing of lights.

Objectives:

1. Use Directional Light to simulate sunlight.
2. Use Area Lights to simulate the reflected light off walls, floors, mirrors and windows.

Step 1: Set your project.
Step 2: Start with a clean slate. Either delete the lights in scene Tutorial_9_1.mb, or open Tutorial_8_2.

If you use Tutorial_9_1.mb, remember to not only delete your lights (you could also just turn all their Intensity values to 0), but also make any material adjustments. Specifically, if you used any materials to create glowing light bulbs for instance, make sure you turn the Ambient Color or Incandescence off as well as deactivating the Glow on that material.

Step 3: Create the sun. Do this with a Directional Light (Create > Lights > Directional Light).
Step 4: Rename to Sunlight.
Step 5: Position and rotate Sunlight as seen in Figure 9.35. This essentially is having the light come in through the single window in the room. Note that Figure 9.35 is the front View Panel.

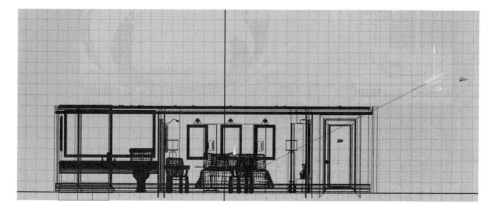

FIGURE 9.35   Positioned Sunlight.

Note that there are actually two manipulators in the scene with the Sunlight selected. This is the directional manipulator (similar to the Spot Light). It is an easy way to aim the Directional Light. Putting that second manipulator right in the middle of the room ensures that the sunlight will be pointing into the room.

Step 6: Activate Use Depth Map Shadows for Sunlight.
Step 7: Render.

 The render will probably be all black. This is because even the plane that is the glass window pane is stopping the light.

Step 8: Select the window pane, turn off Casts Shadows. Remember this is in the shape node of that plane in the Render Stats section.
Step 9: Render (Figure 9.36).

 Raytracing and Maya Software do not calculate bounced light. The light coming off of Sunlight (even with no Decay) is coming in through the window and stopping as soon as it hits the floor, wall, or bed. Nothing is bouncing, and thus the room appears all dark.

FIGURE 9.36 Rendering showing the daylight streaming in from the window; but still revealing a dark room.

Step 10: Increase the Intensity to 6 for Sunlight. Render.

 Giving this Sunlight a very high value will tend to wash out the spot where the rays hit; but this is not a bad thing. In this case it will make the shot look more photo-realistic; a bit of targeted washed areas are often a nice touch.

Step 11: Create a wash of light from the window. Create an Area Light (Create > Lights > Area Light) and position it so that it sits just inside of the window. Make sure that the light is pointing straight inside of the room. You can do this by entering Rotate X = 90 and Rotate Z = 0 in the Channel Box, or by manually rotating it, or by using the manipulator. Rename to WindowWash.

We already have a Directional Light (Sunlight) representing the sun; so why create this new light to put in the window? The Directional Light does a great job of representing the harsh rays of the sun—which you can see with the shadows up in Figure 9.36. However, check out most any window and you will find that besides the direct rays, there is lots and lots of light flooding the room in all angles coming from that window. This is largely because of all the bounced light that is occurring outside. This added Area Light will provide that general wash of light coming into the room.

Step 12: Alter the Attributes to Decay Rate = Linear. Change Intensity to .5.
Step 13: Activate Use Depth Map Shadows. Change the resolution to 32 and turn the Filter Size up to 4.

Using a Depth Map Shadow with a very low resolution and very high filter size will create extremely soft shadows. This wash light should have a very gentle cast and very, very soft shadow.

Step 14: Render (Figure 9.37).

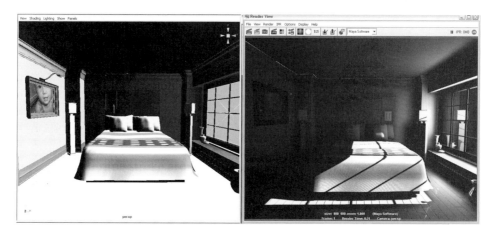

FIGURE 9.37   Rendered results of Sunlight and WindowWash.

Still not there yet, but notice that now there is a nice glow around the window. Note that as soon as you add something like this the View Panel's version of what the lighting scheme provides becomes really bizarre—a perfect illustration of why not to rely on the View Panel's lighting estimate.

Because of this, from here on out, the screen shots will be shown after hitting 6 on the keyboard. This shows colors and textures but not the washed-out lighting estimate.

Step 15: Create bounced light from the floor. Do this with an Area Light (Create > Lights > Area Light).

 The area light will allow for a nice diffuse light. Additionally, you can mimic the surface actually being struck by the sunlight on the floor; that is, you can resize this area light to match the actual light, bouncing surface.

Step 16: Rename this Area Light to FloorBounce. Activate Linear Decay. Adjust the Intensity to .5.

 Why no shadows? Although most accurately, the bounced light off the floor would indeed provide shadows, the way we are using the lights is to provide a gentle wash. By leaving shadows off, we can more easily begin to bathe the room in light.

Step 17: Rotate it 90 along X. You can do this with the Rotation Tool or make the Channel Box visible and enter 90 in the Rotate X input field.
Step 18: Resize and position FloorBounce to approximate the floor hotspot from Figure 9.36. Size and move this light like any other object—with the Move and Scale Tools.

 The idea of this Area Light is that it emits the light that the floor would normally have bounced. By taking a quick look at the rendering produced and shown in Figure 9.36, you can see where the hot spot is—where the sunlight would be striking the floor and reflecting off of.

Be sure that you move this FloorBounce just off the surface of the floor. If it is beneath the floor or on the floor, you can get some strange artifacts poping up on the floor during rendering.

Step 19: Render (Figure 9.38).

 Getting started here there will be some strange results; for instance the undersides of the pillows should not be glowing as they are. In addition, the wall on the left would probably not have such a hot spot as the bed would have blocked a lot of that light. However, the idea here is to gently layer light onto the scene. Some of the good

things that are happening include the blush of light on the lower walls and the ceiling is beginning to receive some light.

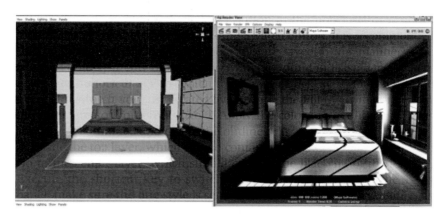

FIGURE 9.38   Rendering and setup of the FloorBounce area light on the floor (pointed upward).

Step 20: Duplicate FloorBounce. Rename to CeilingBounce. Change the Intensity to .35.

Since the ceiling is not receiving much direct sunlight, the light it would be bouncing would be light bounced from other surfaces. So, its illumination would be lower intensity.

Why?

Step 21: Rotate, position and resize CeilingBounce so that it is smaller than the ceiling and right beneath it (Figure 9.39).

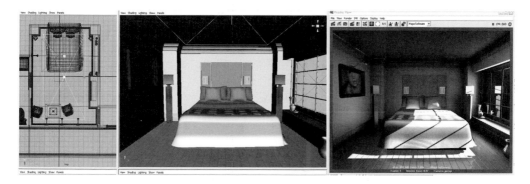

FIGURE 9.39   Results of adding Ceiling Bounce.

The CeilingBounce light is smaller than the ceiling. The reason for this is that the Area Light has a splay. If the CeilingBounce were the same size as the ceiling, it actually would not light the walls that meet the ceiling as well as it does when it is just a bit smaller.

Why?

Step 22: Duplicate FloorBounce. Rename BigFloorBounce. Reduce the Intensity to .2.
Step 23: Resize to fit the entire room (Figure 9.40).

Creating an additional light that represents the floor bounce essentially makes reference to the light that would be bouncing off the ceiling. This bounced light would be at a much lower intensity, but would be a much broader light. Yes, there are two area lights on the floor, but each of these is representing different bounced light.

Why?

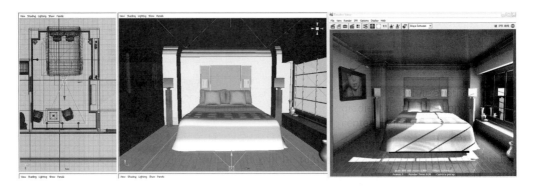

FIGURE 9.40 BigFloorBounce in action.

Step 24: Create a new Area Light. Rename it to WestWallBounce.
Step 25: Activate Decay Rate Linear. Change the Intensity to .2.
Step 26: Rotate, position, and scale it to match the West wall (the wall opposite the window).

Light coming in from that window would bounce off of all the walls, but the wall opposite the window (the west wall) would bounce the most. So placing an area light there is needed.

Why?

Do note that again, the area light is slightly smaller than the bouncing area of the wall. Also make sure that the light is close to the wall, but not in it.

Step 27: Render (Figure 9.41).
Step 28: Create and add bounce lights to the north wall (NorthWallBounce) with an intensity of .2.

FIGURE 9.41   Added WestWallBounce.

Step 29: Add another bounce light to the south wall (SouthWallBounce) with an Intensity setting of .1.

Why? *Why? The north wall (the wall behind the bed) will have received—and thus bounce—quite a bit of light. So the intensity of .2 will represent that well. The south wall is in probably the darkest part of the room, so it should have a much lower intensity.*

Step 30: Render (Figure 9.42).
Step 31: Adjust. As you look at the rendering setup, you may find that you find the scene to be too dark, or too bright. Turn the Intensities down (or up) of the lights that may be contributing the overly dark or bright feeling of the room.

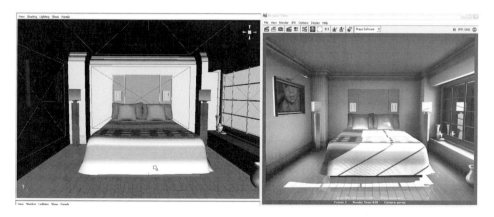

FIGURE 9.42   Rendering with several Areas Lights representing the bounced light on various walls.

Adjusting the lights and doing test renderings is always part of the fun. The lighting tests you do will vary widely depending on what your monitor is, what its settings are, if you are on a Mac or PC, etc. Rendering tutorials are always a bit tough as what appears on the author's monitor may not be the look you get on yours. Adjust to taste.

RELATIONSHIP EDITOR—LIGHT LINKING

Step 32: Select Relationships Window > Relationships Editor > Light Linkings > Light Centric.

As we were building the lighting scheme we took some shortcuts in making the bounced lights not cast shadows. One of the problems with this is things like the bottoms of the pillows on the bed are really well lit by FloorBounce—which they should not be.

Maya allows you to define which objects are going to receive light from what lights. As we have built the lights, one of the options in the Attributes Editor for each light is "Illuminates by Default." We have left this on for every light. But now, we want to go back and tell lights like the FloorBounce to not light the bed.

Figure 9.43 shows what the Relationships Editor looks like for light linking. On the left are the lights in the scene. On the right are all the objects in the scene. When you select a light on the left, objects that are lit by that light are highlighted on the right. For now, every light you select on the left will highlight every object on the right.

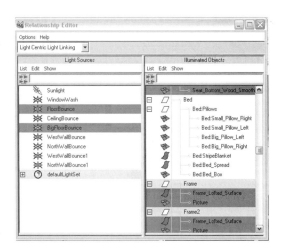

FIGURE 9.43 Relationships Editor for setting up lights not illuminating certain objects.

Step 33: In Light Sources column (the left) select FloorBounce, and Ctrl-select BigFloorBounce.

Step 34: In the Illuminated Objects column (the right) find the objects that are your bed.

Step 35: Click on each of the objects that are your bed. This will deselect them (Figure 9.43).

 By deselecting the objects that are the bed, we are telling Maya to not light any of the objects that are the bed with either FloorBounce or BigFloorBounce.

Why?

Step 36: Now activate shadows for FloorBounce and BigFloorBounce (Figure 9.44).

 Now that these lights on the floor are not going to be blocked by the bed, they can go ahead and cast some shadows. Doing this will help to put some of the depth back into the scene.

Why?

The scene is starting to feel like a daytime light is coming into the room. However, there is one big problem that totally destroys the illusion—the view out the window.

FIGURE 9.44   Activated shadows for FloorBounce and BigFloorBounce.

Cycs

 Cycs is short for cyclorama. Cycs are an old theatre technique in which a depth and space that do not really exist are intimated through a painted drop. In 3D we can do the same thing to help plug holes in the visual scheme like seeing out a window during the daytime.

Why?

Step 37: In the top view create a curve similar to Figure 9.45. Do this with the CV Curve Tool.

The idea here is to create a curve that when made into a curved wall will provide a good look from any angle in the room. From the window, you should not be able to see the edge of the cyc; this is why a gentle curve does just the trick and is preferable to a flat plane.

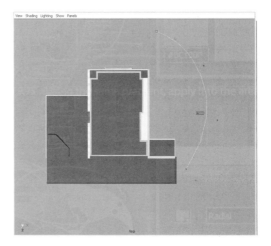

FIGURE 9.45   Cyc curve.

Step 38: Duplicate the Curve and move it up in space (Figure 9.46).

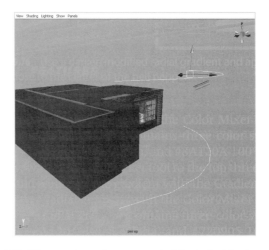

FIGURE 9.46   Second curve needed for Lofted Surface.

Step 39: Select both curves and select Modeling | Surfaces > Loft (Options). Make sure to reset settings before hitting Loft (Figure 9.47).

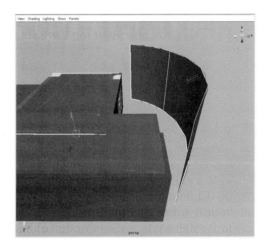

FIGURE 9.47   Lofted cyc

Step 40: Rename to Cyc. Delete its history and delete the curves.

Step 41: Create a new Lambert material named Cyc_Material.

ON THE CD

Step 42: Import into the Color and Incandescence channels the image Cyc.tif (found on the CD-ROM in the Amazing_Wooden_ Man project folder (in the sourceimages folder of course).

ON THE CD   Why?

This image is just a stitched-together image of photos of my backyard. You can really use any image you would like here; but this image is included on the CD-ROM, and you probably already have it on your hard drive.

Why import it into both Color and Incandescence? This material will actually not be lit. It should not be beholden to any of the lights in the scene and should not cast or receive shadows. Ambient Color will allow this material to have no lights on it, but still show up as though it were fully lit.

Step 43: Apply Cyc_Material to Cyc (Figure 9.48).

Step 44: Select Cyc and make it not cast or receive shadows. Double-click cyc to open its attributes in the Attributes Editor. Find the CycShape Node, and expand the Render Stats. Turn off Casts Shadows and Receive Shadows.

Why?

If Casts Shadows remained on, this cyc would actually block the light coming from the Directional Light (Sunlight). Remember that the Directional Lights come from an infinite distance away.

If Receive Shadows was turned on, this surface could potentially show shadows that were cast by lights inside the room. This would make for a strange sight to see the shadow of the window on the trees outside!

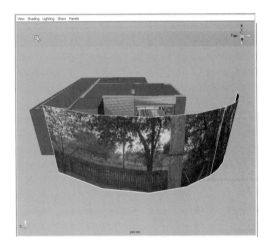

FIGURE 9.48   Cyc with material applied.

Step 45: Use the Relationship Editor to make the Cyc be lit by no lights. Do this by selecting all the lights in the Lights column (including the defaultLightSet), and then deselecting the Cyc on the objects column.

 Since this object has a material that has got Incandescence active, it has its own **Why?** *inner light. There is no need for Maya to calculate light for this object.*

Step 46: Render (Figure 9.49).

FIGURE 9.49   Rendering with Cyc.

Why?
As you move the camera inside the room, you should be able to see the cyc holding up out the window. If you can too easily see edge (tops or bottom or edges) you may need to resize the cyc.

Also note that when you render you might be getting a whole lot of reflection on the inside of the window (because of the brightness of all the lights placed in the scene). If this happens, just select the material that is assigned to the pane of glass and turn down the reflection settings.

Tutorial Conclusion

So there it is. Ironically the lighting scheme that has more light actually uses fewer lights. However, each of the lights used in this day-time lighting scene are providing a general wash of the scene.

Thinking in terms of painting with lights and general washes of light is often the best solution to scenes that have heavy primary light sources. Since mental ray is so long on rendering (and really beyond the scope of this book), this fake bounced light provides some very comparable results.

So over the course of these tutorials, we have placed most ever type of lighting instrument that Maya provides. You have adjusted where they point, how they cast shadows, and how they decay. You have adjusted color and intensity to create more than standard white light. Most importantly, you have added a sense of ambiance to what was a very stale and boring scene.

Lighting can almost be another character in a still or animation. Taking good time to create the lighting scheme of a project always pays dividends. As you move forward, do not short change or cheapen your project by lighting it poorly.

CHALLENGES, EXERCISES, OR ASSIGNMENTS

1. The daytime lighting scheme is a sort of midday light (bright, near white). Light the scene for sunrise. (Hint, the angle and color of the sun will be different).
2. Light the scene for sunset.
3. What sort of interesting scheme could be developed for the bathroom—especially around the mirror?
4. Add ambiance to the hallway; how could that be lit to indicate an upscale apartment, or a scary run down one?
5. Light your own scene (if you have been modeling one). Try lighting it for day, night, sunrise, and sunset.
6. How would any of these scenes be lit differently for a romantic evening? Candles anyone? How would the colors change; how far would the light from the candles throw?

ORGANIC MODELING

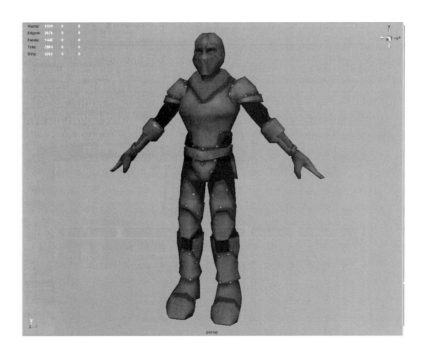

There has been a lot covered so far. You have created a room from scratch including modeling techniques using NURBS and polygons. You have created custom materials to apply to this room and controlled through effective UV Mapping the way these materials laid across these objects. Most recently, you used Maya's lighting tools to bring the room to life—to give it a depth and visual complexity. As fun as this process has been, though, the real challenge begins when you begin to deal with objects that are not man-made.

Organic modeling, texturing, and animating uses many of the same tools as we have explored in earlier chapters. However, the number of polygons and the amount of refining these polygons need begins to jump considerably when working with organic shapes.

In this chapter, we are going to be tackling two models. Each model will become progressively more complex and require more tweaking. In the first, we will actually create our Amazing Wooden Man (Figure 10.1). Although potentially he could be a segmented model with different polygon meshes representing different parts of his body, for illustration's sake (and for the benefits of future rigging), we will instead model him as a single mesh.

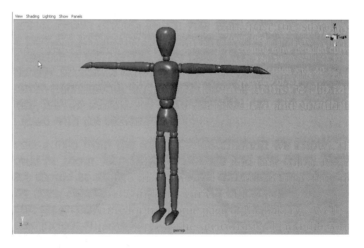

FIGURE 10.1   Completed amazing wooden man.

In the second tutorial we will model a game model (Figure 10.2). The reason a game model is a good one at this point is because of its limited polygon count. Games must render polygon meshes (characters and maps) in realtime. Because of this, a manageable poly-count becomes extremely important. But after you have hashed out a game model, a more complex model becomes much more intuitive to tackle.

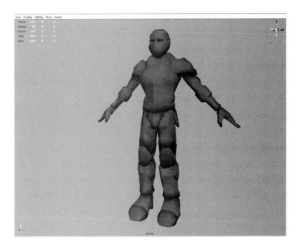

FIGURE 10.2   Completed game model.

Ultimately, in the next chapter we will look at adding textures to these models, as we have done in Figure 10.3. We will tackle UV Mapping and creating custom texture maps that can add all sorts of visual complexity to those drab polygons.

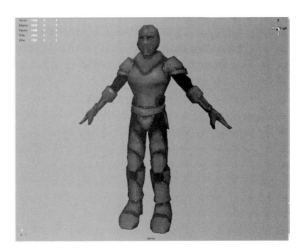

FIGURE 10.3   Textured game model.

These tutorials are not easy. Organic modeling is not easy—it takes good technique, a lot of time, patience, and a good eye for form. Remember that organic modelers did not start out as fantastic modelers—you have to work to get that way. If it was easy, anyone could do it, and you would not be reading this book. Give yourself some time and know that each attempt and project will be better than the last—so your best work is yet to come.

TUTORIAL 10.1   MODELING THE AMAZING WOODEN MAN

Objectives:

1. Create a single mesh character.
2. Create forms using Extrude Face.
3. Master the Mirror Geometry Tool.

Step 1: Set your project. Obviously this can be built right within the Amazing_Wooden_Man project we have been using up to now.
Step 2: Create a new file. Save it as "Man."
Step 3: Create the base shape. Create a new Polygon Primitive Cube with Subdivision Width = 2 and Subdivision Depth = 2. (Create > Polygon Primitives > Cube (Options).

Why? *Even though later we will be smoothing this surface, having just four sides to any organic shape is terribly limiting. By having eight sides, suddenly squarish-looking forms can be made to look much more round. More importantly, with that extra row of points down each side, you can get much more detailed shapes.*

Step 4: Round the form. In the top View Panel select the horizontal middle row of points and scale them in the X direction to match Figure 10.4.
Step 5: Continue rounding. Again in the top View Panel, select the vertical middle row of points and scale them in the Z direction to match Figure 10.5.

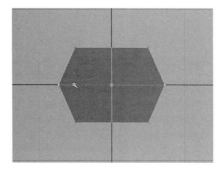

FIGURE 10.4   Rounding the form by scaling horizontal vertices.

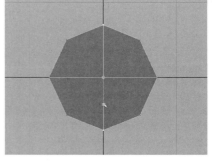

FIGURE 10.5   Scaling the horizontal oints to round the form.

You can see that very quickly we are starting to get a much more rounded shape. Of course, this could also have been done by creating a cylinder—except that a cylinder has triangles at its caps—rather than the quadrangles we now have.

Note that smoothing might also have been a temptation to use at this point, but that would have left you with rounded tops and bottoms; these flat caps at the top and bottom will ultimately be much easier to work with as we work down the body.

Step 6: Scale the entire object a bit more flat in the Y.

Step 7: Extrude the top of the head. Select the top faces and Extrude Face. Resize a bit to make the top of the head (Figure 10.6).

 Remember that if it has been a while since you use the software or anyone else has used the software, or just to be safe—make sure that you have Polygons > Keep Faces Together checked. Multiple selected faces will then stay together when you extrude.

Step 8: Finish the head shape. Select the faces on the bottom of the form. Extrude Face, and then resize to match Figure 10.7.

Step 9: Create a Smooth Proxy. In Object mode, select the object and press Ctrl-` or select Modeling | Polygons > Smooth Proxy.

 Since ultimately this model will need to be smoothed, you do not want to wait too long before creating the smoothed version. As soon as you create a smooth version, often adjustments will need to be made.

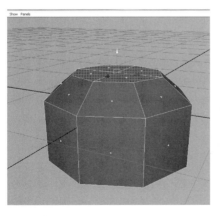

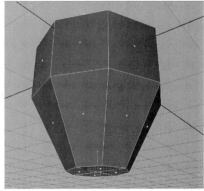

FIGURE 10.6 Extruded faces that have been resized to make the top of the head.

FIGURE 10.7 Extruded faces out the bottom of head to define form.

Remember that if you have not used Smooth Proxy in a while, or have used it on another project, or someone else has used your machine, make sure that you reset the settings for the Smooth Proxy before applying it to the form.

Step 10: Label the objects. In the Outliner will be a group called pCube1 SmoothProxyGroup. Children of that will include the low-poly and high-poly versions. Label them HiPolyMan and LowPolyMan.

Step 11: Add the smoothed version to a referenced layer. In the Layers Editor, create a new layer and name it Smooth. Click the second column until the R (for Reference) appears. In the Outliner select the smoothed version (HiPolyMan) and then right-click on the Smooth layer and select Add Selected Objects from the pop-down layer.

 As we work, the low-poly version will be the model edited. When working with Smooth Proxies, make sure that you do not swap between editing the high-poly and

Why? *low-poly version as it tends to make a mess of the streamlined node structure in Maya. In this case, we will be exclusively editing the low-poly version.*

However, since both are right on top of each other it can become very easy to accidentally select the high-poly version. By placing it on its own layer and making it a (nonselectable) Referenced layer, you can avoid selecting unwanted objects or components.

Step 12: Adjust the form with vertices. Select and adjust any vertices or collections of vertices to refine the shape created thus far (Figure 10.8).

 Note that the position of the vertices is actually what ties the low-poly and high-poly versions together. If you select the low-poly version as an object and resize it, the

Why? *high-poly version will not update. But if you select all the vertices (right-click on the object and select Vertex from the Marking Menu—and then marquee around all the vertices) and scale the group of vertices—the high-poly version will get bigger or smaller. After you have created a Smooth Proxy, make sure you always work with components—not objects.*

Head to Neck Transition

Step 13: Select the polygons on the bottom of the head.

Step 14: Extrude the faces—but not away from their original position. Select Modeling | Edit Polygons > Extrude Face—but do not pull the manipulators to move the new extrusion away (Figure 10.9).

 So what is the point of extruding without extruding away? Remember that one way to define how sharp or soft a corner is on a smoothed poly mesh is how close the sub-

divisions on the low-poly mesh are to each other. By creating an extrusion right on top of itself, there is very little distance between the subdivisions (none actually). The net result is the bottom of the head ends up being flat.

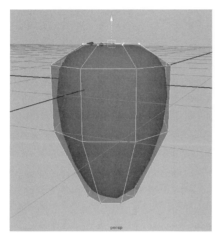

FIGURE 10.8   Adjusted low-poly version—adjusted by scaling and moving vertices.

FIGURE 10.9   Added extrusion without moving away from original position. This provides a sharp bottom to the form.

Step 15: Extrude Face again. You can do this by pressing g on your keyboard to activate the last used tool. Again, make sure to not pull this extrusion away.

Step 16: Swap to the Scale Tool and scale these extruded faces smaller in place (Figure 10).

Why swap to the Scale Tool? Largely this is a matter of convenience in workflow. If you were to use the Scale Tools within the Extrude Face Tool, the default would scale in just one direction at a time and they would not be scaled in the middle of the form. True, you could click the little blue dot that is part of the Extrude Face Tool to swap from local to global, but it is just as quick to press r (to swap to Scale Tool) on your keyboard. Adjust the workflow to your liking.

Step 17: Extrude, move and scale faces twice to create the neck joint. To do this, press g to activate the Extrude Face Tool again. Press r to switch to the Scale Tool and scale the faces outward so that they are slightly smaller than the bottom of the head. Press g to activate the Extrude Face Tool again, and this time, pull the new extrusion down in Y (Figure 10.11).

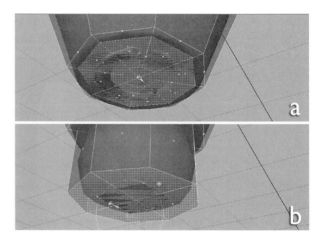

FIGURE 10.10   Extruded and scaled faces; note that they are not extruded away, but remain right on the surface.

FIGURE 10.11   Extruded neck with two new extrusions—the first still right along the face of the bottom of the head (a), and then a second still on the same plane but much larger (b).

Step 18: Create another crisp connection. Again, Extrude Face, scale (Figure 10.12a), then Extrude Face, scale again to create the top of the shoulders (Figure 10.12b).

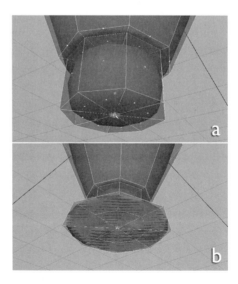

FIGURE 10.12   Additional connection for the bottom of the neck (a and b).

Torso

Step 19: Extrude down to create the body. Do note that it has five extrusions (Figure 10.13). Each of these is simple Extrude Face and then moving and scaling the extruded faces down to create the form.

Why? *Five extrusions actually are fairly significant. Remember that we carefully constructed the head with two subdivisions along depth and width? Here the five extrusions are done for that same reason. Because you have two extrusions up where the arm will come off of the form, you will be able to create an arm that has 8 rows of points allowing for a much more detailed form.*

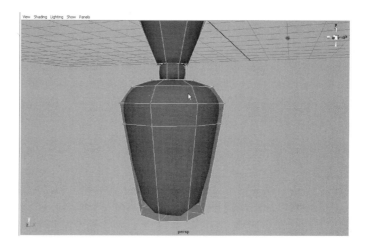

FIGURE 10.13   Extruded body form.

Arms

Step 20: Select the polygons that will become the arm. Choose any side and pick the four polygons shown in Figure 10.14.

Why? *Later, in steps to come, we will be cutting this form in half and mirroring the completed side. Because of this, creating the arm on just one half of the character is all that's needed.*

Do note that in order to get the eight rows of points, we need to select four polygons and not try to build the arm off of just one.

Step 21: Extrude and scale the start of the arm. Modeling | Edit Polygons > Extrude Face. Switch immediately to the Scale Tool (r) and scale the new extrusion to match Figure 10.15.

After you extrude these faces, you will probably have a bit of a hard time seeing them as they will look like they have been swallowed up in the high-poly version. If you need to, pull them out and away temporarily with the Move Tool so you can see them and scale them into the form you want. Be sure to move and rotate them back onto the side of the body when you have found the shape you are looking for.

Remember that to get these faces flat and square, you may need to scale not just in the Y and Z directions but also in the X.

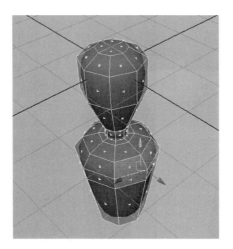

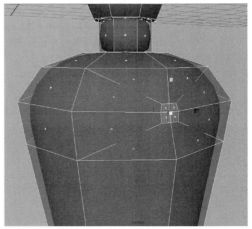

FIGURE 10.14   Selected faces that will become the arms.

FIGURE 10.15   Extruded and scaled faces that will become the arm.

Step 22: Adjust the vertices to create a round shape. Switch to Vertex mode and adjust the vertices either one at a time (via the Move Tool) or in groups (via the Scale Tool). The results should look round like Figure 10.16.

Yes, you could round off the arm later, but doing it now ensures that all of the extrusions you make from here on out to the end of the arm are already rounded—it is a huge time saver in the long run.

Step 23: Extrude out to create the shoulder ball. Select the four faces, and use the Extrude Faces Tool to extrude out to create the arm ball. Note that unlike the neck, this one was created with three extrusions—the first just a bigger version of the original 4 faces (Figure 10.17a), the second to give the socket some roundness (Figure 10.17b) and the third to close off the form (Figure 10.17c). Do not worry about getting an exact sphere.

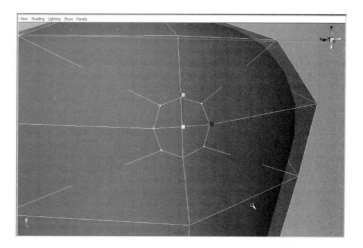

FIGURE 10.16   Rounded arm start.

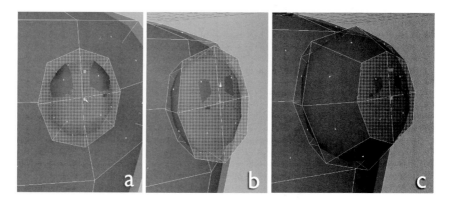

FIGURE 10.17   (a) Creating the sharp connection. (b) Giving the arm roundness. (c) Finishing off the form.

Step 24: Create an overlap for the upper arm. Do this with a series of Extrude Faces. Note that the first one actually extends out (Figure 10.18a), while the second extents back over the shoulder ball (Figure 10.18b). Continue extruding out (Figure 10.18c).

Step 25: Extrude out to the elbow (Figure 10.19a). Add extra Extrude face to make end crisp (Figure 10.19b).

Step 26: Repeat the overlapping steps of step 24 only in reverse. Extrude and scale (Figure 10.20a). Extrude up into the arm (Figure 10.20b). Extrude back out and extrude to create the elbow (Figure 10.20c).

Step 27: Extrude down to the wrist.

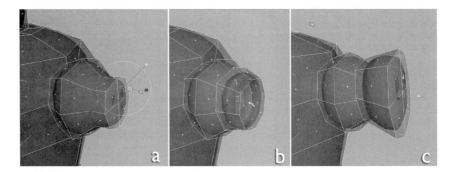

FIGURE 10.18   Creating the overlapping upper arm. (a) Create a bit of an extension. (b) Second extrusion moves back over the shoulder. (c) Third extrusion back out to start the arm.

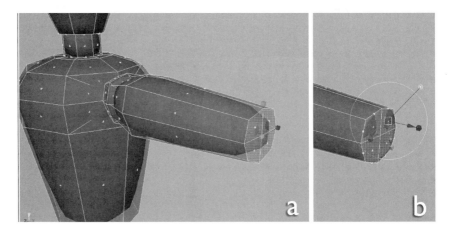

FIGURE 10.19   Extruded to elbow.

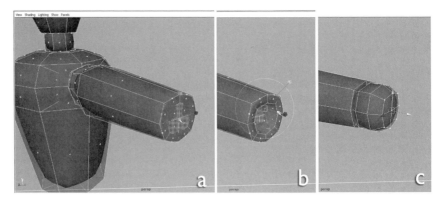

FIGURE 10.20   Continued extrusions to create elbow.

Step 28: Create the wrist, and a hand (that looks like a hot dog) as shown in Figure 10.21.

Step 29: Select rings of vertices and scale them to approximate Figure 10.22.

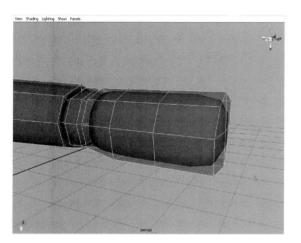

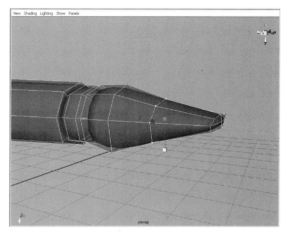

FIGURE 10.21   Rough hand.

FIGURE 10.22   Beginning of sculpted hand.

Why?

There are actually lots of ways to get the hand shape that we will eventually see here. However, in anticipation of potential animation, it is important that we think in rings of polygons (edges and vertices). Without a ring, there is no place for a joint to deform a mesh. So giving the hand three rings of extrusions will allow for future rigging that will allow the hand to bend if we need it to.

Also note that in this step, the scaling of the vertex rings was done only along the y-axis.

Step 30: Select the vertices that would be the palm of the hand. These are all the vertices across the bottom of the form (Figure 10.23).

Step 31: Snap vertices to grid with out Retain Component Spacing. Double-click the Move Tool. In the Attributes Editor, turn off Retain Component Spacing. Hold x down and move the vertices down in the Y direction—they will all snap to the same plane (Figure 10.24).

Step 32: Refine the form. Move the vertices down a little (no need to snap now that they are all level). Now refine the other vertices to approximate Figure 10.25.

Step 33: Make the palm flat. Select the faces that make up the palm (Figure 10.26), and again use Extrude Faces (without moving them).

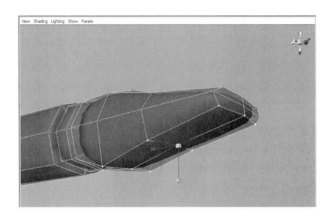

FIGURE 10.23   Selected palm vertices.

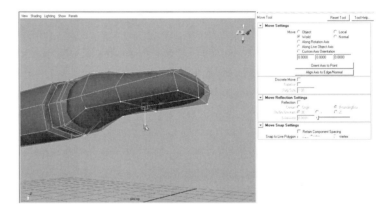

FIGURE 10.24   Snapping the palm vertices to the same plane in Y.

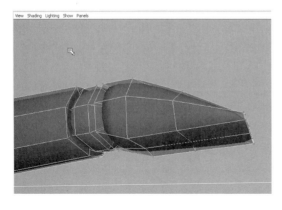

FIGURE 10.25   Rough hand with a bit of refinement.

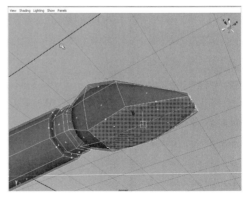

FIGURE 10.26   Flattened palm.

Note that you can make all sorts of tweaks with the hand to get just the form you want. Do make sure to make the tweaks; there is enough geometry in this low-poly version to allow for any form you want.

Also note that at any time, you may want to see what the high-poly smoothed version looks like without the low-poly caged around it. Remember the keyboard shortcuts for this are ` and Shift-`. In Object mode select the low-poly mesh, and press `—the low-poly will hide. Press ` again, and the high-poly version will be hid just showing the low-poly version. Press Shift-` and both will be visible.

Trunk

Step 34: Extrude the belly and trunk areas. Use the same techniques listed previously to get the hard edges of one part to another (Figure 10.27).

Be sure that you have an extra extrusion on the bottom of the trunk to get the hard edge. Also remember that if you forget to do something like that, you can go back and using the Cut Faces tool, you can make a new slice very close to the extant edge and get the same tight cornered results.

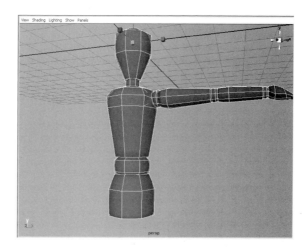

FIGURE 10.27   Completed belly and trunk.

Legs

Step 35: Select the two polygons that make up one half of the bottom of the trunk (Figure 10.28).

Remember that we are only modeling half the character. If you were to select all four polygons at the bottom of the trunk and then extruded them (as we are going to do in the next step) you would be left with one big joint instead of two hip joints.

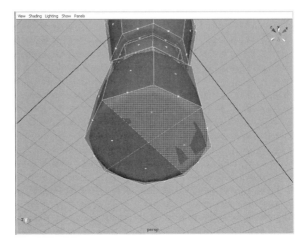

FIGURE 10.28   Selecting the polygons that will become the legs.

Step 36: Extrude and reshape to start legs. Modeling | Edit Polygons > Extrude Face. Then resize the polygons right along the same plane (do not move them up or down in Y (Figure 10.29a). Then, switch to Vertex mode and reshape the two polygons to a rounded shape (Figure 10.29b).

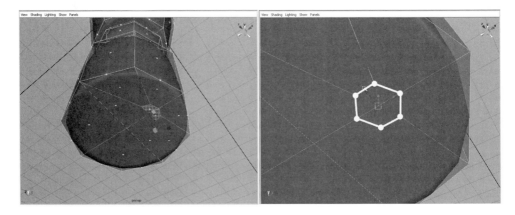

FIGURE 10.29   (a) Extruding and rescaling the faces that will become the leg. (b) Adjusting the shape to form a rounded form from which to build the leg (highlights added).

As discussed earlier, getting the rounded shape early avoids the process of having to round the entire leg one vertex row at a time later.

Notice that this time we are working with a six-sided shape instead of the eight-sided shape we worked with in the upper body. This is not of great concern, and you should still be able to get a nice rounded form.

Step 37: Extrude Face down to create the thigh, knee, calf, and ankle (Figure 10.30).

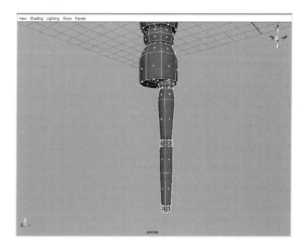

FIGURE 10.30   Extruded leg.

Foot

Step 38: Select the faces that make up the very bottom of the ankle. Extrude them and scale them only in the width (in this case along the X). Give it your best guess in width as to how wide the foot will be. (Figure 10.31a).
Step 39: Select the outlying vertices and move them so you are left with a tighter form (Figure 10.31b).

Rearranging the vertices down on this surface will give us a cleaner mesh to start building the foot from. It also helps to point out any issues with how sharp the edge of the ankle sphere shape is. You can make adjustments as needed.

Step 40: Extrude the (now) bottom two faces twice. Each time be sure to move it down in the Y direction (Figure 10.32).

This seems like a strange start to a foot doesn't it? The plan here is to extrude out front to create the foot and toes, and extrude out the back to create the ankle.

There is no need to always be linearly building in only one direction; sometimes starting in the middle and working out in both directions is just the ticket.

Two extrusions seem like we are adding unnecessary geometry; but it really is adding geometry needed to get the right form. By making sure that this surface has the necessary geometry, we can avoid having to go back in later and splitt and cut.

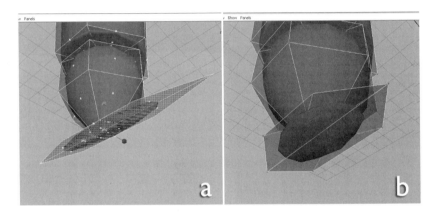

FIGURE 10.31   Creating the start of the foot.

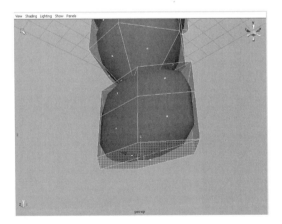

FIGURE 10.32   Start of the foot. Note two extrusions.

Step 41: Select the six polygons that are the front of the foot and extrude them out three times. Each time, resize and move to get a rough foot shape (Figure 10.33).

Note that in each of the screenshots, the Move Tool is being used to move the extruded faces out. The process used in those shots were Modeling | Edit Polygons > Extrude Faces and then immediately w on the keyboard to swap to the Move Tool. This way, the new extrusions move all along one axis (in this case Z) rather than splaying out along the normals as would happen if you used the default move functions of the Extrude Faces Tool.

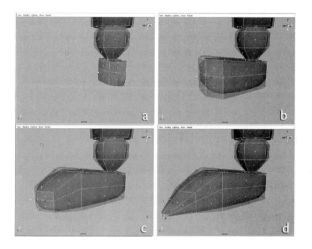

FIGURE 10.33   Foot start.

Step 42: Adjust vertices to get desired foot form (Figure 10.34).

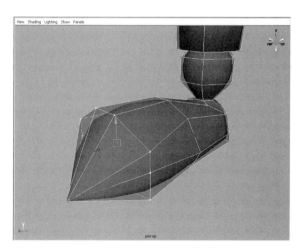

FIGURE 10.34   Adjusted foot—note no heel.

It is never fun to read, "adjust until it looks right," when reading through a tutorial. **Why?** *But when working with organic forms, sooner or later this has to happen. It would just be too laborious to have 100 steps of "grab this vertex and move it so many units to the left, then grab this one and move it up, etc." Remember that the goal here is to understand the tools, not to make a perfect copy of the model included in the figures or on the* **ON THE CD** *CD-ROM. Tweak to your liking and adjust your model as you go along.*

Step 43: Extrude the heel from faces on backside of foot (Figure 10.35).

Step 44: Adjust form to taste.

Step 45: Flatten the heel. Select all the vertices on the back of the heel and use the Move Tool (with Retain Component Spacing off) to snap all the vertices to one plane (Snap to Grid by holding x down).

Step 46: Create a truly flat heel edge. Select the faces that make up the heel and Modeling | Edit Polygons > Extrude Face—and do not move the new faces (Figure 10.36).

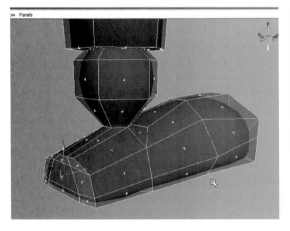

FIGURE 10.35   Backside of foot.

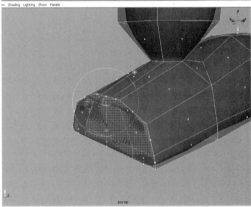

FIGURE 10.36   Flattened heel created with added Extrude Faces.

Step 47: Flatten the foot bottom. Select the vertices that make up the very bottom of the foot. Snap them to grid (with the Move Tool). Then select all the faces that make up the bottom of the foot and Extrude Faces (Figure 10.37).

Step 48: Make adjustments. As you work it is sometimes hard to step back and make sure all your proportions are right. Take a moment now to lengthen, squash or make other adjustments to your model as a whole.

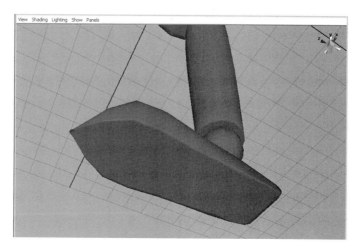

FIGURE 10.37   Flattened foot bottom. Note that this figure shows the smoothed high-poly version for illustration purposes.

Mirroring Geometry

Step 49: In the front View Panel, swap to Faces mode and select all the faces on the side of the model that you did not built the legs and arms on (Figure 10.38). Delete them.

Step 50: Ensure that all the middle points are at true center. Switch to Vertex mode, and select all the vertices that are right on the plane that you wish to mirror the geometry across (Figure 10.39).

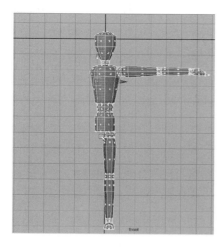

FIGURE 10.38   Selecting one half of model.

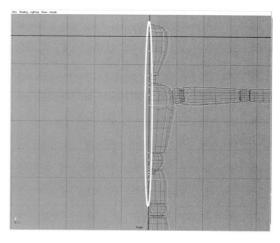

FIGURE 10.39   Selecting the vertices that exist along the mirror axis plane.

In a step or two we will be mirroring the completed half. In order to get a clean mirrored piece of geometry you must have a clean seam down the middle. You may already have all of these points on the middle truly on the middle, but often during the modeling process vertices will get shifted. If the center vertices are not truly on the center, the model ends up with tucks or splits along the mirrored axis. So this is the start of the process of making sure that the center is clean.

Step 51: Snap them to the center (the X Axis in this case). Double-click the Move Tool and turn off Retain Component Spacing in the Attributes Editor. Hold the x key down and drag just the X directional handle. This might snap the vertices way off course, but keep holding the x key down and snap them back to the x-axis.

We are only doing this on the body. Do not do this for the legs; in this model (shown in Figure 10.39) there are some problems with the leg that we are going to have to sort out—but you want to make sure that you are only snapping the points along the seam to the middle. The legs will be separate so you want to make sure that those vertices are not on the center.

Step 52: Adjust any vertices or collections of vertices that should not be on the mirror axis. You may not need to do this if all the vertices that make up your leg are indeed on only one side of the mirror plane; but in this case they were not. Select them and move them in the X direction over so they no longer overlap the x-axis (Figure 10.40).

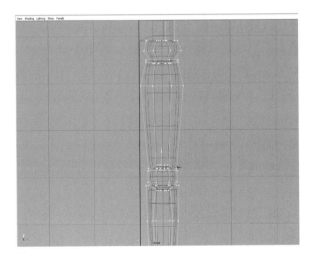

FIGURE 10.40   Futher preparing for mirroring by ensuring that there are no points overlapping the x-axis that should be separate.

Step 53: Mirror the geometry. In Object mode, select your man, and select Modeling | Polygons > Mirror Geometry (Options). If this is the first time you have used this tool, or if someone else has used your machine—be sure to use Edit > Reset Settings. Then in the Polygon Mirror Options window check the –X radio button (if you have been mimicking this layout). Click the Mirror button (Figure 10.41).

The Polygon Mirror Options is actually pretty dynamic with a good collection of useful options. The default Mirror Direction setting is +X; but in this tutorial, we have been building in the +X direction—so changing the setting to –X will make sure and mirror it out along the –X direction. Notice, however, that you can set up the Mirror Direction in any direction you wish.

Also note that by default Merge With the Original is active (as well as Merge Vertices). Since we are looking for a single mesh at the end of this function this is just what we want—this will leave us with one seamless mesh.

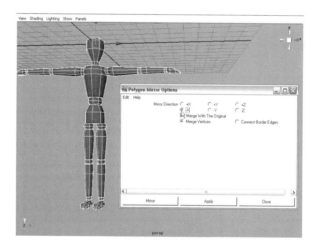

FIGURE 10.41   Mirroring the character.

Step 54: Adjust as you see fit.

Almost always, after a form is mirrored, proportions that you thought were right suddenly do not look so right. When you mirror, it is often a good idea to take a moment to readjust to make the model look like you planned.

Step 55: Delete History. Select your LowPolyMan and select Edit > Delete by Type > Delete History.

Before deleting history, Maya has been keeping track of everything you have done with new nodes attached to the form for every tweak, every cut, and every move you have made. Once in a while—when you are reasonably comfortable with the progress you have made, deleting the history associated with the object can help keep things clean.

Tutorial Conclusion

In the course of this tutorial you have created a single mesh character— one character that is one unbroken collection of polygons. True, this particular shape could have been reached a lot of different ways (a bunch of polygon primitive spheres, and some lofted surfaces); however, this workflow is the same sort of workflow you would use to create a game model, or a much more complicated high-poly form.

TUTORIAL 10.2   GAME MODEL

Objectives:

1. Create a single-mesh game model.
2. Use Image Planes to create correct proportions.
3. Continue to work with Extrude Faces to create appropriate topology.

Setup

Step 1: Define a new project. Select File > Project > New. . . Name the Project Game_Model. Choose a location. Click on Use Defaults and then click Accept (Figure 10.42).

Why? Since we are creating a new object and will be using new textures and since this game model will probably not be used in conjunction with other scenes we have built, creating a new project will help keep our other project files tidy. It will also help keep this project organized in all the right ways.

If this model were going to be imported into our room, it would make sense to save it within the room project. However, as an independent scene, it works better as a sovereign project.

Step 1 includes all the details of setting up a project. If you need a more detailed breakdown of how to setup a project again (including the whys of the whats) be sure to check out the earlier chapters where setting up a project is covered in more detail.

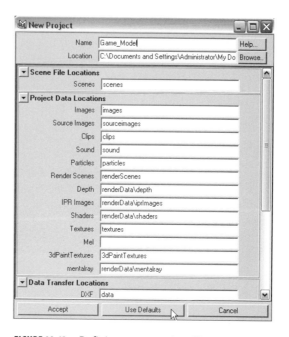

FIGURE 10.42   Defining a new project file.

Step 2: Save the file as Character. Choose File > Save. This should take you automatically to the scenes folder inside your Game_Model project file. If it does not, you will want to redefine or reset your project before continuing. Enter Character in the File name input field and press Save.

ON THE CD

Step 3: Copy the contents of the sourceimages from the CD-ROM to your own sourceimages folder. On the CD-ROM open ProjectFiles > Chapter10 > Game_Model > sourceimages. Select the contents of this folder and copy them to your own sourceimages (make sure it's the sourceimages folder for your newly created Game_Model project).

Why?

There are several important files in this sourceimages folder. Remember that this holds any texture files used in a scene (and in this case includes the finished painted texture for the character) but it also includes any images that are going to be used as resource. In this case we will be using a character design by Will Keetell and we will want to have the drawings he made to help us determine the location of the polygons we are about to create.

Placing these files in your own sourceimages folder will make them easy to find and easy to place within Maya.

Step 4: Import GameCharacterFront.tif into the front View Panel. Press spacebar to open up all four View Panels. In front, choose View > Image

Plane > Import Image. . . This should open up to your sourceimages folder within your Game_Model project file. Select GameCharacter-Front.tif from the files there and press Import.

Step 5: Import GameCharacterSide.tif into the side View Panel. In the side View Panel, repeat the process (View > Image Plane > Import Image…) and choose GameCharacterSide.tif.

The results shown in Figure 10.43 show some important things. First, you now have the sketches that we will be building off of imported into the panels that they will be of most use. It is important that you can see these Image Planes in the persp View Panel to start out with, because it allows you to double-check and make sure that your side and front views match up. Although we will not keep it that way for long. . .

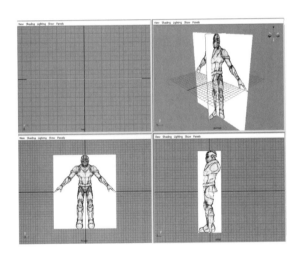

FIGURE 10.43   Imported Image Planes.

Step 6: Hide Image Planes in persp View Panel. In the front View Panel select View > Image Plane > Image Plane Attributes > imageplane1. In the Attributes Editor under the Image Plane Attributes section, click on "looking through camera." Repeat this for the side View Panel.

Once you get ready to start modeling, it can be very distracting to have these big Image Planes sitting in the middle of your perspective space. Ultimately, these drawings are orthographic and so are really most useful in the front and side views anyway. Making the Image Planes only visible in these views gives you the best of both worlds.

By the way, there are some fairly important issues surrounding preparing an image for use like this, be sure to take a look at Appendix C.

Step 7: Activate Poly Count for Heads Up Display. Choose Display > Heads Up Display > Poly Count. This will give you added information on your scene (Figure 10.44).

View	Shading	Lighting	Show	Panels
Verts:	0	0	0	
Edges:	0	0	0	
Faces:	0	0	0	
Tris:	0	0	0	
UVs:	0	0	0	

FIGURE 10.44   Heads Up Display including poly count.

So why all this extra visual garbage on the interface? Well, usually, you do not want extra noise like this; however, this is a game model and so the poly-count will be important. Although the number of polys games and video cards can render in real time continue to climb, modeling for games still requires one eye to be on the poly count. The Heads Up Display allows you to define what information is interactively displayed as you work. Poly count of course allows you to see how many polys you have built so far.

Notice in Figure 10.44 that there are actually three columns. The first indicates how many Vertices, Edges, Faces, Tris, and UVs there are in the scene total. The second indicates the number of components in the selected polygons and the third represents the total selected components.

Let us assume for the sake of this tutorial that we are aiming at creating a model for use in Unreal Tournament 2004. With this assumption, let us aim at keeping the character's poly-count to fewer than 3000 tris. Remember that when Maya renders a scene it must tessellate all polygons—which means that it converts all polygons into triangles. Most game engines will also only "see" triangular polygons (tris). So the Tris value is the one to keep a close eye on. Although we will be building largely with four-sided polygons (represented by the Faces number), the Tris number must remain below 3000.

Step 8: Create a new Polygon Cube. Create > Polygon Primitives > Cube (Options). Make sure to give Subdivisions Along Width and Subdivisions Along Depth a value of 2.

Remember that 2 subdivisions along width and depth allow for a much easier rounded shape to be found. Some artists prefer to start with larger numbers of subdivisions; and still others prefer to start with fewer. This value is a good middle ground, and although we will undoubtedly need more subdivisions along both width and depth before we are done, this allows us to remain as low-poly as we can for as long as possible.

Why?

Step 9: Rename to Character.

Head

Step 10: Move the head. The cube will be automatically created at 0,0,0, but the character's head is much higher than that. Use the Move Tool to reposition the cube at about the head (make sure to do this by moving only along the y-axis (green handle).

Step 11: Round the shape by scaling rows of vertices in the top View Panel (Figure 10.45).

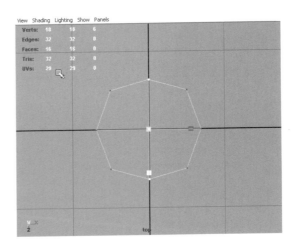

FIGURE 10.45   Rounded shape.

Rounding when there are just a few polygons can save lots of time in the long run. Although most every vertex will need to be tweaked over the course of the tutorial, the shapes are often easier to see if you start closer to what it will eventually become.

Why?

Step 12: Use X-Ray to better see the forms. In the front and side View Panels activate Shaded mode by moving your mouse over those View Panels and pressing 5 on your keyboard. Then, in each View Panel choose Shading > X-Ray. (Figure 10.46).

The Image Plane we are using has a high contrast—very dark lines. Often this is of great help in the modeling process, but it can also make for some tough-to-see moments if you are dealing in just wireframe. However, if you use straight Shaded modes to view things in, you cover up the very resources you have imported. X-Ray is often a good compromise as it allows you to see your shape a little better, but still allows you to see the reference drawing beneath it.

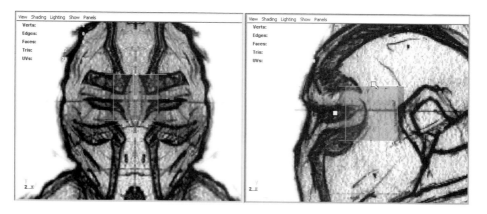

FIGURE 10.46   Activating X-Ray for front and side View Panels.

Step 13: Slide your Image Planes in the front View Panel back. Select View > Image Plane Attributes > imageplane1. In the Attributes Editor, scroll down to the Placement Extras section and expand. In the Center input fields enter –30 in the third column (the Z direction).

What was happening in Figure 10.46 is that you could only see the front half of the rounded cube. The Image Plan remember, was set at Z = 0; so since the cube was half in front of the Z axis and half behind, you were only seeing the front. By adjusting the third column of the Center input fields, you are moving the Image Plane back 30 units in the –Z direction. The result: you can see your entire cube.

Step 14: Slide your Image Plane in the side View Panel back. Repeat the process for side View Panel; only this time enter -30 in the first column (the X direction). This should yield an image like Figure 10.47.

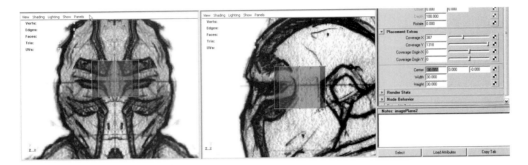

FIGURE 10.47   Adjusted Image Planes.

Step 15: In Object mode, rotate and scale Character to match Figure 10.48.

 How to begin a character is largely a personal preference. You may find that you attack different characters in different ways. Since this character has such distinctive lines in the face via the helmet with such strange curves, in this case, an approach of extruding the form works best.

Why?

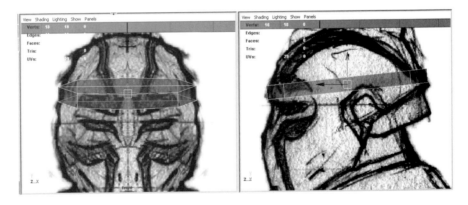

FIGURE 10.48   Scaled and rotated box; just to set up the construction.

Step 16: In Vertex mode, tweak vertices to rough out form. Right-click on the Object and select Vertex from the Marking Menu. Select and move vertices in the front and side View Panels to rough out the first draft of this ring of polygons (Figure 10.49).

 Unfortunately, in tutorials like this there are the inevitable, "tweak the vertices to taste" steps. They are the steps that just can not really be more effectively defined and it is up to you and your understanding of form to successfully execute. The first

Why?

time around a human form can be especially tricky; so if you are not too familiar with anatomy, just give it your best shot this first round. As you do your second, third, and fourth characters you will begin to see the form a bit more accurately.

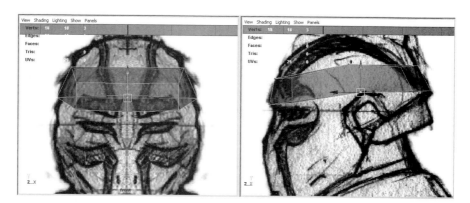

FIGURE 10.49   Roughing out the first round.

Step 17: Select and extrude the faces on the top of the head. Switch to Faces mode (right-click on the object and select Faces from the Marking Menu). Select the faces on the top of the form. Make sure that Modeling | Polygons > Tool Options > Keep Faces Together is checked. Choose Modeling | Edit Polygons > Extrude Face. Use the manipulator to pull the new faces up and away (Figure 10.50).

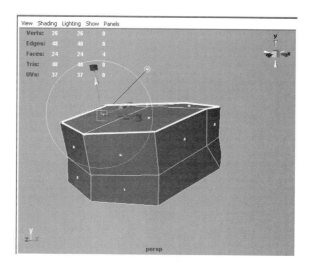

FIGURE 10.50   Extruding the top of the head.

Step 18: Tweak new vertices to match reference (Figure 10.51). Remember to do this switch in Vertex mode.

Why? *When extruding in this case, do not worry too much about getting the shape just right to start with. The tweaking comes via the vertex adjustments. Remember, here you are still looking for a basic general shape. You are looking at maintaining good poly-counts as well as finding the right form. Be sure that, in addition to finding the profile, you look carefully at the front View Panel (in conjunction with the persp View Panel) to determine how wide each set of vertices should be.*

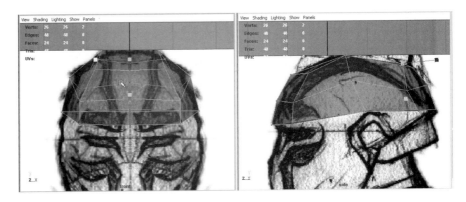

FIGURE 10.51   Adjusted vertices.

Step 19: Extrude the faces along the bottom of the head downward. Switch to Faces mode, and select the four faces on the bottom of the head. Use Extrude Face to extrude them down a bit (Figure 10.52).

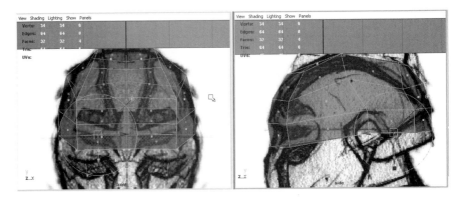

FIGURE 10.52   Extruding down to start filling out the head.

Step 20: Tweak vertices to allow for head shape. Notice that the back vertices are finding the edge of the first helmet ledge. Also notice that the vertices at the very front are defining the bridge of the nose (Figure 10.53).

There are some problems beginning to develop here. Notice that from the middle of the eye (in the side view) to the back of the ear piece is a very, very long distance. Although not always absolutely necessary, a nicely distributed polygon mesh is preferable in both modeling and animation. Get too far a distance between rows of vertices and it can become very difficult to get the sort of detail needed to define the form.

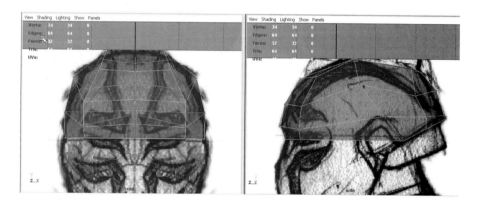

FIGURE 10.53   Tweaked added vertices to find back of helmet ledge and nose bridge.

Step 21: Use the Split Edge Ring Tool to create new subdivision. Modeling | Edit Polygons>Split Edge Ring Tool will activate the tool. Click and drag on one of the horizontal edges to create a new Edge Ring, which subsequently creates new vertices and faces available for editing (Figure 10.54). Tweak new vertices.

Notice the placement of this new ring is approximately at the front of the ear area. This will provide the geometry we need for that ear piece, as well as added geometry to create the curvature of the head.

Step 22: Select the front four faces on the bottom of the shape. This does not include the two under the back ledge of the helmet (Figure 10.55).

With the new edge ring, you now have extra faces that you can extrude out to continue down the head without disturbing the shape you have created on the back of the helmet. We will come back to that area, but for now—as we rough out the general shape of the head—we can leave that as it is.

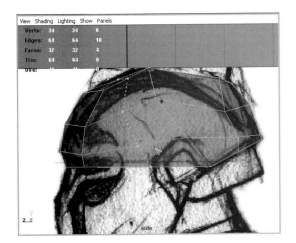

FIGURE 10.54 Adding extra edge ring.

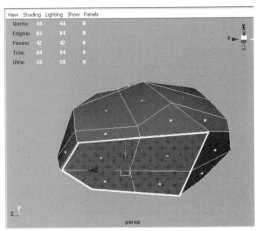

FIGURE 10.55 Selecting front faces (not back of helmet).

Step 23: Extrude Face and tweak to create shape and nose shape (Figure 10.56).

Why? Note that again, there is developing a very wide span between the edge ring that drops down through the middle of the eye (in the side view) and the ring that runs in front of the ear.

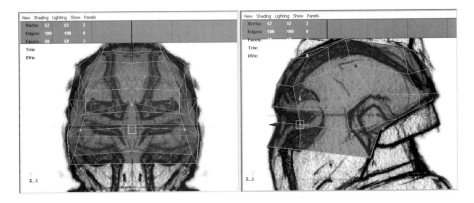

FIGURE 10.56 Adjusted new extruded faces.

Step 24: Use Split Edge Ring Tool (Modeling | Edit Polygons > Split Edge Ring Tool) to create new ring of edges (Figure 10.57). Tweak to find form.

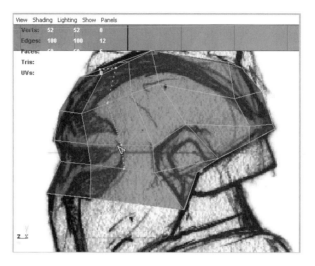

FIGURE 10.57   New edge ring.

Step 25: Extrude Face down to complete face area. Remember, tweak after every extrusion (Figure 10.58).

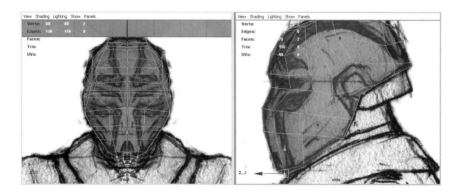

FIGURE 10.58   Extruding and tweaked head.

Step 26: Select the polygons that approximate the extra helmet ledge (Figure 10.59).

Step 27: Extrude the faces, but do not extrude yet—just scale. Select Modeling | Edit Polygons > Extrude Face, but instead of using the manipulator to pull the polygons away, use the scale handles to scale the faces a bit smaller to create the ledge (Figure 10.60).

Step 28: Extrude Face, and move down to create the ledge (Figure 10.61).

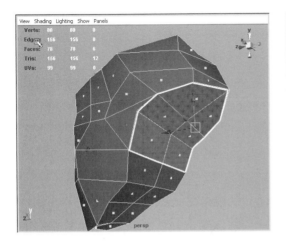

FIGURE 10.59   Selected faces for the helmet edge.

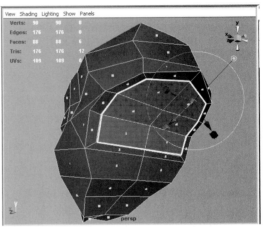

FIGURE 10.60   Using Extrude Face Tool but creating ledge using the scale handles on the Extrude Face manipulator.

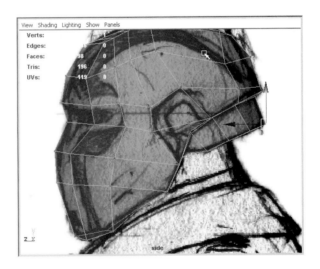

FIGURE 10.61   Finishing off the helmet ledge.

Neck

Step 29: Select a broad collection of faces for the neck (Figure 10.62).

 Why so many? Well, these faces will extrude down to create the neck and will also be the same number of polygons we extrude down to create the body. A decent num-
Why? *ber allows for the approximation of rounded forms.*

Also, we are assuming this guy is fairly buff beneath his armor and thus will have a decently thick neck.

Step 30: Extrude Face and scale to make faces smaller against old faces and create second helmet ledge (Figure 10.63).

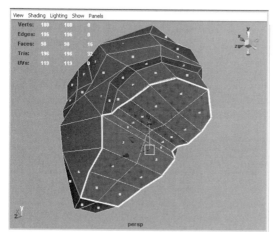

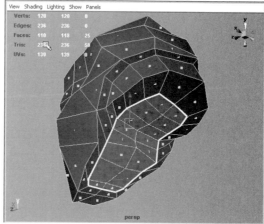

FIGURE 10.62   Selecting the faces that will become the neck.

FIGURE 10.63   Extruded faces also scaled (using Extrude Face scale manipulator handles).

Step 31: Extrude Face again; move faces down to create neck (Figure 10.64).

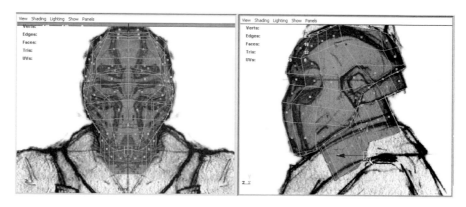

FIGURE 10.64   Extruded neck.

Although there will be a lot of tweaking here, sometimes it is just easier to work with new vertices if they are pulled away from other dense collections of polygons. Pulling it way down as seen in Figure 10.64 just makes for easier selection.

Why?

Step 32: Tweak bottom ring of vertices to match neck-collar intersection. Remember that the collar will intersect the neck a little below where the reference shows the top of the collar to be (Figure 10.65).

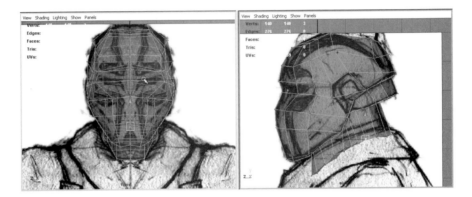

FIGURE 10.65   Tweaked neck.

Collar

Step 33: Select, Extrude and tweak the faces on the bottom of the neck to create the high point of the collar (Figure 10.66). Then Extrude and tweak again to create bottom edge of collar.

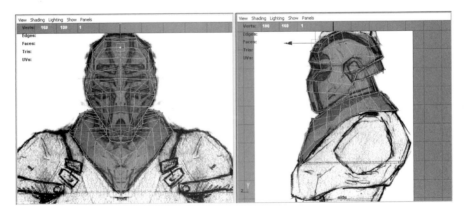

FIGURE 10.66   High point of collar created from extruded faces on bottom of the neck. Then additional extrude for collar edge.

Simplifying Setup

Step 34: Delete bottom faces. Select the faces on the bottom of Character (the ones you just finished working with to create the collar). Delete them.

Step 35: Delete Character's right half (your left). In the front View Panel, select the faces on Character's right side and delete them (Figure 10.67).

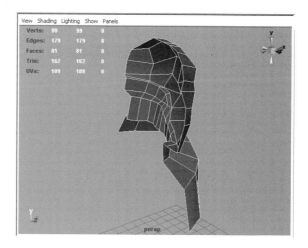

FIGURE 10.67   Results of deleted bottom polygons and character's right side deleted.

Seems strange to delete all those polygons we had been working with doesn't it? Well, it is a little bit, but there is a method to this madness. As we have been working on the head, generally vertices could be adjusted in pairs (selected from the side View Panel). However, as we start down the chest and across the shoulders we would literally need to edit one side of the body and then repeat the process on the other side. This is really much more work than we should need to do for a symmetrical character.

By deleting one half of the character we can start working down creating just one half of Character for the rest of the body. Later we will look at duplicating the extant half to show us what the character looks like whole.

As we start working out the arm, selecting all the faces along the bottom of the form every time can get quite laborious. Now that we simply have a ring of edges on the bottom we can make use of Maya 7's new Border Edge and Ring Selection Tools. Then we can make use of Extrude Face's sister tool, Extrude Edge.

Torso

Step 36: Select the bottom loop of edges. You can either do this by switching to Edge mode and selecting them one at a time, or by using the Edit > Select Border Edge Tool.

The Select Border Edge Tool is really a nice addition to Maya. With the tool activated, click the first edge of the bottom of the shape, and then click the last edge. Maya will then automatically select all the edges in between.

Why?

Step 37: Extrude out to the shoulder. Use Modeling | Edit Polygons > Extrude Edge and extrude the edges outward in all directions.

As your model becomes more complex, the angles between faces become more dramatic. The result is often that the Extrude Faces and Extrude Edges Tools begin to break down. When this breakdown occurs, after you have told an edge to be extruded, if you use the Extrude Edge manipulators, the edges will either do nothing, or some will go up while some go down.

This is fairly easy to work around. After you have activated the Extrude Edge (or Extrude Face) Tool, immediately switch to the regular ol' Move Tool, or the Scale Tool can work well here too. Move or scale these new faces out and away; they can really be moved or scaled out in any direction as you will need to tweak each one individually anyway. Getting them moved out just makes them easier to grab and move.

Step 38: Tweak vertices into place (Figure 10.68). Note that these should be tweaked out to the edge of the shoulder pad.

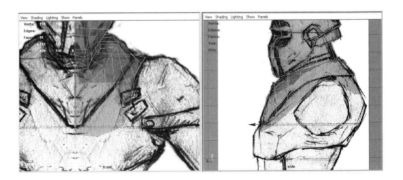

FIGURE 10.68   Beginning of chest. Note not to extrude the shoulder pad.

Step 39: Select the edges that are not part of the arm joint (all those that those that do not run up against the shoulder pad). Be sure to look at Figure 10.69 and the highlighted faces.

*The idea of the next few steps is to close off the area where the arm will grow out of.
At the same time, we will be building down the chest and back, but we are going
to need to wrap some faces down around the armpit where they will eventually
join. As we do this, we do not want to keep building out the arm. So selecting a very
specific collection of edges and extruding those will be key.*

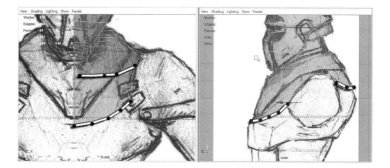

FIGURE 10.69   Select edges not involved in defining the arm joint.

Step 40: Extrude Edges downward (Figure 10.70). Modeling | Edit Poly-
gons > Extrude Edges. You should be able to just use the Y handle of the
Extrude Edges manipulator to pull all the edges down and out.

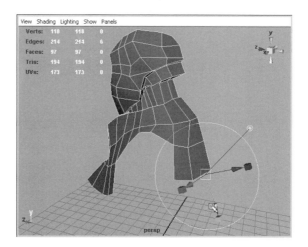

FIGURE 10.70   Extruded edges.

Step 41: Tweak vertices (Figure 10.71). Move these new vertices into
place to indicate the meaty part of his chest, and the deepest part of his
back. In both the front and back, be working the inner-most vertices
around the arm joint.

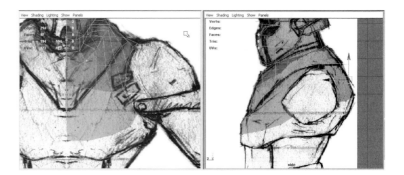

FIGURE 10.71   Tweaked vertices to begin working around arm.

Step 42: Repeat. Select nonarm edges, Extrude Edges, and tweak. This should bring your inner arm pit points almost together (Figure 10.72).

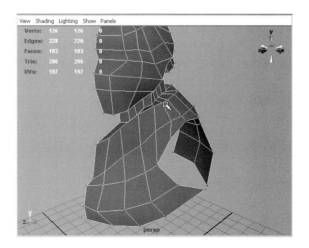

FIGURE 10.72   Results of second extrusion and tweak.

Step 43: Close armpit. Select the two vertices that are closest under the arm pit. Choose Modeling | Edit Polygons > Merge Vertices (Options). Turn the Distance up high (10 or so) and press MergeVertex (Figure 10.73).

Why?

Merging the vertices closes off the hole which makes the arm hole a continuous ring of edges that can be extruded and manipulated. It also closes off the bottom, so we have an unbroken line of edges on the bottom of the form that we can extrude down to create the rest of the torso.

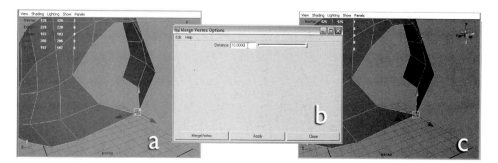

FIGURE 10.73   (a) Selecting the armpit vertices. (b) Settings for the Merge Vertices Tool. (c) Results of the MergeVertex function.

Step 44: Continue extruding down to complete the torso above the belt. Repeat the same steps of selecting the bottom ring of edges and extruding them down followed by vertex tweaking. Look for general shapes; do not worry about matching each line of the form (much of the muscles and things like that will be accomplished via the texture). Extrude down to the belt (Figure 10.74).

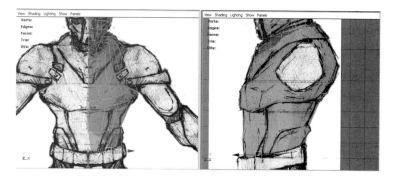

FIGURE 10.74   Completed general torso.

Why?   *What details to include and what not to when you are on a poly-count budget is a tough one. In general, the best strategy is to keep fairly rough the first time around the form. So things like the kidney pads sticking out of his belt on his back are left out (as are things like the ear piece and the eye sockets)—for now. When we have the character roughed out, we may find we have polys to spare and can go back and add detail. At this time the Tris column tells us there are 278 tries, which means that with two halves we have 565 total tries. For as much as we have done of this model, chances are we will have some polygons to spare and will indeed be able to go back and add details like the nose and eyes and certain protective gear.*

However, it is almost always easier (and more fun) to go back and add detail than to have to go back and decide what to have to leave out.

A general rule to consider is that if a piece significantly changes the profile of the character, include geometry; if not, leave it out the first time around as it may be able to be handled with texture.

Step 45: Create the belt. This can be done with three extrusions. One that extrudes outward for the top of the belt, one that covers the width of the belt and another for the bottom edge. See Figure 10.75 for a progression.

When you are working around the belt, you will probably notice that there are some real discrepancies between the front and side views. In the best-case scenarios your front and side views will always match perfectly, but in the real world often they do not. When this happens, be sure you are taking a close look at the persp View Panel so you can be sure you are understanding the 3D space and can make some judgment calls to make sure the belt has a constant thickness and depth around the body.

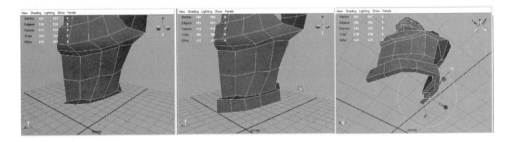

FIGURE 10.75   Belt construction.

Crotch and Butt

Step 46: Extrude down to create the crotch and butt. This will take a few extrusions; but be conscious of the topology (the polygon organization) and try and match Figure 10.76.

Why?

The organization of the polygons here becomes important when it comes time to an-imate. Although it might be easiest to just start extruding down in a solid grid, the way that the anatomy of the hip runs will dictate how the joints will need to be de-fined inside of this poly mesh. And if the polygons are organized inappropriately, the deformation of those joints will become very problematic.

Notice that in Figure 10.76, the crotch has not been closed. There is still a gap there. There are a couple ways to close this; one is via the Merge Vertices method we used earlier. The other is to create an entirely new polygon to bridge that gap.

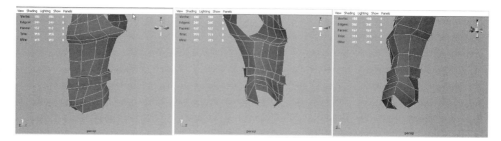

FIGURE 10.76 General crotch and butt area.

Step 47: Append to Polygon to close the gap. Maneuver around so that you can clearly see the area of the crotch. Switch to Object mode. Choose Modeling | Polygons > Append to Polygon Tool. Click on one of the edges (Figure 10.77a), then click on the edge of the other side of the gap to be bridged (Figure 10.77b). Press Enter to complete and exit the tool.

Why not just add a couple for extrusions and then merge vertices? Well, as you can see from the images, the extrusions to get down to the bottom of the crotch have already moved the outer thigh-polys way down the side. Additional extrusions would slide that even further down which would cause real problems when it came time to animate.

By using the Append to Polygon Tool, the gap is bridged in the crotch (where there is no need for many polygons as it will rarely be seen) without having to continue extruding down the leg.

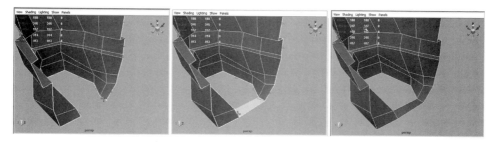

FIGURE 10.77 (a) Starting the Append to Polygon process by clicking on the starting edge. (b) Indicating where the polygon should be bridged to. (c) Final result.

Step 48: Tweak and adjust the crotch geometry for the 'speedo' look. Adjust the vertices to get as close to making the polygons look like a speedo as possible (Figure 10.78).

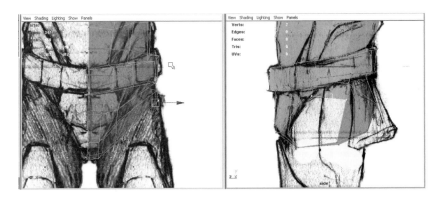

FIGURE 10.78   Adjusted crotch vertices. Adjusted to help facilitate future animation.

Step 49: Add needed geometry. Activate the Split Polygon Tool (Modeling | Edit Polygons > Split Polygon Tool). Split the front side of the thigh up to the belt (Figure 10.79). Remember to use this tool, click on an edge (slide to the corner under the belt) and then click on the next edge, and then the next, and so on. Press Enter to complete and exit the tool.

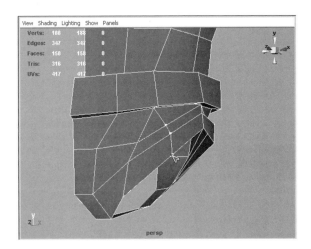

FIGURE 10.79   Adding extra geometry to the front of the thigh.

 What?! This seems to break all sorts of rules. First it creates a triangle and creates a cluster of polygons meeting at one point under the belt. This is true; however,

places like under the belt are good places to tuck this sort of thing. If this were not a game model and was going to be smoothed, this would be a bigger problem. But since it is a game model and is much more what-you-see-is-what-you-get, an occasional triangular face is acceptable.

Ultimately, the tradeoff is that now there are more edges to build the leg off of. As we have been adding places where new appendages can break off (like the arm and leg) we loose edges. This is a way of regaining some of those.

Step 50: Repeat on back side across the butt (Figure 10.80).

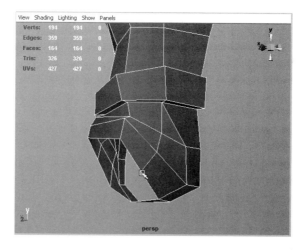

FIGURE 10.80   Added geometry with the Split Polygon Tool.

Housekeeping and Negative Duplicates

Step 51: In the front view, select all the vertices that should be right in the middle of the character. Double-check that you have them all selected in the persp View Panel—select any there that you missed. Also make sure that you did not grab any that should not have been selected (Figure 10.81).

Why? *We are going to make use of a technique to provide a mirrored instance here in a bit. However, as we looked at earlier in order to have a clean mesh, we need to make sure that the points that are on the axis of symmetry are indeed right on X = 0.*

Step 52: Snap to the YZ plane (or X = 0). Double-click the Move Tool in the Tool Box. In the Move Snap Settings section, click off Retain Component Spacing. Hold the x key down and use the X handle on the manipulator to snap all the points to X = 0 on the grid.

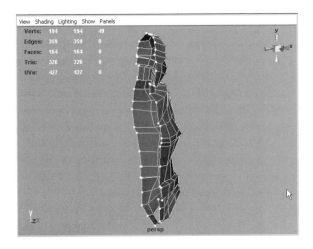

FIGURE 10.81 Selecting the middle vertices.

 Be sure to only use the X (red) handle of the manipulator. Since Retain Component Spacing is off, if you snap using the middle handle, all the points will collapse to one point of the grid.

Step 53: Duplicate in the –X direction. In Object mode, select Character. Choose Edit > Duplicate (Options). Change the Scale X (first column) to –1. Make sure that Geometry Type is set to Instance. Click Duplicate (Figure 10.82).

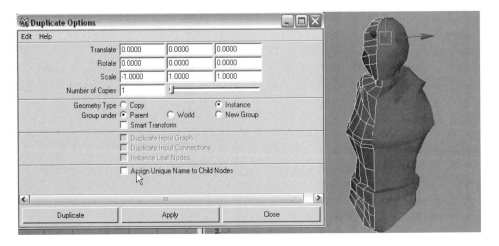

FIGURE 10.82 Mirroring the geometry using a negative duplicate.

There are several ways to get mirrored geometry. We have looked at many of them. One is to use Mirror Geometry—this is not what we want here as it is a static function—if we make changes to the one side, they are not replicated to the other. The second is through options within the Smooth Proxy Tool. However, we do not want to smooth this shape, so a Smooth Proxy would be inappropriate. The third is via the method shown in Step 55.

The Scaling in -1 ensures that the image is the mirror of the original. Think of scaling the object so that it's scale in X is closer and closer to 0 (it gets thinner and thinner), if you keep scaling beyond 0, the object begins growing out the other side—in a mirror of what it was before scaling.

By creating an Instance of one side any changes we make to the original will be automatically updated on the other.

Step 54: Adjust via vertex tweaks (Figure 10.83).

If you have been building just one half of the shape, it can become quite hard to get a really good idea of what the form will look like whole. Inevitably, when you first mirror the shape, you find that there are some adjustments needed; perhaps the chest is too thin too fast, or the face is the wrong shape. Take a moment and tweak the vertices on the character's left side (which will update on the right) to get the shape closer to what you would like it to be.

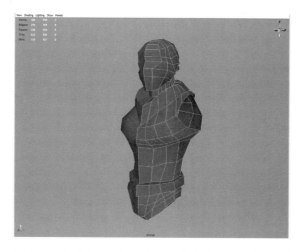

FIGURE 10.83   Adjusted tweaks needed after negative duplicate.

Shoulders and Arms

Step 55: Select and extrude the edges around the arm hole. Extrude straight out first (Figure 10.84). Tweak to create the start of a sort of capped sleeve with the polygons across the top of the shoulder being noticeably longer than those in the arm pit.

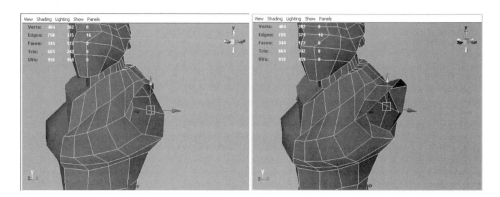

FIGURE 10.84   Starting off with the arm.

Step 56: Repeat a couple of times working out towards the edge of the shoulder armor. Remember that there will probably be a cluster of vertices in the armpit to allow for the longer polygons to stretch across the top of the shoulder.

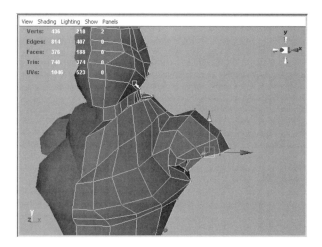

FIGURE 10.85   Capped shoulder.

Step 57: Extrude the armor border. Do this similar to the belt. Create three extrusions to get the ledge in there (Figure 10.86).

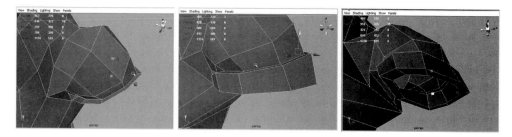

FIGURE 10.86   Creating the shoulder ledge.

Step 58: Continue to extrude the edge loop down to create the general shape of the arm. Do not worry about every detail of the armor, but do make adjustments when there are large changes in the profile (Figure 10.87).

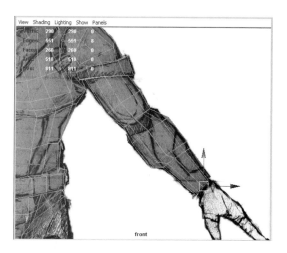

FIGURE 10.87   Arm roughed out through continued edge extrusions.

Step 59: Tweak, tweak, tweak. If you create the general arm shape in the front view, there are undoubtedly some adjustments that need to be made in the persp View Panel. Take a moment to make the adjustments that make the form more correct.

Hands

Step 60: Continue to extrude down to create the hand. You will probably need four or five extrusions to rough out the hand. Be sure to take a look at the persp View Panel to adjust the width of the hand as you go along (Figure 10.88).

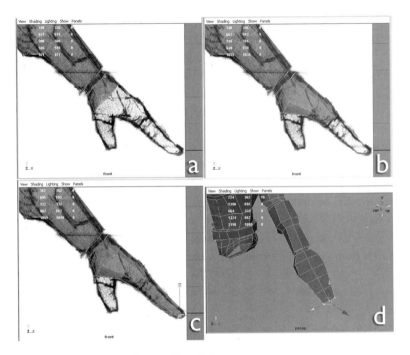

FIGURE 10.88 Progress of general hand shape.

Why?

Seems like a pretty goofy hand, eh? Remember that this is a game hand. First of all in most cases there is no need for articulated fingers. The mitt look usually does just the trick (although some games call for a trigger finger too). When you are running around trying to avoid a rocket to the gut, the fingers on the guy shooting the rocket are the least of your worries. Because of this, you can get away with a low collection of polygons in the fingers.

However, the hands will still need to grab a hold of guns and other objects, so you need to be sure and give them places to bend at. In this case, be sure to give the fingers a few places where there are rows of vertices to allow a joint to deform the poly-mesh.

Step 61: Close off finger tips. Find the end of the last extrusion. Using the Append to Polygon Tool (Modeling | Polygons > Append to Polygon Tool) close off the edge (remember to use this tool by clicking on edges). Figure 10.89 shows one possible polygon organization.

Step 62: Extrude out the thumb. Do this by selecting the faces shown in Figure 10.90 and extruding (Modeling | Edit Polygons > Extrude Face) out twice to create the general shape of the thumb.

Step 63: Tweak the hand and thumb into shape (Figure 10.91).

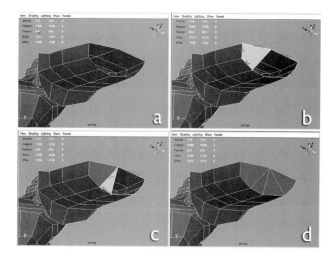

FIGURE 10.89   Closing off the finger tips.

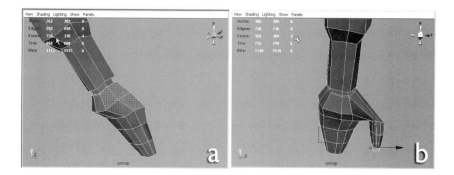

FIGURE 10.90   Extruding out the thumb.

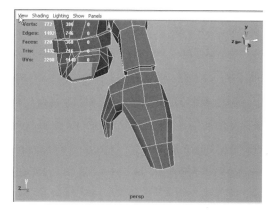

FIGURE 10.91   Tweaked hand and thumb.

Legs and Feet

Step 64: Create the basic shape of the leg through extruding the edge loop that starts the leg off the torso. Figure 10.92 shows the edges to select and a very general shape for the legs. Note that these are just extrusions that match the general shape of the leg as seen in front and side View Panels. Tweaking as you go is always a good idea.

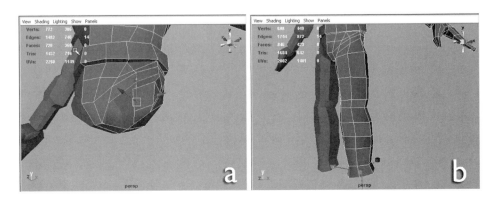

FIGURE 10.92 The leg extruded.

Step 65: Make rough adjustments to approximate the armor. No need to be exact, but if there are some rows of point that are close to where a crisp line of the armor would be, adjust a little to make them fit (Figure 10.93).

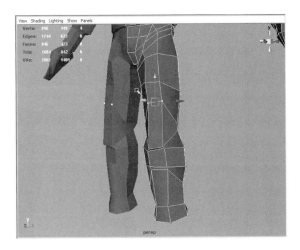

FIGURE 10.93 Adjusting rough shape to generally fit pieces of armor.

This is not a technique you would use with every character. However, with an armor-laden form like this, taking a few minutes to tweak these points to mimic geometry that will need to be in place can pay big dividends later when we attempt to model the armor.

Why?

Step 66: Extrude down to create the stump that will be the foot (Figure 10.94).

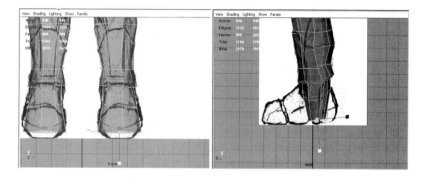

FIGURE 10.94   Creating the start of the foot.

Step 67: Close up the bottom of the foot. In the same way we closed the finger tips, use the Append to Polygon Tool to close up the hold on the bottom of the stumps.

Step 68: Extrude out the front and back (extruding faces) to create the general feet shape (Figure 10.95).

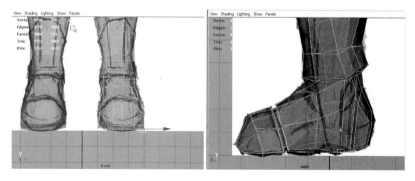

FIGURE 10.95   Extruded foot.

Details

Step 69: With an eye on the first column of the Tris in the Heads Up Display, add geometry as you see fit. This can include areas like the ear piece, eye sockets, added armor pieces, etc. This is largely up to you but do not let the Tris value go over 3000. Figures 10.96–10.101 include some updates.

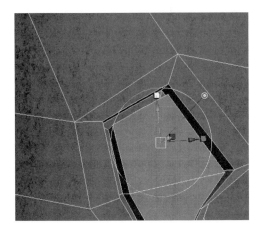

FIGURE 10.96 Added detail to the ear piece.

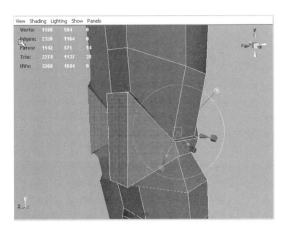

FIGURE 10.97 Adjustments to extrude the knee pads out.

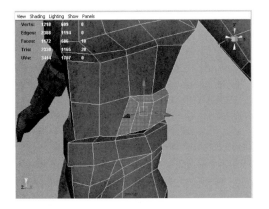

FIGURE 10.98 Extrusion of the kidney pads.

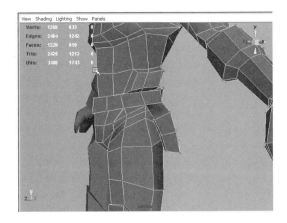

FIGURE 10.99 Creating the butt protectors.

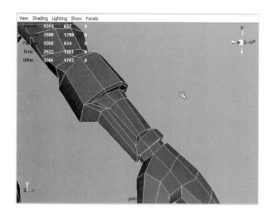

FIGURE 10.100   Added detail to forearm guides.

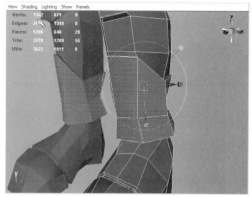

FIGURE 10.101   Added shin guards.

Step 70: Soften Normals. Select the entire character in Object mode. Choose Modeling _ Edit Polygons > Normals > Soften/Harden (Options). Click All Soft (180) and then click Soft/Hard (Figure 10.102).

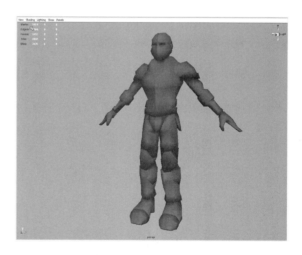

FIGURE 10.102   Softened normals.

Not all game engines support softened normals, however the UT2004 engine does, so we will make use of it here. Softened normals often times produce a model that appears smoother than by default. The actual hard edge between faces tends to be softened, making a model appear much more detailed with a high poly-count than it actually is.

Notice that this causes a few problems. First, there is a very clear seam down the middle of the character—not to worry as we will fix that later after we have UV mapped this character. The second problem is that there are some overly black spots (that will largely go away with texture, but we will also adjust with hardened normals). The third problem is that it makes everything soft. There are some places, like the edge of armor, that we will still want a hard edge.

Step 71: Harden selected normals. Select a loop of edges (say where the color and torso meet) that should have a hard edge. Select all the way around the collar. Select Modeling _ Edit Polygons > Normals > Soften/Harden (Options). Click on All Hard (0) and then on Soft/Hard. Figure 10.103 shows a before (a), selection (b), and after (c) illustration.

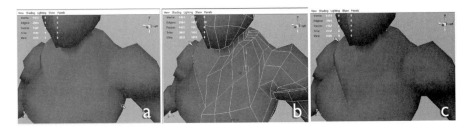

FIGURE 10.103   Results of hardening normals on an edge loop.

Step 72: Repeat normal hardening on other areas of the model that should have crisp edges (Figure 10.104 shows several examples).

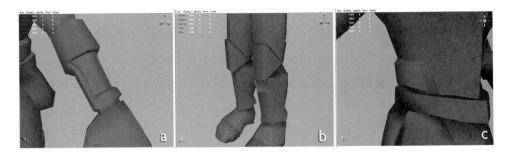

FIGURE 10.104   Hardened normals resulting in crisp edges.

Tutorial Conclusion

ON THE CD

And with that, the basic form is roughed out. On the sample file at this point, the total Tris count is 2842—meaning that we have a few hundred polygons to spare. On the CD-ROM in the ProjectFiles folder in the Game_Model folder (scenes folder) is the model created for this tutorial. It is saved at various times long the way so you can take a look at what changes were made and when. At the end of this tutorial, it is saved as Tutorial10.2.mb.

Remember that the key to this sort of model is really trying to create the illusion of complexity with few polygons. When you create your own game model, the first times through often times you find that you may have been able to save polygons here and there after you are done. But the more game models you create the more familiar you become with your style and where you can most effectively use polygons.

In chapters to come we will texture this model and rig him for animation. With the eye to topology that we have developed here, we should have quicker and easier jobs tackling both of those tasks. ✂

CHALLENGES, EXERCISES, OR ASSIGNMENTS

1. Take a look at Figure 10.105. See the notches? How would you go about creating these on the Man created in Tutorial 10.1?

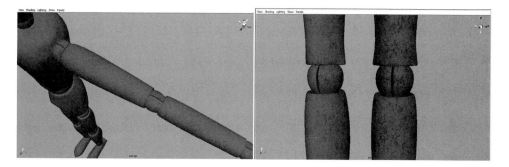

FIGURE 10.105   Added detail to Tutorial 10.1.

2. What other details could be added to the character from Tutorial 10.2? Remember, there are still quite a few Tris to spare.
3. Design your own game model. Follow Appendix C to prepare your image and model it.

11

ORGANIC TEXTURING AND UV MAPPING

Wwe have looked at texturing before. You know all about shaders, materials, the various types of materials (Blinn, Phong, Phong E, Anisostropic, Lambert, and so on). You also know how to create a new material and apply it to an object. We have even looked at ways of changing the size of a particular shader (and texture) across a surface via Projections and its associated modifiers. If any of this sounds foreign, take a look back at Chapters 7 and 8 where the basic ideas of texturing are covered in more depth.

In this chapter, we are going to look at how to use many of the techniques we have covered in the past to texture more complex and organic shapes. Along the way, there are some important theoretical issues surrounding UVs and Maya's ability to modify them that will make a big difference in your ability to place custom textures.

"3D" TEXTURES AND SHADERS

3D is in quotes here because most people hear of 3D shaders and think, "Well, all the shaders are 3D aren't they? I mean that's the medium we're dealing with here!" But it turns out that many shaders and textures are really two-dimensional (flat) that are simply wrapped around, or pasted, onto a 3D form. There do exist some shaders and textures, however, that are 3D in how they interact with objects. Rather than wrapping around a form or shape, these 3D textures penetrate the form in a much more volumetric way. Think of it as a sort of colored fog that leaves a residue on polygons (or NURBS) that a rendering engine can illustrate.

For an example of this, try this little minitutorial.

| **TUTORIAL 11.1** | **TEXTURING AMAZING WOODEN MAN** |

Objectives:

1. See 3D textures in action.
2. Create a 3D texture and adjust the default settings to fit project.
3. Apply the 3D texture and adjust the placement and size.
4. Understand the difference between 3D and 2D textures.

Step 1: Set your project. In this case, you will be texturing the mannequin modeled in Tutorial 10.1 in the previous chapter. This is part of the Amazing_Wooden_Man project. Chose File > Project > Set...Find where you have Amazing_Wooden_Man project (the project that included the interior as well) and click the OK button.

If you have not been working on a bunch of other projects, you may be able to find this via the File > Recent Projects menu. This can allow for very quick selection of projects that you have been working on lately.

Step 2: Open your Man. In this example, we are using Man-Extra.mb, which you are welcome to use, or you can use the results of your own efforts from Tutorial 10.1.

Step 3: Adjust the organization to allow you access to the smoothed version. Depending on your setup, you will want to hide your LowPolyLayer and turn off the reference (the R in the second column of the Layers Editor), so you can have access to the high-poly smoothed version of Man.

Why texture the high-poly version? Good question. In reality, if we were going to be animating this character we would usually apply the material to the low-poly form as that would be the form we would be animating. When you use the Smooth Proxy command, you can make sure that textures translate up to the high-poly version. However, since this is a minitutorial, and we are just looking at the simple concepts of 3D textures, the high-poly version makes for a quicker illustration that looks good.

Step 4: Right-click on Man and choose Materials > New Material > Phong from the marking menu. This will open the material in the Attributes Editor.

Step 5: Rename the material WoodMaterial.

Step 6: Create a new Render Node for the Color channel. Remember to do this click on the checkboard button next to the Color attribute.

Step 7: In the Create Render Node window, in the 3D Textures section click the Wood button. This will open the attributes for this new node in the Attributes Editor.

Step 8: Adjust the Filter Color, Vein Color, and Grain Color to taste. No need to post a screen shot of the settings in gray scale as they would just show up as gray swatches; but take a look at most artists mannequins and you get the idea. The Filler Color is more of a yellow, the Vein Color is a peach color, and the Grain Color is a lighter brown.

Step 9: Press 6 in the persp View Panel. Remember that 6 shows the model with textures (Figure 11.1).

There are several things to observe at this point. First, the way that Maya shows the texture being applied to the surface is often pretty weird. Swatches of color seem to stretch around the head, big dark spots appear on the arms, and so on. Do not fear though, this renders out pretty nicely.

The second thing to note is the big green box that is sitting around the man's head. This is actually a 3D placement node (actually called place3dTexture1). You may have noticed this in your room as you were building and texturing it. This is actually the node that controls the size of the 3D texture node (in this case the wood). This node can be selected directly in the View Panel of the Outliner and moved, scaled or rotated.

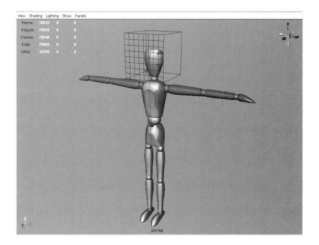

FIGURE 11.1 Results of using a 3D wood texture.

Step 10: Zoom in on a section of the object and take a render (Figure 11.2). You should be able to see how the wood texture is wrapping around and through the object all at once.

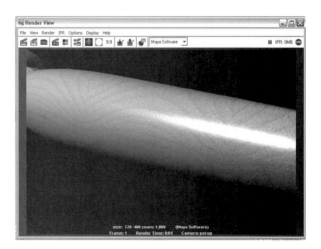

FIGURE 11.2 Rendered arm showing the results of the wood 3D texture in the Color channel.

Step 11: For fun, resize the 3D texture node with the place3DTexture1 node. Select the green cube surrounding the character's head (or select place3DTexture1 in the Outliner). Use the Scale Tool to resize it (Figure 11.3). Rerender (Figure 11.4).

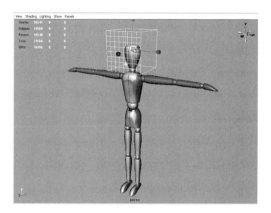

FIGURE 11.3   Rescaling the 3D Texture node wood via the place3DTexture1 node.

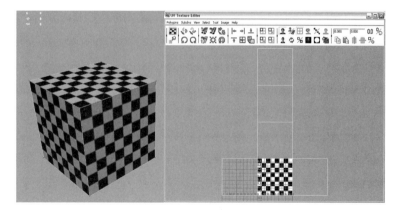

FIGURE 11.4   Results of rescaling the node smaller.

 If you rescale the place3DTexture1 node smaller, you will see more vein more often across your surface. Make it larger and the grain will get so big, you may see the dots across the surface.

Why?

Step 12: Save the file as Man-Textured.mb.

Tutorial Conclusion

Pretty simple eh? Wood (as Maya includes it) is a procedural shader created not through reliance on a bitmapped image but created through mathematical procedures. The benefit of this sort of texture is that it is very adjustable on the fly and you can easily and quickly make adjustments to the color, vein, age, grain, and so on. Also of use is that you do not have to worry much about how the texture is applied across the surface; it largely looks correct as it penetrates the surface. The last problem is that something that is created that easily within the program can very quickly have a very generic look. Since everyone can access the exact same controls, the same wood tends to pop up in a lot of projects which can turn off an experienced eye (like an employer's).

UVs

Generally, the best materials (without an extensive knowledge of programming to create custom shaders) are created from scratch. This can be done through painting programs or through photographs. We have looked at how to create such things in Chapters 7 and 8 for use on the walls and furniture.

But, in those cases, we were generally working with fairly simple forms. It is very easy to define how a material falls across a flat wall as it only needs to project in really one direction. Using the Modeling | Polygon UVs > Planar Mapping function allows for easy and simple placement. But what happens when the shape is more complex; say as complex as the game model we created in Tutorial 10.2? The solution—and how most 3D applications solve the problem—is through UV manipulation.

So what is a UV? Well, it is more of a "where" than a "what." UVs are coordinates across the surface of a 3D shape. Think of UVs as the latitude and longitude of a form; generally (before a lot of polygon editing), the U wraps around the surface like latitude lines and the V wraps vertically like longitude lines.

So why are they important? Well, UVs allow you to define where a texture is to be attached to a surface. Think of a texture as a handkerchief. When the UVs on a surface have been properly defined, Maya (or any 3D application) then knows where to pin the handkerchief on the surface. UVs are plentiful, so this allows for lots of pins so that the texture is settled into place across the surface just as you want it—no pinching or stretching.

Where are UVs? In general, UVs are at vertices. That is, where polygons meet, there is a UV coordinate. You can see UVs in the View Panels, or in a tool called the UV Texture Editor.

The UV Texture Editor is available via Window > UV Texture Editor...Figure 11.5 shows the UV Texture Editor open with a simple cube displayed. Note that by right-clicking on an object in the UV Texture Editor, you can choose to select Edges, Vertices, Faces, or UVs. By default the UV Texture Editor represents these selections by different colors—UVs are green, vertices are yellow, and faces and edges are highlighted orange.

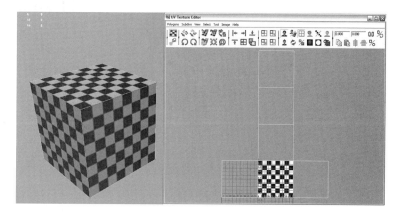

FIGURE 11.5 The UV Texture Editor and the components selectable via the UV Texture Editor.

Notice that in Figure 11.5 the cube does not look like a cube at all—well, not an intact one anyway. What you are seeing there is an unfolded version of the cube. Each of the planes have been laid out to make a 3D form 2D accessible. When you create a simple polygon primitive (like this cube), the vertices and UVs sit in the very same places. Each vertex has a corresponding UV.

Notice that there is only one copy of the actual texture (the checkers). Implied in the UV Texture Editor is that when the edge of the texture are reached, Maya automatically tiles the texture to fill the rest of the polygons. So, you have the same number of polygons on each side of the cube as the same 8x8 checker pattern is repeated once on each face.

Within the UV Texture Editor UVs can be selected (right-click and select UVs from the marking menu, then marquee around desired UVs) and then moved, scaled or rotated (Figure 11.6). Notice that the texture stays still, but as the UVs are manipulated, the texture appears to shift across the surface of the cube.

Consider Figure 11.7, which shows a polygon primitive sphere. See how the polygons (and thus the UVs) are all nicely laid out so that they fit neatly within the top right quadrant of the UV Texture Editor?

You would expect forms that Maya creates by default to have good UV layout; however, things get more complicated once you start working through more complex shapes. Take a look at Figure 11.8. Look familiar? It should as it is the game model from Tutorial 10.2. However, look at the mess that is the UV Texture Editor. Polygons lying on top of each other, some way out of the texture space (the top right quadrant).

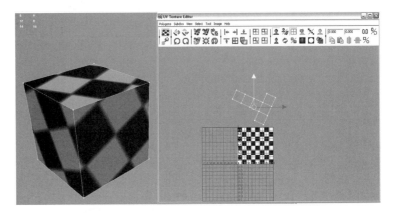

FIGURE 11.6   Rotated, moved, and scaled texture and its resulting cube.

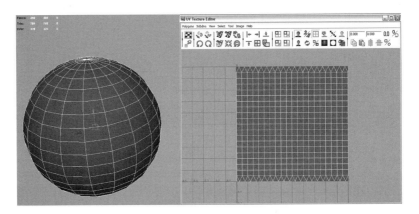

FIGURE 11.7   UV layout for a polygon primitive sphere.

This may not seem like a big problem when using the default gray lambert1 material. However, once any texture is applied (say a quick checkerboard), the results are disastrous (Figure 11.9).

Notice that in some places (like across the chest) some faces have checks stretched way out, while others are highly bunched. In other places like the head, you can see one row of checks stretching across entire polygons. All over the head and at places like the collar, there are polygons that are gray—the texture does not appear in those places at all—those polygons do not even have UVs.

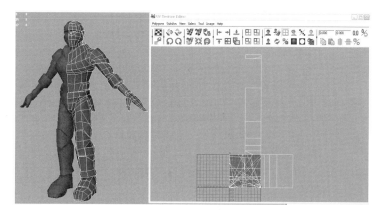

FIGURE 11.8   Character from Tutorial 10.2 and his corresponding UV layout.

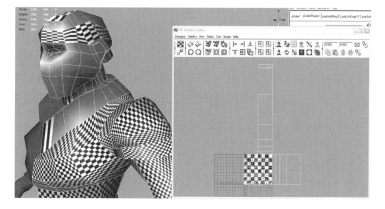

FIGURE 11.9   When a texture is applied using the UV texture layout we were left with in Tutorial 10.2.

If we were always dealing with solid colors for materials this would not be a problem. However, for most higher level 3D, custom textures are a necessity. In game models, the texture is a large part of the effectiveness of a character. It is incredibly important that the texture is applied to every polygon and that no polygons are sharing texture space or left out of the texture space all together.

UV MAPPING

The process of defining or reworking the UVs is called UV Mapping. Most of the tools for this process are available in the Modeling > Polygon UVs menu (in versions earlier than Maya 7 they were in the Modeling > Edit Polygons > Texture menu).

The goal here for our game model is to take control of all the UVs for the form and get them all to fit into the texture space shown in the top right quadrant of the UV Texture Editor. When this layout is complete (a sample is shown in Figure 11.10), we can export that UV layout into a paint program where we can decide exactly what color, bump, specular, and so on appears and is rendered on every single polygon—all thanks to the UV coordinate system.

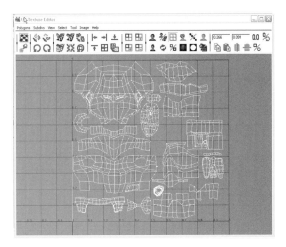

FIGURE 11.10 A completed UV layout.

The benefits are big; but the process can be a bit laborious. There have been some newer tools to emerge recently including Maya's Unfold UVs option (which we will not cover here—it is beyond the scope of this book and requires a very specific workflow unique only to Maya). Other tools like Wings and Modo have developed some very nice UV unwrapping options that can simplify the UV Mapping process. Lots of people model in one program, UV map in another, animate in a third and still render in a fourth. Just another testament to not become too software-centric in the 3D approach.

In the rest of this chapter we will be tackling the UV Mapping process in a very traditional way. There are several benefits to this. First, it allows you to really get down and dirty and understand how UVs work and how to get them appropriately unfold, and second, these are some techniques that you can transfer to other applications. So with an eye to general technique rather than software-specific button pushing, let's get started.

TUTORIAL 11.2   UV MAPPING GAME CHARACTER

Step 1: Set your project. Either use File > Project Set (and find your Game_Model project folder) or select it from the File > Recent Projects menu. In either case we need to be back using Game_Model as your project folder (the project folder from Tutorial 10.2).

If you would like, you can find the files used for this tutorial on the CD-ROM in the ProjectFiles folde. Check in the Chapter11 folder where you will find another Game_Model project file. You can take the contents of the scenes folder and sourceimages folder and copy them to your own to update your project file to match those we will be using for this tutorial. Included there is a file called Tutorial11.2Start.mb which is essentially the results of Tutorial 10.2 but cleaned up a little bit.

Step 2: Open the results of Tutorial 10.2 (or you can use Tutorial11.2Start.mb).

Step 3: Delete the mirrored side. Select the character's right side (the negative duplicate) and delete it.

Why? *This figure is generally symmetrical. So to do the UV layouts, we only need to layout one half of the character. After the one half is laid out, we can duplicate the other half and simply mirror the UV layout. We can still make the character look more realistic and asymmetrical when we paint the texture.*

Step 4: Delete the history of Character. Since this is the only object in the scene, select Edit > Delete All by Type > History.

Why? *All those extrudes, vertex merges, and tweaks are recorded as part of the history of Character. This is usually quite a long list of nodes at this point, and it will keep things snappy if you get rid of them. As we begin to lay on various projections onto this character we want to be able to quickly snag past projection nodes; having a clean slate to start out with makes this a simpler process.*

Step 5: Create a new Phong Material called CharacterMaterial. Right-click on Character and select Material > Assign New Material > Phong from the marking menu. Rename it CharacterMaterial.

Why? *You can also do that via the hypershade if you would prefer. The labeling just keeps it clear which materials will be applied to what objects but avoiding nodes with identical names.*

Step 6: Import a Checker render node into the Color channel. In the Attributes Editor (which should be displaying CharacterMaterial's attributes) click on the checkboard button for Color. Click the Checker button in the Create Render Node window.

Step 7: With your mouse in the persp view, press 6 on your keyboard to see the effects of this texture.

Why? *Why are we using checker; it doesn't seem like a very buff texture for a warrior? Well, this is only a temporary texture. Later we will replace it with a custom-painted one; but for now, the checkers help us see some important things. With a checker pattern you can very quickly see if the texture is being stretched or squished at any point along the surface. It also lets you see if there is a consistent distribution of texture across the surface (as you can see if the size of the checks is the same across the entire mesh).*

Step 8: Open the UV Texture Editor. Window > UV Texture Editor…

Mapping the Head

Step 9: Select approximately the faces shown in Figure 11.11. Switch to Faces mode and select a collection of faces that make a sort of quarter of a vertical cylinder.

FIGURE 11.11   Selecting first projection selection.

Why? *This is not a random selection of polygons. The first projection we are going to use is a Cylindrical Mapping (a good one for most organic shapes). To effectively use a Cylindrical Mapping we need to have a collection of faces that are at least part of a*

cylindrical shape. Notice that none of these selected faces wrap under or over the face; just around.

Step 10: Cylindrical Project the UVs. Choose Modeling | Polygon UVs > Cylindrical Mapping (Figure 11.12).

FIGURE 11.12   Results of default Cylindrical Mapping of UVs.

Why?

Figure 11.12 has some added highlights. The manipulator handles associated with the Cylindrical Mapping are a bit tough to see with textures enabled, but it is important to see this shape and its handles.

These handles are important as they allow for the manipulation of the projection. However, they are sometimes difficult to see just in Maya and even more difficult to see in a book.

A couple quick notes about this new Cylindrical Mapping Node and its manipulators. Right after you use the Modeling | Polygon UVs > Cylindrical Mapping command (or any of the projection commands) you will immediately have access to the manipulators that allow you to visually adjust size and placement for the UVs. There are actually two different sets of manipulators to be had. In general, you do not want to use the default manipulators—but rather those available via the little toggle switch shown in Figure 11.13.

These second collections of manipulators are similar to the traditional Move, Scale, and Rotate Tools seen with other tools like the Universal Manipulator Tool and the Extrude Face Tool. There is a light blue circle around the move/scale handles that will activate the ability to rotate the projection, while the move/scale handles allow you to move or scale the half cylinder that represents the projection.

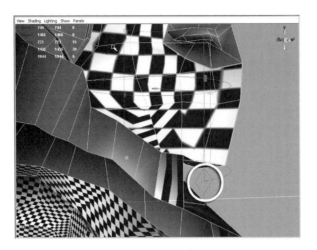

FIGURE 11.13 The toggle that allows for a second collection of manipulators for the Cylindrical Mapping Node.

Remember that you can toggle back to the first set of manipulators by clicking the same little red toggle button again.

Also of important note, if you accidentally click away from the manipulators, they disappear. A quick Ctrl-z will often bring them back; however if they do not, you can regain them in one of two ways. First, you can simply select the faces and reapply the mapping (it will overwrite any old mapping nodes). Second, in the Channel Box, you can select the projection node and then make sure you have Show Manipulators selected in the Tool Box and you will be back in manipulator business.

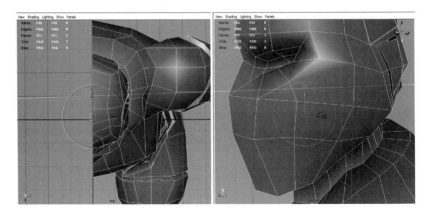

FIGURE 11.14 The second set of manipulators available with the Cylindrical Mapping Node. Note that the texture is hid for this screenshot.

Step 11: Activate the alternate modifier handles and rotate, scale and position the projection so that it creates equal size checkers across the cheeks (Figure 11.15). Be sure that the center of the projection is on the Z axis (X = 0).

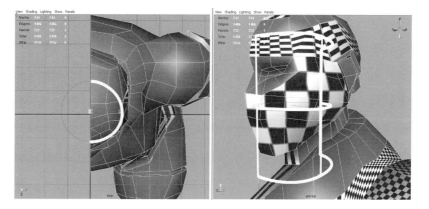

FIGURE 11.15   Rotated, scaled, and moved projection to create constant texture across selected faces.

The size of the checkers here are largely arbitrary. The purpose here is to try and be able to see even texture distribution; so you want to make sure that you can see enough checkers in each projection to be able to determine that.

Because we are only UV Mapping one half of the character, it will be important that the UVs along the center of the figure are in a straight line to allow for easy sewing to the other half. Making sure that the center of the Cylindrical Mapping is X = 0 or along the plane of symmetry will ensure that this is the case. The other half of making sure that you have a clean line of UVs is to make sure that the projection is rotated 90 degrees so that the open end of the Cylindrical Mapping shape is on the open side of the character.

Some tips about adjusting the manipulator. Remember that these faces do not make up an entire cylinder, just a part of one. So often times moving the projection (via the move manipulation handles) a bit in the Z direction (actually done by moving the red X handle since the projection should be rotated 90 degrees) will help distribute the checks a bit better. Also, when the manipulator is indeed at X = 0 and when you have moved it back a bit, you will probably find that the checks are not square. Be sure to use the scale manipulator handles to stretch the handles and thus the checks into perfect squares.

Additional notes about this manipulator are that it can be adjusted numerically in the Channels Box. If your Channels Box is visible (turn it on with the buttons in the top right corner of the interface), and right after you have projected UVs, you will see a node called polyCylProj1 with a collection of input fields beneath it (Figure 11.16). The settings used for Figure 11.15 are shown in Figure 11.16. Notice that the Project Center X = 0, Rotate Y = 90 and Projection Horizontal Sweep = 180. The other values may vary a bit depending on how you modeled your character.

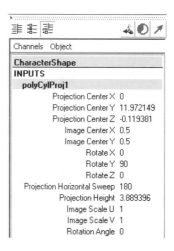

FIGURE 11.16   Using the Channel Box to numerically input changes to the Cylindrical Mapping Node.

Ultimately the goal is to have perfectly square checks with little or no distortion across the surface of the projected faces.

Step 12: In the UV Texture Editor, move the newly projected faces aside out of the top right quadrant. Press w to activate the Move Tool and drag the manipulator to move the faces (actually the UVs represented by those faces) out and away from the mess of the rest of the UVs (Figure 11.17).

Why?

Yes, we are now moving UVs out of the area where they must eventually end up at. However, this is a valuable thing to do as it allows you to easily see the UVs and later to manipulate them in ways that will allow you to attach them to other UVs. If they remain in the middle of the quadrant it becomes impossible to work with.

Step 13: Select the faces shown in Figure 11.18 (or close to these). With your mouse over the persp View Panel, press 5 to hide the textures for a moment and select the ring of polygons shown in Figure 11.18. They should be generally in a cylindrical shape.

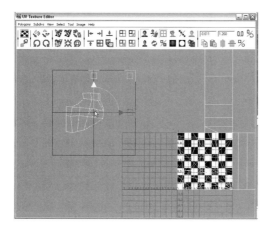

FIGURE 11.17   Moving UVs away for ease of access.

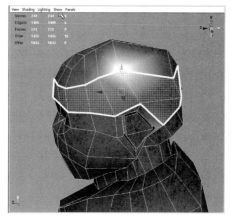

FIGURE 11.18   Selection for next projection.

Why? *Why these? Which polygons to select when for what projection is a tough call. As you work, you will begin to see areas that will be a good candidate for a certain type of projection. On one hand, you could make a lot of little small projections (and then have to do a lot of sewing) to get ultra-accurate projections, or make big huge selections and then get some stretching—but you would have to do little sewing. The compromise is finding big enough collections of polygons to minimize the number of projections—but small enough to allow for accurate projection.*

Step 14: Press 6 to show texture again.

Step 15: Cylindrical Project with options. Choose Modeling | Polygon UVs > Cylindrical Mapping (Options). In the Polygon Cylindrical Projection Options window, turn off Automatically Fit the Projection Manipulator. Change the Rotation for Y (the second column) to 90 (Figure 11.19).

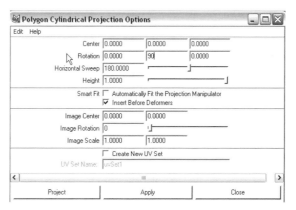

FIGURE 11.19   The Polygon Cylindrical Projection Options to save time with manipulators.

We know from earlier steps that we want the center of the projection to be at 0. We also know that we need the projection to be rotated 90 degrees. While we could get the projection center at 0 and rotated 90 degrees using the handles, doing this in the Options can avoid having to fool as much with the manipulators or the Channel Box. There is still some adjustment that will need to be made, but two of the big ones (center and rotation) are all done.

Step 16: Adjust projection to find correct proportions of checks. Because of the settings in the options window, the projection will probably be down around his hips. Click on the toggle for the alternate manipulator handles for the projection and use the move Y handle (the green one), to move the handles up around the head. You will probably need to use the scale Y handle to scale the projection taller to get the checks square. Resize until they are approximately the same size as the first projection on the cheek (Figure 11.20).

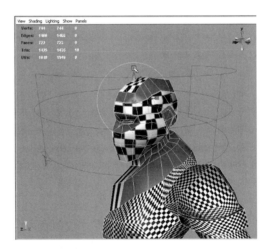

FIGURE 11.20   Results of additional tweaks.

Step 17: In the UV Texture Editor, move these newly projected UVs away to the left (Figure 11.21).

Again, the point here is to get those areas we have worked out away from those we have not. Notice that in your UV Texture Editor, only those newly projected faces will be visible. However, once you have them moved off and away, click anywhere in the UV Texture Editor where there is not a face and you will see all the faces/UVs.

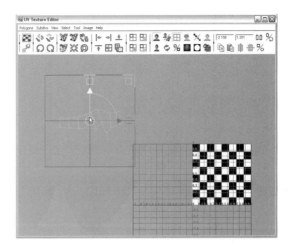

FIGURE 11.21 Moving newly projected UVs away from mess.

Step 18: Move the UVs of the new projection close to those of the old. Right-click on the most recently completed collection of UVs and choose UV from the marking menu (11.22a). Marquee around any UV there (Figure 11.22b). Ctrl-Right-Click and select To Shell from the marking menu (Figure 11.22c). Press w and use the Move Tool to move them down close to the first projection, which should give you something like Figure 11.22d.

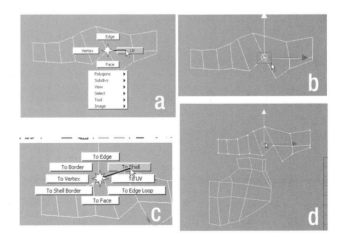

FIGURE 11.22 The process of selecting a collection of UVs.

Yes, we could have selected the UVs by just dragging around the collection of them.
Why? *However, this method of selecting one, and then having Maya pull out the shell is*

useful as we get more complex. You can use it at any time to collect any set of UVs that are sewn (attached) together.

Step 19: Identify shared edges. In the persp View Panel, click on the edges that are shared between the two projections (highlighted in Figure 11.23). Notice that they highlight (twice) in the UV Texture Editor.

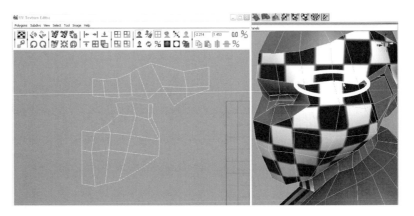

FIGURE 11.23   Finding where the shared edges are in the UV layout by selecting them in the View Panel.

Step 20: Adjust the top collection of UVs so the edges are closer in size. In the UV Texture Editor, right-click on the top collection of UVs and select UV. Select the top shell of UVs and press r to activate the Scale Tool. Rescale so that the shared edges of each shell are close to the same size (Figure 11.24).

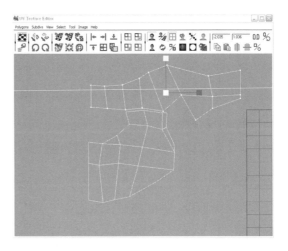

FIGURE 11.24   Rescaled UVs.

Why? *We know that these edges are shared; that means in texture space they should be the same size. Often when dealing with the checkerboard pattern, the checks can end up bigger than the selection and it can be tough to see if the sizes are right; sometimes it is easier to see and make adjustments in the UV Texture Editor.*

Step 21: Sew the shared edges together. In the UV Texture Editor, right-click and select Edges (Figure 11.25a). Choose the edges that are shared (Figure 11.25b). Choose Polygons > Move and Sew UVs (Figure 11.25c).

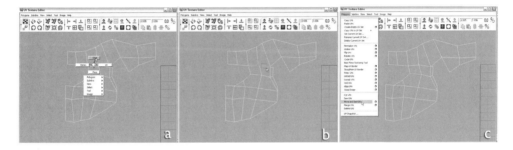

FIGURE 11.25 The Sew UVs process.

Why? *What does this mean? Well, now, the shared edges are indeed one edge. What this means is that the texture now crawls unobstructed across the two projections. It makes for one continuous UV Map for all the UVs we have mapped to this point. For places like the face this will be important. When a surface is solid, there should be few or no seams (UV seams) across its surface.*

Step 22: Select all the faces associated with the ear piece. Note that this may include some faces already mapped (Figure 11.26). Make sure you are looking straight at these faces.
Step 23: Planar Project the UVs. Select Modeling | Polygon UVs > Planar Mapping Options. Since you are looking straight at the faces, select Mapping Direction as Camera. Press project. Use the regular manipulator handles (the red boxes) to resize so that the checks match the rest of the head (Figure 11.27).
Step 24: Sew the new faces into the rest of the mapped face. In the UV Texture Editor move the new faces over towards the others. Switch to UV mode and scale and rotate the collection of UVs into where they belong (Figure 11.28a). Choose Polygons > Move and Sew UVs (Figure 11.28b).

Why? *Now we are breaking some rules. On the one hand we have some well- mapped faces that face the camera. However there are also the recessed faces that give this shape depth. Usually we would want to map those individually, but in this case,*

there is little need. As those recess faces will hardly be seen, we will never see the stretching that will occur there as those faces share an infinitely thin section of texture space.

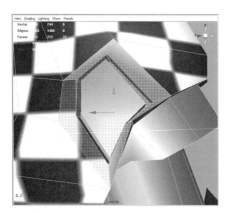

FIGURE 11.26 Selecting ear piece faces.

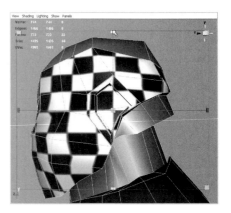

FIGURE 11.27 Results of Planar Mapping and tweaked manipulators.

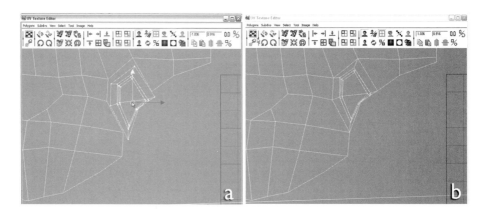

FIGURE 11.28 Aligning and then moving and sewing ear UVs into place.

Step 25: Repeat for the eye (Figure 11.29). The recess faces here are also acceptably not mapped as the eye sockets will all be black.

Step 26: Continue mapping the rest of the head. Note the limitations shown in Figure 11.30.

Why? *Because of the complexity of the head, there either needs to be several seams where you can split off sections of the UV, or you will have some stretching. With many characters, especially those with hair, the seams are preferable, as you can nest*

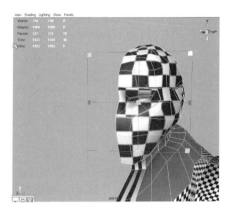

FIGURE 11.29   Mapped eye.

FIGURE 11.30   Stretched and deformed UVs at head top.

them into the hair line or other places where the texture will naturally be changing. It becomes more difficult with a character like this with a chrome-dome. In this case, we have chosen to allow for some deformation (rather than seams) across the back of the head. In part this is because it is unlikely that the back/top of the head will be seen much; and it is preferable to a seam running at the top of the forehead. For other characters this would be a different choice.

Step 27: Map the entire helmet head area. Use both Cylindrical Mapping and Planar Mapping (Figure 11.31).

Why? *Figure 11.31 shows the mapping created after the entire head and helmet is mapped. Notice that there is a separate piece up at the top—this is the second back*

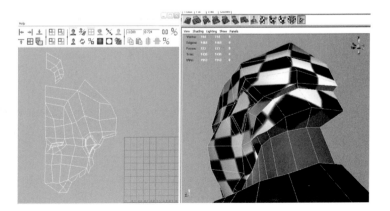

FIGURE 11.31   Mapped head and helmet.

ledge of the helmet. Since the plan is to make this a separate material, this is a nat-ural place for a seam. Also note that the bottom of the map is "dirty." There are ragged UVs flopping around the bottom. These are the faces that make up the un-derside of the chin and jaw. These will rarely be seen and will actually be colored a solid black. Because of this, there is no need to worry about seams.

Although technically the extra helmet ledge and chin bottom could be mapped (and should for nonhelmeted characters); in this case it saves loads of time and has-sle to allow these particular UV collections to be separate or free.

Step 28: Clean up seams. In the UV Texture Editor, select all the vertices that should be on the center seam (Figure 11.32a). Activate the Move Tool (w) and then hold the x key down and move along the X (actually the U) handle.

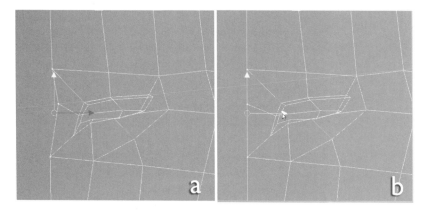

FIGURE 11.32   Adjusting and cleaning up seams.

If you have been careful in your projections and made sure all your Cylindrical Mapping functions were at the X = 0, you should not have many stray UVs. How-ever, sometimes as you Move and Sew UVs there can be a little shifting of UVs. So taking a moment to clean up the center seam can do loads of good.

Why?

Mapping the Leg

Step 29: Cylindrical Map the knee pad. Press 5 to hide texture for a second. Select all the faces that make up the outside ring of the knee pad (do not worry about the recessed faces). Choose Modeling | Polygon UVs > Cylindri-cal Mapping (Options). Turn Automatically Fit the Projection Manipulator back on. Click Project (Figure 11.33). Press 6 to turn textures back on.

Step 30: Using the default projection manipulator handles wrap the pro-jection completely around the knee. Do this by grabbing either of the red handles and dragging it until it meets the other (probably around the back (Figure 11.34)).

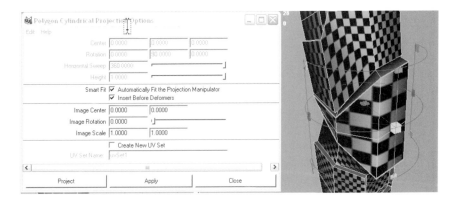

FIGURE 11.33   Results of default Cylindrical Mapping.

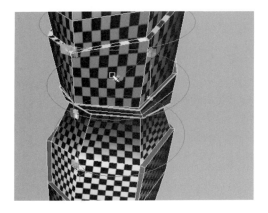 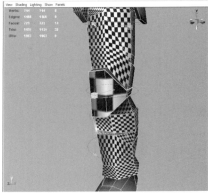

FIGURE 11.34   Wrapping the projection completely around the knee pad.

FIGURE 11.35   Rescaling the projection to create even texture.

Step 31: Scale the projection to make square checks. Do this by grabbing the green blocks of the manipulator to resize vertically (Figure 11.35). Remember to be looking for checks that are the same size as they are on the face.

Why?

This could also be done using the alternate manipulator handles; it is up to you. Sometimes things can be done with either set of manipulators, sometimes only one will work. Sometimes the best solution is to use a bit of both and enter values in the Channel Box. For instance, you could enter 360 into the Projection Horizontal Sweep input value in the Channel Box (the input fields would be way at the bot-

tom of a long list by now—so scroll down); or, you could do it visually as we have just done.

Step 32: In the UV Texture Editor move the newly mapped UVs away to the side.

Step 33: Map the thigh pad. Select the faces that make up the thigh pad (make sure to go all the way around the form). Select Modeling | Polygon UVs > Cylindrical Mapping.

Step 34: Adjust to wrap completely around pad and rescale to make square checks (Figure 11.36).

Step 35: Rotate projection to place seam along back inner thigh. Along the middle of the default manipulator is the line that connects the two red blocks. Click and drag this line to rotate the projection (Figure 11.37).

FIGURE 11.36   Projected UV Map on thigh pad.

FIGURE 11.37   Rotating projection to be aligned with back inner thigh.

Why?

When we were mapping the head we were aiming to create a seam that is easily masked later in the process. When working on things like the arms and legs the seam will always be there. The map has to unwrap and break somewhere. The key is to find where to place this seam.

In the case of the knee pad, the small of the back of the knee was where the projection placed it—and made sense as it is small and tough to see that area. However, for the thigh pad, the back center would be a bad place to have it and would easily be seen since it is such a large area. Rotating it around to a more inner-thigh area tucks it into an area where it will be less likely to be seen.

Step 36: In the UV Texture Editor move the newly mapped UVs away to the side (Figure 11.38).

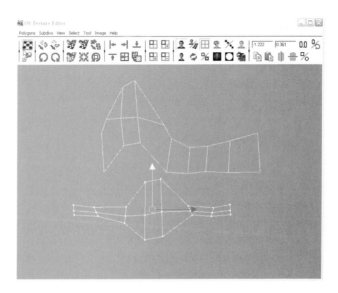

FIGURE 11.38   Moved knee (bottom and selected) and thigh (top) UVs.

 Notice that we are not sewing these together. If the thigh and knee pads were a unified surface we would need to do this to keep the texture from showing seams. However, this character uses separate pieces of armor, so a seam is actually preferable here. And, to our advantage, it makes the mapping faster.

Why?

Step 37: Finish mapping the leg. Do this with multiple Cylindrical Mapping functions for different pieces of armor (Figure 11.39). Be sure to adjust the seam to the most appropriate place on each projection.

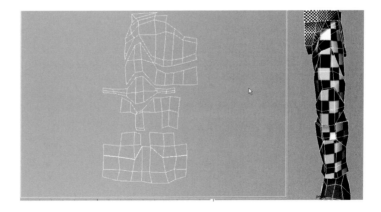

FIGURE 11.39   Mapped leg.

Note that in the UV Texture Editor, each of the mapped areas has been moved over and generally lined up. Of course, nothing is sewn together here (largely because there are faces that make up the recessed part), but the pieces are tucked in together fairly tightly. Part of this is so that you do not waste any texture space. You do not want to have Maya keep track of any texture space that you do not have faces on. The second reason is later as you paint the texture map for this, it will be important to be able to tell what is what. By generally organizing the upper thigh on top and the shin on the bottom, it becomes easier to tell which collection of UVs are for what part of the leg.

Step 38: Map any leftover leg faces (if you have any). This is a bit of a tricky technique, but it works really well. In the UV Texture Editor right-click and select Faces from the marking menu. Still in the UV Texture Editor, select all the faces of the leg that you have mapped (these will also highlight in the persp View Panel). Now, in the persp View Panel, hold the Shift down and marquee around the entire leg. This will deselect the faces that were selected (and consequently already mapped) and select those that were not (which were the faces that were not mapped). The result will be all the ledges of the recessed parts of the armor will be selected (Figure 11.40).

Pretty snazzy huh? Actually using the UV Texture Editor to select hard-to- reach polygons can be a very effective tool. Often bouncing between the two using the Shift-to-deselect-previously-selected and select-previously-unselected faces (or inverse selection) is a quick and very effective way to make sure you have found and mapped all the faces.

Step 39: Planar Map these faces by the Y axis. Choose Modeling | Polygon UVs > Planar Mapping (Options). Change the Mapping Direction to Y Axis. Press Project.

Step 40: Move and scale this blob of UVs into a small space of available texture space (Figure 11.41).

These recessed parts of the armor are where we are going to start the rust look. Because these faces are not seen much, and generally they will contain just a solid rust color, we do not need to spend a lot of texture space on the faces, nor a lot of time mapping and sewing them all into place. We will look at how to make the texture seamless from the edges to the front of the armor later.

FIGURE 11.40   Selected nonmapped polygons.

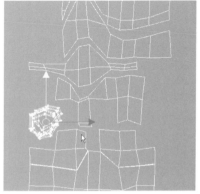

FIGURE 11.41   Mapped recessed faces.

Arms

Step 41: Map the arm using the same technique as you did on the leg. Look for parts that are clearly one particular piece of armor or skin. Note that because the arm is aimed down at an angle, you will need to rotate the projection to get the cylinder of the projection to really act as a sleeve down the arm (Figure 11.42). This is most easily done with the alternate manipulator handles. Work up to the cuff of the shoulder pad, and down to the end of the wrist (Figure 11.43).

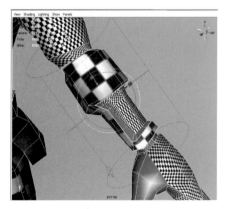

FIGURE 11.42   Results of rotated projection.

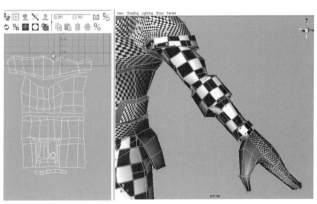

FIGURE 11.43   Completed arm.

A few tips: 1) Some sections will need a cylindrical projection that wraps clear around the arm and sometimes it will only need to wrap around part of it. 2) Remember that sometimes it is easier to see your selection of faces when the texture is turned off (so press

Why?

5 to show only flat shaded—select your faces—and then press 6 again when its time to project). 3) Do not worry too much about the edges (recessed) faces of the armor—give it a simple projection so that it can be given the simple rust texture later.

Step 42: Map the top of the hands with a Planar projection. Select the faces on the top of the hand (not the thumb) and choose Modeling | Polygon UVs > Planar Mapping (Options). Activate Fit to Best Plane and click Project. Tweak the manipulator handles to get even distribution (Figure 11.44). Finally, make sure to move the UVs in the UV Texture Editor off to the side.

Step 43: Repeat for the palm. Select the faces that make up the palm and again choose Modeling | Polygon UVs > Planar Mapping (no need to do options as Maya remembers your last settings for this tool. Tweak the manipulator handles to get good distribution. Finally, move the UVs in the UV Texture Editor so the two halves of the hand are close to each other (Figure 11.45).

FIGURE 11.44   Mapped hand top.

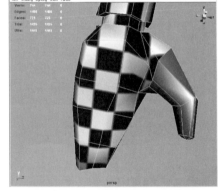

FIGURE 11.45   Mapped palm.

Why? *This technique does not always work for hands, but usually for game hands you can get a quick result via two quick planar maps like this. The seam which runs along the outside edge and between the thumb and fingers is rarely seen. With careful texture painting, it becomes even more invisible.*

Step 44: Map the thumb with two Cylindrical projections for the two sections of the thumb (Figure 11.46). Be sure to work on getting the seams along the same edge on the inside of the thumb. In the UV Texture Editor, move both projections away to the side and then select the common edges (the bottom of one projection and the top of the other). Use Polygons > Move and Sew to attach them.

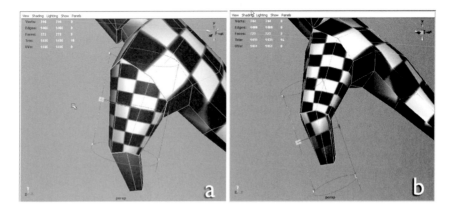

FIGURE 11.46   Mapped thumbs.

 There are an awful lot of checkers in the screenshot shown in Figure 11.46— more than there should be really. Often when working on an object that is going to be sewn together or that needs some specific detailed work, it is alright to let the texture appear smaller than usual. It helps you to define if your four projections do indeed share a relative size.

Once the area is complete, you can arrange the pieces (Figure 11.47) and then select all the UVs and scale them down to make the hand (in this case) share its appropriate share of the texture space.

Why?

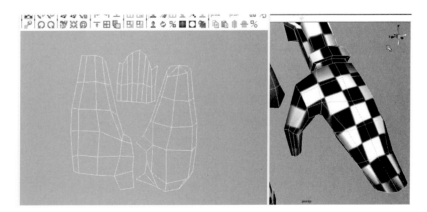

FIGURE 11.47   Completed hand. Notice that the checker size now matches that on the arms.

Step 45: Map the shoulder pad. Do this with two Cylindrical Projections (the faces for each are shown in Figure 11.48a and 11.48b). Make sure the seam is underneath in the hard-to-see armpit. In the UV Texture Editor, use Move and Sew to sew the two projections together.

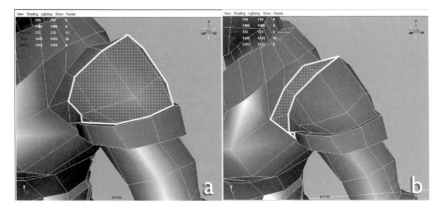

FIGURE 11.48   Projection faces to select and project using Cylindrical Mapping.

Step 46: Organize. In the UV Texture Editor take a minute to start to organize shells of UVs. Figure 11.49 shows the shells created so far. Notice that on the top left are the shells that are the arm. Notice that the hands are at the bottom and the shoulder pad is at the top. Even though these shells do not have to be fused together, organizing them a little bit goes a long way when it comes time to paint.

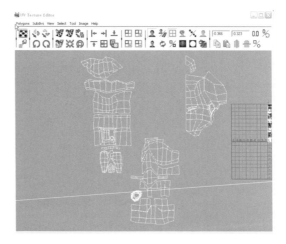

FIGURE 11.49   A bit of organization in arranging shells goes a long way.

Chest and Crotch

Step 47: Map the chest (sans the kidney pad and collar). This can be done several ways, but try doing it with three projections; one around the stomach area, one around the pecs and one on the top of the chest (Figure 11.50).

FIGURE 11.50   Three projections to rough out the chest.

Step 48: In the UV Texture Editor stitch the projections together and make the center UVs snap to the grid (Figure 11.51).

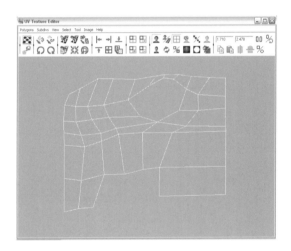

FIGURE 11.51   Using Move and Sew to make the chest one solid UV shell.

Mapping this chest will be a lot like mapping the head. The front of the chest is the likely place to try and make this seamless, so you need to make sure that the UVs along the front are completely flat. The backside will have a seam, but the back will be less crucial (like the back of the head).

Why?

Step 49: Map the kidney pads as a separate Cylindrical Mapping function.
Step 50: Map the outside edge of the belt and the butt guards (Figure 11.52).

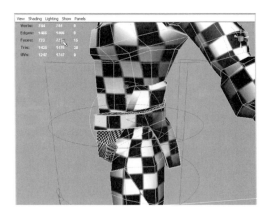

FIGURE 11.52   Mapped belt outer ring of faces.

 Mapping the outside ring of faces is fairly easy as it fits into the shape of a cylindri-cal projection quite easily. The bigger issue here that we need to solve is the top and **Why?** *bottom of the belt.*

In other spots on the model we could get away with not worrying about the re-cessed (top and bottom of rings of polygons) faces. But here, the belt is too prominent to go without. So we will need to get the outside ring of faces to seamlessly connect to the faces on the top and bottom of the belt.

Step 51: Select the faces on the top and bottom of the belt.
Step 52: Use a Planar Projection via Modeling | Polygon UVs > Planar Mapping (Options). Activate Fit to Bounding Box, and change the Map-ping Direction to Y Axis. Press Project. Adjust the manipulator to get a good size of texture (Figure 11.53).

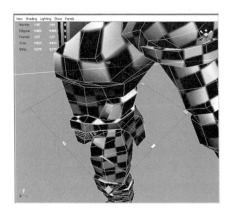

FIGURE 11.53   Results of Planar Mapping on the faces on top and below the belt.

Step 53: In the UV Texture Editor, move the projection aside, and separate the shell that is the top of the belt from the shell that is the bottom of the belt (Figure 11.54).

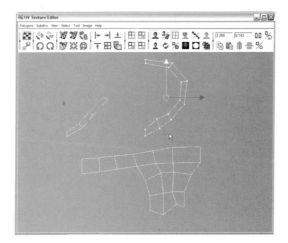

FIGURE 11.54   Separated top and bottom projections. The shell on the bottom is the belt and butt protector.

When the projection was made along the Y axis, both the top and the bottom belt faces were projected upon. This meant that their UVs were right on top of each
Why? *other. By selecting any one UV, and then Ctrl-right-clicking and selecting To Shell, you could find the shell that was either the top or bottom collection of faces. By moving either of those to the side, you can much more easily see each shell of UVs.*

Step 54: Cut the UVs of the top and bottom shells. Do this by choosing each of the edges that separates each face in the UV Texture Editor. Choose Polygons > Cut UVs. Then you can select one UV, Ctrl-right-click and select To Shell from the marking menu. You can then move a shell that is composed of just one face away from the others. You can repeat this moving one face at a time for all the faces (Figure 11.55).

Step 55: Use Move and Sew to sew each of the free-floating faces to the main belt/butt pad shell (Figure 11.56).

Looking better, however, you can see that clearly there is a problem as the polygons along the top of the belt (and bottom) are split. In each of these splits you would end
Why? *up with a seam. This is largely unavoidable in situations like where there is a hard corner between faces that need to have an unbroken texture. The way that you can lessen the problem here is to avoid the seam, but allow for a little stretching via some added sewing.*

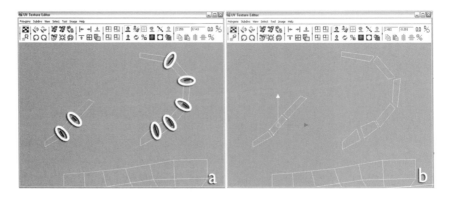

FIGURE 11.55   Using Cut UVs to separate a projection into individual polygons.

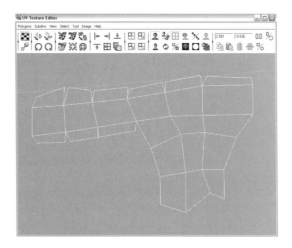

FIGURE 11.56   Results of using Move and Sew to attach faces from top and bottom of belt to the main belt shell.

Step 56: Sew the split edges of top and bottom faces. Select the shared faces between each of the split faces along the top and bottom of the belt (in the UV Texture Editor). Choose Polygons > Sew UVs (Figure 11.57).

The difference between Move and Sew UVs and just Sew UVs is that Move and Sew will take a shell and attempt to move it into a position without distorting either shell too badly before sewing them together. The Sew UVs command just takes the shells at whatever place they are and split the difference between UVs that are to be joined. In this case Sew UVs does just what we need as it joins the UVs together without distorting other parts of the belt shell.

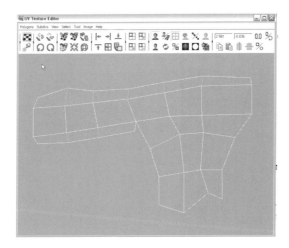

FIGURE 11.57   Result of Sew UVs to rid the belt of seams.

Step 57: Repeat this process for the edges of the butt guard (Figure 11.58).

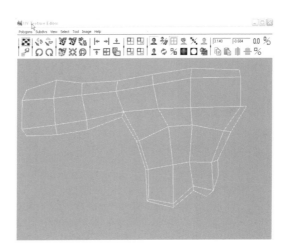

FIGURE 11.58   Added UVs for edge of butt pad.

Step 58: Map the crotch. Do this with a collection of Cylindrical and Planar Mapping functions. Again, remember that you need to have a clean inner edge. Be sure to sew the various projections together in the UV Texture Editor.

 Do not worry too much about exactness in the crotch area. Chances are no one is going to spend too much time looking at that area in the middle of a game and lots

of the crotch area (most of the butt) is covered up by the butt guard. So if you have some stretching of the UVs don't sweat it.

One note though; notice that in Figure 11.59 the checks are small—which means that at the time of that screenshot, the UVs that made up the crotch were taking up a lot of texture space. But these smaller checks allow us to easily see if there is stretching—something we would not be able to see if the checks were really big. However, after all the mapping is done and the crotch area is all one, be sure to take the shell that is the crotch and reduce its size in the UV Texture Editor to get the checks uniform with the rest of the model.

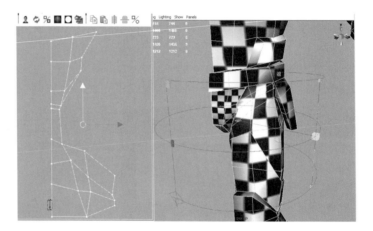

FIGURE 11.59   Finished crotch.

Miscellaneous

Step 59: Map the collar, neck and shoes. You know most of the important techniques by now. Remember that the collar and neck need to be setup with a clean line of UVs along the middle of the model (Figure 11.60).

Step 60: Check for missed nonmapped UVs. If you have been careful and mapped every face, there should be nothing left in the top right quadrant of the UV Texture Editor. To check, in the UV Texture Editor switch to Face mode. Marquee around the top right quadrant. If anything there turns orange, you missed something. Take a look to see whether it is anything important. If you find important faces have not been mapped, map them with a quick Planar Mapping and then go sew them into place. For faces that you can not even find in the model, you might have found a face that is hidden or otherwise too small to matter in the big scheme of things. Scale these faces (in the UV Texture Editor) very small (as they should not take much texture space) and put them aside.

Step 61: Check for faces without UVs. In the UV Texture Editor, switch back to face mode and marquee around all the shells—everything you can see there. This selects all the faces that have UVs. Now in persp View Panel, Shift-marquee around the entire model. This will select any faces that were not selected in the UV Texture Editor—which will point out any faces that do not have UVs assigned to them. If nothing selects, you are in the clear. If something does select, again, do a quick Planar Mapping and get it stitched into place where it belongs.

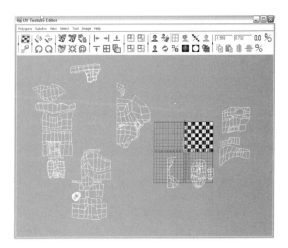

FIGURE 11.60   Completed mapped character—sort of.

Mirroring the Model and UVs

Quick note about the mirroring process we are about to embark on. In most games, artists do not usually mirror the UVs. They create one set of UVs for one half of the model, then create a texture map that covers that one half of the model, and then simply use it twice (mirrored for the other side). This gives them the most texture space to create more detailed textures.

However, for nongame models it becomes really important to be able to mirror the UVs to create nonsymmetrical textures. For this reason, in this section we will mirror the model and UVs so you can create asymmetrical textures.

Step 62: Delete History. Edit > Delete All by Type > History.

Now that the model is mapped, we no longer need it to keep track of the infinitely long list of projections and tweaks.

Step 63: Mirror the Character. Choose Modeling > Polygons > Mirror Geometry (Options). Make sure to change the Mirror Direction to –X. Also make sure Merge With the Original and Merge Vertices are activated (Figure 11.61).

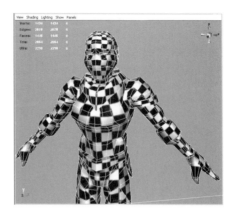

FIGURE 11.61 Results of Mirrored Geometry.

 This will reveal a very checkered character. Of special note is that the texture is an exact mirror of itself. Note that in the UV Texture Editor it seems as though nothing has changed. However, try this:

In the UV Texture Editor, switch to UV mode (right-click and select UV from the marking menu). In the face area, click (do not marquee) on any of the UVs of that shell. Ctrl-right-click and select To Shell from that marking menu. Now switch to the Move Tool and move the shell to the side. You should see that suddenly here are two identical sets of UVs (Figure 11.62)!

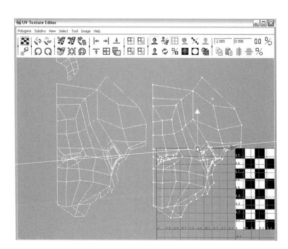

FIGURE 11.62 Identical sets of UVs that were lying on top of each other now separated.

 This is important to know. After mirroring geometry, you have two sets of disconnected UV shells identical and right on top of each other. We need to get things like the face and chest so that it is one solid surface unwrapped (not two halves on top of each other).

Step 64: Mirror one set of UVs in the UV Texture Editor. In the head area, make sure you have separated the two mirrored sets of UVs (if you have not see the Why? box above). Select the UV shell of the UVs that represent the character's right side (Figure 11.63a). Still in the UV Texture Editor, select Polygons > Flip UVs (Options). Make sure the Direction is set to Horizontal and click Apply and Close (Figure 11.63b).

We need to make sure that the two inside seams are facing each other so that we can sew them together. It can be a little disconcerting that after you apply the Flip UVs option, everything disappears—don't panic, just switch to UV mode and click away and everything will come back.

Why?

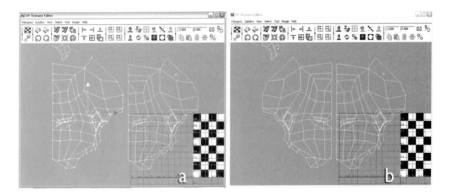

FIGURE 11.63   Flipped UVs.

Step 65: Sew the two shells up. In the UV Texture Editor, switch to Edge mode. Select the edges down the center of the two mirrored shells (these edges are now shared). Use Polygons > Move and Sew UVs (Figure 11.64).

And violà! Now when you look at the head in the persp View Panel, you will see that no longer is there one copy of the checkered texture mirrored, but a smooth tex-tured checker that runs all the way across the face.

Why?

Step 66: Repeat for the helmet ledge, neck, collar, chest, belt and crotch shells (Figure 11.65).

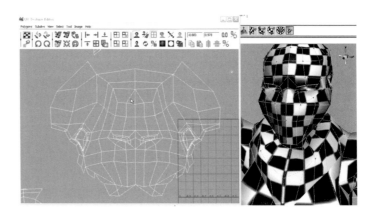

FIGURE 11.64   Stitched together head.

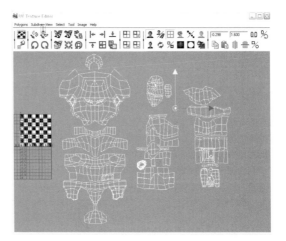

FIGURE 11.65   Completed UV Mapping. Notice the left column of shells are all mirrored and stitched.

Endgame

Step 67: Resize and place UV shells in UV Texture Editor. In the UV Texture Editor select Image > Show Image (which will turn the image off). Select all the UVs by marqueeing around everything. Resize them all (with the center resize handle) until they are closer to the size of the top right quadrant. Arrange the shells so that they make the most use of the texture space but still make sense to you as to which shell is which (Figure 11.66).

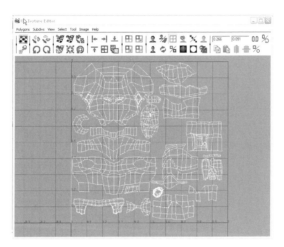

FIGURE 11.66   Laid out UVs.

Some rules: 1) Make sure to only move entire UV shells. Do not just move certain UVs or all your mapping with be for naught. 2) Do not rescale any one shell. You **Why?** *can resize everything together, but you carefully spent the last few hours trying to make sure that the checker material was evenly distributed across the surfaces. If you rescale one shell and not the others, you are redefining that distribution. If the checks were small enough to see you would see checks of all different sizes if you start rescaling only certain shells. 3) Make sure that all the UVs fit inside of the top right quadrant.*

Step 68: Output the UV map. In Object mode, select the character in persp View Panel. Then, in the UV Texture Editor select Polygons > UV Snapshot. . . .Change the Size X and Size Y to 1256 and the Image Format to TIFF. The other values should be fine (Figure 11.67).

What is a UV snapshot? A UV snapshot is a sort of map. Creating a UV snapshot is creating an image that indicates where all of the UVs for a particular object are. **Why?** *You can use this snapshot (Figure 11.68) to then decide where to paint to place different colors or bump on what particular polygons.*

Notice that Maya outputs the UV Snapshot to the images folder of your project file. The file it exports is called outUV. The UV Snapshot dialog box allows us to define the size of the snapshot and the format this image will be in. A 1256x1256 texture map is about a middle-of-the-road size for many games. Saving the UV Snapshot as a TIFF allows you to open and edit the file in most paint programs (including Photoshop, Illustrator, and so on).

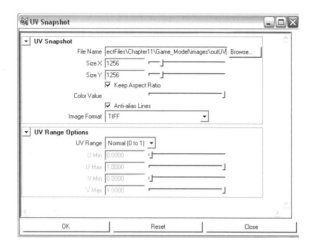

FIGURE 11.67   Outputting the UV Snapshot.

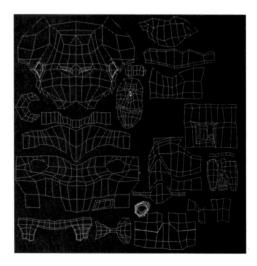

FIGURE 11.68   UV Snapshot.

Tutorial Conclusion

So there it is; the mapping anyway. Figure 11.69 shows a sample painted texture map created using the UV Snapshot created in the last step. In Maya, if the checkerboard render node is replaced with this texture, the results are seen in Figure 11.70. For more details on this process and preparing your texture file from the UV snapshot, take a look at Appendix D.

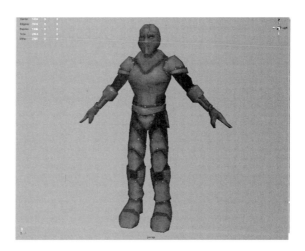

FIGURE 11.69   Textured character.

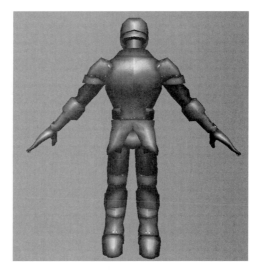

FIGURE 11.70   Additional view of textured character.

CHALLENGES, EXERCISES, OR ASSIGNMENTS

1. Work through Appendix D and create a custom color texture for this character.
2. Create a custom bump map, specular channel, and anything else to give the character extra depth and pizzazz.
3. Use these techniques to map your own character built from the challenges of chapters past. Output the UV Snapshot, paint a new texture and reapply it.

12

CHARACTER RIGGING AND SKINNING

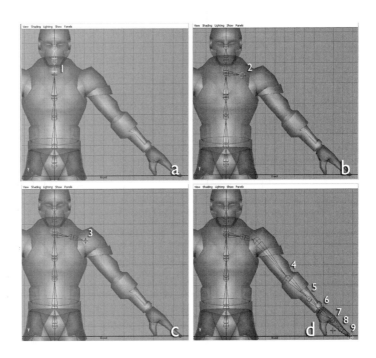

S o we have now modeled rooms. We have modeled characters. We have textured both the room and the character, including the complex system of UV Mapping. We can now put texture exactly where we want on a model. We know how to do still renderings and lighting schemes that bring a visual dynamism to a scene. All of this is important, but where the fun *really* starts is in animation.

This chapter is dedicated to setting up characters to enable the kind of interesting character animation that draws most people to 3D in the first place. This part of the process is often handled by technical directors within large studios. Oftentimes interesting programming techniques are used to further facilitate a rig (the tool that allows for a character to be animated). Mel Script (a form of Maya's scripting language) can be used to automate everything from center of balance to expression driven facial blendshapes.

But just because high-end rigging is usually handled by programmers does not mean that you should not get a handle on the basics. In fact, being a good team player often entails understanding at least a little bit about what the other team players do—and who knows; maybe getting started with 3D animation is the first step toward a future career as a technical director. And in any case, you cannot effectively animate a character without at least a bit of rigging and skinning.

So what is the difference? You may have heard a whole slew of terms thrown around when it comes to character animation: IK, FK, kinematics, rigging, skinning, and so on. In order to understand these terms it is important to start out with the Maya element that is involved in all of these processes—the Joint.

JOINTS

In the past few chapters you have created a character (or two) out of a collection of polygons. The problem is that these polygons are static; other than you moving the components around, there are no reliable ways to bring these polygons to life without some sort of deformation object. Deformation objects—like joints—allow you to, well, deform a collection of polygons; reliably move vertices.

Technically speaking, in 3D, joints are where bones connect. Most 3D applications work with the idea of creating and editing bones that in turn deform polygon meshes. Maya, somewhat controversially focuses not on the bones that deform but rather the joints that connect these bones.

RIGGING

Rigging then is the process of placing joints and defining how they work. You can rotate joints, move joints, and even scale them. You can set up various control mechanisms that allow you to indirectly control bones or collections of joints. IK (inverse kinematics) is one such mechanism. It allows you to move one object that in turn controls two, three or more strings of joints connected by bones. This can be a great time saver as you only need to move and key one object rather than manually rotated every joint to get your character into their pose.

To understand placing and rigging joints, consider the following minitutorial.

TUTORIAL 12.1   RIGGING A BASIC IK CHAIN

Step 1: Create a new File. File > New Scene. . .
Step 2: Change to the Animation set of pull-down menus. Either press F2, or select Animation from the Status Line at the top left corner of your interface.
Step 3: Activate the Joint Tool. Animate | Skeleton > Joint Tool (Options). Reset the settings.

The Joint Tool can really be thought of as the Place Joints Tool. At the most basic level, it allows you to place joints. The default setting makes sure you do not inherit anyone else's tweaks.

Step 4: Place three joints simulating hip, knee and ankle. In the side View Panel click three times placing joints that approximate Figure 12.1. Press Enter to exit the Joint Tool.

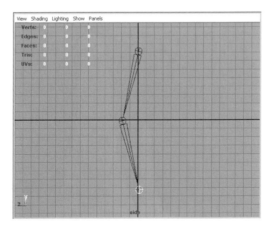

FIGURE 12.1   Placed joints using the Joint Tool. Place the joint by LMB clicking.

Why? *Make sure to not make these joints in a straight line. Give the knee joint a bit of a bend to begin with by placing it a bit in front of the hip joint. This will make the process of IK setup much easier.*

Step 5: Play with the joints. Switch to the Rotate Tool and then select and rotate the joints to get an idea of how they work. Notice that they function just like any other object. Also notice that the ankle joint is the child of the knee joint and in turn, the knee joint is a child of the hip joint. See the hierarchy in the Outliner (Window > Outliner) as shown in Figure 12.2.

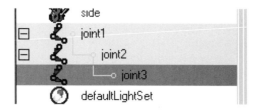

FIGURE 12.2   Outliner showing the hierarchy of the joints.

Step 6: Rename the top joint to HipJoint. The second to KneeJoint, and the third to AnkleJoint. This is most easily done in the Outliner.
Step 7: Setup and IK Chain. Activate the IK Handle Tool (Animate | Skeleton > IK Handle Tool (options) reset settings). Create the chain in the side View Panel by first clicking on HipJoint and then clicking on AnkleJoint (Figure 12.3).

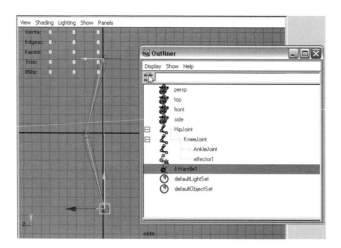

FIGURE 12.3   IK handle and resulting Outliner changes.

The IK Handle Tool allows you to technically create an IK handle; but in order to
Why? *create the IK handle, Maya creates the IK chain. The basic idea of an IK chain is that instead of having to rotate manually each of the joints to get the leg to say, kick, you can grab the IK handle (the child-most element) and use the Move Tool to move it which then drives the rotation of the joints within the IK chain.*

Step 8: Play with the IK. Select ikHandle1 in the Outliner, and then in the side View Panel, use the Move Tool to move the IK chain. See how the HipJoint and KneeJoint are both rotating based upon the single move function?

Step 9: Ensure Sticky is activated for the IK Handle. In the Outliner, double-click on the ikHandle1 icon (not the name)—this will open the attributes for the ikHandle in the Attributes Editor. In the IK Handle Attributes section turn Stickiness to sticky.

Step 10: Make the leg dance with its foot on the floor. Select HipJoint and use the Move Tool to move it around. Notice that the ikHandle1 (with Stickiness enabled) makes the end of the chain stick to the ground. If you imagine this as a leg this is what would really happen; if you moved the hip up and down, side to side, the foot would stay still.

Step 11: Do not close the file; we will be using it in the next minitutorial.

Tutorial Conclusion

And there you have it. Your first rig! OK, so it is a pretty simple one, but many of the core ideas were accomplished. You created joints and created an IK chain to control those joints. Establishing joints and setting up controls is what rigging is about.

SKINNING

Skinning is the process of assigning vertices to joints. Allowing joints to control collections of vertices means that when the joints rotate, the vertices move with it. This allows you to bend an otherwise static collection of polygons.

The hardcore details of skinning will be covered more in later tutorials, but to get a quick look at the idea of skinning, consider the following minitutorial.

TUTORIAL 12.2   SKINNING A LEG

Step 1: Still within the rigged leg created in the last tutorial, create a polygon cube (Create > Polygon Primitives > Cube (options). Make sure its Subdivisions Width, Height and Depth are all equal to 1.

Step 2: Position the cube over HipJoint. Rescale and rotate the cube so that it is bigger than the HipJoint (Figure 12.4).

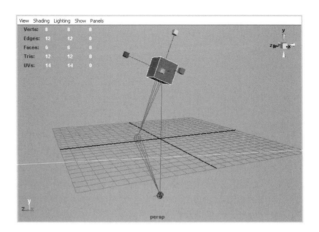

FIGURE 12.4   Start of the leg.

Step 3: Model a basic leg. Do this by switching to Modeling and use Extrude Face to extrude down the shape of the joints to create a very simple leg shape. Do make sure that you have at least the three segments shown in Figure 12.5 around the knee.

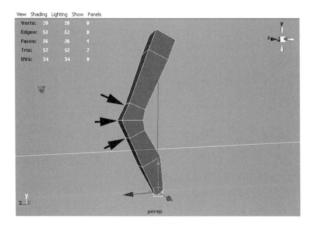

FIGURE 12.5   Simple leg made from extrusions. Note the three subdivisions around the knee.

Remember that polygons do not bend. The only place a mesh can bend is where the polygons meet—at edges or vertices. By making sure that you have three subdivisions around the knee; you are giving Maya three places to split the deformation

Why?

among. With only one subdivision there, the knee would collapse on itself when de-formed.

Step 4: Bind the joints to the leg. In the Outliner, select HipJoint and then Ctrl-select pCube1. Choose Animation | Skin > Bind Skin > Smooth Bind (options). Reset the settings. Click Bind Skin.

Step 5: Now select either HipJoint or ikHandle1 and use the Move Tool to move them around. The joints should now deform the leg geometry (Figure 12.6).

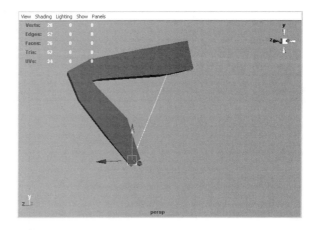

FIGURE 12.6   Leg being deformed through joints driven by IK.

Tutorial Conclusion

Pretty easy, no? Ok, so when you have a more complicated setup—like two legs—it is not quite this easy. However, this does show the way that joints deform a polygon mesh. In tutorials to come we will deal with working through the ideas of controlling exactly how much influence each joint has over each vertex. This can help avoid problems of moving the toe joint and having the tip of the nose move.

RIGGING AND SKINNING A BIPEDAL CHARACTER

The rest of this chapter will be dedicated to rigging the game character from the last two chapters for animation. The overall process will go like this: we will create the joints that belong inside the character, organizing, positioning and naming as we go. Then we will make use of IK chains in the legs to control the joints that make up the legs and feet. After we have rigged the joints and are pleased with the movement and control it affords us we will bind the character to our rig. The default bind is hardly ever the best bind, and we will make use of Maya's Paint Skin Weights Tool to get down and dirty with the vertices to determine how the vertices will be controlled. At the end we will have a character that is easily and quickly deformed through our rig with armor that bends as it should and joints that deform as they ought to.

A few caveats before we begin though. We are using a sort of hybrid of techniques here for the sake of learning. Some game engines require a very specific collection of joints organized in a very particular way. The naming can be important, the sizing can be important, and the organization can be important for successful transfer into a game. In the coming tutorial we will be using a fairly generic but useful flow to create a very generic but useful rig. Although it may (or may not) be usable directly in a game, it will allow us to start animating in the next chapter.

 **TUTORIAL 12.3   RIGGING THE GAME CHARACTER**

Objectives:

1. Create a custom rig for the game character.
2. Create joints for a simple full body rig.
3. Create simple IK chains for the legs.
4. Master the Mirror Joints Tool.

ON THE CD

Step 1: Set your project. Make sure you are using Game_Model as your project. You can either use the last saved version of your game character, or you can use Tutorial12.3Start.mb off the CD-ROM.
Step 2: Delete History. Select Edit > Delete All by Type > History.

Why?

From here on out you should not delete history. Once you bind the joints to the skin, you will have created a node that facilitates this bind. If you delete the history of the file, you break this connection. If you use things like blendshapes (facial deformers), you must also have an unbroken history. Because of the upcoming nodes that must remain—it makes for easier and faster workflow if your mesh is clean without any baggage or history.

Step 3: Optimize your workspace. Turn off Display > Heads Up Display > Poly Count. In side and front View Panels, make sure that X-Ray is enabled (Shading > X-Ray).

Why?

There is no longer a need to keep track of how many polygons are in the scene; and although it can impress your friends and family when they glance at your screen, a cleaner workspace can really speed up the workflow.

As we begin to create the joints we will be creating them inside the character. A shaded, but X-Ray-enabled character can make it much easier to see the organization of the joints we are about to place.

Step 4: Create the spine. In the side View Panel create a string of joints that approximate Figure 12.7. Do this by using Animation | Skeleton > Joint Tool and clicking to create the curved shape of the spine. Be sure to start from the bottom and work up.

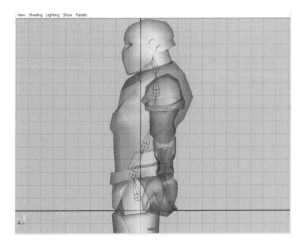

FIGURE 12.7   Spine.

There are several important things to note about creating this spine. First, the actual number of joints is not particularly important—a few more, or a few less, no sweat. Second, be very, very sure that the first joint you place is the bottom one and that it is placed in the side View Panel at about the middle of the hip. This first joint will become the parent of all the other joints in the rig and its placement is important. Third, make sure to have one joint at about the center of the shoulders. Fourth, make sure you have a joint at the base of the neck and one at the base of the head.

Note that when you create the joints from the side View Panel, they are centered right along the YZ axis—right up the middle of the body, where they should be.

Step 5: Rename these joints. Label the bottom most (the first and parent most in the Outliner) as Root_joint. Label the joints up to the joint in the middle of the shoulders as Spine_joint#. Label the joint at the middle of the shoulders as Chest_joint. Neck_joint is the joint at the bottom of the neck and Head_joint is the joint at the base of the head (Figure 12.8).

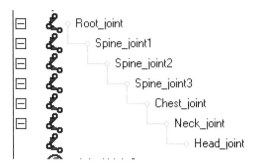

FIGURE 12.8 Outliner with renamed joints.

 There is no special significance of these names. Largely they are just rather intuitive names for their location. However, as we move on through the tutorial, it will be necessary that we both understand which joint we are talking about.

There is something a little bit counterintuitive about the setup so far. Be sure not to be tripped up by the fact that the Outliner lists the joints from parent-most down to child-most. Which means that Root_joint, which is in the bottom of 3D space in side View Panel, is the top joint listed in the outliner and that Head_joint is displayed at the top of the chain in 3D space but the bottom of the list in the Outliner.

Step 6: Create the clavicle, shoulder and arm. In the front View Panel, create a chain of 8 joints that extend from the spine to the tip of the fingers. Start by activating the Joint Tool and then click first on the Chest_joint (in the front view). This establishes that you are going to be building a new chain of joints off of that joint. Then click on where a clavicle bone would be, and continue on to create shoulder, elbow, and one in the middle of the forearm, wrist, and three more in the hand (Figure 12.9).

 Be careful that that first click is right on the Chest_joint. If you are off by just a little bit, you will create a new joint rather than create a new chain as a child of the Chest_joint. Make that first click, right in the middle of the joint. You will know you have got it as the joints above the Chest_joint will highlight.

Most of these joints are fairly intuitive except for the strange joint in the middle of the forearm. This is basically a twist joint. Look at your arm and rotate your wrist. Notice that your elbow does not twist at all—but the twist is facilitated by the complex bone structure real people have. This twist appears to happen about in the middle of the forearm. So this middle forearm joint (#5 in Figure 12.9) will never bend, just rotate to facilitate a twist.

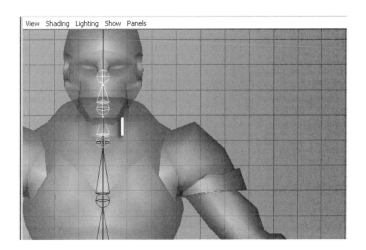

FIGURE 12.9   Creating the arm chain of joints.

Step 7: Name the L_Clavicle_joint, L_Shoulder_joint, L_Elbow_joint, L_Forearm_joint, L_Wrist_joint, L_Hand_joint, L_Finger_joint, and L_FingerTip_joint (Figure 12.10).

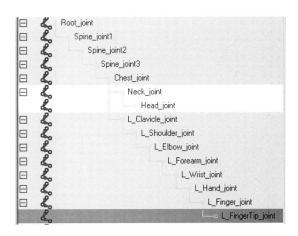

FIGURE 12.10   Named joints.

Why?

The L_ stands for "left"—the character's left. Providing this distinction helps when selecting joints via the Outliner (or in places like the Graph Editor or Dope Sheet).

Do make sure and note how the hierarchy is organized both in the View Panels and the Outliner. This new collection of joints is a child of the Chest_joint; which also has another chain of joints (Neck_joint and Head_joint) attached to it. This is as it should be, as you would never move any of the spine joints and not want the neck and shoulders to rotate with it.

Step 8: Tweak joins in top View Panel. Move and rotate the new left side arm joints so that they fit the geometry a bit more (Figure 12.11).

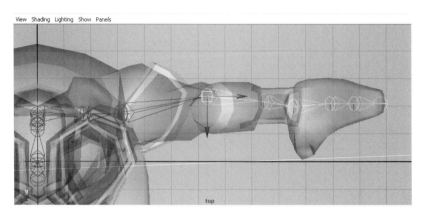

FIGURE 12.11   Tweaked joints to match the arm shape.

Technically the joints do not need to match the geometry at all; however it often makes things a bit more intuitive if the joints all have a bit of bend in accordance **Why?** *with the nature of the geometry.*

Step 9: Create the leg joint chain. Do this from the side View Panel. Activate the Joint Tool and create a chain of 5 joints. Do not start this chain off of any extant joints. Notice in the subset that the new leg joint is a bit behind the root joint. Make sure that every joint has a bit of an angle—do not make them in a straight line (Figure 12.12).

Creating this joint chain in the side View Panel is important. This joint chain will use IK to control it and although there are other ways to define which way joints **Why?** *are allowed to bend within an IK, the easiest way is to give Maya a hint as you create the joint chain. By creating the chain in the side View Panel, and making sure that upon creation the knee joint is bent and the ankle joint is bent, you let Maya know that those are the directions the IK should bend those joints. It also indicates to Maya that you do not wish it to rotate in the other directions.*

Step 10: Rename to L_Hip_joint, L_Knee_joint, L_Ankle_joint, L_Ball_joint, L_Toe_joint.
Step 11: Position L_Hip_joint chain. Select L_Hip_joint in the Outliner. In the front View Panel move the joint (and subsequently its children) in the X direction (drag the red handle) so that the joints actually sit inside the leg (Figure 12.13).

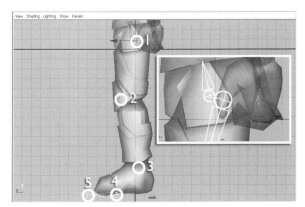

FIGURE 12.12   The leg joints.

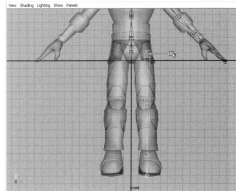

FIGURE 12.13   Moving the leg joints so that they actually sit inside the leg.

Step 12: Parent the L_Hip_joint chain to Root_joint. Do this in the Outliner by either MMB-dragging L_Hip_joint to Root_joint; or by selecting L_Hip_joint and then Ctrl-clicking on Root_joint and choosing Edit > Parent. Either way the results are shown in Figure 12.14.

Why?

A few important things happen here. First, look closely in the Outliner and see the long vertical line indicating that L_Hip_joint is now a child of Root_joint at the same level as the Spine_joint1 chain. The second is notice in the front View Panel that a new bone has been automatically created between Root_joint and L_Hip_joint. When you parent one joint to another, Maya automatically creates the bones to connect them.

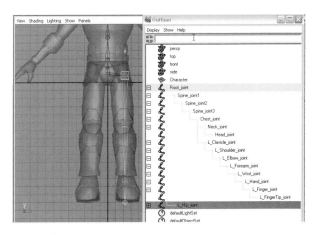

FIGURE 12.14   Newly parented L_Hip_joint now a child of Root_joint.

Step 13: Setup an IK chain from L_Hip_joint to L_Ankle_joint. Activate the IK Handle Tool (Animate | Skeleton > IK Handle Tool). In the side View Panel click once on the L_Hip_joint and then again on L_Ankle_joint.

Step 14: Setup an IK chain from L_Ankle_joint to L_Ball_joint. Activate the IK Handle Tool again, and in the side View Panel click once on the L_Ankle_joint, and then on L_Ball_joint.

Step 15: Setup an IK chain from L_Ball_joint to L_Toe_joint (Figure 12.15).

 You will need to trust on this one for a minute. An IK chain between just two joints seems rather silly; but in a bit we will be rigging this area to allow for some rather
Why? *important foot roll setups.*

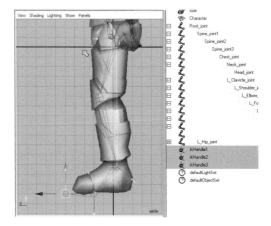

FIGURE 12.15   Three IK chains and the resulting three ikHandles.

Step 16: Rename ikHandle1 to L_AnkleIK, ikHandle2 to L_BallIK, and ikHandle3 to L_ToeIK.

 Again, effective naming can really speed up your animation process as it makes it much easier to grab the objects you need. Take a minute to see how things are orga-
Why? *nized in the Outliner. At this point, all of the joints are children of Root_joint, while the three IK handles are outside of the hierarchy all together. This is just as it should be as it allows you to move the IK handles independently of the body—this will allow you to plant the feet and keep them in place without them sliding on the floor.*

Also note that thus far, we have only been rigging one side of the character. This is by design as we know that the character is symmetrical. Maya has some really snazzy Mirror Joints Tools.

Step 17: Select L_Hip_joint in the Outliner. Choose Animation > Skeleton > Mirror Joint (options). In the options window (Figure 12.16)

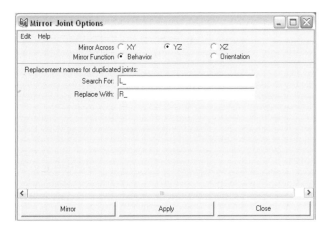

FIGURE 12.16   Settings for Mirror Joint Options.

change the Mirror Across setting to YZ. In the Search For: enter L_ and in the Replace With: enter R_. Press Mirror.

If your character is indeed looking forward, the mirror plane is the YZ one. What this window also allows us to do is tell Maya to not only mirror the joints, but re-label all the joints or IK handles it finds with L_ with an R_. Note that the Mirror Function is set to Behavior—this means that it will also duplicate the IK chains associated with the L_Hip_joint chain.

Why?

Step 18: Group L_AnkleIK, L_BallIK, and L_ToeIK. Select these three IK handles in the Outline and press Ctrl-g. Rename the new group L_Foot.
Step 19: Change the group L_Foot manipulator location to the heel of the left foot area. With the group L_Foot selected, press Insert to move the manipulator location for the group. Move it to the heel of the left foot. Be sure to line it up in both the side and front View Panels (Figure 12.17). Press Insert again.

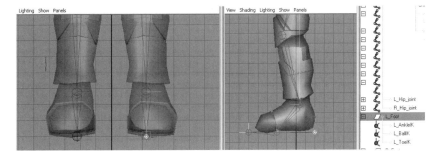

FIGURE 12.17   L_Foot group with altered manipulator.

Step 20: Repeat for R_Foot. Group R_AnkleIK, R_BallIK, and R_ToeIK. Rename to R_Foot. Change the location of the manipulator for the group to the heel of the right foot.

Step 21: Test the leg rig. Select L_Foot (the group), and use the Move Tool to move the group of IK handles. The chain should function as a leg. Make sure to press Ctrl-z (Undo) to replace the group back at its default position (Figure 12.18). Repeat for both legs.

Step 22: Continue to test by moving Root_joint. Select Root_joint in the Outliner. In any View Panel, move the joint (actually the whole chain). The feet should stay planted and not slide through the floor. If they do slide through the floor, select each of the IK Handles and turn on Stickiness in the Attributes Editor (IK Handle Attributes section). When it's working, you should be able to do as shown in Figure 12.19. Be sure to undo (Ctrl-z) to get the Root_joint back to its original position.

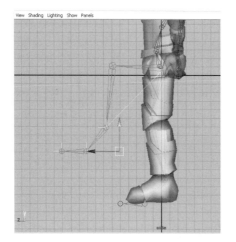 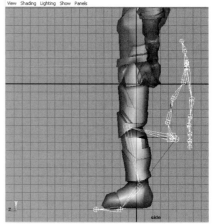

FIGURE 12.18   Testing the leg rig.   **FIGURE 12.19**   Working IK rig.

Step 23: Mirror the clavicle and arms. Select L_Clavicle in the Outliner. Choose Animate > Skeleton > Mirror Geometry (options). Make sure the options were set as before and press Mirror.

Step 24: Hide geometry to get a look at the rig. In persp View Panel, select the Character (the object—not any of the joints). Press Ctrl-h to hide it (Figure 12.20). You should be able to see your entire rig. Press Shift-Ctrl-h to unhide the Polygons.

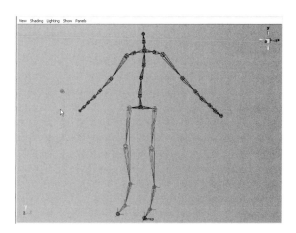

FIGURE 12.20   Completed rig.

Tutorial Conclusion

And with that you are rigged. A very simple rig, but a rig nonetheless. Many rigs will include objects that allow for easy selection of groups or joints. Some have automated Set Driven Keys that allow for quick changes in the clenching of fists, or SplineIKs for even distribution of bends or twists in the spine. Unfortunately these techniques are beyond the scope of this volume; but if you have a real interest in the rigging process, those are some of the key words to look for.

SKINNING

While we have a good start, the joints right now move but do not change anything in the scene. Before we can really bring the character to life we need to make sure that the joints are actually attached and are deforming the character. In the following tutorial we will look at how to do just that.

Before we get into the nitty gritty, there are few ideas we should talk about. First, once you have bound a skin to a series of joints, you need to start thinking of things from the vertices' points of view. You are now telling vertices what can influence them and how they are to be influenced. In fact, when you bind the polygons to joints, the polygon character will gain a new node called skinCluster. This skinCluster Node stores the info about how the vertices are manipulated.

Inevitably the initial binding has problems as Maya tries to decide which vertices are bound to which joints solely on distance. Maya has provided a tool called the Paint Skin Weights Tool that will allow you to change which points are influenced by which joints. It is a visual painting system that you will see in the tutorial to come. It can be frustrating to use at times; but is a very intuitive way to adjust skin weights.

TUTORIAL 12.4   SKINNING THE GAME MODEL

Objectives:

1. Use Smooth Binding to attach joints to model.
2. Adjust skin cluster via the Paint Skin Weights Tool.
3. Prepare ready-to-animate character.

ON THE CD

Step 1: Open the results of the last tutorial. Or if you would like you can open Tutorial12.4Start.mb from the CD-ROM (ProjectFiles > Chapter12 > Character_Model > scenes).

Step 2: Bind joints to Character. In the Outliner select Character and then Shift-select Root_joint. Choose Animation | Skin > Smooth Bind (options). Reset the settings and then change the Max Influences to 3. Press Bind Skin.

In general the default settings for the Smooth Bind are great. The Max Influences default setting of 5, however, indicates how many joints a vertex may be influenced by. In most cases (except for those involving very complex spines (which we do not have), you do not need any one vertex being influenced by more than 3 joints.

Why?

Step 3: Test the binding. Bend him all out of shape. Move Root_joint, the L_Foot group and the R_Foot group, Rotate various spine joints and especially the clavicles, shoulders and wrists. We are looking for ways to break him, so go at it (Figure 12.21).

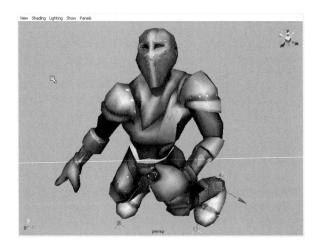

FIGURE 12.21   Bend out of shape.

There are a few things that you will be able to see are working well, and some things that need adjustment. Many of the areas that need adjustment are best seen when the joint is in motion; this makes it tough to show in a book. However, some,

Why?

like the bending of the collar, can still be seen even in stills. In any case, there are enough problems to know that we will need to adjust the skin weights.

Step 4: Get the character back to where he was—his Bind Pose. Do this by undoing multiple times (Ctrl-z) or by zeroing out the Translate and Rotate values for Root_joint, L_Foot, and then R_Foot. Then select Root_joint and choose Animation | Skin > Go to Bind Pose.

Why?

The Bind Pose is pretty important. It is the rotation values of the joints when they were bound. There are several functions including Influence Objects that require the joints to be at their Bind Pose to do. Using the Go to Bind Pose command works for joints not being controlled by any other means. In our case, the upper body fits just this bill. Maya can rotate them right back to the value they were at when the joints were bound. However, the lower body is more complicated. The joints of the legs are being controlled by the IK setups. So Maya cannot return those joints to their Bind Pose by itself. This is why you must return the L_Foot and R_Foot groups back to their Translate X, Y, and Z = 0 position. This returns the joints to the rotation value they were at when they were bound.

Step 5: Open the Paint Skin Weights Tool. Select Character (the polygon mesh). Choose Animation | Skin > Edit Smooth Skin > Paint Skin Weights Tool (options). This will present options for the tool in the Attributes Editor (Figure 12.22).

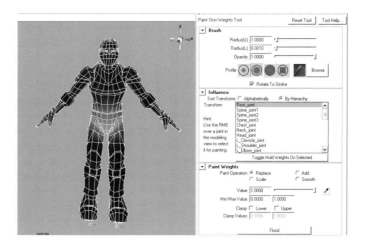

FIGURE 12.22   The Paint Skin Weights Tool.

Why?

A note about how this tool is organized: In the Attributes Editor you will see several sections relevant to how the tools work. The top area works with the size, pres-

*sure and shape of the virtual brush that you will use to paint weight on or off. Al-
though—as we will look at in a bit—the best method is to actually not use these
Brush sliders but instead hold the b key down and drag in the View Panels to increase or decrease the brush size.*

*Below this is the Influence area. This is a fairly important area. The main list
should look familiar as it is a list of all the joints attached to the skin (poly mesh—
Character). When you click on a joint in the Paint Skin Weight Tool, the View
Panel will update to show the influence of that joint. More correctly, the vertices
that are influenced by that joint will turn white—the areas of the model that are
black have no influence. Points may share their influence among several joints and
so there are lots of levels of gray. The whiter a section of the model, the more it is influenced by the selected joint in the Paint Skin Weights Tool window.*

*Below that is the Paint Weights section. This allows you to decide what effect
the brush has on the vertices you are painting. You can replace the vertex's value
completely (in reference to the selected joint), you can Add, Scale, or Smooth the
value. Add and Scale are intuitive; but Smooth is still important. Smooth essentially
takes the value of a point and shares it among the points around it.*

Let's look at it in action.

Step 6: Adjust some known absolute areas like the head. In the Paint Skin
Weights Tool Attributes window, select Head_joint. This will make the head
mostly gray—it should be solid white. Hold b down and drag your mouse
over the View Panel (persp usually works best) to resize your brush to a
manageable size. Make sure your Paint Weights section has Replace active
with a Value of 1. Paint the head so that it turns completely white (Figure
12.23). Note that you are painting vertices; so aim for those as you work.

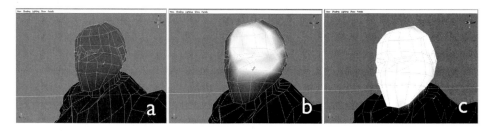

FIGURE 12.23   Painting the skin weight of the head.

*Gray sections of a skin weight indicate a sharing of influence by multiple joints;
which is good for things like elbows and knees as it indicates a gentle bend. However, some parts of the body—like the head—do not share influence as they never
actually deform. The head moves, but should never bend—thus is should have all
of its influence assigned to the Head_joint. Since a vertex has a total influence of 1*

to give (it can share this amid numerous joints), painting the head in at 1 means that all those points influence are with the head joint.

Step 7: Test the new skin weight. When you think you have the head painted completely white so that the vertices that make up the head have a Value of 1 (complete allegiance to the Head_joint); test it by selecting Head_joint from the Outliner and rotating it. If the head rotates and there is no deformation on the head you know you were successful. Do not worry if other areas (like the collar) also move when you rotate the head—stay focused on whether the head deforms or not.

So why did we have to do that? Well, remember that in the Smooth Bind Options window, we told Maya that each vertex could share its influence among 3 joints. The vertices on the head were simply sharing their influence with 3 close joints (maybe the neck and shoulders). Part of Painting Skin Weights is going back and telling certain parts of the body to limit themselves to only be influenced by one joint.

Why?

Step 8: Repeat this process for other nonbendable section. Select the joint where things like the shoulder plate should be assigned to (L_Shoulder_joint and R_Shoulder_joint) and then paint them in completely white. Figure 12.24 shows a few examples; basically anywhere on this model that is armor will have the convenience of having 100 percent of its influence lent to just one joint. After all, metal armor does not bend.

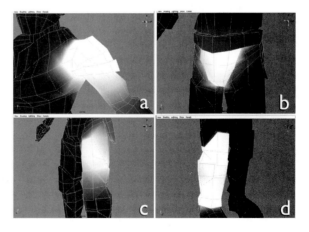

FIGURE 12.24 Samples of areas that should be painted all white—all of their influences assigned to one joint.

Notice that as you do this, a joint may have its influence felt to far; you may see vertices that are gray that you know should not be influenced by the joint you are

Why?

working on. Resist the temptation to paint them in at 0—do not paint them black. In general, always paint additively with a high Replace value.

The best analogy is that you are painting positively and telling points where to be. If you paint a vertex to be 0 for a particular joint, you are essentially saying, "I don't care where you go, but you can't be here." The vertex shrugs his shoulders and then heads off—to where, you have no idea. Which often means you discover the same vertex camping under the influence of another unwanted joint later. It is much better to be painting positively all the time, telling vertices where to be influenced so that they will stay put.

Step 9: Paint the smooth bending sections. The chest is an area where each of the vertices will probably lend a bit of their influence to several joints. Start by selecting Spine_joint2 in the Paint Skin Weights Tool Attributes window (12.25a). Paint a solid white stripe around the vertices that are most clearly around the area of Spine_joint2 (Figure 12.25b). Next, change the Paint Weights section to Smooth and press the Flood button twice (Figure 12.26).

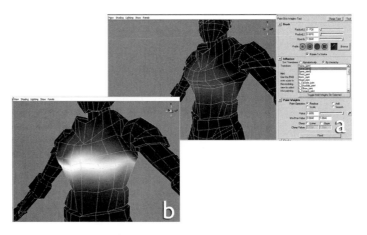

FIGURE 12.25   Roughing out the smooth section.

Why? *The first part of this step gives Maya a center of influence—area that is most clearly influenced by the selected joint. The flooding softens the influence out from that epicenter of influence. By working up and down the spine in this way, you can get influence well shared among the vertices on the chest by joints that make up the spine.*

Often when not dealing with armor-clad characters this technique works well in areas like the knees and ankles as well. This will help you get more natural bending surfaces.

Step 10: Continue to work around the character; testing as you go. Do some painting, do some testing. Repaint, retest.

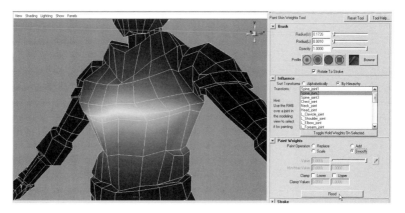

FIGURE 12.26   Using the Flood Smooth to soften the selection.

Tutorial Conclusion

Seems early to be stopping the tutorial; but alas, the Painting Skin Weights Tool process does not lend itself well to book form. It does not even lend itself well to lecture or video training. It is best understood by doing.

In this tutorial we have covered the concepts that make for successful Skin Weighting. However, since it uses a paint brush metaphor, it also has very soft-edges as far as a tutorial goes. It is not exact; and the way someone else paints will probably not be the exact vertices you paint. So take the concepts and dig in. The more you paint and adjust—then test the results—the more the process will become intuitive and successful.

GENERAL TIPS ON THE PAINT SKIN WEIGHTS TOOL

- Remember that Paint Skin Weights will only work on a polygonal object. Select Character before selecting Animation _ Skin > Edit Smooth Skin > Paint Skin Weights.
- You are always painting vertices. Remember this as you are trying to get a region white—its not a matter of how carefully you paint a face, it will not turn white until you paint the vertices that make up that face.
- Sometimes the best way to get access to vertices is inside the character. Remember that it is hollow and sometimes overlapping points or even those more difficult to reach (in crevasses and so on) vertices can be reached easily and quickly on the inside of the mesh.
- Remember that it is a process. The first time painting the character is rarely the final time. Lots of testing and repainting is always needed.
- The Paint Skin Weights Tool also works when the character is posed. You can bend a joint, then select the Character, activate Paint Skin Weights Tool and then paint the skin. As you change the skin

weights, Maya will interactively update to show how the vertices are snapping into new influences.

- New to Maya 7 is the ability to use multicolored display. When the Paint Skin Weights Tool is activated, open the Display section and activate Multicolor Feedback (Figure 12.27). This will display the weights by color—each color indicating the influence of a different joint. This can often be really nice for fine tuning.

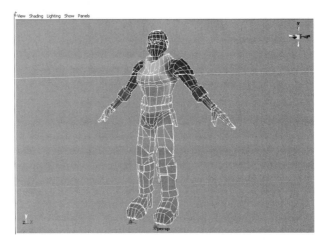

ON THE CD

FIGURE 12.27   Results of active Multicolor Feedback. Not much to look at in grayscale; but be sure to check it out in your file or on the CD-ROM.

CONCLUSION

Ultimately, the things that you have done right and wrong during the rigging and skinning process become (sometimes) painfully clear during the animation process. Suddenly skin weights that are too broadly painted raise their ugly head; and at the same time, delicate successes become clear to the trained eye. The results of this tutorial will be no different.

In the next chapter we will start to tackle animation. In some of the tutorials we will be animating this character. As we do, undoubtedly you will find problems with your rig, or the one presented here, or both. Adjusting the skin weights is luckily a very flexible method that can be done at any time. If halfway through the walk cycle, you discover that the thigh skin weights are just not right; you can adjust on the fly and not loose any of your animation. This sort of flexibility is why many consider Maya the premiere character animation tool of the industry.

Challenges, Exercises, or Assignments

1. Of course, continue to tweak the skin weights for this character.
2. Pose your character in a variety of action poses (Figure 12.28) and try and determine where your weighting holds up or breaks down (adjust when needed).

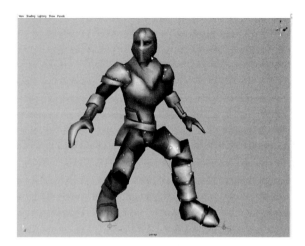

FIGURE 12.28   Posed character testing skin weight problems.

3. Weight your own custom characters created as parts of challenges past.

13

ANIMATION AND CHARACTER ANIMATION

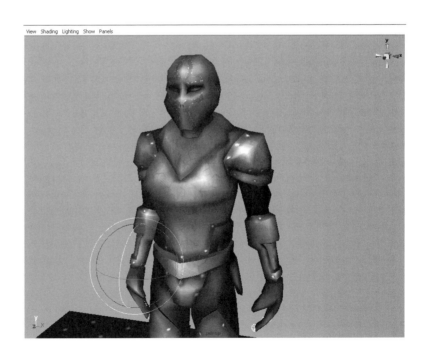

Animation is where things get really exciting. Although modeling, lighting, rendering, rigging and skinning are all incredibly important—how things move is usually more important than what moves.

Now, this does not mean that animation fixes all. No amount of good motion can completely cover a poorly conceived or badly modeled mesh. And if the skinning is bad, all the motion will only serve to point out problems in weights. But there have been many a beautifully constructed, textured, lit, and rendered model that ends up looking like ultra-novice fodder due to bad animation.

Animation is tricky. Animators—especially character animators—are in high demand because there are not a whole lot of really good ones out there. Lots of people master modeling, quite a few learn texturing well, and many attempt animation but it takes a keen eye and lots and lots of study of physics, motion, and character to really bring polygons to life.

THE DISNEY PARADIGM

Walt Disney did not invent animation. In fact he himself was more of a story guy than an animator. The real animator who actually drew the frames of animation was a man named Ub Iwerks.

Ub had followed Disney through three started and failed studios. Each time, Disney would secure financing to start a studio, and each time missed the right formula. Finally though, Disney worked through the details of securing the ability to sync sound to his animation projects. Ub animated *Steamboat Willie* using this new sound-sync method and the project caught the imagination of Americans. Several successful projects followed, most all completely animated by Ub.

So what does that mean "animated by Ub?" Animation (all moving pictures in fact) is simply a series of still images shown in rapid succession. Each of the still images is just a little different than the one before it and after it. Our eye interprets these quickly showing images as motion. In traditional cel animations (named for the celluloid that the frames were drawn on), the animator must draw a whole lot of frames to get motion. For instance, film today runs at 24 frames per second (fps). For every second of animation, the animator must draw 24 drawings. Ten seconds of animation means 240 frames. You can see how labor intensive this method becomes.

Ub, as one of Disney's oldest partners, was—deservedly—his highest paid animator. But having your highest paid animator draw the thousands of frames needed for each animated short made little business sense to Walt. Ub, although a very, very fast draftsman, insisted on drawing every frame of early classics like *Skeleton Dance* and *Steamboat Willie*. As the shorts became more and more successful and the demand continued to rise, Walt Disney wanted to move towards a much more Henry Ford-like model of animating.

The idea would be to have Ub draw the most important frames—the key frames. If Mickey walked into the scene and jumped over a log, Walt wanted Ub to draw a couple foot falls, the squash and stretch of the hop, the frame at the top of the hop and a few frames to define the poses as he landed. Then, Walt would pay a junior animator to come in and draw all the frames in between. The idea here was to have the lowest paid animators draw the most frames allowing Ub to define the action and timing of more animated sequences in less time.

Well, Ub did not like this idea. He felt it lessened his art and eventually he and Disney split. (Ub went on to start his own ill-fated company; and eventually rejoined Walt and headed some very important special effects efforts for Disney's later live action/animation mix efforts like Mary Poppins.) But alas this method of having a master animator set key frames, and an in-betweener (sometimes called a tweener) draw the remaining frames is a method that took hold and is in use to this day.

But there is more to this story than merely antecdotal enjoyment. This workflow has become part of how computers think of animation. You are the master animator. You decide what the key frames are. The computer becomes the junior animator—the in-betweener who fills in the frames between the key frames.

In Maya this idea is realized using the terminology of just *keys.* In Maya, you set keys at various frames. Each of these keys define a particular occurrence, pose, or position at a certain point in time.

MAYA'S ANIMATION INTERFACE

Maya's animation tools are deep and actually hidden all over the place. The default interface includes a few animation tools that are worth mentioning before we get too far. Figure 13.1 shows the bottom of the interface that Maya includes by default.

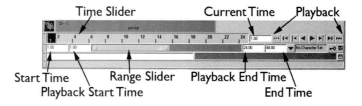

FIGURE 13.1   The animation tools visible at the bottom of the Maya interface.

The top part with the numbers and black box is the Time Slider. Each of the numbers represents a frame which can roughly be translated into a point in time. Usually, by default, Maya presents 24 frames—which in film is one second. The black box (which actually becomes smaller as you show more frames in the Time Slider) is the Current Time Marker. By clicking and dragging the Current Time Marker, you are changing the point in time that the View Panels will display. So if the Current Time Marker is at 1—you will see the state of your digital creation at that point in time. If there is animation, it will be updated in the View Panel as you scrub along the Time Slider. The input field at the far right of the Time Slider indicates which frame the Current Time Marker is on. You can enter numerical values here to change the position of the Current Time Marker.

To the right of the Time Slider and Current Time input field are some fairly familiar buttons very much like your VCR or DVD player. They allow you to play your animation forward and backwards, to skip ahead or back one frame at a time (the triangle with a bar), one key at a time (the triangle with a red bar), or jump to the beginning or end of your animation (the double-triangles).

Below this are a collection of input fields and sliders that show how much of the Time Slider is being shown. The first input field there is the Start Time. It represents the first frame of the animation. The second is the Playback Start Time. This represents the frame at which Maya would start playing the animation if you press the Play Forward button.

The long bar with two blocks and numbers is called the Range Slider. It is a numerical representation of how many frames of the total frames of an animation are being shown in the Time Slider. If you grab the Range Slider by clicking and dragging, you can change the frames that are being shown in the Time Slider. On the Range Slider you will see two numbers, the first number represents the first frame shown and the second represents the last. If you click and drag either of the squares next to the numbers you can increase or decrease the number of frames being shown in the Time Slider. Remember that the frames shown in the Time Slider are those that would play back when you press the Play Forward button. So with the Range Slider, you could narrow in on a collection of frames that you wanted to work with, or broaden what was played back to show more frames.

To the right of the Range Slider are two input fields. The first is the Playback End Time—the last frame on the range slider and the last frame of the Time Slider. The second is the End Time, or the last frame of the total animation. Either of these can be changed by changing the values in the input fields.

The next section says No Character Sets. Character sets can be a powerful organization tool, but we are not going to work with them much here as our scenes will be fairly simple. But as your scenes increase in complexity, make sure you take a look at how this tool works in Maya's documentation.

Next to this is the Auto Keyframe Toggle. Auto Keyframing is one animation technique that many animators like to use that can speed up the animation process. It functions on the assumption that once you have set a key, if you change the time and make a change in your scene that you must want to key that change. If you are careful this can save you some keystrokes along the way; however, oftentimes it creates key frames you had not planned on. Additionally, it tends to make for some rather dirty animation—that is too many keys assigned to attributes that do not need to be keyed. So, in the tutorials to come, it has been left off. However, you might give it a try to see whether it fits in with your workflow once you get going in your animation processes.

Maya allows for many ways to set keys. Pressing s on your keyboard sets a key; however, it sets keys for all sorts of attributes. Pressing s will set Translate, Rotate, and Scale keys when you might only want to be animating the movement or the scale. The biggest problem with pressing s is that you end up with may many more keys than you need; and when it comes time to overlap animation or do any sort of fine editing, you have to wade through mounds of keys that you would not have to if you set your keys a bit more judiciously.

The alternative method is via Shift-w to set a translate key, Shift-e for a rotate key, and Shift-r for a scale key. Although some animation requires using the s keyboard shortcut, most simple animation is more effectively done via the Shifts.

One final note on setting keys. In Maya, almost everything is animatable. This means that most every attribute can have a key set for it. If you select an attribute in the Attributes Editor or in the Channels Box and then right-click on it; a drop down menu that includes Key Selected will appear. You can use this method to set keys for everything from visibility to IK on/off to texture attributes.

Next to that is a button that opens the Animation Preferences. We will look much more at this in the tutorials to come.

Below this is the Command Line, Command Feedback and the Help Line. Unless you plan to manually type commands, the Command Line and Command Feedback are usually not of tremendous help to beginning animators. However the Help Line can be of great use—as you have probably discovered—as it shows the name and often a brief description of any tool that your mouse is sitting upon.

One final note about these animation tools. You can hide or show them using Display > UI Elements.

There are two other tools that you might like to use in animation—the Dope Sheet and Graph Editor; but they are best understood in action so we will wait and tackle those in the context of the tutorials.

TUTORIALS

A few notes about the upcoming tutorials. Animation is an incredibly sophisticated art form. Far more sophisticated than can be covered adequately in one, two or ten chapters. Most animators have worked for years to get motion that is even close to believable (even highly stylized motion)—and it is downright silly to think that you can get a good grasp on it in the course of one book or one semester or even one year of training. This is not meant to be discouraging—just the opposite in fact. As you work along and through the mechanics of how Maya allows you to make things move, focus, for now anyway, on getting them to move—and do not worry too much if the first draft seems a bit dodgy. The best work is your future work and once the tool becomes transparent for you, the technique and art of effective animation will be easier to focus on.

Remember that animation is the process of reanimating. The first draft is never the final draft and new details and possibilities will become evident every time you play through a collection of frames. Further, as you study more on animation and become conscious of important elements of animation in the work of others, you will see more possibilities and tweaks in your own.

So have fun. Look for tool mastery here in these tutorials. The true life of motion will come in time and practice.

We will be tackling several general animation techniques. First we will look at the classic—but deceptively complex—exercise of a bouncing ball. Then we will look at having the game character do a simple walk. Through these processes we will look at many of the main tools that Maya has to offer. However, remember that this is just a look at the tools. Keep working to be able to truly infuse life into these models.

TUTORIAL 13.1   BOUNCING A BALL

Objectives:

1. Organize a simple ball for effective animation.
2. Animate position, scale and rotation.
3. Simulate believable weight, energy, and gravity.
4. Illustrate effective anticipation, stretch & squash, and other basic animation principles.

Step 1: Define a new project. Create a new project (File > Project > New) called Ball_Animation. Be sure to Use Defaults.

Although we will not be using any textures or other sorts of input nodes, we will be outputting files. We will need to render the animation as a string of stills. Without a well-defined project, Maya will store these stills in strange places that you would have to search for later.

Step 2: Create a new scene. Save it as BallHop.

Step 3: Create a new (default settings) polygon sphere. Create > Polygon Primitives > Sphere (options). Reset Settings (should be a sphere that has a Radius of 1, and Subdivisions Axis & Height of 20).

Step 4: Rig the ball. Move the manipulator to the bottom of the ball by pressing Insert and then holding v down (to snap to vertex) as you drag the manipulator to the bottom of the ball (Figure 13.2). Press Insert again.

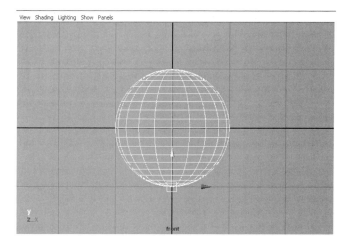

FIGURE 13.2 Rigged ball with manipulator at the bottom of the ball.

Why?

The default positioning of the manipulator, and thus the point at which all manipulation would happen around is at the geometric center of the sphere. This means that if we scaled the sphere it would lift up off the bottom and shrink in from the top to get smaller. But, since we are working on trying to simulate real-world physics it will be important for the sphere to generally be attached to the ground.

Having the manipulator on the bottom of the ball means that we can snap to the ground plane. It means that when we rotate the sphere it rotates around the point that it touches the ground, and when we scale, the sphere will scale down and up from the ground—not the middle of the sphere.

Step 5: Move the sphere up to the ground plane (Y = 0). Hold x down (snap to grid) and move the sphere up so that the bottom of the sphere is at Y = 0.

Step 6: Create a plane and resize it big enough to give you room to hop. The exact size is unimportant (Figure 13.3).

Step 7: Set your animation preferences to Real-Time playback. Click on the Animation Preferences button, or access the Animation Preferences through Windows > Settings/Preferences > Preferences and then clicking on the Timeline Preferences of the Settings category. In the Playback area, make sure Playback Speed is set to Real Time.

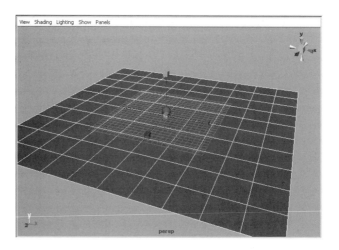

FIGURE 13.3 Added plane for a floor.

 Depending on who used your computer last, Maya could be set up in various ways in regards to playback. In general you want to see your playback in real time—more or less as it would appear rendered. However, sometimes when your scene gets complicated, Maya can not show you every frame in real time, so it drops frames when playing back in the View Panels to still get all the information in in real time. In situations like that you may also be more interested in seeing every frame than seeing Maya's attempt to play it in real time. Notice that within Playback Speed you can have Maya play the animation back by showing every frame, or by playing back twice as fast or half as slow.

Step 8: Change the Time to 30 fps. Still in the Preferences window, click the Settings Category. Change the Time from Film (24 fps) to NTSC (30 fps). Click Save.

 By default Maya is set up for film; but in general beginning animators will not be outputting their work to film; and generally will be preparing it for TV viewing. In the U.S., NTSC is the standard which runs at 30 frames per second.

This actually has great advantages as 30 is generally an easier amount to split up and multiply than 24.

Step 9: Make the total animation 3 seconds. Change the End Time input field to 90 (3 seconds at 30 frames per second is 90 frames total).
Step 10: Show all 90 frames in the Time Slider. Either stretch the Range Slider from 1 to 90, or enter 1 in the Playback Start Time input field and 90 in the Playback End Time (Figure 13.4).

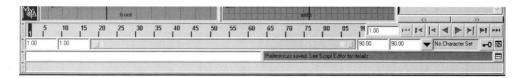

FIGURE 13.4   Time Slider setup.

 For short animations like this, it is often easiest to visualize everything at once. Being able to see all 90 frames and the keys we will set helps to establish the big picture. If a clip ever ends up being hundreds or thousands of frames long, you may need to change the Range Slider quite a bit; but in many cases you can show all the frames all the time.

Why?

Step 11: Set a Translate key at frame 30. Either drag the Current Time Marker to frame 30 or enter 30 in the Current Time input field. Press Shift-w.

 Why set the key at 30? We will be adding some animation later to the beginning of the animation; setting our first key at 30 tells Maya, "okay, for the first 30 frames, do not do anything." This gives Maya its first set of instructions as frame 30 that says, "start here."

Why?

There are several things that happen when you set this Translate key. First, in the Channel Box, the keyed sections will highlight in orange (the Translate X, Y, and Z should now highlight). Second, a small red line will appear in the Time Slider (you may have to move the current time marker aside a bit to see it). This red line represents the key you just set.

Step 12: Move the Current Time Marker to frame 60, move the sphere along the Z axis –12 units, and set a Translate key (Figure 13.5).

 This is the standard process of animating. Give Maya somewhere to start (in this case at Z = 0 at frame 30), then move the Current Time Marker to define a new when, make changes to the scene (in this case move the sphere 12 units along the Z), and record those changes (Shift-w to set a translate key).

Why?

This should create a new key at frame 60 that you can see with a new little red line. If you scrub across the Time Slider you can see the ball sliding back and forth along the ground. Or, if you press the Playback buttons you can play the animation to see the movement.

Step 13: Refine the motion by adding a key at frame 45. Move the Current Time Marker to frame 45. Move the sphere up around three units (Figure 13.6). Press Shift-w.

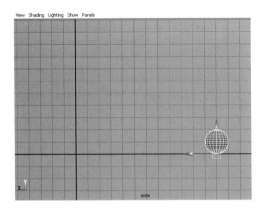

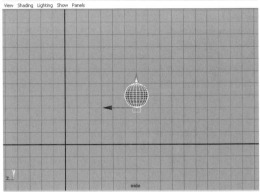

FIGURE 13.5 New position of ball.   **FIGURE 13.6** Refining animation with additional keys.

Yes we could simply have created these keys linearly; but it is important to understand that keys can be set at any time—including between extant keys. You can refine and redefine motion by adding new keys at anytime along the way Essentially this is the basis of an animation technique called pose to pose.

Why?

Step 14: Add rotation to the sphere throughout the animation. Figure 13.7 shows some additional refining of the animation. 13.7a shows frame 30. Rotate the sphere so that it leans into the jump it is about to embark on—press Shift-e to set the rotation key. Then at frame 60 (Figure 13.7b) rotate the sphere back so that it is making sure its bottom is the first part to press the ground. Press Shift-e to set the second rotation key.

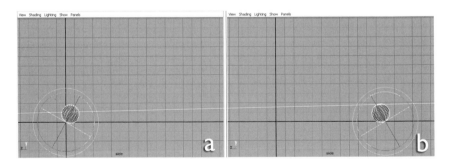

FIGURE 13.7 Additional keys for rotation at frames 30 and 60.

So note that here we are adding rotation keys at the same place as the position keys. You will not see anything dramatically different in the Time Slider, but the Channel Box will show that now the Rotate channels are keyed as they will be orange.

Why?

Step 15: Add stretch to the hop. At frames 30, 45, and 60 add scale keyframes (Shift-r). Stretch on lift off (frame 30), resize to normal (frame 45), and stretch again in preparation for impact (frame 60). Figure 13.8 shows a suggested scale progression.

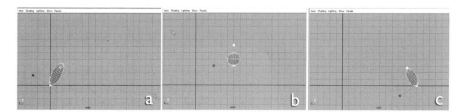

FIGURE 13.8   The Stretch of the hop.

Step 16: Add squash and rotation before hop. Move the Current Time Marker to frame 26. Rotate the sphere back to Rotate X = 0, and squash the sphere (Figure 13.9). Press Shift-e and then Shift-r to set both rotations and scale keys.

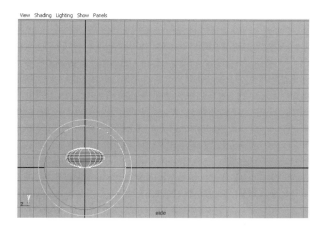

FIGURE 13.9   Rotating and squashing the sphere in preparation of the hop.

Sometimes you want to layer animation—set keys for the position and then later go back and add keys for rotation. At other times, you can do all your rotation, scaling and moving at once and then set keys for all at that same frame. In reality, usually animation overlaps and rarely do rotation, scale, and position keys happen at the same time—however, as you rough out your animation, it can save some time to lay all the initial keys down in easier-to-manage simultaneous frames.

Why?

Previous to this step you had already defined the stretch, this is the squash that at the beginning anticipates the stretch.

Step 17: Add squash at the end of the hop. On frame 62 set a rotation (at Rotate X = 0) and scale key to get the ball squashed as it lands and back to normal (Figure 13.10).

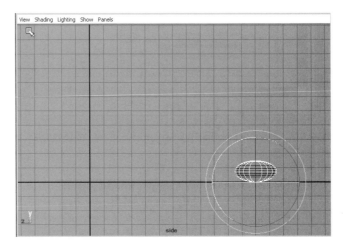

FIGURE 13.10   Squash and rotation at the end of the hop.

Step 18: Add anticipatory stretch and squash before the hop. Figure 13.11a shows frame 13 with rotation and scale keys. Figure 13.11b shows the state at frame 19 (again rotation and scale keys).

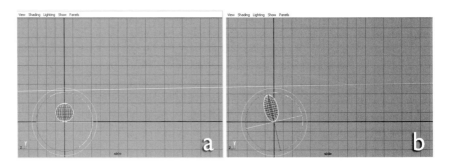

FIGURE 13.11   Giving a bit of stretch and squash (and rotation) before the ball actually hops.

Why? *How did we know that frame 13 and 19 were our target frames? Well we don't— really. These are guesses at how the timing will actually turn out. There will un-*

doubtedly be some tweaks to the timing later. These are largely arbitrary times that give us a rough approximation of the little ready-to-hop jiggle before the hop. Later you can get the timing just right.

Step 19: Add the posthop jiggle. Figure 13.12a shows frame 66, and figure 13.12b shows frame 72. This gives a bit of extra jiggle of the weight after the ball hits the ground.

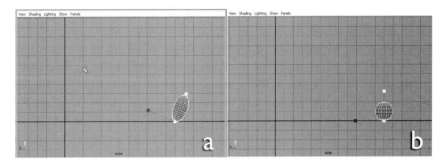

FIGURE 13.12   Giving extra shifting and reaction of weight to the posthop frames.

ON THE CD

Step 20: Playback to see your progress. This is saved as Step19.mb on the CD-ROM if you would like to see the comparison.

Adjusting Curves—The Graph Editor

Step 21: Show the Graph Editor. Choose Window > Animation Editors > Graph Editor. Figure 13.13 shows the graph editor with pSphere1 selected.

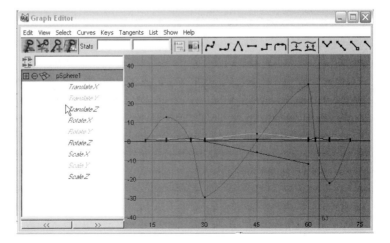

FIGURE 13.13   The Graph Editor of the animation thus far.

The Graph Editor is one way to adjust keys within Maya. In the left you will see selected objects and beneath that the particular attributes that have keys. In the main area—the graph—you will see keys represented by black dots with colored curves connecting the dots. The curves represent the interpolation between keys—which essentially means the frames that Maya is in-betweening for you. You maneuver in the Graph Editor just like in the View Panels, with the Alt-key and mouse buttons.

Maya attempts to make motion as fluid as it can by default. This is why the interpolation is curvilinear. However, sometimes this default interpolation makes movement too smooth. For instance, when the ball is finishing squashing and stretching for its liftoff, the moving off the ground feels soft and sluggish. Similarly, when it lands, it feels like it is landing on a cotton ball. Neither have the pop that occurs when something jumps off of or lands on a hard surface. The Graph Editor will help us adjust those issues.

Step 22: Display only the Translate keys. Under sphere, select Translate X, Translate Y, and Translate Z. The other keys will hide in the graph.
Step 23: Press f to frame these keys. Notice the green curve indicates the path the sphere takes in the Y direction.
Step 24: Marquee around the key at the start of the Y curve. This will select the key and show its tangents.
Step 25: Weight the tangents. In the Graph Editor select Curves > Weighted Tangents.

 By default the curves are nonweighted. This means that each of the points (our keys) along that curve have no more influence over the curve than any other. This means that although we can adjust the tangent's (or, using more familiar terminology, the Bezier handles of a control point) directions, we are powerless to adjust the length of the tangents to give one key more influence over the interpolation. Weighting a curve allows us that option.

Notice that we selected a key, but made an adjustment to the entire curve.

Step 26: Free the Tangent Weights. In the Graph Editor choose Keys > Free Tangent Weight.

 Freeing the tangent weight allows us to now grab a tangent and pull it longer or shorter to more aggressively control the interpolation.

Step 27: Zoom in on the first Y key. Manuevering in the Graph Editor works just like it does in the View Panel. Alt-LMB+MMB drag will allow you to dolly in.
Step 28: Select the out-tangent (the tangent to the right of the key) by marqueeing around it.

Step 29: Switch to the Move Tool (w) and MMB-drag the tangent to approximate Figure 13.14.

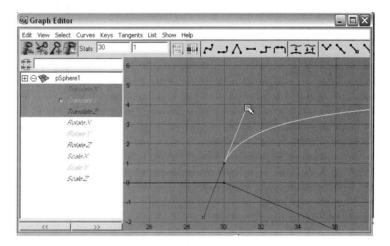

FIGURE 13.14   Adjusted tangent using the Move Tool.

Without the Move Tool being activated you will be unable to adjust tangents in meaningful ways. Often students forget this and cannot figure out why the Graph Editor is broken. If things are not working like you want them to in the Graph Editor make sure you actually have the tool you need activated.

Why?

   Note that the Graph Editor using the methodology of LMB to only select. If you wish to alter something it is almost always using the MMB.

   Adjusting the tangents like this will make the sphere appear to burst off the ground.

Step 30: Select the key at the end of the Translate Y curve. Free the Tangent Weights.
Step 31: Adjust the tangents to mimic Figure 13.15.

This will make the sphere appear to stick its landing.

Why?

Step 32: Resize the Graph Editor and focus on the Translate Y curve. Resize your Graph Editor window (click and drag at the bottom right corner of the window). Select the curve. Press f to frame just the curve.

When the Graph Editor is trying to show you the value over time for X, Y, and Z, sometimes it has to show a lot of the graph to fit it all in. Sometimes, if you can get Maya to show you just one curve, you can get a much better idea of what the interpolation actually looks like.

Why?

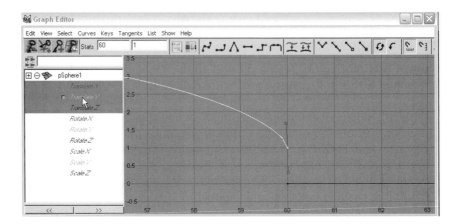

FIGURE 13.15 Adjusted tangents for the key at the end of the Translate Y.

Step 33: Refine the curve to match Figure 13.16. Refine by selecting and adjusting the tangents that control the curve.

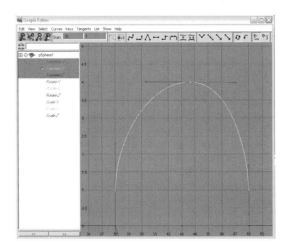

FIGURE 13.16 Adjusted Translate Y curve with better focus.

Step 34: Playback. Notice the quick launch and good stick in the landing.
Step 35: Adjust keys values in the Graph Editor for the Z value. As you look at the distance the ball is hopping, it appears to go too far (it floats). Select Translate Z in the left side of the Graph Editor and press f to frame it. Marquee around the last key of the Translate Z curve (this one appears as a line). Notice in the Stats section at the top of the Graph Editor; it should read 60 (frame number) in the first input field and -12 (value in Z) in the second. Change the second input field to -8.

Notice that you would also visually move the key up in the graph section by MMB-dragging. But entering the numerical value allows us to keep things a bit cleaner.
Why?

Step 36: Delete the middle key of the Translate Z curve. Select the key by marquee-selecting around it and press delete.

 As you adjusted the last key, the straight line that is the Translate Z becomes a curve. This means that the ball would hop a long way at first, and then suddenly die off. For simplicity's sake, here we will assume that the ball travels at a constant rate in Z for the entire hop. Deleting the middle key gets the Translate Z curve back to a linear line.
Why?

Step 37: Close the Graph Editor.

Step 38: Adjust the timing in the Time Slider. In the Time Slider, Shift drag over all the keys (Figure 13.17a). Drag the triangle at the right end of the now red selection to the left. This rescales the selected keys (rescales them around the first selected frame).

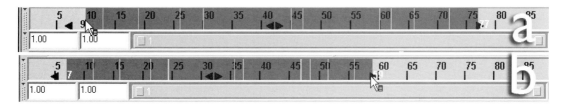

FIGURE 13.17 Selecting (a) and rescaling keys (b).

 Rescaling keys changes the time between each key. If the number of frames between keys are fewer, the motion happens faster. Thus, rescaling the selection of keys in the Time Slider smaller makes for faster motion.
Why?

Notice that this is not an exact science at this point. Scale, press playback, adjust again. Look for getting the animation to feel right in its motion.

Notice that you can rescale the keys with the triangle at the beginning or end of the red selection. But also note that in the middle of the red selection is a double-arrow that you can use to simply move these keys to a different point in time.

Playblast

Step 39: Create a Playblast. In the persp View Panel, move your camera around into position so you can see the entire hop. Change your Range Slider to include only the hop and not the extra frames after the hop is done. Choose Window > Playblast… (options). Reset the settings. Change the Scale to 1. Press Playblast (Figure 13.18).

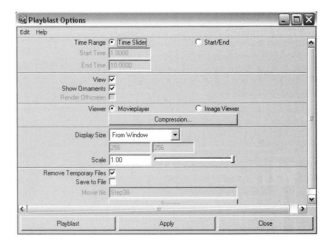

FIGURE 13.18   The Playblast Options window.

Playblasts are previews of an animation sequence. They do not render a scene using Maya software or the other more time-intensive output methods; however, they do create a minimovie that allows you to view the animation. In this situation, where there are not many polygons, this is less of an issue as Maya can probably play the animation in realtime in your View Planes. However, in more complicated scenes, Maya will be unable to Playback every frame in realtime; yet it is very important to see it that way.

A Playblast will save every frame and output it to a movie that you can view in Movie player. Most of the settings in the Playblast Options window are pretty easy to understand. Show Ornaments refers to things like manipulator handles and locators. You can change the Compression of the output movie. You can change the Display size to a numerically defined size (720x480 for DVNTSC for instance). And at the bottom, you can choose to save the playblast rather than just output it as a temporary file (Figure 13.19).

Step 40: Light the scene and render. Put some lights in the scene—make sure they cast shadows. Open the Render Settings window. Change the Frame/Animation Ext to name#.ext. Change the Image Format to Tiff (tif). Change Start Frame to 1, End Frame to 60 (or whatever your last frame of animation is) and change Frame Padding to 2. The other settings (if they are default) should be fine (Figure 13.20).

The Render Settings (previously Render Globals) has a few things that are important to rendering animations. The Frame/Animation Ext area lets you define how Maya will name the frames it renders out. Different video editors allow for different

FIGURE 13.19   Results of the playblast.

FIGURE 13.20 Render settings to render out the ball hopping animation.

naming conventions, but almost all of them will recognize an image sequence when it runs Name#.ext.

Changing from a Maya Tiff to a general Tiff will allow for more video editors to be able to read the files. Start Frame and End Frame are pretty self-explanatory, but Frame Padding may not be. Basically this indicates how many zeros will be placed in front of the rendered frame number. So a frame padding of 3 would render something that was Filename001.tif for the first frame. This is important as it helps computers understand how to sequence frames and not fall for the problem of File1.tif being followed by File10.tif, then File11.tif, and so on instead of File2.tif.

Step 41: Change to Rendering mode (F5), and choose Rendering |Render > Batch Rendering. In the bottom right corner of your interface you should see something that reads like figure 13.21.

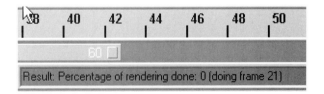

FIGURE 13.21   Rendering in progress.

 You can also see the progress by selecting Windows > General Editors > Script **Why?** *Editor...*

This will render each individual frame and save the file to your images folder in your project folder.

Step 42: View the animation in either FCheck (File > Open Animation) or something like Quicktime Player (Pro Version) (File > Open Image Sequence). You could also import the image sequence into something like Premiere, Final Cut Pro, or After Effects.

Why?

FCheck is Maya's built-in image viewer. It is usually located in the same directory as Maya is—and is accessible usually through Start > Programs > Alias > FCheck. Once it is open, select File > Open Animation. Navigate to BallHop folder (your project file) and find the images folder therein. Select the first frame of your animation and press Open.

FCheck will then read each of the frames into memory—the first time through might be a bit slow. Then once it has them all, it will play the animation (Figure 13.22).

FIGURE 13.22 FCheck in action.

Tutorial Conclusion

Now this is just the most basic of animation exercises. The timing is not quite right yet; the anticipatory stretch and squash and the final jiggle to rest could be tweaked and massaged to a more sophisticated flow. The stretch and rotations could be offset to allow for overlapping motion. The list of tweaks could (and should) go on and on. The specifics of the beauty of motion are just too much to cover in this chapter.

However, in this tutorial you have touched on many of the important tools of Maya's animation work flow. You have set keys that defined movement, rotation, and scaling. You have added keys between keys, before and after extant keys. You have adjusted key positions in the Graph Editor, and used the Graph Editor to control curves that defined the interpolation between keys. You have used the Time Slider to scale and move keys.

Finally you have output your animation as a Playblast and a rendered sequence. Technically, you have touched on all the major tools of Maya's animation paradigm. Yet there is still much that could be covered.

In the next tutorial we will look at using these tools to animate a character. Amazingly, the same basic tools of setting Move, Scale and Rotate keys works in bringing a character to life.

TUTORIAL 13.2   BASIC WALK

Objectives:

1. Organize a character for animation.
2. Use referencing to maintain original character integrity.
3. Use IK to animate lower body.
4. Use FK to animate upper body.
5. Touch upon elements of weight.
6. Animated completed walk.

Step 1: Set your project to Game_Model. This should include the rigged version of your Character.

Step 2: Open your last version of your game model. Make sure this version is rigged and skinned.

Step 3: Return the character to his Bind Pose. Remember that you must do some of this by returning the IK groups to their origin—enter 0 in Translate X, Y, and Z in the Channels Box.

Step 4: Group mesh, IK handles and joints. Choose Root_joint, L_Foot, R_Foot, and press Ctrl-g to group them. Do not include Character in the group. Rename the group Character_Group. Place the manipulator for this group at the bottom center of the feet (Figure 13.23).

Why? *Organizing the character in this way will allow you to put the character into a new position without having to move multiple objects. If, when you get ready to animate, you need to have him walking along a different plane than he was modeled, or in a different direction than he is now, you can just rotate the group that contains everything.*

Remember to not include the Character in the group. At this point, the joints will control everything about the polygons of the character. If you include the Char-

acter in the group, when you move the group, the polygons will get movement orders twice—once for the polygons themselves and once for the joints. This will cause the polygons to move twice as far as the joints.

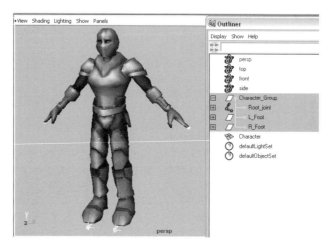

FIGURE 13.23   Organizing the file though grouping.

Step 5: Save as GameModelReady.mb.

We will be making use of Maya's referencing system. The core idea behind this is that you can reference Maya files in other Maya files. This is different than simply importing files as referenced files can be updated at any time.

In this case we will be referencing GameModelReady.mb into another file GameModelWalk.mb that we will actually do the animating in. In fact, we could reference GameModelReady.mb into as many files as we would like. The benefit of this is that if we find along the way that there is a problem in the skin weights or anything really; we can make the changes to GameModelReady.mb, and all the places where it is referenced—the changes will also be in effect.

This does several things for us. First, it keeps the original GameModel Ready.mb clean without any keys or other garbage. Second, if you are working on a narrative project you will probably have many Maya files that represent various shots. If you discover you need to have this character with red armor instead of blue; you only need to adjust one file to have the changes in all of the shot files.

Step 6: Create a new scene. File > New Scene…
Step 7: Create a plane for the ground. Make its Width 50 units and Height 200 units. Create a material to apply to the floor. Make sure it is something with a bit of texture (maybe checkerboard or modified bulge or something like that).

Although not totally necessary, you get a much better idea of the motion if the floor beneath the character actually has some pattern to it. It allows you to see ground being covered.

Step 8: Create a Reference. Choose File > Create Reference (options). Reset settings and click Reference. This should open you to the scenes folder inside your project folder. Choose GameModelReady.mob and press Reference (Figure 13.24).

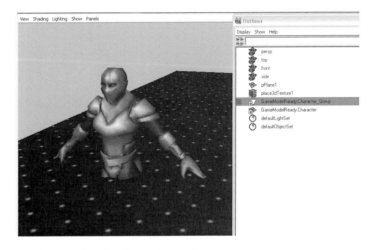

FIGURE 13.24 Results of creating a reference.

Note that there are a few things that are different about the scene now. First, the Character and its associated joints and IK handles are all in the new scene—although they are in a poor location (part way through the floor, and so on). Second, notice in the Outliner that the icon next to GameModelReady:Character_Group has a little blue dot on it. This indicates that this is a referenced object.

Referenced objects have some restrictions. One big one is that you can not delete the file by just pressing delete. To get rid of referenced files you need to use the Reference Editor (File > Reference Editor. . .). Here (Figure 13.25), you can turn a referenced file off, so it does not appear in the file; or you can right-click on a reference and choose File > Reference > Remove Reference.

Step 9: Move GameModelReady:Character_Group into position standing on the floor (Figure 13.26). Select GameModelReady:Character_Group and use the Move Tool to position him. The exact location is not important but do make sure he is standing on the floor.

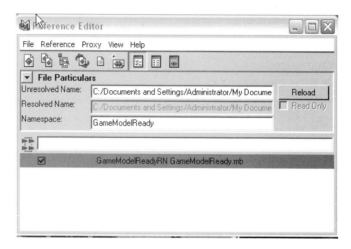

FIGURE 13.25   The Reference Editor that allows you to control, turn off, and/or remove referenced files from a scene.

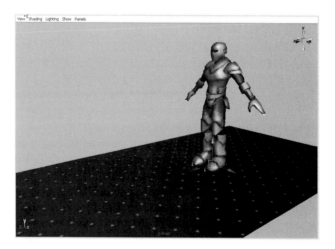

FIGURE 13.26   Positioned character.

Step 10: Make the scene 90 frames long, and make sure you are animating at 30 fps. Change the number of frames in the End Time input filed next to the Range Slider. Open the Animation Preferences and in the Settings Category, make sure to change the Time to NTSC (30 fps).

Step 11: Organize the Outliner. Expand GameModelReady:Character_ Group. Minimize GameModelReady:Root_joint, minimize GameModel: Ready:L_Foot and GameModel:Ready:R_Foot. Your outliner should look like Figure 13.27.

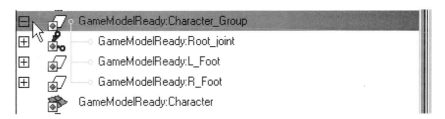

FIGURE 13.27   Organized outliner.

To keep the reading easier, the GameModelReady has been omitted for the rest of the tutorial and just the part of that referenced file we will be using is listed. So remember, when you see list L_Foot it means GameModelReady:L_Foot in your Outliner.

Roughing out the Movement

Step 12: Record a Translate key at frame 1 for L_Foot. Remember to do this with Shift-w.

Remember that to define animation, we must define a key at the beginning and end of each section of animation. In this case the L_Foot is going to make the first move, but we must give it a place and time to start.
Why?

Step 13: Record a Translate key at frame 1 for Root_joint.

In this first part we are going to animate the legs moving and taking the general body with it. So we need to give the Root_joint a key to start with as well.
Why?

Step 14: Move the Current Time Marker to frame 5. Move Root_joint forward and down a bit (Figure 13.28). Record a Translate key.
Step 15: Still at frame 5, move L_Foot to approximate Figure 13.29. Record a Translate key.
Step 16: At frame 10 record a Translate key for L_Foot (Figure 13.30a) and Root_joint (Figure 13.30b). Remember to set the Translate key after each movement.
Step 17: While still at frame 10, set a Translate key for R_Foot.

Frame 10 is where R_Foot is going to start to move. So we must give it a key here to know when to start its movement to where.
Why?

Step 18: At frame 15, position and set a Translate key for R_Foot and Root_joint (Figure 13.31).

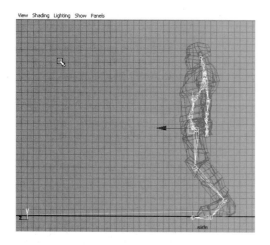

FIGURE 13.28   Moving the body forward in the walk.

FIGURE 13.29   Moving the foot to passing position.

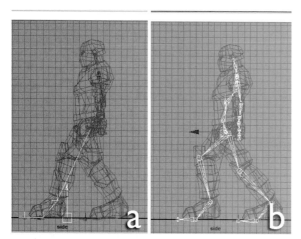

FIGURE 13.30   Pose at frame 10.

FIGURE 13.31   Passing pose for frame 15.

Step 19: At frame 20 record a Translate key for both R_Foot (front foot) and Root_joint in a pose matching Figure 13.32.

Step 20: Set a Translate key for L_foot at frame 20.

Between frame 10 and 20, the L_Foot has been on the ground and not moving. Setting a Translate key at frame 20 tells Maya, "ok, you have instructions at frame 10 to be in this place and at frame 20 to still be in the same place; so don't move during that time."

Simultaneously, it gives Maya a key to know when to start the movement of the L_Foot again.

Step 21: Set a Translate key for R_Foot and Root_joint at frame 25 to match Figure 13.33.

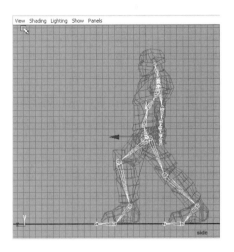

FIGURE 13.32   Right foot fall at frame 20.

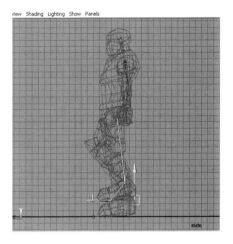

FIGURE 13.33   Passing position for next step at frame 25.

Step 22: Set a Translate key for R_Foot (front foot now) and Root_joint at frame 30 to match Figure 13.34.

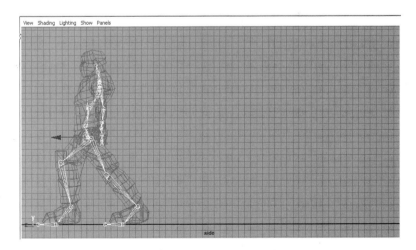

FIGURE 13.34   Pose at frame 30.

Step 23: Repeat the steps until frame 90. The general pattern is this: Both feet are on the ground every ten frames (frames 10, 20, 30, 40, 50,

60, 70, 80, 90); every five frames between those, the moving foot is in the air at about the ankle height of the planted foot. Remember that every time both feet are on the ground (every ten frames) both feet must have a Translate key recorded.

Refining the Foot

Step 24: Set a Rotation key at frame 1 for L_Foot. Move the Current Time Marker to frame 1, select L_Foot in the outliner and press Shift-e.

 We are going to rotate the foot to mimic the rotation of the ankle during the walk.
Why? *Setting the key at 1 gives L_Foot a rotation value to start from.*

Step 25: At frame 5, set a Rotation key (Shift-e) for L_Foot to approximate Figure 13.35.

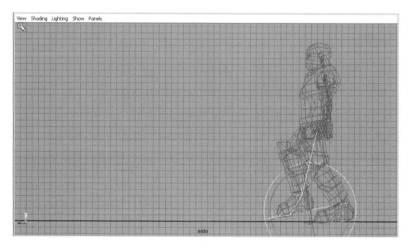

FIGURE 13.35   Rotating the L_Foot. In this case, the Rotate X value is 10.

 This little toe point is really more to anticipate the foot flop that occurs when the foot
Why? *actually touches down. It will make a bit more sense in a few steps.*

Step 26: At frame 10, rotate the L_Foot up to match Figure 13.36 when the heel touches down. Record a Rotation key (Shift-e).

 When we walk, usually the first part of our foot to touch down is the heel. Rotat-
Why? *ing the foot up like this allows us to indicate this visually.*

Notice that in the captions, the Rotate X value is listed. Remember that you can enter numeric values in the Channel Box and then after pressing Enter, press Shift-e to set the Rotation key.

FIGURE 13.36   Rotation of L_Foot at frame 10. In this case, the Rotate X value is –15.

Step 27: At frame 12 rotate the L_Foot flat again (Rotate X = 0) and set a Rotation key (Figure 13.37).

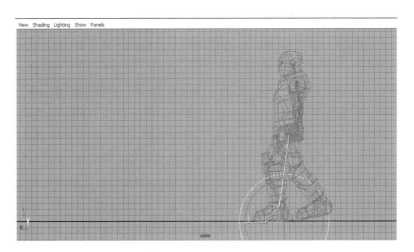

FIGURE 13.37   Completing the foot flow at frame 12 with a flattened L_Foot (Rotate X = 0).

Step 28: Repeat the foot flop for R_Foot. At frame 10 set a Rotation key. At frame 15 rotate down (Rotate X = 10) set a Rotation key. At frame 20 rotate up (Rotate X = −15) set a Rotation key. At frame 22, flatten foot (Rotate X = 0) set a Rotation key (Figure 13.38).

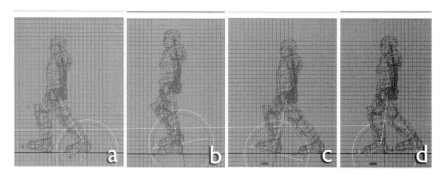

FIGURE 13.38   Setting the foot flop for the right foot.

Step 29: Add the foot flop for both feet for the duration of the walk.

Animating the Upper Body

Step 30: Expand the Root_joint group to show all the joints. Do this in the Outliner and hold Shift down when you click the + sign.

Step 31: At frame 1, rotate the shoulders (R_Shoulder_joint, and L_Shoulder_joint), elbows (R_Elbow_joint and L_Elbow_joint), wrists (R_Wrist_joint and L_Wrist_joint), and hands (R_Hand_joint and L_Hand_joint) to a more natural pose (Figure 13.39).

Step 32: At frame 1 set a Rotation key for the following joints: Root_joint, Spine_joint2, Chest_joint, Head_joint, L_Shoulder_joint, L_Elbow_joint, L_Wrist_Joint, R_Shoulder_joint, R_Elbow_joint, R_Wrist_Joint. The easiest way to do this is to select all of these joints in the Outliner (Figure 13.40) by Ctrl-clicking on each (do not Shift-click as it will select all the joints in between the desired joints) and then when they are all selected press Shift-e to set the key for all.

Step 33: Move to frame 10 and begin posing and setting keys. Rotate the R_Shoulder_joint forward (set a Rotation key—Shift-e) and the L_Shoulder back (set a Rotation key—Shift-e). Rotate the hips via Root_Joint so the left hip is forward (set a Rotation key—Shift-e). Counter with rotating Spine_joint2 (set a Rotation key—Shift-e) and Neck_joint (set a Rotation key—Shift-e). In essence, use the Rotation Tool to rotate each of the joints in the upper body to find the right pose. Remember to set a Rotation key for each bone after you have it rotated where you want it.

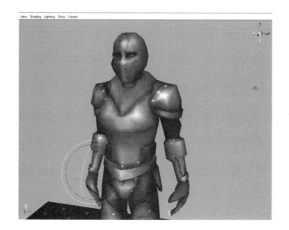

FIGURE 13.39   Rotating the arms into a relaxed pose.

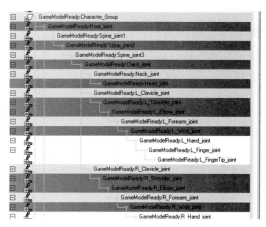

FIGURE 13.40   Setting a key for multiple joints at once.

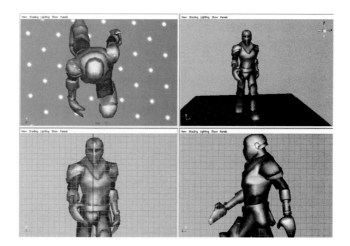

FIGURE 13.41   Establishing the pose for frame 10. Set a Rotation key for each joint you rotate.

Step 34: Move to frame 20 and again pose and set Rotation keys. Basically rotate all the same joints you did for step 31, but rotate them opposite (Figure 13.42).

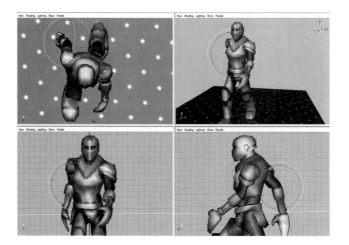

FIGURE 13.42 Rotated upper body for frame 20.

Dope Sheet

Step 35: Select Window > Animation Editors > Dope Sheet…
Step 36: In the Outliner, select Root_joint. Look in the Dope Sheet (Figure 13.43) and expand (hold Shift down when clicking the +) the Root_joint.

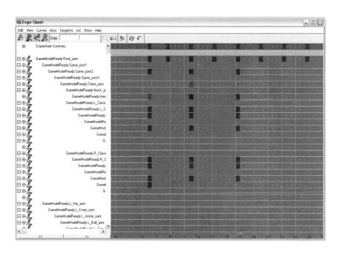

FIGURE 13.43 Dope Sheet showing keys for Root_joint and its children joints.

It is important to realize what you are seeing here. Figure 13.43 shows the Dope Sheet after Root_joint was expanded. You will notice on the left under Dopesheet Summary are all the joints (you can expand that area with the >> symbols on the bottom of that column). To the right are tick marks representing

frames and black or dark gray blocks representing keys. You can marquee-select around any of the keys which will then highlight yellow.

Notice that you can maneuver around the Dope Sheet just like in any other window in Maya. Alt-MMB will allow you to pan around the sheet. Alt-LMB+MMB allows you to zoom in and out to see more or less frames.

Step 37: Expand the keys of Root_joint. Do this by clicking the + in a circle.

Why? We have Rotation and Translate keys for Root_joint. In this case we do not want to duplicate the Translate keys as you already have the movement of that joint as it should be. But we do want to be able to duplicate the Rotation keys. But to do this, we need to be able to see the difference in keys.

Step 38: Select all the keys that rotate the upper body from frame 10 to 20. To do this, first activate the Select Keyframe Tool (Figure 13.44) at the top right corner of the Dope Sheet. Then marquee-select around all the keys from Root_joint's Rotate keys (at frame 10) to the last key visible at frame 10. This will create a light blue box with small range numbers at the bottom (10 and 21). The keys will highlight yellow (Figure 13.45).

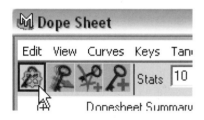

FIGURE 13.44   The Select Keyframe Tool.

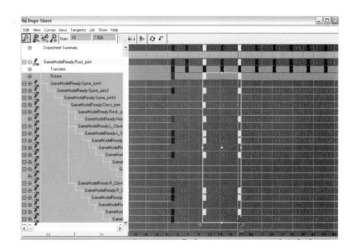

FIGURE 13.45   Selected keys.

Step 39: Copy and paste these to frames 30 to 41. Do this in three steps: (1) Press Ctrl-c (to copy); (2) click and drag the little blue diamond in the center of the selection (it will highlight yellow when you do this), and drag it until you see the range as 30 to 41 at the bottom of the selection box (Figure 13.46); (3) Press Ctrl-v to paste (Figure 13.47).

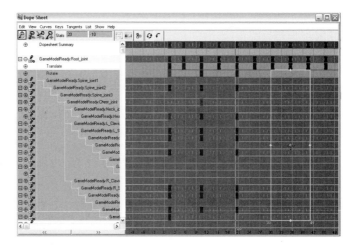

FIGURE 13.46   Moving the selection box to target frames.

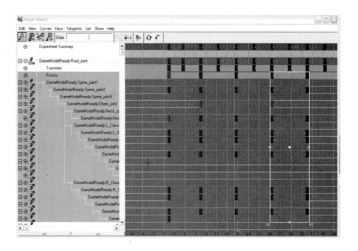

FIGURE 13.47   Pasted frames into target area.

Make sure that you have selected the keys in the Rotate row of the Root_joint. When you paste, if things do not happen as they are described in Step 37, undo (Ctrl-z) and reset your settings for Edit > Copy (options) and Edit > Paste (options) in the Dope Sheet. Repeat step 37.

If all works out right, your character should be swinging his arms and chest correctly up to frame 40.

Step 40: Repeat to frame 90. Each time, select a collection of keys (you can increase the number of keys as you have more) copy them, move your selection indicator and then paste.

Step 41: Tweak, tweak, tweak. There are so many tweaks to make this into a good walk that it could take a book in itself to work them all out. For now, give it your best shot. The art of the walk will come with study and practice.

Step 42: If your machine plays the animation choppy, output a Playblast to see it in real time.

Step 43: Light the scene and give it a render (Figure 13.48).

FIGURE 13.48   Rendered scene with character in motion.

Tutorial Conclusion

It is a start—but just a start. The intricate mechanics of twisting, weight, and overlapping motion that is a walk is not easy and takes a while to master. However, in this tutorial we looked at how to work with IK to control the legs and create a basic walk. We looked at how to work the upper body with FK or basic rotation. Finally we looked at the capabilities of the Dope Sheet to quickly select, move, and copy keys.

CONCLUSION

And with that we wrap up the coverage of Maya in this volume. We have covered a lot of ground in these pages. We have built primitive forms that grew in complexity until we created a room complete with organic furniture. We looked at how to give that furniture more visual complexity with textures and custom-built materials. We also looked at how to give special depth to a scene via lighting that mimicked the lighting in the real world.

We tackled the dynamic world of organic modeling. We created a game character that we created a custom UV map and custom textures for. And finally we looked at how to rig, skin, and animate the character.

It has been a long road, but hopefully over the course of your travels you feel confident with the tools we explored along the way. Remember that tutorials might be a good way to get started learning the tools; but the results can rarely be used in a demo reel; and in fact, at best—if you are completely successful with the tutorial, you have a result that looks just like everyone else who successfully completed the same steps.

The true growth comes when you take these ideas and tools and begin constructing your own projects with your own vision. Only then do you start to find ways to implement Maya's toolset into your own workflow and begin to create the 3D works of art that inspire viewers, win awards and get jobs.

CHALLENGES, EXERCISES, OR ASSIGNMENTS

1. Refine the walk animation.
2. Animate the character with character. Try a cartoon, a fashion model, a jock…
3. Animate the character with an injury. Broken foot? Bruised leg?
4. Animate the character in a run? How does a run differ from a walk?
5. Try a skip, character hop, kung-fu move, jump flip, and so on.

A

CURRICULAR FLOW

The contents of this book were created based upon many years of teaching Maya in the classroom. The tools selected and the tutorials presented are those that provide students a good overview of the tools of Maya, which will allow them to excel faster in their 3D pursuits.

This appendix provides a suggested flow of how much to cover and how fast. In reality, every area has students of varying preparedness. If you are teaching at a community college or university, you may have students who dealt with digital media in high school and can move very quickly. But you may have students who had no training previously and need to back up a bit. You may have prerequisites for a course and do not need to spend much time on Photoshop; or this book could be used for a course in which students have no prerequisites.

If you are using this book as a high school textbook, the literacy of your students will define much about your pacing. If students have machines at home and can supplement their in-class time with homework, you can do more in-depth assignments.

In short, these suggested curricular outlines are just that—suggested. Adjust as you will and remember that this book is meant to supplement classroom instruction—not replace it.

PLAN A: 16-WEEK SEMESTER

This plan makes the following assumptions:

- You are using the book for a one-semester course.
- This is the only semester you will be using Maya.
- You are meeting twice a week for at least 2 hours.
- Most of the work must be done in class.

MEETING	LECTURE	IN CLASS	HOMEWORK
Meeting #1	Course outline, 3D paradigm, Maya introduction	Tutorial 2.1 Primitive Man	Read Chapters 1, 2 Girlfriend, Primitive Temple
Meeting #2	Room creation, basic polygonal modeling	Tutorial 3.1: Room Primitives	Read Chapter 3
Meeting #3	Room creation, component editing	Tutorial 4.1: Boolean Functions in the Room	Read Chapter 4
		Tutorial 4.2: Creating a Table with Component Editing and Extrude Faces	
Meeting #4	Room creation, component editing	Room Checkup; continue modeling furniture	Finish hard furniture in room
Meeting #5	Room creation, NURBS modeling	Tutorial 5.1: Creating Vases	Read Chapter 5
		Tutorial 5.2: Trim	
Meeting #6	Further NURBS coverage	Finish trim and frames in own room	Read Chapter 6 Complete trim
Meeting #7	Advanced polygonal modeling	Tutorial 6.1: Modeling a Sink with	Model sink and soft furniture
		Smooth Proxy	
Meeting #8	Modeling cont'd	Finish modeling room elements	Read Chapter 7
Meeting #9	Maya materials	Tutorial 7.1: Creating a Material	Read Chapter 8 Begin texturing room
Meeting #10	Texturing polygons	Tutorial 8.1: Creating Seamless	Track down textures for room (online)
		Textures	
Meeting #11	Texturing polygons cont'd	Tutorial 8.2: Texturing the Shower Stall	
		Texture bathroom	
Meeting #12	Texturing cont'd	Tutorial 8.3: Texturing the Main Room	Texture room
Meeting #13	Texturing cont'd	Complete texturing room	Read Chapter 9
Meeting #14	Maya lighting intro	Tutorial 9.1: Lighting the Scene for Night	Complete night lighting
Meeting #15	Maya lighting cont'd	Tutorial 9.2: Daytime Lighting	Daytime lighting cont'd
Meeting #16	Maya lighting cont'd	Complete daytime lighting	Daytime lighting complete
Meeting #17	Maya lighting cont'd	Romantic lighting of scene	Read Chapter 10 $\longrightarrow$

MEETING	LECTURE	IN CLASS	HOMEWORK
Meeting #18	Organic modeling	Tutorial 10.1: Modeling the Amazing Wooden Man	Finish Amazing Wooden Man
Meeting #19	Organic modeling cont'd	Tutorial 10.2: Game Model	
Meeting #20	Organic modeling cont'd	Game model cont'd	Finish game model
Meeting #21	Organic modeling cont'd	Game model complete	Read Chapter 11
Meeting #22	UV mapping	Tutorial 11.1: Texturing Amazing Wooden Man Tutorial 11.2: UV Mapping Game Character	UV mapping cont'd
Meeting #23	UV mapping cont'd	UV mapping game character cont'd	UV mapping cont'd
Meeting #24	UV mapping cont'd	UV mapping game character cont'd UV snapshot	
Meeting #25	Photoshop texture painting	Appendix D Paint and apply custom texture	Read Chapter 12
Meeting #26	Rigging/IK	Tutorial 12.1: Rigging a Basic IK Chain Tutorial 12.2: Skinning a Leg Tutorial 12.3: Rigging the Game Character	Complete rigging
Meeting #27	Skinning	Tutorial 12.4: Skinning the Game Model	Complete skinning
Meeting #28	Animation introduction	Tutorial 13.1: Ball Animation	Finish ball animation
Meeting #29	Character animation	Tutorial 13.2: Basic Walk	Animate walk
Meeting #30	Character animation cont'd	Walk complete Animate character hop	Animate hop
Meeting #31	Character animation cont'd	Animate run	Animate run
Meeting #32	Character animation cont'd	Animate strut/skip/fat walk/old walk, and so on	

PLAN B: TWO 16-WEEK SEMESTERS OR A ONE-YEAR COURSE

This plan makes the following assumptions:

- You are using the book for two semesters or a full year.
- This is the only year you will be using Maya.
- You are meeting twice a week for at least two hours.
- You can assign out-of-class projects.

MEETING	LECTURE	IN CLASS	HOMEWORK
Meeting #1	Course outline, 3D paradigm, Maya introduction	Tutorial 2.1: Primitive Man	Read Chapter 1, 2 Girlfriend, Primitive Temple →

MEETING	LECTURE	IN CLASS	HOMEWORK
Meeting #2	Room creation, basic polygonal modeling	Tutorial 3.1: Room Primitives	Read Chapter 3 Room research
Meeting #3	Room design	Present research Begin modeling student room	Continue student room Read Chapter 4
Meeting #4	Room creation, component editing	Tutorial 4.1: Boolean Functions in the Room	Boolean student windows and doors
		Tutorial 4.2: Creating a Table with Component Editing and Extrude Faces	
Meeting #5	Furniture creation	Continue modeling rigid furniture for student room	Read Chapter 5 Student room cont'd
Meeting #6	Room creation, NURBS modeling	Tutorial 5.1: Creating Vases	Student room vases/glasses
		Tutorial 5.2: Trim	Student room trim
Meeting #7	Further NURBS coverage	Finish trim and frames in own room	Read Chapter 6 Complete trim
Meeting #8	Advanced polygonal modeling	Tutorial 6.1: Modeling a Sink with Smooth Proxy	Model soft furniture in student room
Meeting #9	Modeling cont'd	Continue soft furniture	Read Chapter 7
Meeting #10	Maya materials	Tutorial 7.1: Creating a Material Begin texturing student room	Read Chapter 8
Meeting #11	Texturing polygons	Tutorial 8.1: Creating Seamless Textures	Track down textures for student room (online, books, and photos)
Meeting #12	Texturing polygons cont'd	Tutorial 8.2: Texturing the Shower Stall	Texture student room
Meeting #13	Texturing cont'd	Tutorial 8.3: Texturing the Main Room	Texture student room
Meeting #14	Texturing cont'd	Texture student room	Texture student room
Meeting #15	Texturing cont'd	Complete texturing room	Read Chapter 9
Meeting #16	Maya lighting intro	Tutorial 9.1: Lighting the Scene for Night	Complete night lighting of tutorial room
Meeting #17	Maya lighting cont'd	Light student room for night	Student room night lighting
Meeting #18	Maya lighting cont'd	Tutorial 9.2: Daytime Lighting	Daytime lighting for tutorial room cont'd
Meeting #19	Maya lighting cont'd	Daytime lighting student room	Daytime lighting student room
Meeting #20	Maya lighting cont'd	Continue daytime lighting	Continue daytime lighting
Meeting #21	Maya lighting cont'd	Complete daytime lighting	
Meeting #22	Maya lighting cont'd	Romantic lighting of scene.	Read Chapter 10
Meeting #23	Organic modeling con'd	Tutorial 10.1: Modeling the Amazing Wooden Man	Finish Amazing Wooden Man
Meeting #24	Organic modeling cont'd	Tutorial 10.2: Game Model	Game model
Meeting #25	Organic modeling cont'd	Game model cont'd	Game model →

MEETING	LECTURE	IN CLASS	HOMEWORK
Meeting #26	Organic modeling cont'd	Game model complete	Create custom character style sheet
Meeting #27	Organic modeling cont'd	Student character (Appendix C)	Student character
Meeting #28	Organic modeling cont'd	Student character	Student character
Meeting #29	Organic modeling	Student character complete	Read Chapter 11
Meeting #30	UV mapping	Tutorial 11.1: Texturing Amazing Wooden Man	UV mapping cont'd
		Tutorial 11.2: UV Mapping Game Character	
Meeting #31	UV mapping cont'd	UV mapping game character cont'd	UV mapping cont'd
Meeting #32	UV mapping cont'd	UV mapping game character cont'd	UV snapshot
Meeting #33	Photoshop texture painting	Appendix D Paint and apply custom texture	
Meeting #34	UV mapping cont'd	UV map student character	UV map student character
Meeting #35	UV mapping cont'd	UV map student character UV snapshot	UV map student character
Meeting #36	Custom texture	Paint and apply custom texture	Custom Texture
Meeting #37	Custom texture cont'd	Finish custom texture	Read Chapter 12
Meeting #38	Rigging/IK	Tutorial 12.1: Rigging a Basic IK Chain	Complete rigging
		Tutorial 12.2: Skinning a Leg	
		Tutorial 12.3: Rigging the Game Character	
Meeting #39	Skinning	Tutorial 12.4: Skinning the Game Model	Complete skinning
Meeting #40	Rigging revisited	Rig student character	Rig student character
Meeting #41	Skinning revisited	Skin student character	Skin student character
Meeting #42	Setup complete	Test rig and skinning of student character	Read Chapter 13
Meeting #43	Animation introduction	Tutorial 13.1: Ball Animation	Finish ball animation
Meeting #44	Ball of a table	Animate 15 seconds of ball rolling off a table, bouncing, and coming to a stop	
Meeting #45	Ball hitting empty box	Animate 10 seconds of heavy ball rolling on the floor and striking an empty box	
Meeting #46	Ball hitting full box	Animate 10 seconds of light ball rolling on the floor and striking a heavy box	

$\rightarrow$

MEETING	LECTURE	IN CLASS	HOMEWORK
Meeting #47	Family of balls	Animate 25 seconds of a family (father, mother, teenage boy, and toddler daughter) walking along the street	
Meeting #48	Character animation	Tutorial 13.2: Basic Walk	Animate walk
Meeting #49	Character animation cont'd	Animate student character walk	
Meeting #50	Character animation cont'd	Walk complete Animate student character hop	Animate hop
Meeting #51	Character animation cont'd	Complete hop	
Meeting #52	Character animation cont'd	Animate run	Animate run
Meeting #53	Character animation cont'd	Complete run	
Meeting #54	Character animation cont'd	Animate character strut	Complete strut
Meeting #55	Character animation cont'd	Animate character skip	Complete skip
Meeting #56	Character animation cont'd	Animate character run, hurdle	Complete run, hurdle
Meeting #57	Character animation cont'd	Animate character sneak	Complete sneak
Meeting #58	Character animation cont'd	Animate character throwing baseball	Complete baseball
Meeting #59	Character animation cont'd	Animate character punching game character	Complete punching
Meeting #60	Character animation cont'd	Continue character punch	Complete punch
Meeting #61	Character animation cont'd	Animate character over-weight walk	Complete overweight walk
Meeting #62	Character animation cont'd	Animate character old walk	Complete old walk
Meeting #63	Character animation cont'd	Animate character walking into room, sitting on chair	Complete walking/sitting
Meeting #64	Show and Tell	Show and Tell	

NOTES ON EXTRA ASSIGNMENTS

At the end of each chapter of the book is a small collection of extra challenges or assignments. If you are using this book as part of a class, these can make great homework assignments; if you have a class with varying skill levels, these make great assignments to give those a little faster than the others.

If you are not using this book in class and are using it to teach yourself Maya, these still have tremendous use. Remember that when following tutorials, the best you can do is be successful in duplicating the author's production—and, therefore, create an object completely useless for your reel. It is those extra assignments, unique to your reel that will set your work apart from the pack.

B PREPARING IMAGE PLANES

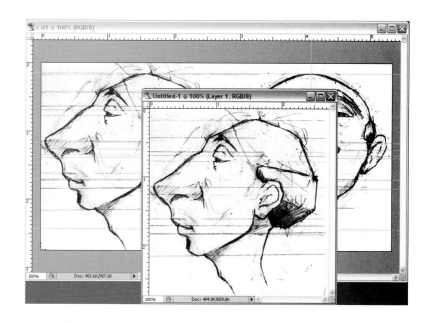

Image Planes can be of tremendous help when modeling. It almost allows you to trace a 3D form onto a 2D drawing. Not only is this of value for your own designs, but frequently in the 3D industry, the modeler is not the designer. However, the modeler is still responsible for maintaining the design integrity of the character designer. Being able to prepare and work with Image Planes is important.

Image Planes are really only as good as the images that are used to create them. These images are only as good as the preparation that goes into them. A crooked image in an Image Plane, or an image with front and side views that do not match up, are worse than useless—they can be a hindrance to your modeling process. Because of this, it becomes very important that good preparation time is put into your images.

There are several goals to keep in mind when preparing an image. First, make sure that the characteristics of the character match in the front and side views. Second, make sure that you are building two images that are exactly the same height. Third, assuming your character is more or less symmetrical, make sure that your front image is indeed symmetrical with the center of the character in the center of the image.

GOAL 1:   MATCHING CHARACTERISTICS FOR FRONT AND SIDE VIEWS

Step 1: Scan your drawing. Make sure that as you (or your character designer) draws the design, draw one view first, and then use a ruler to develop some rough guides. Often many designers find that graph paper can be of great help. Although you can fix a lot of problems in Photoshop, if you start with a good drawing, you are more likely to have success (Figure B.1).

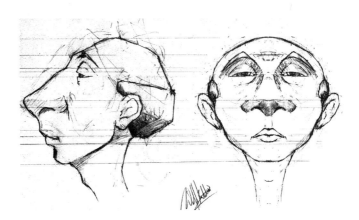

FIGURE B.1   Character design by Willem Keetell (*www.willemkeetell.com*).

Step 2: In Photoshop, press Ctrl-R to bring up the rulers. Drag from the rulers into your scan several guides. Start with one at the top of the head, add one at the chin, the eyes, the top of the ears, the shoulders, the arm pits, the chest, the waist, the crotch, the knees, the ankles, and the bottom of the feet. The more guides you have, the better an idea you will have of the effectiveness of your scan (Figure B.2).

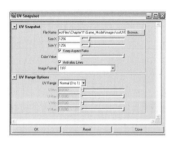

FIGURE B.2   Using guides in Photoshop to determine whether side and front views indeed line up.

Step 3: If the two do not match up well (if the nose of the front view is too high, for example), use the Free Transform tool (select and then press Ctrl-T) to adjust. Note that sometimes you can fudge stuff around a little bit using Free Transform or even Liquefy; but sometimes a drawing is just bad. If you have to spend too much time trying to deform one half of an image; it may just be easier to redraw.

Step 4: Crop the image down to get rid of any extra space or excess canvas created while transforming. Maya can handle a lot of info; however, there is no need to make your video card handle any more info than you need (Figure B.3).

Step 5: Isolate the side view. Use the Rectangular Marquee tool and select the side view. Make sure that your selection goes from the absolute top of the image to the absolute bottom. Now that you have aligned the front and side views, it becomes very important that you do not make one smaller than the other. Copy (Edit > Copy). Create a new file (File > New—click OK in the New dialogue box), and Paste (Edit > Paste). The new document automatically is the size of the copied pixels in memory, so the side should paste right into the right-sized file (Figure B.4).

Step 6: Save as Side.tif. Actually, you can use .picts or .jpgs, as well; although .tifs without compression tend to be very reliable in Maya.

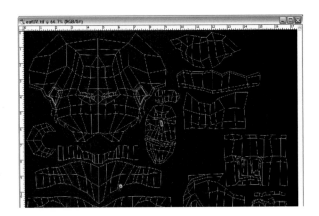

FIGURE B.3 Cropping out unnecessary content.

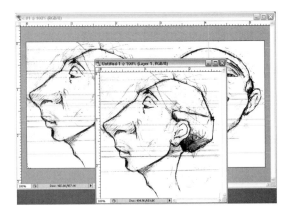

FIGURE B.4 Pasted side view.

Step 7: Back in the main altered scan, select half of the front view. Again, be sure to go from the absolute top of the image to the absolute bottom. Select as closely to the exact middle of the face as you can. (Figure B.5).

Step 8: Copy and paste into new document. Select Edit > Copy, create a new file (File > New), and Edit >Paste it into a new file (Figure B.6).

Step 9: Double the canvas size, making sure to keep the extant pixels to one side (Figure B.7).

Step 10: Paste again. Still in memory should be the one half of your front face. Press Edit > Paste again to paste another copy into your file. It will automatically create a new layer.

Step 11: Choose Edit > Transform > Flip Horizontal to mirror the half face.

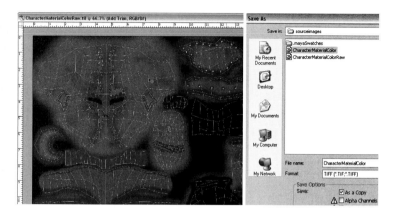

FIGURE B.5   Selecting one half of the front view.

FIGURE B.6   Pasted face half.

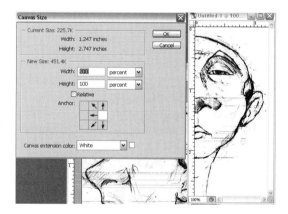

FIGURE B.7   Creating double-wide canvas.

Step 12: Use the Move tool to move the mirrored half face into place. It should snap into place as the image should now be exactly as wide as two half faces (Figure B.8).

Step 13: Flatten your image (Layers > Flatten Image) and save as Front.tif.

Step 14: In Maya, you are now ready to import Side.tif and Front.tif into your Image Planes.

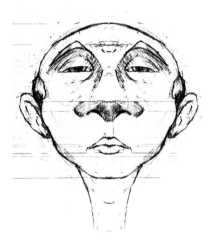

FIGURE B.8   Mirrored and placed half face.

CONCLUSION

Since you carefully cropped out excess pixels and canvas, you can be sure that both of your images are the same size vertically. This means that when they are imported into the Image Planes, they will be the same size, and the front and side views will match up. As you build the polygons that make the nose in the front view, they will match in the side view.

Since you have a mirrored half face, you know the middle of the Front.tif image is the middle of your character. This means that when the image is used as the front View Panel's Image Plane, it will be set so the middle of the face on the y-axis. This allows you to easily create one half of the face and use Mirror Geometry. Remember that most faces are not symmetrical in reality, so you will want to go in and make one half of the face asymmetrical at some point, but you only need to do the raw modeling for one half of the face.

UV SNAPSHOTS AND CREATING CUSTOM TEXTURES

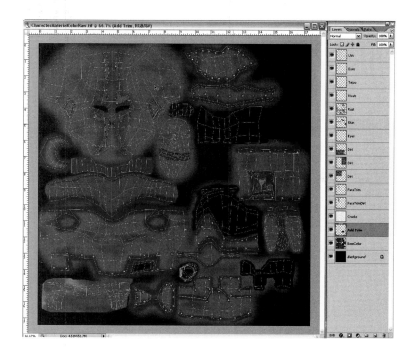

When we left chapter 11, we had looked at how to create custom UV maps that helped us help Maya define where the UVs of a polygon object lay within our texture space. We had created a custom UV layout through various projections (Figure C.1).

Then, within the UV Texture Editor, we used Polygons > UV Snapshot. . . to define an image that we could use in other applications to paint a custom texture (Figure C.2). We used a size of 1256 × 1256 for this game model (although you could use larger maps if you needed to).

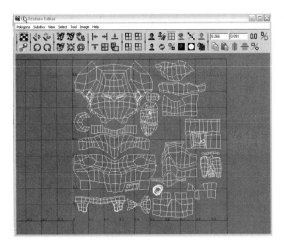

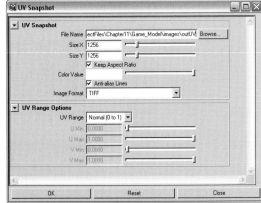

FIGURE C.2   UV Snapshot options window.

FIGURE C.1   Completed UV layout.

The output, which ends up saved to the Images folder in your project, is a regular bitmapped (or raster) image that you can use within your favorite paint of photo editing application. Here, we will use Photoshop, but you can use others as well.

The point here is not how to paint textures—several volumes of books could be written on that idea—but rather to show how to prepare your file for painting. Specifically, we want to use the lines (that represent the polygon edges) to help us define what to paint where, but not paint over them at the same time.

Step 1: Open outUV in Photoshop. Remember that outUV is the snapshot Maya created and will be located in the images folder of your Game_Model project file (Figure C.3). Note, of course, that the white lines indicate polygon edges.

Step 2: Separate the white lines from the black background. You can do this several ways, but Maya has already output an Alpha channel that will be of use. In the Layers palette, change to the Channels tab. Ctrl-click on the Alpha 1 channel. This will select the white lines (Figure C.4).

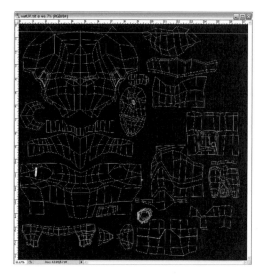

FIGURE C.3   The outUV image.

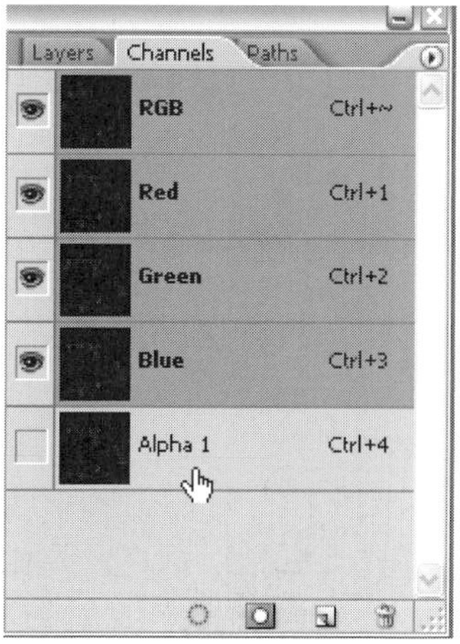

FIGURE C.4   Selecting just the lines that represent the polygon edges.

Step 3: Copy and paste into a new layer. With the white lines selected (done in the last step), select Edit > Copy and then Edit > Paste. This will paste the white lines into a new layer. Rename this layer UVs.

Step 4: Create new layers beneath UVs but above background. Paint on these layers. Notice in Figure C.5 you will see the UVs layer on the very top of the layers. As we paint, we are painting beneath these guides.

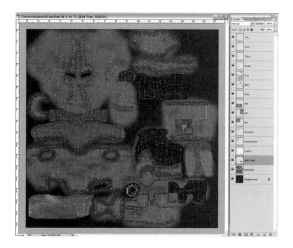

FIGURE C.5   Painted texture with background and UVs in tact.

Step 5: Before saving for use in Maya, make sure that you hide the UVs layer (or you will have the white lines over the top of your model).

Step 6: Save a raw version of your texture with all your layers in case you want to come back and edit.

Step 7: Save CharacterMaterialColor.tif into your sourceimages folder. Be sure to check off Layers and Alpha Channels in the save dialogue box (Figure C.6).

FIGURE C.6   Saving the color texture to the sourceimages folder.

Step 8: In Maya, open the Hypershade and show the input/outputs for your CharacterMaterial. Delete the checkerboard as the texture. Instead, click the checker button in the Color channel (in the Attributes Editor) and choose your newly saved CharacterMaterialColor.tif. The results will be your newly painted texture in which all the color aligns just like it should on the character.

OTHER RESOURCES

This volume is designed to provide an overview of Maya's modeling, texturing, rendering, and animating capabilities. It is just a start to an incredibly deep application. Finding other places to supplement your knowledge gained in this book will be an important step in your Maya progression.

MAYA'S HELP MENU

When you have Maya open, press F1, and Maya's Help menu will open in your browser. It is searchable and can provide some general overviews and descriptions of tools. It also includes several tutorials. It is not the most helpful tool in the world but can often get you on the right track in determining what the names of tools are that will help you in your discussions with others in venues like online forums.

OTHER MAYA BOOKS

Thomson Learning and Charles River Media (*www.charlesriver.com*) have an increasingly large collection of great Maya books. In addition, loads of other publishers have great collections of Maya books on very specific topics. Do a quick search on Amazon.com and be prepared to dig through lots and lots of Maya volumes.

ONLINE TUTORIALS

The Web has brought an incredible library of tutorials to the desktops of anyone with an Internet connection. Some favorites are:

- *http://www.highend3d.com/maya/tutorials*
- *http://www.learning-maya.com/*
- *http://www.tutorialfind.com/tutorials/3dsoftware/maya*

There are loads of others and a quick Google search for "Maya tutorials" will reap a bounty. Remember that most tutorials on the Web are unadjudicated, which means anyone can post them, and they may or may not be accurate. They may or may not be the best way to solve a given problem. But they are usually posted by people who are willing to share their knowledge for free and so they are usually pure in intent.

ONLINE FORUMS

Perhaps the best resource—especially in the rapidly changing world of 3D software—are online forums. These forums usually require you to register, but they contain a vast wealth of information that is searchable. In addition, you can post your own questions about a part of the software that you do not understand or a problem you are trying to solve. Most 3D forums are quite good at helping, and people are anxious to help share their knowledge.

Be sure that before you post a question that you have read the rules for the forum and done a quick search to find out whether the question has been addressed previously; it keeps people friendly and willing to help you.

Favorite forums include the following:

- *http://forums.cgsociety.org*
- *http://forums.awn.com*
- *http://www.aliasusergroup.com*
- *http://www.alias.com/glb/eng/community/home.jsp*

E

ABOUT THE CD-ROM

This CD-ROM is included to assist in learning the content included in this book. It includes all the images printed in grayscale in the book in full color. It also includes all the project files used in the tutorials. Note that when using the Project Files, you will be best served by copying them to your hard drive. Sometimes Maya needs to write back to the project folders and if that folder is only located on your CD, Maya can become confused and behave poorly.

FOLDERS

The files on this disc are organized into folders as follows:

Figures: All of the figures from the book, organized in folders by chapter.
Software: Maya7® Personal Learning Edition™
Projects: The files used for the projects in the book. Notice that there are folders for each chapter's tutorials and The Amazing Wooden Man folder (that includes the project file for multiple tutorials). Note that each of these folders includes the entire project file and should be copied in their entirety to your hard drive.

SYSTEM REQUIREMENTS

This CD-ROM should work with most any CD-ROM-equipped Mac or PC. Note however, that performance within Maya is largely dependent on your processor and video card.

Maya requires one of the following operating systems:

- Windows® XP Professional or Windows® 2000 Professional (sevice pack 2 or higher)
- Red Hat Enterprise Linux 4.0 WS
- SUSE Linux 9.3
- Apple® Mac® OS X 10.3.9 or higher

Maya requires one of the following browsers:

- Internet Explorer 6.0 or higher
- Netscape® 7 or higher
- Safari™

Hardware Requirements

At a minimum, Maya requires a system with:

- Windows: Intel® Pentium® III or higher, AMD Athlon™ processor
- Macintosh: Power Mac® G4 and G5
- 512 MB RAM
- CD-ROM Drive
- Hardware-Accelerated OpenGL® graphics card
- 3-button mouse with mouse driver software
- 450 MB of hard disk space

INDEX